AN INDELIBLE MARK

AN INDELIBLE MARK

FREDERIC KIMBALL

Library of Congress Control Number:		2008905845
ISBN:	Hardcover	978-1-4363-5409-7
	Softcover	978-1-4363-5408-0

This book was printed in the United States of America.

To order additional copies of this book, contact:
Xlibris Corporation
1-888-795-4274
www.Xlibris.com
Orders@Xlibris.com
50077

For Ellen

1

The Sorcerer's Apprentice

The best, according to Sophocles, is not to be born. Henry Stillman's predecessor in his mother's womb took the playwright's shortcut and was aborted in the collision of an American Flyer sled with a Japanese stone lantern under a full moon in December of 1931. Joe and Julia Stillman had done such things before Henry was born—danced in the dawn, tobogganed by moonlight, and skinny-dipped in dark swimming pools; but by the time he knew them, they slept in different rooms—his mother in an warm ocean of pink pillows and soft sheets and his father on an ice-cold porch, wearing a black beret to keep the frost from his brain.

Sophocles' second best, which is to see the light and return quickly whence one came, was not an option for Henry since his successor was the womb itself which turned inside out like a washed pocket to show nothing more was to be expected. His bridges were burned; he was here to stay. He was the fifth of five. As soon as he could crawl, he tried to escape. He was found sitting on the sidewalk, holding the rolled afternoon newspaper. He was locked in his nursery where he reached the mantle of a fireplace from the saddle of his hobbyhorse, pulling himself up by the reins and the thick black mane. Over the mantle was a painting of green water and sandy cliffs topped by two wooden tank towers in stark relief against the grey sky. It was an oblong painting, only a foot high, but nearly as wide as the mantel. He took the painting off its nail and stood it on end as far to one side of the mantle as possible so he could use the exposed chinks in the bricks to climb up the chimney. The ceiling prevented his departure, and they had to get a ladder to bring him down. He was buckled into a swiss leather harness and tethered to the base of his horse by a leash whose length varied directly with his behavior.

He played with an old and much-abused ark whose animals were fortunate to find a mate and more so if the pair had legs enough between them to stand propped against each other in the driving rain, waiting their turn to hobble aboard the ark. Noah and his sons were long lost; Henry had to play both God and man. He begat the Flood, and he abated it. Before the Flood, he had parents and brothers and sisters. Afterward he was an only child, an orphan among animals. His father visited the playroom to observe the silent deluge and returned the next evening with a wood mallet and red peg bench—a reversible plank with two rows of tight-fitting wooden pegs. He sat on the floor with his son and taught him to hammer. Grasping the mallet near the end of the handle, he allowed the weight of the head to fall in a smooth arc whose center was his shoulder. Inertia did the work; he could drive a peg flush with the plank in one effortless blow. He gave the mallet to Henry who tried and failed. His father patiently demonstrated his son's error. He choked the mallet near the head and tried to push the peg down with short, ineffective chops from the wrist. This was the way a woman hammers, he said. He gave the mallet back to Henry who was afraid to hammer in front of his father ever after.

They removed the harness when he was five, and since he stayed where he was put and came when he was called, he was sent to kindergarten with a pink-and-grey rug to nap on. The rolled rugs were stored in a red box so high that only Henry and Ms. Finch were able to see inside it; he was twice the height of his peers and appeared to be in the wrong grade. During the nap period, Ms. Finch called one or two children to her desk to press their splayed hands into medallions of wet clay. She pushed each digit deep into the cold disk, then scratched the name and date on it with a nail. The crock of clay by the sink was the social center of the classroom; the children stood around it like rhinos at a mudhole, sloshing water into the grey muck, squeezing it through their fingers, daubing their faces, pretending they were savages. Henry began to make clay balls the size of golf balls. He hid the dried balls in the rug box under a piece of carpet that was kept for guests. He soon had over fifty balls.

He showed his ammunition to Jimmy Bowes, the president of the class, who napped next to him. Jimmy was a left-hander; he could hit things with a rock that Henry didn't know were there. "See that bottle?" The astigmatic Henry couldn't, but almost instantly he heard it shatter. Jimmy was in love with Sally Partridge, the prettiest girl in the class. Henry was linked, reluctantly, to the largest girl in the class, Donna Hasenclever, who adored him. They did not tell the women about their plan.

Henry chose a day when his father was in the east—he had gone to the very tip of an island in the Atlantic Ocean because a hurricane had blown down the house where Henry was born. While the class played in the yard, Henry and Jimmy sneaked into the classroom and got into the rug box. They stood all the rolled rugs on end like the pickets of a fort, and when Ms. Finch and the class returned for naptime, they were abruptly repelled by a hail of hard clay balls. Henry and Jimmy had seized the rug box. Jimmy scored a direct hit on Terry Strohmeyer, a show-off who threw an eraser at them. Ms. Finch pulled the children to safety in the hall and came back to propose a truce. If they came out immediately, all would be forgotten. Jimmy Bowes tried to climb over the edge of the box; but Henry, who was twice his size, pulled him down and sat on him. "She'll call Ms. Reed," Jimmy protested. Henry said they had enough ammo to last all afternoon. "Then what?" Bowes asked. Belatedly they had begun to think ahead. "I'm giving you to three," said Ms. Finch. "Are you coming out, or do I have to call Ms. Reed?" Henry hurled a clay ball over the parapet of rugs, but he couldn't sit on Jimmy Bowes and aim well at the same time.

Jimmy was still struggling to surrender when the principal, Ms. Reed, came in preceded by Mr. Hughes, the janitor, shielding his head behind a wide coal shovel. Henry had to let go of Jimmy so he could pelt the janitor's stomach, and Bowes escaped over the top. Henry caught him on the neck before he ducked behind Mr. Hughes. The next person through the door was his mother. They had located Julia Stillman at the hairdresser's, and she came with half her hair grey and the other half blue. When Henry saw her, he surrendered, and they walked through a gauntlet of spectators to Ms. Reed's office where Jimmy Bowes was waiting. They were both expelled from kindergarten. Jimmy's family could not be found, so they drove him home in Julia Stillman's black Buick. Henry carried his grey-and-pink rug, and his mother held the clay disk of her son's giant handprint.

Julia Stillman understood why Jimmy Bowes could do such a thing—he was practically an orphan. Jill Bowes thought only of her next house or her next horse, of her youth, beauty, and money. She didn't know if Jimmy was alive or dead. But

Henry had parents who loved him, who devoted their lives to his happiness. Had he stopped to consider who really suffered by his actions? His mother and father. What had they done to deserve such humiliation? Henry was surprised how much his mother disliked Mrs. Bowes who was always nice to him. He looked at the folds of freckled flesh hanging from the crook of her arm that rested on the ivory steering wheel. He puzzled over her half-grey, half-blue hair under her straw hat. It was always brown, and he asked her when it had changed. Julia Stillman took blue-tinted sunglasses from a large handbag beside her on the car seat and put them on. "It hasn't been brown since you were born," she said. He had made her old, and now he made her cry. His father would have to deal with him, she said. He was more than she could handle.

Joe Stillman was from the east. He seemed like a visitor to St. Louis though he had lived there twenty-five years. He read eastern newspapers, the *New York Herald Tribune* and the *East Hampton Star*; he wore three-piece tweed suits; and he talked differently. Everyone was sent to school in the east when they were old enough. But most importantly, Henry's namesake, Uncle Henry, lived in the east. He was called Button, and Joe had just been with him, looking at what the hurricane had done to East Hampton. Main Street was blocked by uprooted elms, and the village was covered with two feet of sand and mud. Button's house had lost a lot of shingles, but the apple tree was still standing. The yacht club dock was found in Stonington, Connecticut, and Jack Cromwell's ketch on a highway in Bridgeport. Henry did not know these people or places, but they were real in his head. The east was Joe's place. St. Louis was his mother's.

Joe Stillman was angry when Julia told him about the rug box. No one respects a bully, he said. Only a coward throws anything at unarmed women and children. But when he heard Henry had been expelled, he started to laugh. It was just the sort of humorless performance to be expected from an outfit run by old maids. Henry could learn more at home watching hens lay eggs or helping Joe in the lab. The mention of the lab caused Julia Stillman to put on her blue glasses. She said nothing as Joe led his son to the basement—to be rewarded for what he and Jimmy Bowes had done. She went upstairs.

The lab was low and dark with a ceiling crisscrossed by pipes and hot air ducts from the furnace in the next room. Two window wells were so filled with leaves and the gratings above so clogged with ivy that no light came in. Machine tools lined one wall—a turret lathe, drill press, band saw. Joe's test bench was a clearing in a jumble of wires and radios. At the center was the cathode ray oscilloscope—a big box with fifty knobs and a tiny round screen that held a jumping green line which danced, fluttered, and spun to sound.

Joe was trying to invent the perfect phonograph. He had givn up listening to live music. Real orchestras were in the east. He believed that Vladimir Golschmann, the conductor of the St. Louis Symphony Orchestra, was trying to make eighty men sound like one hundred. Golschmann was driving the ensemble to intermodulation distortion, and Joe had stopped going to concerts. His phonographs were already better. His tangent tone arm was a legend among engineers who gathered at the counter of Van Sickle Radio Supply downtown. It was said he had taken the push-pull circuit to the limit of the 5Y3 power tube. People called in the middle of the night to ask his opinion on feedback and grid bias. Some nights he did not go to bed, so exciting was the prospect of the perfect fidelity. Henry hoped to become his apprentice when he was old enough to understand electricity.

Joe sat in his squeaky rattan chair, plugged in his soldering iron, and asked him about the battle of the rug box—how large were the clay balls, how long had he dried them, how had he concealed them. He didn't ask why they had done it, but he was merciless about the lack of a plan, a strategy. He gave high marks for tactical surprise—but what have they intended to do next? Henry was stumped. "What did you want to happen next? What did you want to gain?" Henry squirmed.

"Jimmy Bowes was right to bail out. You had no plan. You won the battle, and you lost the war."

"What war?" Henry didn't know about any war.

"The war against women," said his father. It was all new to Henry who had to ask why they were at war with women. "To get them to leave us alone," said Joe. He dipped the tip of his soldering iron in acid flux; it sizzled and made a column of smoke. While he filed the black oxidation from the tip's four faces, he spoke about first things.

"The first thing to know about women is they overreact. The second is they have no sense of humor."

Henry was standing with one knee crooked which made his pelvis uneven. It was a posture that made Julia Stillman tell him to stand up straight, but it reminded Joe of his brother. "You looked like Button just now," he said. Henry was accustomed to the comparison. He was said to be his "spit and image." Joe took off his glasses and polished them with his necktie. “Button got thrown out of Princeton for some fool prank. Didn’t do him any harm, it was a stupid place anyhow.” He got up from his chair, and Henry thought perhaps he might be going to hug him. If he was, he thought better of it. He turned back to his test bench and adjusted a gooseneck lamp over a rack of panels. He never mentioned his son’s expulsion from kindergarten again.

He became all business. “I’m in the market for a first-class test engineer, someone who can hear sixteen thousand cycles and isn’t afraid of hard work.” Henry tried not to seem too eager. Joseph Stillman had been Charles Proteus Steinmetz’s test engineer at Schenectady when the Wizard of General Electric became the first mortal to make lightning. Joe turned on a sweep frequency generator—a high-pitched squeal. The dog barked and ran from the room. Henry could hear over eighteen thousand cycles and got the job. He was also made director of maintenance, which required him to locate burning cigarettes left on the edges of shelves, benches, desks, and machinery. Six or seven were often lit at once.

Joe believed there was a major flaw in the Fletcher-Munson curves, which was, he said proudly, like believing that Lord Kelvin had got the boiling point of water wrong. Fletcher and Munson were Bell Laboratory engineers who had made a landmark description of the relative sensitivity of the human ear to bass and treble stimuli which they expressed in curves showing the steep decline of the ear’s sensitivity to lower frequencies. A bassoon needed twice the loudness to equal a flute. The Fletcher-Munson curves had determined the design of every loudspeaker and crossover network ever made. If the curves were skewed, as Joe claimed, everything based on them was junk. He intended to repeat the experiments with Henry as his subject. With corrected data, Joe would build the perfect amplifier.

The perception of loudness varied with the ear’s response to sounds of varying pitch. Loudness was difficult to quantify and possibly subjective. Henry had to stand for hours at very precise locations while he strained to differentiate one loud noise from another. He had to reposition himself before each blast to ensure he was not standing in a nodal point where the mechanics of wave propagation would cancel the effect they were trying to measure. Joe Stillman recorded the data with a sharp pencil on squared paper. When the curve departed from expectations, he blamed Henry for moving or failing to discriminate precisely. He raised the volume to help him hear better. Sometimes Henry suspected he was turning it up to get Henry to say what he wanted. The older man’s hearing had diminished with age; he wasn’t aware when his tone generators passed the threshold of pain. The noise drove away every living thing. The household fled to the upper stories. The dog cowered on the third floor. His brother and sisters shut their doors. Julia listened with clenched teeth in her upstairs sitting room. The first floor was deserted, a buffer zone used only for meals. But Henry, the test engineer, stayed at his post just as his father had stood by Steinmetz when the first lightning turned the lab's oxygen into ozone and they all passed out. Henry believed what they were doing in the basement was important, and he longed for the day when he could understand it.

But the experiment never ended. One curve implied another. Henry was growing up, but the work dragged on, every night—from dinner to until nine o'clock when Julia called from the top of the basement stairs that it was Henry's bedtime. Immersed in nodal points, beat frequencies, and transient decay rates, both Joe and Henry ignored her. "Five minutes, mister!" she shouted. Five minutes to pull himself away from the hypnotic green squiggles on the cathode ray oscilloscope; the whistles, birdcalls, glissandos, and arpeggios of the sweep frequency generator; the acrid whiff of acid flux in the solder; and the reassuring pall of Lucky Strike smoke that coated everything—a pencil tasted of tobacco if you put it in your mouth. He kissed his father good night—a last bracing whiff of the Lucky Strikes—then reluctantly he climbed the basement stairs, walked through the blue chintz and Chippendale of the dark first floor, up the front stairs, and into a bower of pink pillows, of muffling rugs, mirrors, and glass, and the scents of powder, soap, and perfume: Julia Stillman's bedroom, where his brother and sisters waited for him on their knees around her vast bed so they could begin the nightly prayers for the conversion of Joseph Stillman. The young Judas, with the smoky kiss of his father fresh on his cheek, took his place at the family cabal that asked God to deliver Joe Stillman from the dark cave of rationalism to the light of the Catholic Church.

Henry felt like a traitor praying for Joe's salvation behind his back. In fact, Julia was trying to enlist him as her spy, but he had refused to say anything against the Fletcher-Munson curves despite his own discomfort. Julia was frightened. Something secret and sinister was going on, and either Henry was too young to see it or he was part of it. Joe needed to be saved more than Russia for whose conversion from atheist materialism they also prayed after Mass every Sunday. No one really knew what Joe believed, but they knew it was not good for him. Anyone in their senses, said Julia, could see he was just making noise to scare people away. She wanted him to stop struggling with his demons in the basement and join his family at church. But Joe already went to church, once a year, at Easter. To all but Julia, his annual appearance at Father McBride's parish was a disaster. He tried to stand, sit, and kneel with the congregation; but he soon tired of the intricate demands of Roman worship and sat back smiling, even at the consecration. No one expected him to genuflect and cross himself, but neither did they want him to stick out like a sore thumb. If he was converted and went to church every Sunday, how would he behave? Julia didn't care; she had been put on earth to make Joseph Stillman a Catholic and take him to heaven with her. And her children had been born to help her. God could not remain deaf to the cry of family.

Julia led them in a rosary with a Glorious Mystery before each of the five decades of Hail Marys. She had to read the mysteries from the back of her enormous Roman missal made twice as thick by obituaries, clippings, and holy cards stuffed between its two thousand thin leaves. With the elastic band removed, her missal left a trail of the dead. Remembrance cards fluttered to the floor as she turned the pages—a necrology of the French in the new world (Chouteaus, Chateaus, DeBalivers, Gravois, DesPeres) and the Irish and Englishmen they had married (Walshes, Maffitts, Matthews, McBrides), but nothing for the black Protestant Stillmans. Julia was going to fix that. Armed with her missal, like Moses and his tablets, she spoke for the dead and for the generations to come. Someday Joseph Stillman would rest next to her in the Chateau plot at Calvary Cemetery, united in the sacred earth. But she wasn't taking chances. She sent Henry to Sunday school at Father McBride's to strengthen his mind against atheist influence at home and to prepare for his first communion.

Etienne McBride and Julia Stillman were Chateaus, a family descended from the French fur traders that had come up the river from New Orleans when Missouri was a French territory. The cousins were both educated by the Sisters of the Sacred Heart, an order of French nuns who came to the territory to convert the Indians but ended up teaching reading and arithmetic to the settlers and their descendants. Father McBride lived with his old mother in the country home where he was born, a stone-and-clapboard manor whose drawing room she converted to a chapel for her son. His was the only parish for miles in what had been a county of Baptist and Lutheran farmers until the automobile joined the city with the land. Between masses, he taught catechism on an oak window seat in the entrance hall between the dining room and the chapel. His two Dalmatians, Maud and Charlie, slept at his feet; and a suit of armor guarded a dark staircase that wound from landing to landing until it reached the garrets and gables of the fourth floor. The staircase enclosed a recently installed elevator just large enough to contain Mrs. McBride. Her descent was heralded by a clanging bell. She emerged from the cab swaddled in lace and bedecked with fringed purses in which she kept alms for the children—pennies and olive seeds from the Holy Land. She used two canes—one for support and the other for beating off the Dalmatians who tried to topple her. Her son was tall and lean with bushy grey hair receding deeply on both sides of his forehead, leaving a widow's peak in the center, almost down to his thick eyebrows. His breath smelled of the sacramental wine he had been drinking at masses since six in the morning. Other odors drifted from the back of the house—of cinnamon, sugar, and bacon—the breakfast being prepared for Father McBride while he explained to his catechumens who God was and why He had made them. He could not eat until he had sung the High Mass at ten thirty.

Henry had glimpsed the priest's breakfast from the window seat one Sunday when his mother was late. The glass-paned double doors to the chapel banged open. The organ postlude swelled; and Father McBride, with the chalice and his two acolytes with the processional cross and the censer belching perfumed smoke, swept past the suit of armor, across the hall, and into the dining room which also served as the priest's vestry and altar boy's robing room. Mr. Davis, the organist, and his daughter, the soprano, soon joined them; and when all the cassocks and white surplices and the celebrant's vestments had been hung in an oak armoire, they fell to the feast set out by the housekeepers—sticky buns, eggs and bacon, sausage, and more. Henry was determined to become an altar boy.

He made rapid progress in the spiritual life. He learned to love and fear God, to believe that Satan's rebellion had been successfully contained in hell, that baptism washed away Adam's sin, and that God would receive the pure into everlasting happiness in heaven. He learned to name his sins—disobedience in particular—the root of all evil, Satan's sin, man's first sin, the sin which separates us from God, from our teachers, our parents, and all who love us and want what is best for us. In his first confession, Henry repeated to Father McBride the names of the sins he was taught, a list that would be sufficient to his needs for many years—until the Jesuits opened the gates of knowledge on vistas of unimagined evil. But in the year that he learned the Act of Contrition, he firmly intended to amend his life, to do good, and to sin no more. He became an altar boy when he was eight.

Father McBride taught him his Latin script from a plastic card with the priest's lines in black and the acolyte's in red. He showed him how to wear his costume and how to use the props—the bells, the censer, the wine cruets with their glass stoppers. It was Holy Week in Lent. The statues and crucifixes were concealed in black bags; the bells were replaced by a wood clapper. New rituals had to be learned daily—the Stations of the Cross at night and the Forty Hours' Devotion. Henry spent every free hour at Father McBride's, and on Holy Saturday before Easter, they made holy water together at five in the morning. The ingredients, set out by the housekeepers the night before, looked like a recipe for soup—a big tureen of water, a slice of bread, a lemon, an egg, salt, and several bottles of oil and chrism. Father McBride worked at the holy water like an alchemist, reading Latin over his potion from a dog-eared copy of the *Rituale Romanum*, the prompt book for the mystical theatre troupe to which Henry was apprenticed. "Ad deum qui laetificat juventutem meum." (To God who gives me joy in my youth.) It was true; he was having fun. He forgot he had not been in the laboratory for weeks, but his father was traveling a lot, and he wasn't missed. On Easter, Joe Stillman got his first look at his son, the altar boy, in his cassock and white surplice. Asked for his opinion, Joe said anything could happen on Easter: the dead got up and moved rocks, rabbits laid colored eggs, and his test engineer spoke Latin.

Button died unexpectedly of a stroke or a heart attack, alone in his house in East Hampton, the same day a battleship sank in the Pacific with four thousand sailors. Joe was on the train east before anyone knew. They said Henry had met Button and Aunt Phoebe at the World's Fair. But while he remembered the Trylon and the Perisphere and his first sight of the Empire State Building out the train window just before the train went into a tunnel, he didn't remember Button. Henry thought it was queer for Button to be in East Hampton in the middle of winter.

The war and rationing were wearing Julia down. One son-in-law was in the Pacific and another in the North Atlantic. Button's death was the last straw, and then Mr. Mullin died, a day after Button. Julia went to the service at Father McBride's and let Henry miss half a day at school to serve the Mass for the Dead, which was a gold mine for altar boys. The undertakers tipped the acolytes five dollars if they went to the cemetery.

Henry had never been in a Cadillac limousine in his life. He sat on the jump seat with the pole of the processional cross over his knees and toyed with the silver microphone that was tucked in the plush upholstery. At his feet were the silver bucket for the holy water, the censer with its rings and chains, the charcoal-and-incense pot, the silver shovel for the last dirt, and Maud who was gnawing something under the seat. Father McBride's tall frame was stretched in the backseat, an old overcoat over his cassock and surplice and Charlie on the seat beside him, his head in the priest's lap. His three-cornered priest's hat with a black pom-pom was knocked forward almost to his brows. He frowned at the floor. "Where's the aspergillum?" he asked. Henry looked under the skirts of his own cassock and saw that Maud was chewing the wood-handled silver ball that held a sponge for sprinkling the coffin and mourners with holy water. He pulled it away from her and put it in the bucket where it belonged. "We go clockwise around the grave with you on my left. When we've come full circle, you put down the bucket and give me the shovel. Then you get the censer."

Etienne McBride and Joe Stillman fished together in the Ozarks, and the priest often left a bloody bag of wild duck in their kitchen when he came back from his mother's farm up the river. But things had changed. The parish was filling with young people and children, and the diocese was pressing Father McBride to build a school. Joe was working on a project for the government. Neither man had time to play anymore.

"Is Joe still raising Cain in the basement?" the priest asked. Henry told him how they prayed for his father's conversion around Julia Stillman's bed. Father McBride was surprised. "Does Joe know what you all are up to?" Henry didn't think he did. The priest was silent for a long time, scowling. Then he said there was no harm in Joe Stillman getting religion if he wanted, but he oughtn't do it just because Julia Chateau said he should. "He won't go to hell, the way he is?" asked Henry. They were turning into the cemetery. Maud jumped up on Father McBride in excitement. He let the dog chew at his sleeved arm. "Maud will see hell before your father does," he said.

"We should do some fishing. Tell him that for me." No one had told him about Button, so Henry did. He just shook his head. They stopped inside the cemetery gates to let out the dogs who bounded across graves and markers and chased each other out of sight over a hill of tombstones.

"They ought to be hunting," he said, watching them disappear. Maud and Charlie were waiting for them by the limousine as they came down the stone steps from the grave site, Henry leading with the processional cross and the asperges bucket. Joe Stillman's '37 Ford coupe with its C ration card, a grey salesman's model like a turtle with a shark's mouth, was parked behind the limousine. Joe was standing in the road, his brown felt hat pushed almost to his overcoat collar, a Lucky Strike in his mouth, and his hands thrust deep in his outer pockets. He was mad as hell. When Henry was close enough, he said very evenly, "Get out of that goddam dress, and get in the car. Why aren't you in school?" Henry said that his mother had said he could serve Mr. Mullin's mass. He went to the limousine to leave his altar clothes. Father McBride was rubbing his dogs' ears and listening to Joe.

"Etienne, goddamit, you know better than let Julia make a monk out of the kid."

Father McBride laughed. "For Pete's sake, Joe, we were having fun. Cemeteries are the only time me and the dogs get out of the house."

Joe apologized for shouting at Father McBride as he drove Henry to his school near the airport. Etienne McBride was a decent sort and meant no harm. A first-rate flycaster in fact. But enough was enough. He didn't mean to downplay the importance of religion; making holy water was necessary, but so was generating electricity. He was damned if he'd apologize for his part in the Century of Progress—"Live better, live electrically. Better living through chemistry." These weren't just the slogans of General Electric and DuPont, they were his personal credo. "I think the applied sciences—the doctors and engineers and chemists—have done more than all the priests and philosophers put together to alleviate human misery and make a better world." He never mentioned Button's funeral, but the thought of General Electric put him in such a good mood he gave Henry a lesson in how to take a curve. First off, you can tell a curve is coming before you can see it by the alignment of distant telephone poles. Slow down before the curve so you can speed up while you are in it. Acceleration increases the centripetal force that holds the car in the turn against the force of inertia that wants it to go straight. Never slow down in a curve; you will lose control. The corn rows spun past, opening and closing their brief apertures on a vanishing perspective like the flicker of a movie. Joe loved to drive.

Everybody was doing war work. Jimmy Bowes's father made turrets. Donna Hasenclever's father was an army interpreter stationed in England. Joe was traveling a lot for the government—they were building war plants in Tennessee and in the west to make bombs and ammunition to defeat the Japs and Germans. Joe was leaving his test engineer to guard the laboratory from spies and saboteurs.

But Henry allowed his friends to visit the lab after school; and sitting at his father's test bench, he summoned the jumping green line in the cathode ray tube, the strange burps and chirps of the sweep frequency generator, and the bluish nimbus of the Tesla coil that lit neon bulbs across the room and made your hair crackle as it filled the room with the sweet, prickly smell of ozone, a cousin to the deadly phosgene. He had been waiting his turn for a long time. Now Henry began his own war work.

He invented the electric chair in 1943. It was made of orange crates and tin cans and was installed in the dark room next to the laboratory. His friends lined up outside the chamber to be electrocuted for a nickle. Inside they met the smell of chemicals and the spooky red light used for developing. Henry strapped the victim into the chair and sponged his wrists with salt water where they touched the tin electrodes. Then he signaled Jimmy Bowes in the furnace room to begin cranking a magneto attached to a spark coil that delivered a tingling jolt—a shadow of the 1,700 volts at 250 amperes consumed by the state of Missouri's chair in the death chamber at Potosi. Girls particularly liked the sensation of being shocked. They squealed and shrieked, but they came back for more. Donna Hasenclever spent her whole allowance, and Henry allowed her to go free. He took the electric chair to school and exhibited it at an assembly where he gave a report on early penal electrocutions. The first electric chair was powered by galvanic batteries which many believed only stunned the victim. The cadaver was given to relatives who were waiting at the prison gates with a horse-drawn hearse. They ran the body over bumpy roads until the victim's heart was jolted into life again. So many dead men walked again that New York State mandated a chest cavity autopsy after electrocution. It was not electricity but the medical examiner's knife that stopped the heart forever. "Electricity is our friend!" Henry cried, and to prove it, he picked up two exposed wires with 110 volts AC and showed they would light a bulb. There was a gasp when the ground wire sparked on the bulb base as it made contact. Then Henry touched the two wires with his fingers. Teachers shouted; some children got up. Pandemonium. Joe Stillman had taught him to test a socket for the presence of electricity by putting his finger in it and feeling a tickle. The trick was never to be grounded or to let your head or heart get in the circuit. It always got a reaction when he put his finger in a light socket—people stood clear, as if he were a bomb. Mrs. Ridenour, the principal, pushed George Baumgartner's marimba on stage even though Henry hadn't finished and George wasn't ready.

He invented gunpowder and the recoil cannon in 1944. He waited until his father came home from a trip to introduce the device on the lawn at cocktail hour. The first model was cumbersome because Henry had chosen electric ignition which required a portable power source. About six o'clock, Henry appeared from behind the greenhouse on a red wagon pulled by a Millbrandt gasoline lawn mower. The recoil cannon, a two-inch pipe on a reciprocating carriage, was between his legs. He detached the wagon at ground zero and took the lawn mower to the command bunker behind a compost pile. It remained connected to the device on the wagon by a wire. His parents rose from their lawn chairs to get a better look. He aimed the cannon at an embankment of honeysuckle. Henry began the countdown, backward from ten. Julia thought she heard the telephone and went indoors. Joe casually disappeared behind a tree as if he were going to take a leak. Henry was in the bunker. The air was electric with expectation. Joe saw the dog was quietly sniffing in the honeysuckle, and the last word spoken was Joe shouting "TOBY!" to the dog. Henry touched the wire to the idling lawn mower's spark plug which ignited an exposed bulb filament buried in the powder charge in the cannon, a secret formula of homemade black powder, shotgun charge, and urea fertilizer. Final testing had been going on until late afternoon because the tamper still tended to shoot out of the barrel with a whooshing noise and a fantastic tongue of flame. But Henry was not trying to make a roman candle; he wanted a bang and dreaded a fizzle. His final adjustment was to hold the wadding in with a soft wood bung tapped lightly in the muzzle of the cannon. The unexpected power of the explosion was extremely satisfying until he opened his eyes—there was a smoking crater where the cannon and wagon had been, the lawn furniture was moved around a bit, the front of the greenhouse was caved in and most of the glass broken, the honeysuckle bank was scorched, and the dog wasn't moving. The wagon was a wreck, and a hundred feet away, Joe Stillman was rooting in a myrtle bed with his foot. He soon kicked the remains of the smoking cannon onto the lawn. Henry joined him. The barrel was all that was left—peeled like a banana.

"You're goddam lucky," said Joe.

Toby was not so lucky. They found his collar under the greenhouse. "You saw the goddam dog. Why didn't you stop?" "I don't know." "Not good enough." "I was a prisoner of the countdown." "People like you killed Archimedes."

Joe took Henry to the basement and spoke very seriously. He didn't have a good word for any part of the cannon, which he referred to as a bomb. Not even for the electric fuse. It was a recoil cannon, said Henry. It wasn't meant to explode. Had he used anything for a tamper besides the cotton wadding?

"A soft wood bung."

"That's how you make a bomb," said Joe and refused to say another word about it.

The war was on his mind. There was enough dynamite and black powder being set off in the world without Henry adding his two cents. The war might last for years, until his brother or even Henry was old enough to fight. He hoped his son would never see another bomb in his whole life after the one he had built by mistake that afternoon. Joe Stillman was tired and worried. He sat at his desk polishing his steel-rimmed glasses. His eyes were red.

Henry knew he had stepped on Joe's toes. Dynamite was his father's business. He had left Steinmetz and General Electric to operate coal mines in Illinois. He made himself an expert in the nitrate family of glycerines and studied the ways of shaping gas compression in the boreholes. He invented an electronic switch to sequence the firing of blasting caps that could make a face of coal fall in uniform chunks into the waiting hopper cars. Nitroglycerine and the black powders were as familiar and friendly to Joe Stillman as his Shredded Wheat. He taught the hydrodynamics of compressed fluids at Washington University. He missed the east—he missed Steinmetz and Toscanini and Stokowski and salt water and roasted chestnuts and most of all Button and all the friends he sailed with on Gardiners Bay off Long Island. He had traded all that he loved for coal and corn, muddy water, Julia Chateau, and five children. And now this endless new war and the far-fetched schemes he was hearing about how to end it.

Henry stood uneasily in the doorway, wanting to tell his father he knew he had overreached himself, making gunpowder. Joe saw him hunch his shoulders and shift his weight every so slightly. He smiled. "You looked like Button just now." Henry knew it. But still they couldn't move toward each other. Joe looked away toward the wall behind the drill press. The oblong painting of the cliffs and water towers that had been over the mantle in Henry's nursery had been hanging in the lab for a long time. Button painted it of the western shore of Gardiners Bay where he and Joe sailed from a little club in Amagansett. "That tank on the left, the tall one, got blown away in '38," Joe said.

Julia was righting the furniture and sweeping glass when they came up. She said it was time to speak about what the Chateaus are made of—the steel and flint of the fur men who opened the Mississippi River from the delta to Minnesota and the Missouri River from the confluence above St. Louis to the headwaters of the Platte in North Dakota. "By rights you ought to be locked up," she said. They were too old and too tired to handle him. If the truth were told, they had bit off more than they could chew. They had whelped an armed barbarian with no moral sense, not even a veneer of civilization, only a lust to destroy what ten generations had created. Even Jimmy Bowes didn't try to blow up his home and family, which in his case might be the best thing. Henry was going to summer camp as soon as she could find one. Then boarding school. She meant it. He never lived with his parents again—he visited them. He was governed by surrogates. He was almost thirteen.

CAMP KOOCH-I-CHING

The Kooch-i-ching counselors were afraid when they saw the Mounties' red seaplane with white maple leaves on its wings circling over Lake Wabigoon in Ontario. They weren't much older than the campers, but they had killed a deer at the last campsite and buried the carcass in the woods. The four canoes came together while the young men in the stern seats made the nine boys swear they wouldn't tell. The plane came in low over the remains of a beaver lodge and a forest of dead wood that reached into the head of the lake. As the plane taxied toward them, they could see two Royal Canadian Mounties in their Smokey Bear hats. The plane cut its engine. It was a still, hot day, and the boys were shielding themselves from the sun under ponchos tied to their paddles, which they had been trying to use as sails in a vain effort to avoid paddling to the next portage. It was their tenth day in the wilderness, living on Spam and dried milk, and they were bushed. A Mountie got out of the plane's cockpit and stood on the pontoon, gorgeous in his red coat and shiny black boots. "The war is over!" he shouted. "The Japs have surrendered." The Americans had dropped a new kind of bomb on them ten days ago—an atom bomb. A whole city disappeared in a second—a quarter-million people vanished in a fireball hotter than the sun. The campers cheered. The officer got back in the cockpit, and the plane taxied away, blowing the first breeze toward them they had felt all day. The plane was getting up speed when it flipped over and came to rest nose down in the shallow water. The Mounties were able to stand beside their inverted aircraft and examine the shredded pontoon, which had been ripped by an underwater snag. The counselors decided to make camp nearby and invited the Mounties to stay with them.

Henry and Jimmy Bowes had the third shift of bear watch that night—from twelve to two. Huddled near the campfire, they speculated about the bomb. Joe Stillman had said that an ounce of radium could drive the *Queen Mary* around the world a hundred times. Bowes said flatly that Henry's father was probably in on it—he knew if anyone did, him and Einstein. Henry didn't contradict him. He picked up a twig.

"You know the amount of atom power in this twig?"

Jimmy Bowes's dick, which was always slightly erect, had a left hook in it. It came out the right side of his rowing shorts and started to go back in the left.

"What are you looking at?" he asked Henry.

"Nothing."

"How much power?"

"The mass of the twig times the speed of light squared."

Bowes didn't believe it. "All that in a twig? Bullshit!" Henry had always suspected his prick was shorter than Jimmy Bowes's, and this summer, he had seen it was so. Earlier in the season, Bob Gormely, the director of the junior camp, had called Henry a two-ton bomb with a two-inch fuse. Henry wanted to blow up in the man's face.

They heard a noise by the stream. Jimmy Bowes pulled a burning stump from the fire and loped like a caveman into the dark. Henry found his flashlight and caught up just as Jimmy Bowes shouted, "Drop that, you son of a bitch!" Henry's flashlight caught a bear's red eyes looking at them over the rim of the aluminum butter-and-bacon pot they had tied in the stream to keep cold. He was sitting on his tail in the stream, holding the pot in both paws, eating their butter. They were close enough to smell the bear's awful stench. He finished eating, dropped the pot in the water, got up, lifted his rear leg, and pissed in the stream. Then he slowly lumbered away. The bear reminded Jimmy Bowes of how Kennedy said you get a girl pregnant. The guy puts his dick in the girl's thing and pisses. Henry asked him to be more specific about her thing, which Bowes believed to be a slit that opened or could be forced open. How? With your finger. And you put your thing in her thing? Henry tried to imagine the geometry of the act and the consequences. "Where do you do this? In a hospital?" Jimmy Bowes had a laughing fit, and Henry had to hit him to find out what was so funny. "A hospital,"

Bowes repeated and started laughing again. "You can do it anywhere. The best place is in a car."

The Wabigoon trip returned to camp three days later near dinnertime. They were tired, dirty, and hungry. They had shared their last Spam and dried apples with the Mounties, and the bear had eaten their butter and bacon. Gormely, the director of the junior camp, was waiting for them on the dock. His right forefinger made little ringlets of his pubic hair as he watched them throw their duffle bags and food sacks onto the dock. He never wore clothes before sunset. He was a proud man—bronzed, oiled, and nude except for a Cubs baseball cap and a police whistle on a shoelace around his neck. His body was a textbook of muscles, but he was proudest of his scrotum, which he would stretch before him with both hands to show how tight yet supple and retractable it was—the scrotum of a ten-year-old. No man his age, fifty-three, could boast of a tighter scrotum; and the reason was he had never worn a jockstrap in his life. He hated clothes, especially bathing suits, pajamas, and underwear. He wanted to see a bare ass in every bunk and staged bed raids at all hours to make certain no sissy was sleeping in skivvies or pj's. The lights would suddenly go on, everybody had to fall out of bed, and anyone caught wearing bottoms had to jump in the lake. Second offenders were sent to collect spent shell casings by flashlight at the rifle range deep in the woods among bears, owls, and mosquitoes. The number of shells varied with the offense—seldom less than five hundred—and finding them took hours of buggy boredom. Then they had to be counted into a coffee can Gormely kept locked in his trunk before the offender could go to bed.

The director watched them pull the canoes out of the water and put them upside down on cross arms nailed to pines near the dock. He hadn't said a word since they arrived, and neither had anyone else. He was pissed. When the canoes were stowed, he blew his whistle. "All counselors go to the dining hall. The Mounties want to talk to you. All campers stay on the dock." Gormely stared at the members of the Wabigoon trip with seething rage, his crew cut bristling and his craggy beak sniffing the wind. "Who shot the deer at the Manitou campsite?" His gaze traveled from camper to camper. Shepley, Lane, Smith, Younger, Stillman, Bowes, North, Fischel, Fredericks? Gormely plucked at his scrotum, and the bud of his penis peeked out of its foreskin. They had sworn not to tell. "You'll stand here 'til Labor Day, or tell me who did it."

Five thousand shells each was the penalty for their silence. They headed for the rifle range. It was summer's end, and the area around the firing line had long been picked clean, but a shell casing can eject over ten feet if the bolt is pulled back hard. They were on their hands and knees sifting through pine needles far from the range shelter, but by nightfall, they hadn't found two hundred in all. Their hunger was growing and the light fading; the mosquitoes were out. Inevitably someone, maybe it was Bowes, said Gormely had to go. It was everyone's favorite pastime—killing the director. The classic plan was to drown him (the canoe smashed in a rapids) or crush him (the falling tree on his tent). The need to kill him was urgent and sincere. Terry Shepley worked all night to chop through an immense pine using tiny hatchet strokes to make it look like beavers' teeth, but the tree got caught in the upper branches and refused to fall. The consensus at the rifle range was to torch Gormely's cabin while he slept. What about the other guys in the cabin? And suppose Gormely wakes up? "Chloroform," said Shepley who loved details. North had some signed prescription forms for asthma medicine. They were easy to change, but someone had to get to the drugstore in town. Only Catholics ever went to town—for church. Gormely hated having to let the Catholics leave. They brought back candy and comic books from the town drugstore and corrupted the rest of the campers. Henry was the only Catholic in the group; he would have to do it. He listened to the plan, and he did not like it. Everyone was talking big, and then they'd back out.

"Who's backing out?" Bowes asked angrily. "It was my idea."

"What about the rug box?" said Henry. He had never forgiven Bowes for trying to surrender. First, said Henry, a prescription could be traced. And second, ether was a cinch to make—he had chloroformed his dog with homemade $CHCl_3$. All he needed was nail-polish remover and lime from the latrine. He could buy Cutex after Mass without leaving a paper trail. It was Saturday; they would have ether by Sunday night. They should alert everyone in Gormely's cabin to be ready to leave, then they would jump him with an ether-soaked towel as soon as he was asleep. The beauty of ether, said Henry, was that it burned or evaporated and left no trace.

Gormely let them go to bed at ten o'clock with only 643 shells. The Mounties had taken the counselors to Fort Francis in Ontario to be arraigned.

On Sunday morning after breakfast in the main camp dining hall, Gormely made the day's announcements. He wore jeans and a checked shirt because there were women in the main camp—the director's wife, the cooks, and the camp nurse. A smile played on his weathered mouth while he waited for people to be quiet. There would be no boat to town this morning. Because of the polio epidemic, all town trips were cancelled. The bishop of Duluth had given Catholics a dispensation to miss church for the rest of the summer. They were welcome at the nondenominational services in the shed. His hand went toward his scrotum in a gesture of triumph and grabbed a handful of denim. Henry was relieved. It was a bad plan. Why did only Gormely burn up in the cabin? The Mounties would figure it out; you couldn't even kill a deer in Wabigoon without getting caught. Gormely had to be killed deep in the boondocks in a legitimate accident with very few people around. He knew people hated him. He was careful whom he tripped with—counselors he knew, kids who were still in awe of his scrotum. Campers had been trying to kill Gormely for twenty years; it was easier to wipe out Hiroshima and Nagasaki.

Henry had twelve letters in his mailbox. He took them back to his bunk. Ten were from Donna Hasenclever whose adoration increased as the square of the distance between them. He opened one—her guppies were now bigger than thumbtacks—and threw the rest in his trunk. His mother's letter—written before the war ended—said his father was returning soon and that sugar was coming back into the stores. He didn't finish it. He seldom finished anything; his mind veered or raced ahead. The last was from Joe Stillman written on yellow second sheets of onionskin typewriter paper. It described how a fission bomb worked. Uranium was a heavier cousin of radium and also radioactive, which meant a neutron could get inside the nucleus and make it unstable, yielding two protons or "fission." Henry skipped. Meitner and Fermi had discovered that enough neutrons were released to keep the fission going in a chain reaction, and if Henry remembered his Einstein ($E=mc^2$ where c is the speed of light), he stopped reading. He knew all that. On the second page were drawings of two kinds of bombs: the uranium-235 bomb was "so crude any fool could make one," and the plutonium bomb was "a cute idea" in Joe's opinion. His drawing looked like boards of different lengths stacked together with a ball inside, labeled Cross Section of Implosive Lens. The screen door banged open, and five of his cabinmates stormed in. They saw Henry reading his mail. They all knew about Donna Hasenclever. He tried to hide the letter.

"It's from his girl!"

"Donna."

"With the big boobs."

"It's not!" he shouted. "Leave me alone!"

They jumped him and tried to pry the letter from his hand. He shouted for Bowes who was hanging back in the doorway. "Bowes! Get 'em off me! Help!" Fredericks got the second page, and they all gathered around to look at it. There was immediate disappointment.

"That isn't from Donna."

"What is this shit?"

"Give it back, you guys, it's important!"

Henry grabbed the sheet from them and jumped onto his upper bunk. They looked at him as if he had flipped.

"What's the big deal?"

"Who's it from?"

Henry looked down at them solemnly. "It's the atomic bomb."

Silence. Disbelief.

"You're kidding."

"Bullshit"

"I am not."

"Where did you get it?"

"It's from his old man," Jimmy Bowes spoke from the doorway.

"He knows how the atomic bomb works?"

"I can't tell you," said Henry.

Two of them began to climb onto the bunk. Henry stepped on their hands. He wadded the thin onionskin paper with the drawing of the implosive lens into a small ball and ate it.

Jimmy Bowes bunked below Henry at the far end of Gormely's cabin, which gave them a few seconds' warning if he staged a sudden bare-ass inspection. The night was windless, and the smell of tobacco lingered among the pines. Gormely was smoking down on the dock. He would probably let them sleep. Bowes's head appeared beside Henry's. "Stillman? You awake?" Jimmy Bowes climbed onto his bed. They whispered.

"That was stupendous, what you did with your old man's letter."

"I had no choice," said Henry.

"He invented the atom bomb, didn't he?"

"I don't know," said Henry. "This is the first I've heard."

"Come on! He wrote you how it worked. I saw it."

"A sketch, that's all."

"That's why you ate it. So the Russians wouldn't get it."

Bowes's explanation was as good as any.

"He was at Los Alamos, wasn't he?"

"He was away a lot. He never said where."

Jimmy Bowes said he had known it all along—that Joe Stillman wasn't just some mad inventor playing around with radios and phonographs. That was his cover—to throw you off the track. Jimmy saw through that. Henry admired Bowes's theory. It explained everything.

Bowes was silent. "You know how when you're asleep you can get a hard-on and white stuff comes out?"

"A wet dream," said Henry. "What about it?"

"Okay. Well, you don't have to be asleep."

"What do you mean?"

"I'm telling you. You can get a hard-on wide awake."

"How?"

"By rubbing it."

"Did Kennedy tell you this?"

"I've done it."

"What happens?"

"Semen comes out."

"Semen?"

"The white stuff. Jesus! If you don't believe me, try it. On your stomach, against the sheets. Real slow. It takes about five minutes." It wasn't an efficient way to masturbate, but for the next year, it was the only way Henry knew.

Gormely opened the screen door and came in. Bowes pulled up the sheet over them. "Shit!" he whispered. "He can smell it." "No, he can't. He's been smoking."

Gormely stood a long moment, then walked past the row of beds and steamer trunks toward their end of the cabin. They froze. The penalty for being in someone's bunk after lights-out was a thousand shells, and there wasn't a single one left. Gormely stopped and sniffed. Then he turned back toward his end, stripping off the evening's flannel and denim as he went until he stood by his bunk in his familiar nakedness. Jimmy Bowes dropped into his bed below.

Henry worried about the future. He had learned everything he knew from Jimmy Bowes, but Julia Stillman had just written that she was sending him to a Jesuit boarding school in Maryland. Who would tell him about life?

ST. ALOYSIUS OF GONZAGA

There were two railroads to the east. They ran parallel from St. Louis to Terre Haute, Indiana, where they split, one northeast to the Great Lakes and the other straight over the Alleghenies. The Pennsylvania Railroad was sheer adventure as it breached the Kittatinnies at the Horseshoe Curve just west of Altoona in a breathtaking feat of engineering that Joe Stillman said rivaled the Great Pyramids and the Panama Canal together. Henry was too excited to sleep. He stood for hours in the vestibule of the Pullman with his head out the upper half of the double doors drinking in the sooty wind, waiting for the legendary Horseshoe Curve when the engine and first cars of their train coming down the far side of the curve would pass the last cars still going up and between them, far below, the nested lake of the Kittatinny reservoir. Then the uncoupling at midnight of the New York and Washington sections in Harrisburg and the rude awakening in Baltimore with a last call for breakfast and finally the Washington Monument out the right-hand window.

The school, St Aloysius of Gonzaga, was located in a large Georgian building surrounded by a golf course in the rolling hills of Maryland. It had a columned portico and four floors, the last with a row of dormer windows in a roof topped by a tall-glassed cupola. An adjacent chapel of pink granite and marble had a bell tower beside it even taller than the cupola. St. Aloysisus was Henry's confirmation saint, a choice made by his mother, which he deeply resented. Julia said he was the patron saint of youth, but to Henry, he was the sissy saint. The brief life of Aloysius on page 2011 of her fat missal told how as a young prince in his father's castle, Aloysius was so sickened by the lewdness and blasphemies of the duke and his nobles at the dinner table that he had to excuse himself to vomit in an antechamber.

The prefect of the fourth floor was waiting at the top of the stairs. Father O'Connor was a cheerful man with curly blond hair, a button nose, and a lyrical tenor voice. His left leg dragged behind him as he led Henry to his room. "I limp like Ignatius," he explained. "We were both hit in the leg by cannonballs." His roommate was already in residence, a small, dark, and delicate boy with shining black hair and dreamy soft eyes. "Alfredo de Sanze de Santa Clara de Bogota," said Father O'Connor, almost singing. "Meet Henry Stillman from San Loo-weee, Miz-zooo-ree." Alfredo scowled from behind a chifforobe in the center of the room that marked the entrance to his half. He had laid down a labyrinth of tape on the floor, dividing the space into two sectors with corridors to the door and the only window.

Father O'Connor lived across the hall. When Henry knocked on his door to get a library pass, he found the priest at his desk, wearing a white tee shirt, white boxer shorts, and black socks, garters, and shoes. The room smelled like Joe Stillman's lab—a burning cigarette and the bittersweet odor of acid flux for soldering. Father O'Connor was building a cathode ray oscilloscope from a kit. The chassis, about a quarter assembled, was inverted on his desk.

"I'm becoming a radio repairman on my GI Bill," he said.

"An oscilloscope," said Henry. "My dad has a Dumont."

"Is he a radio repairman?" the priest asked.

"He's an engineer."

"Electrical?"

"And chemical. He teaches gases and hydrostatics at Washington University."

"I teach physics. I'm building this stuff for the lab. It comes with the course."

"Were you in the army?"

"I was a chaplain," he replied.

"My father was on the Mesa, I think. Though he doesn't talk about it."

"The Mesa?" the priest asked.

"With Oppenheimer. The Manhattan Project."

"That was a better place to be than Hiroshima," said the ex-chaplain. "Or Biedenkopf," he added.

"Where's that?" Henry asked.

"In Germany, where I got blown up. By a Bouncing Betty." This was an antipersonnel mine that sprang from the ground when he stepped on it. He was still full of shrapnel—patches of grey under the translucent pink skin of his arm, his cheek, and particularly his legs. His left leg was not much use; it dragged behind him a little and was very sensitive. He hated to wear trousers if he didn't have to. Henry was impressed with the amount of metal in Father O'Connor.

"Did you get the Purple Heart?"

"I sure did. You want to see it?"

He pulled up the left sleeve of his tee shirt to show a bright tattoo just below his shoulder—the Sacred Heart of Jesus wrapped in flaming thorns. The purple heart dripped crimson blood where the thorns pierced it. The tattoo had been made by a legless sergeant in a hospital in England. He wanted to make the chaplain a South Seas hula girl or a Madonna, but he had run out of blue.

For the first weeks, Henry wondered if his roommate spoke English at all, but it turned out the Spanish-speaking students were boycotting the Gringos and their language because the Jesuits would not allow them to speak Spanish to each other. They were there to learn English. Father O'Connor told Alfredo to pick up the tape he put down and to move his furniture against the walls. Henry gradually learned from others that Alfredo's father, Senator Jorge de Sanze de Santa Clara, was the minister of interior and the second most powerful man in Colombia. His mother's family was the richest. They owned the emerald mines and the coffee cartel. They had given the school's enormous marble chapel in memory of Generalissimo de Santa Clara, a descendant of Bolivar. Alfredo had six suits and a uniform with braid, six pairs of shoes, and a tinted photograph of his mother in an oval silver frame on his dresser. Donna Maria Veronica Esmeralda de Medellin had long black hair, large black eyes, red lips, a red dress, and a large but plain silver crucifix on a chain around her neck. Henry had a black-and-white photograph of Joan of Arc taped on the mirror of his dresser. She was bound to the stake in three places, but she strained to free herself. Her bosom, neck, and chin formed a sweeping arc that stretched toward heaven, her eyes closed, her mouth open, a chaste virgin longing to become the bride of Christ in death. The two guardians faced each other from opposing dressers until the Sunday visit of Alfredo's uncle from Bogota, an old man with a white mustache, a cane, and a black fur coat. He climbed to the fourth floor to see his nephew's room, and then took him to the Colombian embassy for lunch. After study hall that night, Alfredo spoke his first English to Henry, one long, lilting sentence ending with its verb, "The imposter saint on your mirror, not even a photograph but a magazine picture, profane and disgusting, of a public whore, should not in the same room with my own mother be." His uncle said that Henry's effigy of St. Joan was a blasphemy, and he should take it down.

She whom the oligarchs called whore was an actress on the cover of a program of a play about St. Joan of Arc he had seen with his mother. Julia was as concerned as Alfredo's uncle for the spiritual state of her favorite actress who had left her husband and children to live in sin with an Italian film producer. But she did not pass up the chance to see her in the flesh and smell for herself whether that flesh was corrupt. Henry saw only St. Joan and smelled only the bundles of burning brush in the cathedral square of Rouen. He was enjoying a brief interval in his life when the temporal and the spiritual reality were a seamless whole, when nothing human was alien to God and the divine design embraced all creation with love and tenderness—Ingrid Bergman, Roberto Rossellini, Dr. Peter Lindstrom, and St. Aloysius of Gonzaga who Henry learned had died very young in the slums of Rome, cradling in his arms the wasted victims of the plague. In this state of beatitude, Henry's picture seemed just as good to him as Alfredo's, and he told him so. The next day while he was at football practice, the picture of St. Joan was defaced with a crude beard and naked breasts.

The breasts of St. Joan or Ingrid Bergman were never far from Henry's thoughts. Sins which seemed so remote when Father McBride had taught him their names now came into focus. It seemed very likely that an impure thought about St. Joan was more sinful than the same thought about Ingrid Bergman, particularly in her degraded state. The Jesuits told harrowing tales of boys called to judgment in the heat of their sin. He would never sneer at the purity of Aloysius again. On Friday evening, he stood in the long line before the confessional of the most popular priest in the school. It was said that Father Kirby understood the problems of students—that he was on their side. When Henry finally got into the confessional, the smell of tobacco was intense. It was a week since his last confession, he said, and recited Father McBride's list of sins—disrespect, disobedience, inattention—the petty crimes of an altar boy. Then he paused.

"Is that all?" Father Kirby expected more.

"I had impure thoughts several times—three times."

"Did you entertain these thoughts?"

"I did, yes."

"And did these thoughts lead to impure actions?"

"Twice, yes, Father."

"Alone or with others?" the priest asked him.

Had he heard him right? "Could you repeat that, Father?"

"Were these impure actions performed alone or with others?"

Henry's mind was a white sheet without a mark on it. He was thoughtless, speechless. What did he mean, impure actions with others? *With others*? An impure action was just one thing, what Jimmy Bowes had taught him, beating off. What was he suggesting? His head was now awash with possibilities. Who? How? Where? What? The priest struck a match. Henry had forgotten where he was.

"Take your time," said his confessor.

"I was alone, completely alone."

Henry escaped the confessional with a trivial penance, five Our Fathers and five Hail Marys, but the priest's question haunted him. Impure actions with others? What did they do? Who were they? How could he meet them?

He found himself looking at people with a new curiosity and suspicion, especially Father Kirby, the director of spiritual life, a grizzled man with short bristly grey hair and an immense Roman nose. He was everywhere—he taught religion, he was the retreat master, he was the chaplain of sodalities, and most conspicuously, he was the chaplain of all athletic teams. For football, he wore a towel around his neck stuffed into the front of his sweatshirt and a baseball hat with a long bill like a platypus. In the prayer huddle before the toss-up of their first junior varsity game, Father Kirby thrust his hand into the center of the players to start a violent pyramid of hands slapped angrily on top of each other while the players intoned the Hail Mary. Then Kirby unleashed his secret weapon. "Virgin of Victory!" he hissed. The players screamed, "Pray for us!" and the huddle exploded with a terrible banshee howl, "KILL, KILL, KILL-L-L-L," that so unnerved the Episcopalians on the opposing team that they lost all will to resist.

Henry returned to Father Kirby's confessional the next Friday to ask him what he had meant by alone or with others. The old man's memory needed refreshing. "Tell me again the occasion of the impure actions." He hadn't asked for details before, and Henry found himself getting in deeper.

"I was looking at a picture."

"Smut from the day students?"

"No, Father."

"They sell dirty magazines to the boarders."

"A photograph, Father."

"Where did you get it?"

"It was from a theatre program."

"The Gayety?" That was the burlesque house on K Street.

"It was a program for a play."

"This photograph, was it of a woman?" His confessor was getting impatient.

"Yes."

"A naked woman?"

"It was of St. Joan."

"St. Joan? Of Arc?" Silence. Henry could feel Father Kirby recoil from his depravity, from the stench of his bestial and profane appetite.

"St. Joan should be a model of chastity for us. Even rough soldiers respected her virgin purity."

"I know," said Henry. "What is an impure action with others?"

"Touching, fondling, exciting oneself or another."

"Fondling another," Henry repeated. He was getting warm; he was on the track. He was also getting an erection.

"Or fondling oneself in the presence of another." There was an edge in his voice, but Henry was determined to get to the bottom of it.

"Who?" he asked.

"Friends, strangers, animals." He could hear Father Kirby wrinkling the cellophane of his cigarette pack. Henry had pressed too far.

"I'd like to know you better, sit down and have a real talk," said Father Kirby. "My door is always open, on the third floor."

Henry should never have gone back to the priest. Alfredo had told the Jesuits he worshiped a profane idol. He could get Henry expelled for sacrilege. His powerful family would offer to build a football stadium or a gym if Henry were sent home. Father Kirby was the hatchet man; his invitation was a trap. Henry was prepared to confess his carnal desires and ask God's forgiveness, but he would never admit that his photo of St. Joan was an improper effigy. It was a sacred image, and he wanted Alfredo and his friends punished for defiling it. He carried the mutilated icon in his pocket for evidence. He approached Kirby's third-floor door three days in a row. It was indeed always open, billowing smoke and laughter. The third day it was quiet, and he knocked and went in. Father Kirby was reading *Life* magazine and eating a Hershey bar. He offered Henry half. "I've been watching you, kid, and I've been wanting to have a talk with you." Henry was ready to run. "Keep your head down, that's the first thing to remember. Never let 'em see your eyes." He was talking about the scrimmage the day before when Henry's head got pushed back, his helmet torn off, and his nose cut which required a visit to Sister St. Hilda, the school nurse, who told him that boys were beasts and should live in the jungle until they learned to behave. Father Kirby's phone rang. He asked Henry if he could stop by the next day. He wanted him to meet a friend.

Kirby's room was crowded again. Through the blue haze of smoke, he saw six or seven upperclassmen sitting on the priest's bed and chairs and desk in the small space. He recognized two seniors—Bill Watts was talking to Larry Gargan, the captain of the football team. Bill Watts was the president of the student government, the prefect of the senior sodality, the leader of the honor roll society, and the senior deacon of the altar society. He walked a few inches off the ground, like Jesus over the Red Sea. He was the only student allowed to carry the great monstrance before the sacred Host was placed in it for Benediction. The whole school watched Bill Watts, like a juggler on a wire. They watched him say grace before meals, standing by the St. Francis Xavier fountain in the center of the refectory. They watched him at football games, chapel services, the Saturday-night movie, the honor roll assemblies. He was beautiful and radiated serenity because he was going to the Jesuit seminary at Woodstock to begin his novitiate when he graduated in June. He had a vocation, which the Jesuits nursed and sheltered like a rare and fragile thing. That was why he seemed to walk on a cushion of air; he was carrying a giant bubble that could burst at the least jiggle. His vocation.

Bill Watts saw Henry in the door before Father Kirby did. He came toward him, and Henry instinctively drew back from respect, or perhaps fear that he might scratch or puncture the almost-visible nimbus of his vocation. Bill Watts was accustomed to that, and he moved to put the lowerclassman at ease. He was about to reach out and touch, even embrace, Henry as Christ did the leper, as St. Aloysius did the victims of the plague. But before contact could be made, Father Kirby was between them in his grey-and-blue varsity letter sweater and his platypus baseball hat. He steered Henry nimbly away from Watts and introduced him to the group as a "fine JV tackle with loads of potential," which was ridiculous; and then, holding him firmly by the elbow so he couldn't get too close, he said to Bill Watts, in a low voice, "This is the fifth former I told you shows a schoolman's grasp of faith and knowledge. A young man to watch." That was code and needed to be cracked. Bill Watts gave him a pensive, exploratory handshake. Henry felt connected to a polygraph. He thought of saints who could read souls and see the cancerous shadow of sin lurking within. Whatever he saw, Watts smiled and put his arm around Father Kirby, a head shorter than he. "Trust this funny old man," Watts said to Henry. "Hold nothing back, and he will let you fly." He left the room, followed by the football team, a kind of earthly ballast to keep Bill Watts from rising heavenward before his time.

Henry was alone with his confessor who rummaged in his desk and found his last Hershey bar. He wanted to admit he had a sixth sense about people. He saw the destiny of Bill Watts when the boy was just nine. His father brought him to the school to visit his elder brother Jack, before Pearl Harbor. He crossed himself; Jack must be dead. Henry shifted uneasily. Moses Kirby, x-rayer of souls, had seen through Henry Stillman the day he walked into the school. "What I saw was not just a right tackle and an ace student but something much more exciting—a prefect of the Junior Sodality of the Sacred Heart." He had to explain. A sodality was a prayer and study group that formed the spiritual core of student life, more important than a hundred football teams.

How wrong the old priest was, a man who knew Henry lusted for Joan of Lorraine and still spoke of him in the same breath with Bill Watts. "I would feel like a hypocrite. I am a very bad person," he said. Kirby brushed aside his protest. "Scruples. Beware of them. Scruples lead to pride, which is a real sin, as when you say, 'I am so worthless even God cannot love me.' Trust me, son, I will tell you when you sin." Henry was deflated; he thought himself as a monstrous sinner. But Father Kirby knew what real sinning was. He heard confessions at the Baltimore Cathedral before holidays like Christmas when the aisles were jammed with the fallen, waiting to confess and return to the fold. "That's when you land the big fish." Henry, a failure at sin, was being offered the consolation of holiness. Kirby asked him to think about it. It was a decision that could change the rest of his life. The confessor had no doubts at all; he had been a priest for forty-three years and never missed a call. Henry would make a splendid prefect and example to the entire school, a sterling successor to Bill Watts, who incidentally agreed entirely with him, that Henry Stillman was a comer.

"A schoolman's grasp of faith and knowledge." They were flattering him, and he knew it. He wasn't a scholar like Aquinas or Duns Scotus, but he could reason. In religion class, Kirby had read an article from *Time* magazine about Dr. Edwin Hubble who predicted the new Palomar telescope would determine whether the universe would expand indefinitely—to infinity—or at some point collapse back into a ball. Was the universe finite or infinite? What did the class think? His peers guessed wildly, but Henry recognized it for a problem in teleology, not astrophysics. It did not take a two-hundred-inch reflecting mirror to know that the universe must be finite because only God is infinite. Father Kirby beamed. The Jesuits were the heirs of the schoolmen—it was a code word for he is one of them a man to watch. Father Kirby had pierced his armor; he knew that Henry had the makings of a Jesuit. If life is an entrance exam to eternity, who would risk eternal damnation for the brief candle of mortal lust and pleasure? There was only one logical choice—to leave the world and its temptations and consecrate everything to God. Ad majorem Dei gloriam.

He became the prefect of the Sodality of the Blessed Virgin, a first step toward a right life. Standing in a black cassock before his peers who sat in the first pews on the Gospel side of the chapel, reading notices from his clipboard, kneeling in front of them, slightly elevated at the communion rail, to lead a rosary with the Glorious Mysteries, he was the next Bill Watts. He was a miniature Jesuit, and he loved it. His classmates who had ignored him or returned his former aloofness with petty meanness suddenly found respect. He knew his elevation was trivial, barely an inch above the rest, but he discovered that the ladder of hierarchy led out of the pit of anonymity. A single rung allowed Henry the perspective to see where he had been and where he could go. He had a destiny. He didn't have to do anything; it radiated from him, this gift of the Holy Ghost. Everyone knew it. It was premature to think of a vocation; Father Kirby would tell him when it was strong enough to withstand the world's gaze. He did not write home about the spiritual developments in his life. Things could change, and besides, he had not yet lived. He wanted to taste the world, like St. Paul and St.Augustine, before renouncing it entirely.

Jimmy Bowes, who was still at school in St. Louis, wrote him about Marla Starker who would let guys take her to the garage and do anything they wanted. Bowes and Henry had independently learned that boys didn't piss in girls; they ejaculated the semen which they discovered at Kooch-i-ching. But the physiology of the union between the sexes remained obscure. Why did they go to the garage? Was Bowes right about people doing it in automobiles? He would find out at Christmas.

MARLA STARKER'S GARAGE

Joe and Julia met the all-coach Jeffersonian in the cantilevered shed of the St. Louis Union Station where the trains backed in from Mill Creek yards outside. A year before the brakes failed on the Anne Rutledge, a New York Central sleeper to New York, whose last car smashed the track-end barrier, jumped four feet onto the station level platform, broke through the iron gates, and rolled across the grand concourse, knocking down a Union News stand. Joe Stillman drove Henry down to see it. Temporary repairs still showed where the flanged wheels had gouged the marble floor.

The drive uptown was gloomy. Just north of the station on Market Street, they passed a wide billboard proclaiming the Mill Creek Valley Title I Urban

Redevelopment Area. On Locust Street, whole blocks of four-story porched tenements from which bright laundry and sheets had flown like the canvas of clipper ships were now rubble. They were tearing down Blacktown. "Where are they putting the Negroes?" asked Henry. He glanced at his father's grim face; he looked neither left or right at the devastation. "Kinloch. Outside the city limits, where they can't vote," Joe said. The population of St. Louis, the twenty-sixth city, was eight hundred thousand, one-quarter Negro. A trip downtown confirmed that St. Louis was falling apart.

They were just inside the back door when Joe asked Henry if he'd like to help run some Fletcher-Munson curves. Julia let out an abrupt and frightening wail. "He's just come home! We haven't seen him for three months. Can't we just sit down like normal people for five minutes without having avalanches and earthquakes? Is that too much to ask?" Joe shrugged and sat down obediently. He took a Bakelite jeweler's glass from his jacket pocket and put it over the left lens of his glasses in order to scan the newspaper a word or possibly a letter at a time. "Cataracts," he said. Julia sat on a couch and crossed her legs. She had what she wanted—all her men keeping her company in her blue living room.

"What are they teaching you?" Joe Stillman wanted to know. "Quadratics, solids?"

"Plane geometry mostly."

"You had that last year. Can you bisect a torus?"

Henry knew Joe thought the Jesuit curriculum was weak on science and heavy on "moral philosophy." He was anxious to show his father how the power of scholastic logic could illuminate physical principles.

"Do you think the universe can expand indefinitely?" he asked.

"Depends on what you use for Hubble's constant, which depends on the total mass of the universe. The jury's still out on that one. It could collapse or expand forever. Why?"

Julia wanted to know if she had heard right. What did they say was expanding? "The universe, Mother."

"Isn't it large enough already? Does everything have to be bigger and better—even the poor universe?" She was nostalgic for Ptolemy. The men ignored her.

"The Jesuits say the universe must be finite because only God is infinite."

"Suppose it isn't?" Joe asked.

"It has to be. An infinite universe is a logical contradiction. QED."

"So if the universe turns out to be infinite, then God doesn't exist. You want my opinion, they're just asking for trouble."

"How so?"

"Why look foolish if you don't have to? Just say God *is* the universe, they're both infinite, and everybody's happy, Hubble and the pope."

"That's pantheism," said Henry. "God is *in* a hydrogen atom. He is immanent in all things, but He must also be above and outside Creation. Before and after. He can't just be a bowl of tapioca or Hubble's constant."

"So call me a goddam pantheist," Joe said irritably. "I didn't know God still had to have a long white beard and a bad temper. I thought we'd left that stuff behind."

"God must be able to know his creation."

"If he knows what's been going on the past couple of years, he ought to be ashamed of himself."

Henry's face was burning with humiliation. He was a fool, and his father knew it. He had no mathematical aptitude, Ohm's law was opaque to him, and even his theology was a sham. Julia came to his defense, making him feel even worse. "I think that was uncalled for, Joe. You asked what he was learning, he tried to tell you, and you tear him down. It's so easy when you don't believe anything."

"Who says I don't?" Joe asked, standing up and mashing out his cigarette. "I believe we're all going to hell in hand buckets while you Pollyannas preach that God's in his heaven and loves us." He went out through the dining room and the swinging door to the pantry. Soon rumblings and avalanches came from the basement. Julia Stillman sat stoically in her blue wing chair as the whole house shook in sympathetic vibration.

"What's eating him?"

"He was so excited you were coming home. He misses you terribly."

"Funny way to show it."

"Sometimes I'm sorry I made him stay out here. There was so much more for him in the east—"

"Is he still teaching?"

"He doesn't know what to do with himself. He wishes he was back at General Electric with his hunch back or wherever that was during the war—"

"New Mexico. He was making the atomic bomb."

"You always say that, but I don't believe it."

"Have it your way. He was fishing for a year and half. I'm going out with Jimmy Bowes."

"Can you at least say good night to him. Go down and just talk to him?" Cascades of jagged sounds exploded from under the carpet.

"I will if he can hear me."

But he didn't go down.

Jimmy Bowes's family had just moved to the center of the city on a private circle of vast homes protected by feudal gate towers and guards. Whites were leaving the neighboring blocks to barricade themselves in armed enclaves. The marble mansion was a copy of the Trianon Palace, and behind it was an equally impressive carriage house and stables where Mrs. Bowes kept her horse, which she rode sidesaddle in a long tartan skirt and a hooded cape, looking like a Gainsborough. Her sculpture studio was over the stables. They had lived in a smaller house when Jimmy and Henry were growing up, and Mr. Bowes worked very hard. The machinists in his aircraft plant went on strike after the war; and for some reason, the longer the plant was closed, the more valuable it became. Big Jim Bowes had nothing to do but drink and play golf. He called himself a "paper millionaire." He was a jowly man with a cowlick that made him part his hair in the middle. The strike didn't bother him. "I'm still in the big house," he said, cupping an oversized glass of scotch in his hands. "More ice, who's in charge of ice?" Jimmy ran to the pantry for ice. Big Jim's attitude toward his workers disgusted Mrs. Bowes who had visited the picket line and passed out homemade donuts to the strikers. She was so warm, concerned, and beautiful that the machinists would have worked for her for nothing. *Life* magazine published a photo of the strikers eating Jill Bowes's donuts.

She sat with Henry on the sofa across from Mr. Bowes who was waiting for his ice. She wanted to hear all about the Jesuits. She thought it was just incredible that anyone could still believe in God; the sheer idea made her tingle. All her life she had wanted to believe in something; she just couldn't. Was that so terrible? What would the Jesuits say about her? He assured her she wasn't alone.

"Oh, Henry, Henry, *Hen*-ry. You *have* your religion. It just makes me so *en*vious, so perfectly envious!" She had a way of saying his name that made it sound almost all right. Mr. Bowes was listening to them with his eyes closed. "Young Stillman!" he rasped. "Don't listen to Jill. She was a goddam Holy Roller when I met her. She had God and the saints coming out her ears. Ask her about those hillbillies down in the Ozarks. Where's the ice?" He closed his eyes again. Mrs. Bowes went on as if he had not spoken, as if he were not there. "Tell me what it's like, having religion," she pleaded. Henry said he would tell her something that he hadn't told to a single person, not even Julia Stillman. The Jesuits had made him the prefect of the Sodality of the Blessed Virgin. "Ohhhhh!" she gasped. Henry knew she didn't know what he was talking about, but it set off Big Jim. "He gets to lay every blessed virgin end to end—" "Shut up!" Mrs. Bowes screamed. "We're *talk*ing!" "Where's the ice?" "What's a prefect, what's a sodality?" Henry explained the spiritual hierarchy, and when she heard that a prefect wears a cassock while performing his sacerdotal duties, she jumped to the conclusion he hoped she would. "You're going to become a Jesuit!" She couldn't believe her ears, but when she thought about it, yes! He would make a wonderful priest! He was so understanding, such a good listener. "I could be a Catholic if there were priests like you. I could even imagine going to confession."

"That's so much bullshit!" said Mr. Bowes. "Where's the goddam ice?" Mrs. Bowes took a beige pillow from the couch and beat Big Jim on the head with it. "You are so goddam negative, you make me sick. Go play squash, get off your fat ass!" He grabbed the pillow and threw it into the hallway. "Come here!" he said, lunging after her, but she easily avoided him. "Goddam! You hear me?" he shouted. She put her hands over her ears and ran from the room passing Jimmy returning with the ice. Big Jim sank back into his chair, exhausted. Jimmy Bowes said they had to get going; they were late.

Jimmy had his father's cowlick, but he tried to plaster it down with Vitalis. He checked it obsessively in mirrors or felt it to make sure no hairs had popped out of their viscous bed. He looked at his cowlick in the rearview mirror as soon as they were in the ancient station wagon. Henry readjusted the mirror so he could see behind. He had to be careful; his learner's permit required him to drive in the company of an adult, and he couldn't get caught.

"What was my old lady screaming about in there?" Bowes asked him.

"Your old man pissed her off."

"Women are so stupid," said Jimmy Bowes.

They got lost in a county subdivision called Buckingham Terrace Estates looking for Marla Starker's house. Bowes had been there twice, but someone else had always driven.

"And she does it in the garage?"

"I swear. You'll see."

There were so many cars in front of the ranch house and attached garage, they had to park six houses away. Dr. Starker answered the door, a meticulously groomed man with gold collar and tie clasps, gold cuff links, watch, and rings. Henry could smell the Alfred Dunhill on him; he had just shaved, but it hadn't worked. Each subcutaneous black bristle of beard was visible on his chin and cheek, ready to erupt. "They're all in the rumpus room," he said, nodding toward some steps to the basement level.

The low-ceilinged room was crowded with a pool table, a pinball machine, and a dozen boys. Some wore letter sweaters, most had coats and ties like Jimmy and Henry. Henry didn't recognize anyone, and there was no sign of Marla Starker.

"Where is she, in the garage?"

"Shhhh!" A fire door on an overhead track rolled back a little, and a dark girl with a gypsy face and masses of black hair slipped through. The counterweighted door began to close again, but a young man coming behind her wedged himself through. Everyone looked at him. He smirked back and joined some friends in a close huddle near a pinball machine. Marla Starker stood alone and very composed. She was wearing a formal dress of stiff, shiny red material cut low in front and tight at her waist, which wasn't small. She was kind of stocky. The dress was short, and her matching shoes were high and spikey. It wasn't a very good getup for the garage, but maybe she was going somewhere later. Her guests ignored her; they were looking busy talking to each other. Henry nudged Bowes. "Does she remember you?" Bowes could tell with his hand that his cowlick had popped up. "I've got to find a mirror," he said and tried to leave, but Henry grabbed him. "Introduce me, will you?" The front doorbell was ringing; more people were coming. Jimmy Bowes jerked away from his grip and ran out. It was just like the rug box. Henry was alone with Marla Starker.

"I'm Henry Stillman."

"Have I ever seen you before?"

"I came with Jimmy Bowes."

"Where is he?

"He went to the john."

"So?"

"I go away to school."

"What do you want to do?"

"You want to go somewhere?"

"Where?"

"The garage?"

"The garage?" She seemed surprised.

"Sure."

"If you want."

She turned and put her shoulder to the heavy door and pushed it back a foot or more. "Watch out. It closes," she warned him. He rushed through behind her before the door slammed tight. They were sealed in the garage with a silver Eldorado and a copper Continental. The Cadillac was still warm and clicking under the hood. The front bumpers of both cars nestled up to a tool bench along the rear wall and Henry waited to see which car Marla Starker would choose. She jumped on the bumper of the Eldorado and sat on the bench next to a battery charger. Henry stood next to her with his foot on the bumper.

"What kind of doctor is your father?"

"A psychiatrist."

"Gosh."

"A child psychiatrist."

"Is that his Eldorado?"

"My mother's."

"What's she do?"

"What d'you mean?"

Henry didn't know what he meant. She had on so much makeup, a blistering red lipstick, and stuff around her eyes, it was hard to tell what she really looked like.

"What?" she interrupted his reverie.

"I was just thinking."

"You just stand there. What's wrong?"

"Nothing. Nothing's wrong."

"So what are we doing?"

"You don't want get in any of the cars—"

"Where would we go?"

"I don't know."

"You have a car?"

"Outside."

"What is it?"

"A station wagon."

"Make and year.

"Ford. Thirty-eight."

"You're kidding!"

"The best car Ford ever made."

She laughed, a real gutsy raucous peal of unbridled disdain whose object subsumed every single thing about Henry, including his vehicle.

"You're wonderful when you laugh," he said.

"Sure," she said, jumping down from the bench. "You've got a real line, whoever you are, a real line." The interview was over.

"So what happened?" Jimmy Bowes wanted to know.

"She was great, really great."

"Didn't I tell you? Didn't I tell you?"

"She was terrific."

"Did she show you her boobs?"

"Terrific, incredible. A great sense of humor too."

"What do you mean?"

"Her laugh."

Bowes was surprised that she had laughed. "Why did she laugh?"

"Something I said," said Henry.

"Don't talk to them," said Jimmy. He was very serious. "They don't like it."

Henry was surprised. "Why not?"

"They don't think you want to make out."

"There are other ways," said Henry, trying to sound confident of his technique.

"Sure," said Jimmy Bowes. "Like ways you learned from the priests."

He longed to ask Bowes about the automobiles in the garage and where she did it, but he couldn't admit his rejection by Marla Starker. Doing it alone seemed a lot easier than doing it with others.

Julia drove him to the Union Station. A redcap took his suitcase. His mother sat behind the wheel of her Buick, the same car that had carried him into exile from kindergarten. She had put on her blue glasses. "You never mention Donna Hasenclever anymore." "She's fat," said Henry. Julia understood. As the senior chaperone of a subscription dance, she was obliged to coax tearful wallflowers from the ladies' lounge and pair them with unwilling boys who had scribbled the names of imaginary partners in their dance cards. "Do you notice anything about your father?"

"He seems full of beans to me."

"He's changed, don't you think?"

"He can still skewer me."

"He wants so much for you to succeed. It must be very difficult for you. His pressure." Henry didn't want to have this conversation. He leaned through the door and kissed her goodbye. But he carried with him the scent of her perfume, Ma Griffe.

THE SHOREHAM HOTEL

Late one night, Father O'Connor shook Henry awake and told him to get dressed without waking Alfredo. The rector wanted to talk to him. Father Maloney was waiting for them in his office on the first floor. A tall and stately man in cassock and spectacles, he held his Holy Office to his chest, his forefinger marking the page of his interrupted devotions. Father Kirby stood by the window. Father O'Connor closed the door, and the rector whispered his news.

Alfredo's father had been assassinated a few hours before. The motorcade of the president of Colombia and his minister of interior, Senator de Santa Clara, had been ambushed by rebels on the highway between Bogota and his estate in Guatavita. The two leaders and their bodyguards were killed. A revolution was in progress, but the army has remained loyal, and Senora de Santa Clara had been able to reach the airport with the remains of Alfredo's father and his younger brother, Raoul. The sensitive mien of the rector became clouded when he mentioned the widow. "Alfredo's family have been great benefactors and protectors of the church and of the Society of Jesus, which makes the present situation most precarious and uncertain. If his mother comes to Washington, we must act with great delicacy." The rector was choking with discretion. He looked to Father Kirby. "You're Alfredo's best friend," said his confessor, which wasn't true. Alfredo didn't even talk to him; his best friend was Sanchez from Guatemala. "You're his roommate. We're counting on you to give him support. The rector wanted you to know the facts." The phone rang. Father Maloney answered it and switched to Latin. He listened solemnly and said, "Benedicite" with resignation. "Donna Esmeralda de Santa Clara arrives tomorrow and will stay at the Shoreham with a party of forty."

"Why not at their embassy?" Father Kirby asked.

"The political situation is unsettled. The vicar-general says the society must not meet with anyone until the situation in Bogota is clear. Alfredo's classmates may, of course, visit on their own initiative to pray for the deceased, present a spiritual burse, and comfort their classmate."

"The Junior Sodality of the Sacred Heart," said Father Kirby with professional pride. "Stillman is the prefect." The rector put a hand on Henry's shoulder. "A spontaneous gesture toward the bereaved Alfredo. Who can fault that?" On the stairs back to the fourth floor, Kirby and O'Connor speculated about the vicar-general's game. "He's hiding behind the kids." "He's dickering with the rebels." "Pius wouldn't let him." "Pius has seen his day. Deo volente." Father Kirby crossed himself as he uttered this treason, either to hasten the supreme pontiff's day or to ask pardon for wishing it. The two men were devout conspirators.

Alfredo was gone when Henry woke up. There were no newspapers in the basement snack store, and the proprietor would not say why. Donohue, a day student, brought the papers from town. Bogota was in flames, and a front-page photo showed the heads of the president and his chief minister on pikes over the gates of the old city. But the papers didn't yet know the widow and the body were coming to the Shoreham Hotel where Henry would lead the rosary for the minister. Henry knew something the world did not know, and he experienced the ineffable thrill of being an insider.

It took five trips of the small private elevator to get all the members of the sodality up to the George Washington Suite of the Shoreham Hotel. When the twenty-five boys were crowded in the front hall, Senora de Santa Clara appeared and greeted them herself. Alfredo's mother was taller than he had imagined and more beautiful in black—a coat with a high collar that lifted her head high and the same silver cross that she wore in the photograph. She towered over Alfredo beside her as she took the hand of each boy and pressed it in her black velvet-gloved hands, silently, looking each in the eye. A dozen men stood at attention behind her—some swarthy with black hair, others grey, lean, and stooped. The uncle was there, in uniform and braid, beside a nurse with a small dark-haired baby. Then they filed into a vast public room where the coffin was set in a hillside of flowers and green leaves blanketing the whole wall. Two oak kneelers with plush red pillows were in front of the gold casket and several dozen folding chairs and were arranged with an aisle between them. The sodality filled the chairs, and Father Kirby nudged Henry toward the casket.

It was coming down Connecticut Avenue in the old school bus that Father Kirby had remembered to tell Henry that each decade of the rosary must be prefaced by one of the Five Sorrowful Mysteries. Henry wrote them on his cuff with a blunt pencil in the dark bouncing bus. He pulled at his left cuff to make sure they were still there, but Senator Jorge de Sanze de Santa Clara was there before him—small, no taller than his son. His hands were folded over a gold crucifix half as big as himself. There were little ventilation holes in the toes of his black shoes. For tropical climate? Bogota—altitude 8,563 feet—cold and wet. With his altar boy's eye, Henry spotted an undertaker lurking behind the greenery. He kneeled, crossed himself, and began the Apostle's Creed. He knew the First Sorrowful Mystery—The Agony in the Garden. Alfredo's father was wearing a very dark blue pin-striped suit. The stripes were subliminal—a grey thread that surfaced briefly every five centimeters. There was a large spray of roses coming out of Senator de Santa Clara's collar where his head should have been.

He was on the third Our Father. Bogota was four hundred miles above the equator. The road from Bogota to Guatavita—two lanes, hairpin curves. They rolled rocks down to block it. The motorcade stopped. A bloodbath. His secretary, his bodyguards, his driver, the flash of the machete. He was on the eighth or ninth Hail Mary when the prayer lost all meaning. He couldn't tell if he was saying it right. It sounded like a mouthful of oatmeal. "Mail Marry mull of mace, the boarders smee smee and smith sky and spit." The beads told him he was done; it was time for a Glory Be and the Second Sorrowful Mystery. He had no more idea than the headless senator what the Second Sorrowful Mystery was. The head was with the rebels, the body with the widow. Someone was smoking in the coffin. He could smell the tobacco; he could see the smoke wreathing up over the roses.

Henry looked at his left shirt cuff; there was nothing on it but a grey blot. "The Second Sorrowful Mystery," he said. There was no hope. Clothe the naked? Bury the dead? They were the Sorrowful Works of Mercy. A voice from the coffin whispered very clearly.

"The Scourging at the Pillar." The voice was right. "The Scourging at the Pillar," said Henry and launched into the second decade of Hail Marys.

"Slow down," said the voice in the flowers. It was Father Kirby. He was in the leaves somewhere, behind the grass mat, under the coffin, invisible, smoking. He was in there on his hands and knees. The Holy Prompter. The Holy Ghost.

The widow and the prefect of the junior sodality exchanged envelopes after the rosary. Henry gave Alfredo's mother a spiritual burse card illuminated by Brother Umber with black and purple roses. It contained pledges of twelve thousand five hundred Our Fathers, twenty-five thousand Hail Marys, and thirty-five thousand Glory Bes, a burse almost as large as the one collected for Pope Pius's crusade against communism. Senora de Santa Clara had tears in her eyes as she pressed a black-bordered envelope into Henry's hand. "Give this to the *compania*," she whispered, "and take care of my Alfredo." She kissed him on both cheeks. He could smell gardenias.

In the bus going back, Henry was wretched. He sat with Father Kirby in the seat behind the driver, Brother Umber, who was sacristan of the chapel, organist, choirmaster, music and art teacher, and bus driver. He had forgotten the Hail Mary and all the mysteries; he was humiliated. Father Kirby said he had been terrific, no one knew a thing, the family was in tears. "Great work. Baptism of fire."

"No! I went blank. I didn't know what I was doing."

Kirby leaned between Henry and Brother Umber's back. "Nobody does!" he whispered loudly. "Half the masses you hear the priest is mumbling gibberish. Tell him, Brother Umber."

"They improvise," said Brother Umber with a professional's disdain for sloppy performance. He had studied piano with Busoni and Leschetizsky and played for Liszt. "Except the cues for the server," he allowed, "that's all they know, like the bars before tutti."

Father Kirby asked for the envelope Senora Santa Clara had given him. It contained a black-bordered card that said, "The family of Senator Jorge de Sanze de Santa Clara, the Republic of Colombia, and the Party Liberacion Nacional thank the Compania del Jesu for their comfort and support. Donna Esmeralda de Santa Clara." There was a check for one hundred thousand dollars drawn on a French bank. Father Kirby put the envelope in his pocket. "I was proud of you, kid. You looked good up there." If that was true, then something was fishy. He couldn't even remember the Sorrowful Mysteries, and no one cared. The priesthood was all show and illusion. They did it with mirrors and wires—raised the dead, cut a woman in two, fed a crowd with five loaves and a dozen fish, disappeared an elephant. Thaumaturges—miracle workers. Why is Christ like Houdini? Because they both died and rose again.

The Jesuits allowed the newspapers back in the snack shop because Alfredo had stopped coming to school. Donna Esmeralda de Santa Clara was on every front page. Bogota was in flames, ten thousand were dead, a civil war was raging. The rebels claimed victory, but Esmeralda de Santa Clara had taken her slain husband's place as leader of the Liberation Party. The army, the church, the business, and the farmers were behind her, she claimed, united against the communists. She demanded recognition of her government in exile and American intervention in Bogota. A rebel spokesman accused the Santa Clara party of being fascist oligarchs who had fled Colombia with three hundred million of the people's pesetas. President Truman was refusing to see her. Donohue brought a forbidden tabloid to school, the *Herald*, that accused Donna Santa Clara of using slave labor in her emerald mines and branding the buttocks of servants who worked on her estates.

Henry was called back to the rector's office after Sunday Mass. "What we say in this room," he whispered, "we say in petto." Secretly, in the breast. The rector slipped his hand inside his cassock over his heart and left it there while he spoke. The Santa Claras were the order's most generous benefactors. A solemn High Mass would be said for the repose of the senator's soul next Sunday. The Maryland Province of the Society of Jesus had a proud record of courage in the oppressor's face. The night a British column burned the White House in 1814, the Society of Jesus gave asylum in this very building to President Madison's fleeing wife. But there was also a time for discretion. The safety of Jesuit institutions in Colombia and throughout the world must be considered. Could he count on the prefect of the junior sodality to be their emissary in a matter of extreme delicacy? They wanted Henry to take back the check Alfredo's mother had given him. Father Maloney's hand went deeper in petto beneath his gown. The society would prefer to be able to say they had never seen it. It had been given to the sodality, but it was far in excess of the sodality's needs, as Henry knew when he opened it, wasn't that true? And on mature reflection, he wished to return it. The hidden hand withdrew from in petto, holding the unwelcome envelope. The rector nodded to Father Kirby who had prepared some reasons why Henry felt the sodality could not accept her honorarium. They rehearsed his speech, gave him the check, five dollars' spending money, and permission to go to the zoo when he was done. Brother Umber would drive him.

Brother Umber's breath was like Father McBride's after four masses on Sunday—he had been drinking the altar wine. It was among his duties to decant the wine from a cask in the chapel's basement and fill the glass cruets for each mass. He drove very slowly, looking through the steering wheel because he was so short. At the Shoreham Hotel, Henry waited an hour in a small windowless room of the George Washington Suite for someone to see him. A soldier took him to another room and closed the door. Glass doors led to a terrace overlooking Rock Creek Park and the zoo. He smelled an intense odor of gardenias before he knew Alfredo's mother was in the room. She was wearing a black robe with white fur around the collar and a gardenia in her long dark hair. "They've sent back the money, haven't they?" she said before he could give her the check. She threw it on the floor and refused to hear his speech. "Henriquez," she said. "It is a beautiful name." Henry hated it. It was a dumb name. He had never liked it. Henrys were simpletons. Henry Schluter owned the Shell station on Clayton Road in St. Louis County. He was bald and simpleminded. Henry was a cartoon character, also dumb and bald. Her first husband was named Henriquez, she said. "He was tall like you, but he drowned, poor Henriquez." *Typical of a person named Henry*, thought the current bearer of the stigmatic praenomen. He intended to change it. "Where are you from, Henriquez?" "St. Louis," he told her. "I have heard of your zoo. We want to have one like it in Colombia with the little apes who smoke cigars and ride motorcycles. How do you call them?" "Chimpanzees," he told her. "Cheemps, yes, how dear! And who was St. Louis?" "Saintly King Louis the Ninth, of France," said Henry, "of whom it was written that he could peer into the inmost fastnesses of the heart." She shuddered. "I hope he doesn't peer into mine," she said. "My heart is black." They looked at the snow in Rock Creek. "There is no winter in Bogota, only in our hearts, like your fathers, your black Jesuits. Why are they so cold, so suspicious? They cannot believe a little token comes from a broken heart. They think everyone must be like them."

She was silent for a long moment. "Oh, let them think what they want!" she said suddenly. She put her hand on Henry's cheek and turned his face away from the park toward her. "Don't let them corrupt you, Henriquez. Watch out for the Black Robes. They are not where the heart is. They know only their heads. There is no truth there. You know that, I can see." She looked at him with kind of mischief that said, "We have a secret." He wondered if what she saw was his erection. She smiled, moved close to him, and brushed her groin against his. "That is where the truth is, boys know more than old men."

Henry needed to leave, but he hadn't delivered any of Father Kirby's speech. "Our sodality can't take money for what comes freely from our hearts. And besides, we have no expenses, we don't—"

"Shhh! Don't talk, Henriquez," she whispered. He prayed, *Mother Most Pure, Mother Most Chaste, Mother Undefiled, Tower of Ivory, House of Gold, Queen of the Angels.* He ejaculated. She felt him come and was not surprised. "My Henriquez was like that. He thought too much." She kissed him lightly on the cheek. "You are a wonderful man," she said, "but you must stop thinking." They were standing a few inches apart, she looking at him and he at the floor, when Alfredo came in. "Wouldn't you two like to go to a movie?" she asked. Alfredo turned and left. She sighed. "What a stuck-up little fellow he has become! I wish he could stay with you and learn to be a man. *Que lastima.*" She let him go.

IMPURE ACTIONS

Brother Umber was reading a pocket score of the Verdi's *Requiem* in the school's Dodge station wagon when Henry returned. A bunch of gladiolas was on the seat beside him. He was a nearly round Catalonian with short white hair. If he had played for Liszt, he had to be at least eighty. Despite his vow of poverty, he had been allowed to bring his Bechstein piano into the order with him. The concert grand sat with its lid locked in an alcove of the refectory where he gave lessons. Julia Stillman wanted Henry to take piano, but after one lesson, Brother Umber gave up. Henry, he said, had absolutely no sense of time. Mozart had such a pupil, the daughter of a wealthy elector. "She was like teaching a rock, and he refused to see her again. The elector begged him, offered him a house and gold, but Mozart chose poverty. Fraulein Knoedler helped kill Mozart," Brother Umber stately flatly. "Ask anyone who must teach."

Henry wasn't interested in going to the zoo. He was feeling weird. He really wanted to take a shower and go to bed. Brother Umber asked if he minded stopping at the Carmelite convent in Georgetown on their way back to Maryland. He wanted to deliver something. Brother Umber was excited. He let out the clutch too soon and stalled the old Dodge five or six times in a row. He was like a camper allowed into town after months in the woods. He got to wear a black suit and tie and a black felt hat, instead of the cassock. He couldn't stop talking. His old teacher, Theodor Leschetizsky, had made Jan Paderewski from nothing—"a tinkler"—but he was hard and cruel. If the wrist was not five inches above the keys, he beat it with a ruler until there was blood. He taught only one finger for two months, then the next. Brother Umber wasn't allowed to play a note of music for two years, only Leschetizsky's exercises. He made a sudden right into a small street, climbed the curb, touched a tree gently, and stalled. He was parked. He grabbed the flowers, saying he would be right back, and disappeared though a small gate in a high wall covered with ivy. He didn't come back. Henry was getting a bad stomachache; cramps doubled him in the seat. He tried to walk. It had been forty minutes. Finally Henry went to find him.

The gate opened on a path to a side door in a chapel behind the walls. The church was lit entirely by the red glow of votive candles burning in ruby glass cups. The narthex of the chapel was separated from the nave by an iron grill ten feet high. Henry could see dimly through the bars, past the banks of votive flames, into the dark nave that had no pews or benches, only kneelers scattered randomly in the vast space. Six or seven nuns in brown habits and white coifs were praying, each alone and facing away from the others. Henry knew about Carmelites; Julia Stillman took her lace to be mended by the mendicant nuns who were cloistered in their convent. When they were hungry, they rang the bell in the tower, and neighbors left food by the grill, just like this one where Brother Umber was speaking rapidly and with many gestures to an old nun behind the bars. She was holding the gladiolas and seemed anxious for him to leave. She looked back at her kneeling sisters frequently. Carmelites are contemplatives—they have taken a vow of silence and can't talk to anyone, even each other. Henry was doubled up like a shrimp from the pain in his abdomen when something happened. The old nun threw a wad of paper through the grill. Brother Umber kneeled to pick it up, and she threw the flowers on top of him, then turned and walked toward the altar. She was crippled and could barely get up a step. A younger nun left her kneeler to help her. Brother Umber was still talking to her back in a romance language Henry didn't recognize. He slipped outside and waited in the station wagon.

The old man was in a rage all the way home, muttering to himself in a rainbow of languages. "People get stupid when they're old, don't ever get old." He was quiet for a few miles, then he said, "Women are tigers, the best way to keep them is behind bars." The excruciating pain was now located in his right side and getting worse. When they got to the school, he hobbled straight to the infirmary to see Sister St. Hilda. It was late Sunday, her day of rest, and the old Sister of Bon Secour let him know nothing could be so wrong with him it couldn't wait until tomorrow. Her chief cure was scorn and disbelief. She loathed disease and especially its seat, the body. She interrogated him like the Wizard of

Oz from behind a baffle of wheeled muslin screens that barricaded the hallway to her cloister. It was never certain exactly where she was or when she might appear. It was a job to get her to actually look at you, but for internal complaints, her manifestation was unnecessary. From her invisible station, she prescribed a punitive enema and supervised it by remote control. The malingerer was sent to a bathroom stall, told to leave a crack in the door through which she passed an enema hose accompanied by a stream of instructions and threats. Henry obeyed and, when he had evacuated the warm emetic, described to her its color and consistency. He was told to flush the toilet, return to his room, take a hot shower, and go to bed. She had never been seen.

The pain grew worse, and by dinnertime, Father O'Connor called an ambulance. Father Kirby went with him, sitting beside the stretcher. With the siren blasting over their heads as they shot down Wisconsin Avenue toward the Georgetown hospital, Father Kirby asked the dying boy if he wanted to make a confession. He couldn't tell the priest that he had sinned with his roommate's mother and maybe it wasn't a sin to come in your pants if he had tried to stop himself. He had prayed to the Virgin, but Aloysius would have run from the room. Henry stayed, indulged himself, let her rub against him. They were conspirators, lovers. Through fur and flannel, they had performed some kind of sex for which sin his glands were rotting, about to explode in the face of his confessor who asked again if he wished to confess. Father Kirby lit a cigarette while he waited. The ambulance driver spoke through the open partition. "Dangerous to smoke back there, Father. Oxygen, ether, you name it." Henry's stomach was cut in two by a jagged bolt of pain. Extreme unction was what he wanted. A blanket absolution, total forgiveness, no questions asked. He knew if he died, he was going to hell.

He woke while they were still sewing him up. First he heard laughter, then he saw gloved hands moving in the glass reflectors of the lights above him. A masked and blood-spattered doctor at his feet said he wouldn't be called Buttonhole Charlie anymore if people could see this mess. That crazy nun should be locked up. An enema for a burst appendix? Homicide. Sheer murder. They joked about his ravaged stomach as if he wasn't there. It occurred to him that he was dead, but a nurse noticed he was awake and warned them the boy was listening. He later saw where the surgeon's scalpel had wandered all over his abdomen, severing muscles and ligaments in the hunt for the burst appendix, which was found just in time to prevent him from learning the consequence of his apostasy had he died. He was relieved he was alive to reconsider his actions.

Nuns, nurses, doctors, and orderlies came and went without warning. He couldn't even pee, and the nuns had to call an intern to put a catheter in his penis. The lights were never off. He thought constantly of Donna Esmeralda and wanted to jerk off thinking about her, but he couldn't get an erection, much less get his hand to it over the bandages, wires, and tubes. His world was unmoored. He had nothing to do but examine his conscience. Was there a god, and if so, did he know or care about Henry's sin, if it was a sin? Had he invented his apostasy just to avoid confession? Was it dishonest for him to remain the prefect of the Sodality of the Blessed Virgin? He closed his eyes, and the form of Donna Esmeralda appeared dressed only in a garland of gardenias that covered her breasts and the silver crucifix below her navel. He heard the voice of Father Kirby close by.

"You look a lot better than you did yesterday. You passed out on us in the ambulance. I had to give you conditional absolution. Hoped you wouldn't mind."

Father Kirby was standing beside his bed.

"Conditional on what?" Henry asked.

"Sincere contrition. They just call it that."

If there was a god, he wanted to cover his bets. "I don't mind, I'm sincerely contrite," he said.

"I knew you were. I've brought a friend, just wants to say hello." He called to someone in the hall. "Come on in, he's awake!" Bill Watts came in and sat on his bed. With a face transfigured by sympathy, he leaned toward him, bracing himself with a hand on Henry's covered knee, which hurt though he tried not to show it. Watts seemed about to kiss him or put his other arm around him; but he only wanted to ask, in a whisper the nuns couldn't hear, if it was true that he had actually taken an enema from Sister St. Hilda. Henry admitted he had. Watts was appalled. "Never, ever, take an enema from Sister St. Hilda. When she hands you the hose, you dribble the water down the sides of the toilet bowl, then put your head in it, so it echoes, and go—" He made a noise like a gaseous bowel movement. Henry laughed, which triggered a stomach cramp so painful an intern gave him morphine to save the stitches, and the nuns made his visitors leave. Julia Stillman telephoned to say she had sent him a railroad ticket to come home for Easter. In her voice, he could hear the sand running through her three-minute egg timer.

He had to live in the infirmary with Sister St. Hilda for two weeks until he was able to walk up the stairs to the fourth floor. His presence taxed the ingenuity of the nun to remain invisible. He roamed the first floor at night to give the nun privacy to eat her supper, which was left on a tray outside the curtained doors. One night he heard the piano in the refectory. The glass-paned doors were locked, but a pantry entrance was open. Brother Umber was playing in the dark. His head was bent over the keys, his left ear practically touching his flying fingers. He seemed to be listening to the keys. He saw Henry and stopped. "Do you want to hear a story? I am the orchestra. A drunk old man comes home all full of schnapps. BOOM DEE BOOM DEE BOOMBOOM!" he sang in his ragged tenor. "His wife lets him in. She is the piano. SHHHH! You'll wake the whole neighborhood!" He played a set of legato, quieting modulations. "Here is your pipe. I'll make some warm milk. Boom Dee Boom Dee Boom Boom. Not so loud. Go to hell, woman, leave me alone." It went back and forth with the piano getting louder and the old man softer, trying to soothe her. "They've changed places now. She is angry. From G, a note in a woman to beware, she descends chromatically. Forty years and what do I get but cursing and drunkenness? Fifths—a mocking chord, a terrible logic. She is about to explode. Comes the trill. Pots, pans, cups, lampshades, everything flies."

The trill was tense. It lasted forever, punctuated by crashes in the treble and bass. Gradually it diminished. "She is legato again. Listen to her two sighs. They are woman, pure woman. The old man comes from behind the door. 'I am sorry,' he says, three times. She accepts him so quietly, and now for the first time they are together. From E to G to E they go, soaring up. It is the most wonderful bar in all music. It does not end, never. There is a rest and then the rondo."

Brother Umber locked the keyboard lid. "A piano should never be locked. Like a church should never be," he said. "But the waiters, they play boogie-woogie, with dirty hands." They walked down the long wide hallway, past the reception hall and the statue of St. Ignatius, to the north wing and the infirmary. Brother Umber opened the door without ringing and called loudly to the sister. "Help, Sister St. Hilda, help quickly! I am wounded in my heart. Blood is flowing in all my veins! Nurse! Sister! Come out! Please!" He sounded like he was dying. From behind the screens of muslin, from her room deep in the rear of the building, came a loud retort.

"Go to your cloister, you drunken old goat!"

"I can't sleep without your blessing," he protested.

Sister St. Hilda appeared from behind a screen carrying her empty dinner tray, which she handed to Brother Umber. "Go wake up the Carmelites with your nonsense and leave decent religious some peace!" The perpetually sour lady was smiling until she saw Henry, and then she started berating him again. "You're corrupting my convalescent! I'm going to have you sent to the missions. To Jamshedpur. The Tamils will eat you on a bamboo skewer. There'll be no more tete-a-tetes with Carmelites then." "*Bon nuit*, Madame," said Brother Umber, and carrying her tray, he closed the door gently behind him.

Alfredo was now a day student, living with his mother at the Shoreham Hotel. When Henry was allowed to return to the fourth floor, he hoped to find the oval photograph of Alfredo's mother; but all his roommate's belongings, the seven suits and the uniform, were gone. Henry went to Father O'Connor's room to ask if Alfredo was coming back. The priest was building a variable sweep frequency generator in his underwear. A certificate of achievement from C. R. Smith, president of the National Radio School, was Scotch-taped on the wall. "The kid's mother will never let him go. She's a tiger," said Father O'Connor. "The poor guy's gonna get eaten." Henry was learning all women are tigers, all men are eaten. He had spoken with no one about his visit to the Carmelites. "Brother Umber and I stopped at the Carmelite Convent, just before I got sick."

"Did you see Sister Annunciata?"

"There was an old nun behind the grill. He took her some flowers."

"That's his wife." Henry hoped he would say more.

"They couldn't see each other for fifty years. Then her order decided why not, they ain't going to run away now."

In return for that information, Henry offered to help solder resistors and condensers into the radio chassis. Father O'Connor was surprised at his skill. "I used to do it for my father." The priest thought his father's line was molecules, fluids, and gases.

"Electrons too," said Henry. "He was Steinmetz's test engineer at General Electric. They made the first lightning, three million volts, 1912." Father O'Connor whistled. "Charles Proteus Steinmetz. Hysteresis. Great man. So what did your father have to do with the Manhattan Project?" Joe Stillman never talked about it. But his specialty was black powders, shaped charges, and electrically sequenced ignition. He learned dynamite in the coal mines. He could blast a seam so it fell in perfect chunks into the waiting hopper cars.

"They say it took a lot of explosives to make a critical mass," said the priest.

"The implosive lens, he wrote me how it worked."

"An interesting man, your father," said Father O'Connor.

"He believes in the expanding universe."

"So do I," said the priest.

"Science is my father's god. He's an atheist."

Father O'Connor looked up from the wiring diagram of the radio kit. Did his father actually say that? Not in so many words, Henry admitted.

"He's a pantheist. He believes God is the universe."

"That's a lot different. Don't go calling someone an atheist without their permission," the priest warned. "No one with half a brain will say there is no God. He can say he doesn't know or he isn't sure. Because nobody is."

"Not even you?"

"We all have our bad days," said Father O'Connor. In the war? Father O'Connor nodded. People said there were no atheists in foxholes, but he had met plenty of men in foxholes who felt abandoned by God. Life seemed meaningless, and death too. Just when the chaplain was at the point of despair himself, God appeared to him. This seemed unlikely, but Henry went along with the story.

"What was He like? I mean, how did He appear?"

"How the Lord manifested Himself to Captain Bill O'Connor," the priest began. "It's a very short story. I got it in my head that I ought to be with a squad that had got themselves pinned down in a barn. They had dead and wounded, which was my job. I had to be with these men. The barn was in a field with Jerries all around it, in the hedgerows and everywhere. I got my assistant and another boy wounded trying to take me across it. I was so angry I picked up his BAR, a kind of light machine gun my corporal was carrying, and I said to myself, *I'm going down there and give those men last rites if I have to kill every living thing in my way*. That was my plan, so help me it was. I took about ten steps, and God appeared and stopped me in my tracks."

There was a catch coming, or Henry hoped there was, so he wouldn't have to pretend to believe the priest had seen God. He went along with the priest's tale. "God actually came down and you saw Him?"

"He didn't come down. He came up."

"What did he look like?"

"He looked exactly like a Bouncing Betty – brown, about eight inches in diameter, gently rotating. He sent me to the hospital to cool off."

Henry liked the story. You could believe it was god or an antipersonnel mine. Whatever it was cooled him off. What he didn't know was which Father O'Connor thought it was. He liked to joke, like he joked about his Purple Heart tattoo, but Henry had discovered it wasn't the idea of the tattoo guy in the next bed. It was a copy from his mother's remembrance card, which he found in a book he borrowed. Same colors, identical bleeding heart, brown thrones, and orange flames.

Theresa O'Connor. Died October 30, 1938.

O'Connor fused the real and the spiritual world and talked to things the way Joe Stillman did. He dropped a pair of pliers and said, "Drop, damn you. You can't fly anyhow." Things were alive, or he imagined they were. He waited a moment for the rebuked pliers to return on their own before he picked them up. If God was everywhere, in everything, he could be in an antipersonnel mine or in the expanding universe.

Father O'Connor was stepping into his cassock to check the hall. "Here's one for you to think about. What's the Great Commandment?"

"Love thy neighbor as thyself, for the love of God."

"Love thy neighbor. Right. But if my neighbor is trying to kill me and make God's earth a hell, is he really my neighbor? Suppose he is the devil. I am commanded to love the sinner, not the sin, but must I love the devil?"

"I don't think so."

"Then why isn't it all right for me to take a machine gun, or an atom bomb, and send these devils back to hell so the world will be safe for the God of Love to return from wherever He's been hiding?"

He opened the door. In the long corridor, a dozen students kneeled by their doorways surrounded by books and papers. They had been caught in some forbidden pursuit during the two hours of study hall—listening to the radio through earphones, reading comics, wrestling with their roommates.

"Or to put it another way, if God is all-powerful, why is He so weak? Or is God really running things? Is He still there?"

"Suppose," said Henry, "we found out that God was gone but decided to go on as if he was still there."

"Sounds like a smart thing to do. He might have just stepped out for a moment."

"But if you really, really knew there was no God anymore—"

"That's real faith—to believe without hope."

"People do that?"

"Sometimes, like in foxholes."

"They lie to themselves, you're saying."

"To an unbeliever, they seem to be lying."

"It's all relative?"

"No. It's the same thing from different angles."

"God or a Bouncing Betty. It all depends."

"You're getting warm. We should talk some more." He went in the hall and looked both ways.

"Everybody up!" he called. "*Raus, raus!* Amnesty. Back to your rooms." The kneeling figures cheered. Father O'Connor limped down the long hall singing in his melodious tenor.

> As she wheeled her wheel-barrow,
> Through streets broad and narrow,
> Crying "cockles and mussels, alive, alive, oh!"

It was no surprise to O'Connor to find atheism and despair in foxholes because he felt the same absence of God in himself. But he didn't quit; he was ready to kill his way into a barn to do his chaplain's duty at the cost of his soul. It didn't surprise Henry, who had risked damnation to conceal his sin with Donna Esmeralda from Father Kirby. The role of junior prefect demanded a much better man than he, but who else was there? Donohue who sold pornography from K Street to the boarding students as Kirby well knew? Henry was flawed, but he was the man. He could strive to be worthy. He saw why he had been chosen; the Jesuits were pragmatists.

In his room, he found Bill Watts stretched out, like a new roommate, on Alfredo's naked mattress. Watts could find his own corner in other people's lives the moment he met them, be intimate in a crowd, or make of his privacy a public event. "Congratulations!" he cried, jumping to his feet when Henry came in. "We've decided on you for the Tower of Ivory, my favorite!"

Watts has come directly from Father Kirby where they had chosen Henry to be lector on the mystical meaning of ivory during the Adoration of Mary held in her grotto behind the chapel on Friday afternoons in May. The centerpiece of

Marian devotions was the Litany of the Blessed Virgin, forty-nine ejaculations to the Virgin of which Tower of Ivory was the twenty-ninth and, with Mystical Rose and House of Gold, the most allusive and needy of explication.

"Congratulations, again!" He took Henry's hand and pressed it to his chest and with his other arm around Henry's back pulled him toward him. "I am very, very proud of you," he said, pressing Henry's head against his shoulder with his free hand. You could call it a hug. "I'll be doing House of Gold right after you. We'll be there together. You have nothing to worry about."

Henry was uncomfortable in the arms of both Bill Watts and of the church. He suspected that the senior prefect had an erection. It was scarce two weeks since he had lost, or mislaid, both his innocence and his faith; and he had barely savored his freedom. He tried to disentangle himself from Watts who was still spinning his web. "You know that next year you'll be the senior prefect. I'm leaving that to you. I'll be watching you from Woodstock." A loud bell signaled the end of study hall. Joe Nitto came in to borrow some batteries, and Watts left.

The Adoration of Mary would be Bill Watt's swan song as prefect of the sodality, and in June he would become a Jesuit novice at the Woodstock seminary. Everyone knew that only those with potential vocations, and the captains of major sports, were invited to speak at the May services in the grotto. The inner circle of sanctity and power was opening to receive him, to suck him into the vortex of faith before he had even lived. His ambition was to be a sinner first and become holy afterward, like St. Paul and St. Augustine who had tasted the best of both worlds.

Things were moving too fast. They had the wrong man to replace Bill Watts. He had to persuade Father Kirby that he was an imposter. On Friday night, he waited in the line for his confessional where he had to listen, even if he smoked or dozed. In his room, he could always get away—with Hershey bars or magazines or phone calls.

"I had impure thoughts about a woman."

Kirby didn't open his eyes.

"You entertained these thoughts?"

"Yes. And impure actions."

"Alone?"

"With her."

Kirby opened his eyes. Henry had his attention.

"You had impure actions with . . . ?" He wanted to know who.

"With Donna Esmeralda when I went back with the check. I couldn't tell you. I don't think there is a hell, and maybe there's no God to send me there. I resign as prefect of the sodality."

He had lit a cigarette.

"What happened between you and Alfredo's mother?

"I was aroused."

"By anything she did."

"We touched."

"I saw the way the lady was acting when I stepped out of the elevator. The rector should never have sent you back there."

"I should have confessed."

"You were entrapped. St. Jerome himself could not resist such a succubus."

"I enjoyed it. I want to do it again. I am a very bad person, and worse, I am a hypocrite."

"I told you before—your weakness is scrupulosity. I hear a lot of confessions, and I know what's going on. You are almost the only student who actually examines his conscience."

"I cannot be like Bill Watts."

"It was Augustine who said it is enough, for now, to avoid crime. He who would put aside sin altogether puts aside not sin but forgiveness."

"St. Augustine said that?"

"Book 9, *Civitas Dei*. For your penance, say five Our Fathers and ten Hail Marys, and pray for me."

The world was all screwed up. Brother Umber was married; Father O'Connor was an atheist; Bill Watts was queer; Father Kirby forgave sins before they were committed; and Henry, who had lost his faith and compromised his roommate's widowed mother, was beginning to feel that he fitted in, that this could be his home. All he had to do, according to Augustine, was stay out of jail. The pursuit of absolute virtue was a sin of pride that could land you in hell. This was a place for Henry.

When, at Easter, Julia Stillman saw the scar on his stomach, she was appalled. The still-red and swollen ridge of the incision meandered across his belly like a lost mole. The surgeon was a butcher; didn't he know where the appendix was? Henry explained his appendix wasn't where it should have been. They had to look for it. And whoever heard of giving anyone an enema for a stomachache, she wanted to know, or a hot shower? That nun must be a medieval monster; that was the only explanation. Julia would never let him out of her sight again. It was a mistake to leave him there after she met his sinister roommate and the crippled priest. She knew then and there that something was fishy. And now they send him home mutilated by Jack the Ripper. It was the last straw. Henry was put in the position of defending Sister St. Hilda's infirmary and the navy surgeon known as Buttonhole Charlie whose incisions were so famously small a sailor was returned to duty in twenty-four hours. Julia reminded him that she had danced with the Kaiser and seen the Hottentots at the World's Fair. She wasn't born yesterday. And he was never going back to that place. "Put that out of your mind."

She didn't know the half of it, but it wasn't a good time to tell her that he was the prefect of the junior sodality on the brink of a vocation. He pushed her hands away from his convoluted scar and zipped up his pants. "You've forgotten why you sent me away. Remember Toby, remember the bomb I built which blew him up and leveled the greenhouse. That's why you put me in an institution."

"That was before. Everything's changed."

"For the worse, Mother. I'm older and more dangerous. You don't want me around—"

"The truth is," she admitted, her icy hauteur melting in a pool before his astonished eyes, "I need you. I've been left alone with Joe Stillman for the first time since Prohibition, and I can't deal with him. I'm fit to be tied."

"What's the matter?"

"He wants to bomb China. He broods about it day and night."

"The Reds are taking over."

"There are so many things to really worry about."

Her real worries were the Germans, Jews, Negroes, and nouveau riche who had taken over antebellum French St. Louis from the Chateaus. Communism was not on her list.

"I'll talk to him."

He asked about China over cocktails. Joe wanted to rain atomic bombs on Peking, the Great Wall, the Forbidden City, and the Hong Kong tailors.

"All this to keep Chiang Kai-shek from being pushed into the sea?"

"Of course not!" he said. But mention of the generalissimo had galvanized Julia Chateau whose idol was Madame Chiang Kai-shek and the Soong sisters. It all made sudden sense. Joe was trying to protect them.

"Julia! Be quiet. Let me talk to Henry." He favored preemptive nuclear bombing of the mainland because this was the moment, our last chance, before Russia or China got the A-bomb and dropped it on us. He had written the *Post-Dispatch*, but they were all Reds and would never print it.

"How long will it take the Russians to make a bomb?" Henry asked him. Joe took off his glasses and rubbed his eyes.

"The U-235 gun bomb. Any fool can build one. All you need is plain vanilla uranium, thirty pounds or so. Could take three or four years. The implosion bomb, that's a horse of a different color. It takes plutonium, which doesn't grow on trees, and lots of luck unless—" He left them hanging in suspense while he replaced his glasses and looked around him to see if his audience was still listening. Julia's eyes had glazed with any reference to foreign affairs or technology, but Henry was wide awake. "Unless what?" he asked.

"Unless Oppenheimer and his crowd, you know what they are, don't you? They're Reds. His brother, his wife, all their friends. I wouldn't be surprised if they already gave Russia the bomb. The cat's out of the bag in my opinion. That's why I'm leery of bombing Russia. We just don't know. But China's a sitting duck. You watch though. We're too goddam soft and sentimental to defend ourselves."

Henry took issue. "Truman used the bomb against Japan. What's so soft about that?" "Who?" Joe Stillman asked. The thirty-third president was never mentioned by name in the Stillman household, and the reference to him unleashed a furious tirade against "the bankrupt haberdasher from Kansas City, a cipher, a Shriner, a man who wears a bow tie, a man with no class."

"At least he can't be a traitor to his class—if he hasn't got any," said Henry, referring to a conviction they held even more earnestly about the thirty-second president whose name was seldom uttered either. Julia Stillman put on her blue glasses. Joe Stillman got up again.

"Who in hell you think you are, coming back here and treating us like a joke?"

Now Julia was on her feet and at his side. "Joe, he didn't mean it that way. He's too young to know about the Depression. He doesn't know what we went through."

"Then he ought to listen and keep his mouth shut."

Henry flushed. All words, words, words. They had danced through the Crash, drinking bootleg bourbon from Hermann, Missouri, and spent the Depression building a giant house in the country and having babies. It was Roosevelt and the New Deal and the graduated income tax they hated. Henry was fed up with their fairy-tale version of history; he was making his own.

"Fine with me. I'll keep my mouth shut. I'm taking a vow of silence. And poverty, chastity, and obedience while I'm at it." They stared at him.

"What's that mean?"

"It means I'm thinking of becoming a Jesuit."

"You're sixteen, for crissake!" said Joe.

"So was St. Aloysius."

"Who's that?" Joe looked at Julia.

"The sissy saint. Mother named me for him."

He put out his cigarette. "This is all your goddam doing," he said to Julia Chateau.

Julia eyed Henry with deep suspicion. "Is this serious?"

"They made me the prefect of the Sodality of the Blessed Virgin."

"That's just a prayer group," she said to Joe, trying to minimize the news.

"Father Kirby thinks I have a vocation."

"That's what he's paid to think," said his father. "And his shills are telling you he's right. That's their racket, for god's sake! They're selling you a lot of snake oil. It's time you wised up."

"Let me talk to him, Joe."

His father went to the basement. Julia had put on her dark glasses. There was no air in the house; Henry could barely breathe. He didn't see how he had ever lived with them.

"Nothing would make me happier or prouder than for you to become a priest," she said. Faced with someone who said the exact opposite of what she meant made him want to get in a car and drive until it ran out of gas. He decided to give it one shot, then go look for Jimmy Bowes.

"I don't think you are happy that I have a vocation."

"I'd be ecstatic if you really had a vocation, but I don't think you do."

"How do you know? How can you say—"

"You don't even go to communion. You're about as religious as a coat hanger. Why did you tell your father all that?"

"Because I want to be someone he can't push around, that he respects or at least he's afraid of—"

"Henry, Henry, Henry, he'd be totally lost without you. You're the thread he hangs on."

She took off her glasses to dry her tears. It was the second time he'd made her cry.

"Forget everything I said," he told her.

"I'd be glad to," she replied.

"Just don't try to stop me from going back." He left the house and drove to Jimmy Bowes's place where he found only a yardman who said the family was in Boca Raton for Easter.

They went to Mass at Father McBride's parish on Easter Sunday. It was a cliff-hanger whether Joe Stillman would consent to the annual embarrassment, but he came. Etienne's mother had finally died, and Joe wanted to give his condolences. Joe made a date with the priest to go fishing, and on the way home, Julia told them things from the backseat about the late Mrs. McBride that Henry would never have guessed. The old lady, when she was widowed, had bribed the archbishop to ordain Etienne and let him make a parish chapel in the living room of their country house so he could take care of her. Etienne was just an overgrown boy, a Huckleberry Finn who wanted to fish and hunt with his dogs and drink wine in the mornings. Religion, when you got down to it, was work for altar boys, not grown men. She was speaking to Henry, but she was really letting Joe Stillman know that she had no investment in Henry's vocation; it was none of her doing. He imagined the scene they would make if he told them that in a month he would be standing in a black cassock before a bower of bright forsythia, like Aloysius in his garden at Gonzaga, birds twittering in the mild May, about to deliver before the entire school a meditation on the Tower of Ivory which he had been writing on the train, oblivious even of the Horseshoe Curve. Ivory. White, pure, strong, unstained, chaste, immaculate. *Macula non est in te.* Why tell them? It was better to go it alone, like Aquinas. St. Thomas's family also opposed his vocation. They tried to rip off his Dominican robes, and when he escaped, his mother hired brigands to kidnap him. She made his brothers lock him in a tower and tempt him with lascivious strumpets whom Thomas set on fire. Angels bound his waist with a cord so tight his head and heart were separated forever from the beast below the belt. Though large as an ox, fellow Dominicans rescued the saint by lowering him in a basket from the tower. Henry held his breath, but his vocation was not mentioned again, even on the drive to the Union Station. Joe and Julia Stillman waved to him from the platform.

ON THE LOOSE

It never occurred to him to suspect they had made a deal, even when only a week later Joe Stillman appeared at the school in Maryland, unheralded, in a Diamond cab. He wore his tweed suit and carried a large box with the Tesla coil which they had discussed giving to the school for the demonstration of static electricity. He said he was in Washington on business and wanted to show Henry the sights on the weekend. But he hoped to meet the physics teacher who was building the sweep frequency generator, if he was around. "He sounds like a regular guy."

Father O'Connor was on his way to Baltimore to buy war surplus radio equipment to build a seismograph. He met Joe in his old army khakis. He told his father how happy he was to meet him and then said something that made Henry want to dig a hole and crawl in. "Your boy is very, very proud of you, Mr. Stillman. He's lucky to have a father he can admire." Joe said that was nice to hear, but he was surprised that his children had kept up their religion despite his godlessness. Father O'Connor wasn't surprised. "Isn't God just a father who loves his children? Maybe you gave them a good example in spite of yourself." Joe showed him the Tesla coil, and they all went to the rector's office where Father Maloney accepted the gift for the school. Joe insisted on showing them how to work it. The oscillator hummed, the blue field glowed around the secondary coil, and the hair of the three men waved and crackled in the electrostatic wind—one in his tweeds, one in a black soutane, and one in a khaki shirt with the faded image of captain's bars on the collar. "The coil generates around twenty thousand volts," Joe said. "My!" said the rector. Actually Joe was behaving like a pack rat—a Rocky Mountain rodent that always leaves something to replace what he steals; a pine cone will be found where a toothbrush had been left. In this case, Joe left the Tesla coil in place of Henry.

It was not until they were in the cab to Washington that Joe told him they were going to New England. "I want you to see Building B at Schenectady where Steinmetz made lightning." Henry smelled a fish. "What else?" They might look at some schools. "I want to stay here," he said. Joe was unshaken. Henry owed it to himself to know what else there was in the world, and if he didn't like what he saw, fine. Nothing lost. They'd all be the wiser. "Mother chose the Jesuits. I like them, and I want to stay." Joe shook his head. He couldn't play one parent against the other anymore. The way the world was going (to hell in hand buckets), they all had to pull together. "Your mother and I both feel that education is the only thing we can give you. The government will take everything when we die. Won't matter a plug nickel who you are or where you're from. It's what you know and who you know. That's the new ball game. Union Station," he said to the driver.

In New York City, they changed stations and took the New York Central to Albany where they went to a hotel. In the morning, they took a cab to Schenectady and drove around the General Electric Company. He showed Henry Building B. Henry expected an ominous structure, like Castle Frankenstein, but Building B was of ivy-covered brick, granite trim, and mullioned windows. It looked like part of a college. They went by Steinmetz's old house on Wendell Avenue where Joe had roomed on the third floor, fresh out of Yale. Then they took the Boston and Albany east to Massachusetts. Joe had worked in General Electric plants in every town they passed—Troy for marine propulsion, Hudson Falls made transformers, Pittsfield turbine generators. They got off in Greenfield, Massachusetts, in a wet spring snow, and took a taxi thirty miles to meet Frank Boyden, the headmaster of Deerfield Academy who showed them his school. "You'd be a large fish in a small pond," Joe said on the way back to Greenfield.

More railroads, change of stations in Boston and the Boston and Maine Railroad to Prescott Academy in Oldfield. "You'd be a small fish in a big pond." They didn't look at any of the Episcopal church schools like St. Paul's where Joe had gone; he thought Henry had enough religion to last him his life. It was time to learn something. Oldfield had a colossal chapel with a spire as high as a radio tower. The director of admissions downplayed the chapel. The benefactor who donated the modern campus wanted to build a chapel, and the school gave in. Quid pro quo. "They just sing anthems in there; and Barney Nugent, our minister, talks about fair play. Totally nonsectarian. Less religion than you get on a dollar bill." The older men laughed. They were strangers, but they understood each other. They were New Englanders. What Henry hadn't learned was that a New Englander always says less than he knows.

In Boston again, Joe took him for seafood at the Old Union Oyster House near the North Station. Henry refused clams and oysters. Joe prophesied that after Henry had been at Oldfield for a year, he would eat nothing else. Henry tried to order a baked stuffed lobster despite Joe's advice that a fresh live lobster from Maine should only be boiled. Though he was looking forward to the buttery crumbled crackers, he reluctantly agreed. Their boiled lobsters lay in puddles of curdled milky fluid mixed with intestines and lobster eggs on large elliptical plates. Henry poked at his with a fork. "Watch me," said Joe as he dismembered the crustacean like an anatomy lesson. He ripped off the claws, cracked the second joints, and removed the meat with a pick. Then with both hands, he broke the back in two pieces and drained them over his plate; the chest cavity spewed out fluid, roe, and hot water. With his forefinger, he removed the tail meat in one piece, then pulled out a sac in the chest cavity, and held it in his thumb and forefinger for Henry to see. "The brain," he said, "poison." He put the chest section with its dangling feelers and dripping innards directly to his mouth and began sucking. "You'll get the hang of it," he promised. Henry knew his father hoped he would learn to be a New Englander. "I liked Oldfield," Joe said. "I wish I'd gone to places like that. They look like straight shooters to me." Joe Stillman had been expelled from St. Paul's School because he was the only one to admit he went ice-skating in the middle of the night. His companions, one his best friend, remained silent and were never discovered. Joe Stillman, who had been punished for telling the truth, never entirely trusted people or institutions again.

Oldfield sent entrance examinations, which the registrar at St. Aloysius administered outside his office on the foyer opposite the statue of Ignatius. For three hours, Henry scribbled in a desk chair like an adulterer in the stocks. Teachers, religious, and students whispered as they passed and stared at the boy with a scarlet *A*, for apostasy.

Father O'Connor looked over his shoulder at a quadratic equation he was trying to simplify. "Two x minus y squared equals y cubed minus x, you jerk." He was rooting for Henry to escape. So was Father Kirby for whom his intended defection to Protestant New England offered the moral strategist a fresh opportunity to reverse the Reformation. Henry would be sent as a spy and agent provocateur into the enemy camp. He would be a Jesuit in petto. Kirby was nostalgic for the society's golden age in the Counter-Reformation when undercover Jesuits infiltrated the courts of Europe and performed such daring sabotage that the order was suppressed by outraged monarchs. It had never been the same since the Restoration. Henry would be the pope's time bomb hidden in the soft underbelly of atheistic materialism. He wouldn't hear of Henry not speaking in the Virgin's grotto. It would mark the departure of his two proteges, Watts to the novitiate and Henry underground.

Cherry blossoms, dogwood, the sweet scent of fresh mowed grass on the greens and fairways. The senior and the junior prefects of the Sodality of the Blessed Virgin, both tall and grave, one blond and fair, the younger, dark haired with tortoiseshell glasses, a touch of El Greco's Grand Inquisitor. Their mentor and confessor, Father

Kirby, half their height, like a scrappy terrier bouncing up and down in spiritual excitement. Brother Umber leading his a cappella choir in the Marian liturgy.

Crowns of angels round thee gather,
Sweetest Virgin of the May.
Macula non est in te.

Tower of Ivory, House of Gold, Ark of the Covenant, Gate of Heaven, Morning Star, pray for us. A swan song for both prefects.

It was not the end of Julia Stillman's world that Henry was going to Oldfield. Between the bungled appendectomy and his suspicious vocation, the bloom was off Jesuits. She had given him the best catholic education she could. There was no more she could do but rest in peace.

It turned out that Jimmy Bowes was going to Oldfield too. When Mrs. Bowes heard that Henry was leaving the Jesuits, she was confused. "I thought you were going to *be* a Jesuit!" He made her sit down to hear his story. "I realized when I was about to die that there was no heaven, no hell; and if there was a god, he had forgotten us." She screamed as he knew she would. Her reaction was important because she was the only person, besides Joe and Julia, who knew he had ever intended to take Holy Orders. "I'm on a roller coaster!" she gasped. "You said at Christmas you were going to be a priest and now—now—I can't believe you're sitting there telling me this. I depended on you. You are the only one who has faith. You just can't, Henry, you can't lose it. I won't allow it! What do the Jesuits say? Can't they help you?"

"The Jesuits are atheists too," he said, driving in the last nail. "Henry! Don't tell me such things!" She put her hands to her ears and ran from the room. But she came right back. Her face was flushed, and her nostrils were flared with passion. "Henry Stillman, take back everything you've said, or I won't let you in this house again."

Henry took a deep breath, and then he described Harlow Shapley's classification of line spectra of variable Cepheid stars from old photographic plates dating back to the last century. You could drive a truck into Jill Bowes's wide-open mouth as he told about the mysterious dislocation of the red frequencies, the Doppler effect, and the theory that Edwin Hubble advanced to account for it. Distant galaxies were accelerating away from each other at speeds that would soon approach the speed of light. The universe was expanding. Mrs. Bowes was transfixed. "What does it all mean, Henry?" "It means that God is dead," said Henry. "The divine corpse stinks in putrefaction." Mrs. Bowes made herself another drink and sank into the sofa.

"How can you say that? It's so terrifying!"

"Nietzsche said it in *Also Sprach Zarathustra*."

"I'm completely wrung out. I'm shaking."

She exaggerated, but she was definitely in his spell. He wasn't making any sense, and it wasn't the right book of Nietzsche, but it made no difference; the effect was the same. Could he do this to anyone or just to someone who was overwrought and susceptible, like Mrs. Bowes? Could he do it to Marla Starker? If he knew her wavelength—if he had the right hook—he could. Jimmy Bowes was dead wrong. Women love to talk. Mrs. Bowes was worried about him. "Oh, Henry, Henry! What will Julia Chateau say when she finds out you are an atheist?"

"I'm never going to tell her."

"Mothers know, believe me. They know everything. Be careful."

"You are the only one in the whole world who knows."

"Why, why, why, Henry? Why me?"

Why indeed? Wasn't it odd that his only real confidant in the world was Jimmy Bowes's mother? He took a guess.

"Because you understand me," he told her. Her eyes became cloudy, and she closed them tightly. She squeezed his hand.

"It will kill Julia Chateau if she ever finds out." What would? That he was an atheist, or that Jill Bowes knew all about it? Both. Mrs. Bowes enjoyed being a wedge between Henry and Julia. She liked mischief. His mother must never know as long as she lived. If she discovered he had lost his faith while he was with the Jesuits, she would not let him go to Oldfield or even out of her sight, and his grand design would crash. His plan was to recreate himself, free of Julia and her church. It was time to make a break, to choose sides, and he chose Joe Stillman's. He would go to Oldfield; he would read Joyce and D. H. Lawrence and do physics and chemistry, and to calm his aching soul, he would study the Upanishads as Oppenheimer had in his dark hours at Göttingen and on the Mesa. And if that didn't work, he could always be a Jesuit in petto. The sky was the limit, and his heart sang. Henry the Apostate was out of his cage and on the loose!

2

OLDFIELD

Julia Stillman pulled Henry up the platform of the Union Station toward the locomotive, away from Jimmy Bowes who was being lectured by his mother and Big Jim Bowes who was arguing with Joe about how to keep the Chinese Reds from pushing Chiang Kai-shek into the sea. "Give 'em a taste of Hiroshima, they'll get the message," said Joe in deadly earnest. "Moscow could have something to say about that," Big Jim warned. The Soviets had unexpectedly tested their first plutonium bomb the previous summer, but Joe Stillman was undeterred. "I'll bet they don't have but one or two, like we did in '45. I say call their bluff." Henry wanted to listen to the men, but the locomotive ahead was sending clouds of impatient steam into the vast roof of the train shed, and Julia Stillman had put on her blue sunglasses. "I want you to promise me that you will go to Mass. I told them at Oldfield if you don't go to church on Sunday, I want to hear about it. It's who we are. We don't have a choice."

Oldfield was both the town in Massachusetts and synonym for Prescott Academy, founded in 1779 by Josiah Prescott on Oldfield Hill, the town's highest ground where the first colonists had settled in 1631 for security from the red man and to be nearer to God. Josiah's younger brother, Samuel, had ridden with Paul Revere and Dawes. Revere was the elder Prescott's partner in a powder mill, which prospered in the revolution and furnished the means for the school's first building whose delicate fan windows and graceful white cupola were designed by the architect of the statehouse and whose brass hinges, locks, and weather vane were made by Revere himself. The school now straddled Main Street for half a mile—four quadrangles of brick buildings, rouge red and flecked with the leach of lime. But Main Street turned alabaster white as it left the hill. The merchant's mansions, the Doric columns, and soaring spires of church and meetinghouse pierced the canopy of elms.

Henry lived in Gookin House, on Main Street halfway down the hill, a yellow clapboard home where the Reverend Leverett Gookin wrote the notorious Arminian tract against the Trinity for which he was banished to the frontier and a gruesome death in the Indian raids on Deerfield in 1704. It was only a few more blocks to the center of the modern town and St. Joseph's Roman Catholic Church next to the railroad station where the Boston & Maine crossed Pequonit Creek. The steam laundry was across the tracks by an old mill that now made overshoes and tennis balls, belching acrid, greasy smoke even on weekends. Railroads had brought coal, soot and immigrants, as well as St. Joseph's Church, to pilgrim Oldfield, and church, laundry, station and mill were all grimy brick, gloomy as St Louis University on the edge of the Mill Creek railroad yards. But on the hill, the red brick mills of the mines still basked in the sun and were cooled by breezes in the elms. And nothing rose nearer to God than the copper spire and gold-plated weather vane of the Laughlin Memorial Chapel.

The director of admissions didn't shoot as straight as Joe Stillman thought. There was more religion than he admitted. Chapel was compulsory for everyone, daily except Wednesdays, in the third period. It was heralded by the tolling of the chapel's giant bell: a double clap every fifteen seconds for three minutes, then a single stroke every five seconds for another minute, and finally a series of staccato blows accelerating to a frenzy. Stragglers rushed to be inside before a sudden silence preceded three stately blows, the doors were locked and attendance taken by scholarship students in the organ loft who checked empty seats on a master seating plan. As the organ prelude reached a crescendo of cement-shaking chords on the thirty-two-foot pipes, Henry contrasted this spectacular din of bells and organ with the cool Gregorian modulations Brother Umber improvised with his feet while twisting backward on his organ bench to pass out parts and instructions to the choir behind him. In the Laughlin Chapel, the choir stalls faced each other with the pulpit between them. Henry strained to see the organist at his console below the left stall. A mane of red hair bobbed above the music rack, and from time to time, he caught sight of a bushy red mustache when the organist half rose to reach distant stop knobs. There were three high-backed chairs behind the lectern and doors on either side in the wood paneling. As the prelude ended, the left door opened and B. Barnard Nugent, the school minister, made his entrance. Something about him was familiar—the short bristling hair, the prehensile Roman nose like the searching proboscis of an anteater, and the angular puffed chest of a man who lifts weights. It was Bob Gormely, the director of the junior camp at Kooch-i-ching, all got up like a judge in black robes. But Barney Nugent did not begin with a hymn to his scrotum. He kept his hands on a Bible bigger than a laundry box and waited for eight students in maroon corduroy jackets, tan chinos, and dirty white buck shoes to march up the aisle and take their seats in the front pew, four to the left and four to right. They were the student deacons, positions of honor reserved for campus big wheels—athletes and extracurricular leaders. On Sunday, they collected the wicker baskets of offerings, which supported a school for troubled youth in Harwell, a mill town of temptation and danger ten miles north that was off limits to all students.

The minister opened the Bible and read the lesson. "He whose testicles are crushed or whose male member is cut off shall not enter the assembly of the Lord. Deuteronomy, chapter 23, verse 1." He paused. His effect was electric; he was the focus of a thousand eyes. "What did Moses mean?" he wondered and paused again. Finally the minister answered himself. The words put him in mind of Pete Gray, the one-armed outfielder for the St. Louis Browns. Henry knew nothing about Deuteronomy, but he and Jimmy Bowes had seen Pete Gray play at Sportsman's Park. The Reverend Nugent thought that any man able to catch a ball with his left hand, put the ball in his mouth, stick his glove under his stump, take the ball from his teeth, and field it to second base could never be said to be crushed by adversity or severed from the grace of God—not while he had the will to fight. "But let's not fool ourselves. Moses means what he says. There are no eunuchs in heaven, no pansies, no cowards. You men have got to cut the mustard. But the lesson of the Christ, the meaning of the Messiah and the new dispensation, is this: it's not what you've got down your pants or up your sleeve that makes you a man, it's what you have in your head and your heart. And on that score, Pete Gray is more than a man. He is winner on the playing fields of the Lord." After that, they sang all four verses of Hymn 519 about a god who stands in the shadows, watching the innocent being sent to the gallows by an unjust ruler.

Then the minister said, "Let us bow our heads in prayer." They bowed, and he prayed, addressing himself directly to God, man to man, off the cuff, on the fly, an intimate discourse that seemed recklessly presumptuous to Henry who was accustomed to the mediation of the saints and the silence of contemplative prayer. Nugent had Father Kirby's casual cockiness with heaven, but the Jesuit would have spoken first with the Virgin and asked her to pass it along. The minister asked for a dozen things including a mild winter and victory over Islington Academy in their traditional football rivalry. He berated himself and the community for ingratitude and offered his bare back for scourging. Henry stole a glance at the speaker. The unbowed man was talking to a god not in heaven but over their heads and behind them. Henry turned to look. There was a short man, possibly a dwarf, standing in the open door to a shallow balcony above the wide doors over the center aisle. He wore a cardigan sweater buttoned up to his chin, a cloth cap, a muffler, and seemed to have just come out of the cold. He nodded his head vigorously to all of Nugent's flattery, apologies, and demands as if the minister were speaking directly to him. He was Nugent's god. When Henry turned back toward the pulpit, the minister was looking straight at him. Their eyes met. Henry bowed his head quickly. The organ postlude was even louder than the prelude—a thunderous, algebraic cacophony as sere as the yellow leaves that were the only color in the clear panes of the tall chapel windows. Bach, Deuteronomy, and the Protestant Reformation—cold comfort. It looked like snow.

In the vestibule, the small man in the cloth cap stood halfway up a stairway to the bell tower above. He watched the crush of students trying to wedge out the three doors and down the broad steps, the organ still thundering behind them, the snow blowing before them. A heavy ring of keys hung on his belt; he was a janitor or custodian. Metal-rimmed glasses slipped down his small reddened nose. One eye looked up, the other down.

From the chapel steps, Henry spotted Jimmy Bowes walking with friends on a diagonal path to the library. He had seen Bowes only once since they arrived, in the dining hall with the same people—Thorndike and Sedgewick, Bostonians he had met on Nantucket. Bowes made friends easily; he knew someone wherever he found himself. Henry had not made a single friend at the Jesuits, nor was he close to anyone in his family; his sisters and brother were strangers to him. When he thought about it, Bowes was his only friend and maybe Donna Hasenclever whose letters he never read or answered. In thick or thin, she'd be there, waiting. But you couldn't count on Jimmy Bowes. In a pinch, he would always side with the crowd, like in the rug box in kindergarten, like at Kooch-i-ching. Jimmy Bowes had to be popular or dead. Still, Henry ran to catch up with him.

"Who did that minister remind you of?" he shouted before he got to them. Bowes turned in blank surprise.

"Who?"

"Gormely! I thought he was going to pull out his scrotum right there in the pulpit."

The Bostonians looked at Henry with such distaste that Bowes had to explain they once knew a guy who was always showing off his balls, not saying they had planned to kill him. "He's a humbug," Henry warned them about the minister. "He pretends he's talking to God, but he's really praying to a dwarf in the balcony, a wall-eyed homunculus." Henry was becoming excited and loud.

"It's no big deal," said Bowes, trying to quiet him.

"Why's the guy so hot and bothered?" Thorndike asked.

"I'm not hot and bothered," said Henry, even louder. "I'm just saying the jerk was selling his snake oil to the janitor."

"What's the poor man's offense?" Sedgewick wondered with patrician boredom.

"Pete Gray, for one thing," Henry answered him. "He doesn't know the first thing about Pete Gray. To begin with, Gray never put the ball in his mouth."

"Who cares if some one-armed 4-F stuck the ball in his mouth or his ass?" Sedgewick asked with condescending languor. Bowes intervened. "Don't argue with him. He just hates the minister because he's Protestant. Stillman's a mackerel snatcher, that's all this is about."

Bowes had it backward—he hated mackerel, not Protestants. He had a deep Catholic hatred of fish of any kind—a dead, stinking thing washed up from the sea as punishment for our sins. And Bowes knew Pete Gray didn't put the ball in his mouth because they had both seen him play at Sportsman's Park. Bowes was sucking up to his new friends, and Henry was on his own. He took an abrupt right fork in the path and nearly ran to be away from them. The fork led to a loading dock behind the Commons, a building containing four vast dining halls. A man with a day's growth of black beard below a starched white skullcap was smoking by the swinging doors to the kitchens. He waved. He was the chef who carved meat on a maple block at the head of the steam tables from which women spooned the meal into the partitions of plastic trays. Henry had told the chef how much he loved the crisp skin and fat of a roast, which was routinely trimmed off and thrown in a bucket. This chef saved some for Henry, hidden under a parsley garnish. As he waited his turn, Henry would watch him carving a roast, a considerable feat because he had no fingers on his left hand, only a thumb and knuckled stump. His unopposed thumb, unable to hold a fork or knife, still managed to supply all instruments. It pinned the roast while his blade slid back and forth against the guide of his stumps, slicing the meat, which he served on the flat face of his carbon steel knife. Henry wondered if his fingers had been chopped off by a knife or cleaver or severed by a machine. If Henry had lost his fingers, he would have avoided cutting and slicing the rest of his life, but this man had a perverse joy in his work and a generosity the other cooks lacked: he gave larger portions, not just the fat and skin. His good spirits made one forget what his work had cost him. He reminded Henry of Karl Bissinger, the St. Louis candymaker whose arms and chest were encrusted with thick keloids of fibrous red scar tissue caused by a vat of boiling syrup spilled over him by an assistant. Sugar's gaunt and crippled martyr still loved his candy and customers, especially fat ladies to whom he gave opera creams and children who were rewarded with chocolate-covered molasses lollipops from a tray behind the counter. A box of Karl Bissinger's molasses lollipops arrived on his birthday at Camp Kooch-i-ching barely two weeks before the war ended. He shared them with Jimmy Bowes. He never would again.

The opportunity to set the record straight about Pete Gray arose unexpectedly when he discovered he was assigned to religion class with the school minister. The director of admissions had also neglected to mention the compulsory Bible classes taught by local clergymen including the Reverend Nugent. He met his class in a cold basement lecture room under a grid of frigid steam pipes. Bowes, Thorndike, and Sedgewick sat down front; but Henry took a seat as far back as he could find, certain he would be recognized as the one who discovered the preacher was praying to the janitor. Nugent's duffel coat was buttoned to his chin by peg fasteners in loops of rope. He rubbed his hands together and kept moving. "We're here to read the Old Testament," he began, his breath crystallizing in the air. "Thirty-nine books about the Jews. Why should we Christians study the Old Testament? What business is it of ours? Who cares about the Jews? Let's hear it. Speak up. Anyone." He waited. "The Jews killed Christ," someone said.

"The Romans killed Christ in the New Testament. We're studying the Old Testament. Adam and Eve, the Flood, Moses. The history of the Jews." Nugent was impatient.

"The Old Testament explains where we came from, why we're here," said someone else.

"The *Mahabharata* explains where we came from. The head of Buddha or Apollo or from fire. They're all good stories, good as Genesis, but not *our* story." He searched the young faces, rubbing his freezing hands. "Gentlemen, why are we Christians? And I presume at least some of us call ourselves Christians. Why are we interested in a book about the tribulations of the twelve tribes of Israel? You back there, with the glasses, what's your name?" He was looking at Henry. Nugent recognized him.

"Stillman, sir."

"Any ideas, Stillman?"

"Christ was a Jew," Henry answered.

"Freud was a Jew, Einstein's a Jew. Is that why we read the Old Testament?"

"No, sir. But Einstein never claimed to be the new Messiah. Or Freud, either." Nugent stared at him.

"Don't be so sure about that. You seem like a guy with a lot on your mind, you and Einstein. You come from New York, Stillberg?"

"St. Louis, sir."

"Missouri! The Show Me State." His tone mingled disdain and amusement. "You root for the Redbirds?" Henry lied. "The Browns," he answered, relishing the palpable contempt that filled the room. "Mr. Stillberg from St. Louis is a fan of the Browns, gentlemen." A few of his classmates sniggered, but Nugent kept an expression of sanctimonious neutrality, waiting for the Browns fan to justify himself. "Yes, sir, I am," Henry proclaimed proudly and added, "And Pete Gray never put the ball in his mouth."

"Where did he put it?"

"He caught it with his mitt, tossed it up, tucked the mitt under his stump while the ball was in the air, then caught it in his bare hand and fielded it."

Nugent stared at him, disbelieving. "First off, Gray didn't have enough stump to tuck a matchbook."

"I saw him, sir."

"You and who else?"

"Jimmy Bowes. In Sportsman's Park. A lot."

"Who?"

"Jimmy Bowes, sir." He pointed to Jimmy Bowes who was slumped down in the front row, head buried in his chest, pretending he wasn't there.

"You a friend of Mr. Stillberg here?"

"Yes, sir."

"Stillman, sir," Henry corrected him.

The minister glanced his way. "That's what I said," and turned back to Bowes.

"And you saw Pete Gray play in Sportsman's Park?"

"Yes, sir."

"Did he hold the ball in his mouth?"

"He might have, sir. I don't remember." It was Bowes's chance to confirm how Pete Gray had really fielded a ball, and he let his best friend twist in the wind. Nugent shook his head and walked to the blackboard. "Let's see if Mr. Stillberg knows any more about the Old Testament than he does about baseball. Tell us about the new Messiah. Who's it to be? Einstein, Joe DiMaggio?"

What Nugent was fishing for was as obvious as what Father Kirby had wanted to hear about the expanding universe, but Henry didn't want to be his patsy. "Christians believe the birth of Christ fulfills the prophecy of Isaiah that a Messiah would be born of the House of David, making the Old Testament prophesy the New, whereas the Jews—"

Nugent cut him off. "The god of the Old Covenant promised a Messiah to the Jews! The New Testament fulfills the promise of the Old. Why didn't you just say so?" He was off and running with the Pentateuch, the Law, its authorship, its historicity. Christ was a shadowy Essene pacifist, too fond of paradox, the pale-and-effete synthesis of the grand dialectic which obsessed the minister, the dialogue between Moses and God. The authors of this desert drama—P, JE, and D, as they were named by biblical scholars—were they historians or propagandists? He pulled down maps of the desert; of the Tigris and the Euphrates; of Babylonia, Egypt, the Nile; of wandering tribes, captive tribes, and lost tribes; photographs of papyrus, pots, and urns. He was a spiritual archeologist, slogging neck-deep in sand, shards, and illegible glyphs. He had photos of the Dead Sea Scrolls that spoke of a Teacher of Righteousness, who might have been a precursor of

Christ. But it was the covenants of Abraham and Moses that obsessed him, the seminal events which foreshadowed his own dialogue with the Almighty, which he conducted not from a mountain but from Oldfield Hill. The Dissenters who founded the Massachusetts Bay Colony had made their own covenant with God to lead them from bondage in England to the Promised Land. And a hundred years later, as their descendants struggled to throw off the last colonial chains, Josiah Prescott, a member of the Massachusetts congress during the Revolution, made another covenant. He promised to found a school to instruct youth in "the great end and real business of living," which was to serve and magnify the Lord, if the Lord would bless these strong white Protestant men with beauty, riches, children, and long life. In the dialectic of history, "in the strife twixt truth and falsehood," the men of Oldfield were assured of victory. They were the Chosen. Nugent had been ignoring Henry's raised arm for several minutes, trying to get to his punch line before the class ended. "What is it, Stillman?"

Covenants had been made and broken so fast, he had lost track, Henry said. First God favors the Jews, then the early Christians, then the Roman Church, and suddenly he sides with the Reformation and the Dissenters. Henry wanted to know what happens to old covenants when God decides to make a new one. Nugent stared at him. "What happens when you default on a contract, Mr. Stillberg is asking. The repo man comes and takes away your car, that's what happens." The class laughed, and the bell rang. "The road to hell is paved with broken covenants, ask any Israelite." More laughter. Henry felt the heat of his own red face in the freezing basement. He hated B. Barnard Nugent more than Gormely. It surprised him, the depth of his hatred. Bowes and his friends were leaving. The Chosen. If Joe Stillman had not polluted his pilgrim stock by marrying a Catholic, Henry might have been among the elect and able to laugh with Barney Nugent at the repossessed vehicles of the unsaved, the passed over, being towed away. But he was a registered Roman Catholic who had to check in at the ten o'clock Sunday Mass at St. Joseph's Church down by the railroad station and the overshoe factory on Pequonit Creek.

Mike Squillace, the football coach, looked up as Henry pointed to his name on a large ledger sheet spread on a card table in the cold vestibule of St. Joseph's. He and a Spanish teacher, the only Catholics on the faculty, took turns taking attendance of Catholic students who were excused from the Sunday service on the hill. "Tackle or guard?" he asked. You didn't have to play football to go to church, so Henry pretended he hadn't heard. "Stillman," he answered. "Tackle," Squillace guessed correctly. "What d'ya weigh?" "A hundred and fifty-five." "Ever throw a hammer?" Henry shook his head. He had never heard of throwing a hammer except in anger. "See me in the cage next week," Squillace said. Henry went inside though most of the students signed in and left. The coach didn't care. St. Joseph's had a garish friendliness—the smell of incense and candle wax, the bright pinks and blues of the plaster saints, the tinkle of bells and the drone of a mournful electric organ, and a stream of announcements from the pulpit: births, deaths, bans, breakfasts, suppers, clubs, teams and packs, a pastoral letter from the archbishop excommunicating all who voted for Proposition 6 which would legalize the sale of contraceptives and 3.2 percent beer on Sunday. At communion, the whole church filed to the altar rail. Henry got up too, but he drifted to the back; he was ready to leave. He was a little skittish about the sacred wafer. It gave him a twinge, like the vampire's involuntary shudder in the presence of garlic. He called it a Pavlovian response to the forms and symbols of his former faith.

Henry walked along a road by the railroad tracks which soon hooked left up a hill by a steeply sloping cemetery below a white-spired church. At the church, it joined School Street and became a wide, shaded street of nineteenth-century homes that ended at Main Street where the campus began. Passing Norton Seminary for Young Women, a squat Romanesque school behind ivied walls of the same Civil War vintage as the steam laundry and the mills, he was overtaken by a boy he had seen in the Commons eating alone and reading a newspaper. He was smoking right on the street, which was forbidden, and Henry hoped he would pass him, but he fell in silently with Henry's stride, and they climbed the hill together. He had a prematurely aged and crooked face with an involuntary smile which deceived people on first meeting him because he appeared to be friendly. He finally introduced himself as Adam Kornfeld, the Inquiring Reporter. He wrote a column in the *Oldfielder*, the student newspaper, called Nut in a World Shell.

"This is an interview," he said. "Are you a Catholic?"

Henry, who had long planned to declare himself an atheist, was surprised to discover it was more exciting to claim membership in a despised minority which worshiped in the wrong end of town with the soot of locomotives and the stench of the overshoe company. But before he could answer, the Inquiring Reporter asked a second question.

"Can you curl your tongue?" He demonstrated, making a cylinder of his tongue between his lips.

"I'm a Catholic," Henry answered, "are you?"

"I'm a Marxist, but I say I'm Catholic to get away from Bach."

"You aren't really Catholic?"

"I hate Bach, don't you?" He thought Bach was a German barbarian who had written even uglier music than Beethoven. Bach made his ears bleed; he couldn't listen to anything written after Palestrina. Henry was keeping a list of things he didn't know: Bach organ fugues, James Russell Lowell (author of Hymn 519), Deuteronomy, Giotto, Calder, Increase Mather, the Essene community at Qumram, Ulrich Zwingli, and Palestrina. Nor did he understand why someone with a Jewish name would go to a Catholic church just to escape Bach, so he asked him.

"You want me to go to a synagogue, like a good Jew? I'm not a good Jew. A, I hate Jews, and B, hanging around Jews can get you killed, if you haven't noticed. I feel safer with Catholics. That's why I'm walking with you."

"Is it safe to be smoking?" Henry asked.

"We're both lower middlers. Our only safety is in a safe-deposit box. You're from Kansas City." Henry shook his head.

"Ottumwa." Wrong.

"Say r-o-o-f," Kornfeld demanded.

"Roof," said Henry, to rhyme with "woof."

"Kankakee. Jefferson City."

"St. Louis."

"St. Louis. Goddam! Had you bracketed? The next round would have been in. St. Louis Browns, Pete Gray. Have you ever heard more crap from one man than Barney Nugent? He does that Moses bit every year, first chapel, same timing, same schtick. You can bet the student deacons don't have crushed balls. Real jocks. Big wheels. This place is sick." He offered Henry a cigarette, which he took.

"Can we smoke here?"

"No," said Kornfeld, lighting up.

"I saw Pete Gray play," said Henry. Kornfeld wasn't interested. "Pete Gray was some one-armed 4-F Bill Veeck hired because everyone else was in the army. You know the only good thing about St. Louis? The Union Station—largest cantilevered train shed in the world. And the Eads Bridge. Longest tubular steel arch ever made. Five hundred twelve feet. What's the matter? Are you afraid to light up?"

"You forgot the zoo," said Henry.

"Great zoo. First natural habitats. Moats. No bars."

"The chimpanzees."

"Tasteless, disgusting. Animals should never ride motorcycles. Or wear clothes. Do you believe in the Trinity?" Kornfeld asked.

"No."

"The Real Presence?"

"No."

"Papal infallibility?"

"No."

"How can you call yourself a Catholic?"

"I was baptised. It leaves an indelible mark."

"Like circumcision."

"I'm circumcised," said Henry.

"That's really weird," said Kornfeld.

"Why?"

"Everybody's circumcised. If the Nazis came to America, how would they know who to kill?"

"I'm trying to lose my faith."

"I've never believed in anything."

"I thought it would go out like a light." In church, Henry had realized it wouldn't. His faith would have to erode, like a mountain. He was stuck with it.

Kornfeld qualified his previous disclaimer of any belief. "Marx maybe."

They had reached the top of the hill where the campus begins, and Henry still held his unlit cigarette in his palm. Upperclassmen could only smoke at the invitation of a master in his rooms. Lower middlers couldn't smoke at all. Kornfeld noticed his unlit butt. "What's the matter, you afraid?" Of course he was; he didn't want to be thrown out. And he was embarrassed to admit he really didn't smoke. Joe Stillman smoked enough for the entire family. "Young Stillman, you're taking this place too seriously. You won't survive." But he stamped out his own cigarette before they crossed Main Street. They were at the entrance, in a low stone wall, to a great lawn trisected by diagonal paths, the legs of an equilateral triangle whose base was Main Street and whose altitude was the axis of the campus symmetry, terminating at the majestic stone steps to Josiah Prescott Hall, the white-pillared building with the tall cupola and cold radiators where he had compromised himself with Barney Nugent over the dialectical necessity of Christ. Steel fence stakes, called soprano poles, were planted every ten yards along the asphalt paths to guide the snowplows. "Walk me to the inn," Kornfeld commanded. He wanted to pick up his *New York Times*.

The Oldfield Inn, a block past the chapel, had a barnlike roof whose columned overhang formed an arcade along Chapel Street. The front desk of the inn sold newspapers and private-label candies, maple sugar leaves and a chocolate-covered wintergreen bar with the specific gravity of lead. Five telephone booths in an alcove behind the front desk were the lifeline home for students unable or unwilling to write. Kornfeld sat in a booth smoking while he discarded unwanted sections of the *Sunday Times*, keeping only news, sports, book review, and the Sunday magazine, which he gave to Henry. "The girdle gazette. Good for whacking off." Forty pages of tall models in diaphanous underwear. Before he folded the paper, he showed Henry the front page. The lead story on the right was about the U.S. Army withdrawal from Korea. It was filed from Seoul and said, "Special to the *New York Times*. By Adam Kornfeld." "That's my father, he's covered MacArthur since Bataan."

"Do you live in Japan?"

He shook his head. "I haven't seen him since 1939, the World's Fair. We had lunch at the Aquacade."

"I went to the Aquacade," said Henry. "My parents took me."

They left the inn and crossed the street. "Where *do* you live? With your mother?"

"Nowhere, really. You should come out for the *Oldfielder.* Assignment meeting Wednesday nights. Basement of the library. Will I see you?"

Kornfeld abruptly left him and headed straight for the library on a forbidden diagonal across the vast expanse of grass. Walking on the grass was almost as great an offense at Oldfield as smoking. He had a death wish and also a bad habit for a reporter; he didn't wait for answers.

Henry himself had been waiting for the opportunity to discover whether his tongue curled. He had tried with his mouth closed, but he couldn't tell. It seemed to wrap itself around his finger, but he needed a mirror to be sure. The chapel bell began to toll—the double clap, *bong*-rest-*bong*, that should have continued for three minutes, but didn't. The Sunday regimen was different. It was ten of eleven; this was perhaps a warning peal to give worshipers time to comb their hair, find a necktie, and be in their seats. People were already streaming from the dorms and the library. Plews, who lived next to him in Gookin House, was crossing Main Street behind a group of Norton girls whose choir sang with the Prescott choir. He was wearing his Sunday necktie. Plews had seven ties on seven nails and wore them consecutively so you could tell the day by his tie. Henry joined him.

In the vestibule, the tolling from above and the strident and military organ from inside mixed in a heady cacophony. Student deacons exhorted worshipers to hurry through the three inner doors. Henry darted up the stairs where the janitor had stood when he first saw him and found himself in a square room with a conference table and a grand piano and two half-opened doors, one to the little balcony where he watched the custodian listening to Nugent's prayers and a second in a far corner, to a narrow staircase with a patch of light at the top and a cold draft coming down. It led to the belfry. There were six staccato blows on the big bell and silence from above. Henry withdrew from the doorway. The organ inside had also climaxed. The little man in his cloth cap and ragged mittens came out the door and saw Henry. He was Quasimodo. He rang the bells. They looked at each other for a long moment. Henry wasn't supposed to be there. Then the dwarf unwound a thin scarf from his neck, rubbed his gloved hands together, and went in the balcony door, leaving it ajar. Henry went downstairs to the now-empty vestibule, took a program from a pile, and left. The next Sunday, B. Barnard Nugent would preach on the life and thought of Martin Luther, the fifth in a survey of the world's great religious leaders.

On the back of the program, he learned that the Laughlin Memorial Chapel was the gift of Joseph Laughlin, class of 1871, and was completed in 1937. It had a spire and weather vane 180 feet high and a bell of eight tons cast in Elmira, New York. The custodian and verger of the chapel was Quintus Elmo.

ON THE MESA

The cage was a cathedral of sport under a pyramid of glass at the other end of the campus. Mike Squillace and his coaching staff were processing the students into the fall sports program. Books and clothes were left in rows of neat piles while the owners queued in their underwear for cardiopulmonary endurance tests and posture photographs of toothpicks pasted at right angles to their spines. Henry, who had been poked, photographed, rebuked for body fat and bad posture, now faced a line of coaches with clipboards waiting for him. A voice behind him said, “Sign up for tennis. Courts are a mile away, no one checks them. Smoke, read, even sleep.” He barely recognized the naked Kornfeld, a thin skeleton in boxer shorts. Before Henry could answer, Mike Squillace was all over him like a Labrador, squeezing, pinching, sniffing, licking, and accusing him of concealing the fact that he had been right tackle for St. Aloysius.

“I can’t play football. I don’t like it, and I’m no good.”

“It’s there in your record. JV right tackle.”

“I want to play tennis.”

“Tennis? Big guy like you, tackle for St. Aloysius, what are you afraid of?”

The coach’s face came close to his, separated only by the bill of his baseball cap pressing Henry’s forehead, his narrowed eyes seething contempt and his nostrils pulsing synchronously with his chest. Henry could only hope their shared faith might stay his hand, but the real reason Squillace didn’t hit him was that someone was coming toward them with a slight limp. There was no mistaking his English teacher. Besides, the limp Paul Forbes was almost six and a half feet tall. A coach’s clipboard was clamped under his arm though Henry had no idea what he coached. He usually wore faded denim work clothes, no necktie, needed a haircut, and met his class under a tree outside his basement classroom because he couldn’t stop smoking for fifty minutes, though he claimed it was because he enjoyed the Indian summer. Henry would never have supposed he had an interest in sports.

“You can’t have ’em all, Mike. I’ve had my eye on Mr. Stillman.”

“Mud in his eye, that’s what he needs.”

His English teacher took his physical measure. “Long legs. Sprint, broad jump, high hurdles?” Henry shook his head. “Shot put, discus, hammer, javelin?” Mr. Forbes was trying to find a slot for him in track, but Henry was no help. “He’s got shoulders for the hammer,” Forbes said, but Squillace wasn’t interested. “This winter maybe. We need his weight on the JV line.”

“What is a hammer?” Henry was belatedly curious about his alternatives.

“Iron ball, sixteen pounds, with a five-foot wire and handle. Spartans used it to kill each other. Come out for track and field. I’ll watch out for you.” His final offer.

“Sorry, Paul,” said the head coach. “The JV’s got him. I promised Ralph.”

“I want to play tennis,” said Henry.

"Next spring. Now clear out. You're done."

Kornfeld was waiting for him at Salem Street. "I saw you talking to Paul Forbes."

"He wants me to go out for track."

"You know who he is, don't you?"

"My English teacher."

"Pole vault. World's record. Five point four seven two meters, fourteen feet one and three-quarters inches. Gold medal, Los Angeles Olympics, 1932. Where have you been?"

"So what's wrong with his leg?"

"I heard his wife shot him. You going out for track?"

"I have to play football."

"You're a rotten football player."

"How did you know?"

"I knew you stank first time I saw you. In church."

"We met on School Street. By Norton."

"I saw you first in church. I followed you."

"Why?"

"I wanted to meet a Catholic. I told you."

"I hate football."

"You'll be killed," Kornfeld spoke slowly and with deep conviction. "Coaches are paid to put x number of bodies on the field and x number on the bench, and they don't care if you're blind with one leg. *You* are the only one who cares. And me."

"Why you?"

"I have plans."

"What are they?"

"I can't tell you yet. But don't get killed. Stay on the bench."

They walked to the Commons, which was just across the street. Henry steered them toward the lower right hall where he always ate. Kornfeld stopped. "Why do you eat down here? It's dark and noisy."

"It's not noisy."

"You can hear them mashing potatoes."

"I like the cooks—"

"They're all the same."

"The head chef, the one with no fingers—"

"They're in the mashed potatoes—"

"He gives me skin and fat."

"He'd slice off his thumb for you."

"He likes me. That's why I eat down here."

"Because you're doomed, like he is."

Dinner was pot roast, mashed potatoes and gravy, peas and carrots, kaiser roll, butter patty, apple crisp, milk, tea, or coffee.

Kornfeld watched the chef give Henry a slice of fat and crisp skin from the top of the roast. He refused anything from the man. By the line's end, he had peas, carrots, and coffee on his tray. Kornfeld dropped his *Times* on the table and sat. "Fat is disgusting. You shouldn't eat it." Henry stuck out his curled tongue.

Kornfeld was unimpressed. "Three out of five can do it."

"Why haven't you seen your father since the World's Fair?"

"I can tell where he is from the *Times*. Tokyo, Bangkok, Okinawa, Shanghai."

"He doesn't write?"

"No."

"And never comes home?"

"I have no home. I told you."

"Where's your mother?"

"My family is boring. Tell me about yours."

"You wouldn't like them."

"Why not?"

How to explain. It wasn't an attractive sight, the picture of Joe and Julia Stillman seen through the eyes of a homeless Marxist Jew. He had only one Jewish friend in St. Louis whom his mother had treated as she would a child ignorant of his leukemia. "A time will come when you won't see Richie anymore," she mourned, meaning that a curtain falls between Christians and Jews, inexorable and natural, like the Rocky Mountains. It was a waste to tell her she was anti-Semitic. She was just trying to teach him what life held in store. Kornfeld could never forgive these people or understand their fears. Only German immigrants had kept Missouri, a slave state, out of the Confederacy. They put on Union uniforms made secretly at home by their wives and defeated the Southern sympathizers when they tried to seize the St. Louis arsenal. "It's just not a nice place," said Henry, searching for a way to describe people who thought Roosevelt a traitor, Truman a clown, and Negroes the sleeping enemy.

"Bessie Smith was from St. Louis. Jazz, rag."

"First my family feared the Germans, then the Jews, and now the Negro. The whites are waiting for them to rise up, like the Mau Mau, and hack them to pieces in their beds."

"Why don't they?"

"They're too beaten down. They shuffle and wear brown. We have a yardman who has worked for my family since he was a slave."

"Who bought him?"

"My great-grandmother. Only women have property in my family. Men are ornaments imported from the east for their genes, manners, and wit."

"I want to be imported to St. Louis," said Kornfeld.

"No, you don't. You do not want to be a Jew in St. Louis."

"Or a Negro in St. Louis. Tell me about the yardman."

"Robert is eighty-eight and still squirts leaves."

"Explain."

Henry told him how early in the morning Robert starts to move a line of leaves down the driveway with a jet of water from a heavy brass nozzle. The leaves move quickly at first, but soon they flatten and adhere to the asphalt. He squats to squirt; the jet must be close to the ground to get under the back edge of the leaf. By noon, he is talking to the soggy leaves and pleading with them to move. It is not allowed to touch them. The work is contemplative and water intensive, like fishing. By late afternoon, Robert has moved less than a bushel of leaves about twenty feet and used an acre foot of water. Then he goes home. "I could do that," said Kornfeld.

"You could do a lot worse. Robert sent three daughters to college squirting leaves, and a grandson is a postal supervisor."

"Your ornamental father, what does he do?"

He had talked too much and made his family sound like monsters. What he had meant was that the women were rich, but the men worked. His father worked every day.

"He used to mine coal."

"In a helmet with a carbide lamp?"

"In a three-piece herringbone tweed suit, actually, and a brown felt hat. He showed the men at the face how to cut the seam so it didn't collapse, how to blast the coal so it fell into hopper cars in uniform chunks."

"He was an operator, an owner."

"An engineer."

"Where was the mine?

"In Illinois."

"Where John L. Lewis began. Did they have strikes?"

"After the First War. Wobblies and syndicalists shorted the electric cables, cut the air hoses, and struck the railroad. My father delivered the company coal himself, with the company switch engine, stoking the boiler in his Brooks Brothers suit. Pickets shot at the locomotive cab as he pushed the hoppers over the Mississippi to the steel mills in St. Louis. He had to crouch under the throttle to keep clear of bullets from the open windows. At night, he waltzed with his beautiful old-French wife on an outdoor dance floor overlooking the polo field of the St. Louis Country Club. The Roaring Twenties."

"Your family are slaveholders, plutocrats, and strikebreakers," said Kornfeld, not really trying to conceal his infatuation with the privilege he wanted to destroy.

"No more," said Henry. "The mines were sold. Joe Stillman designs coal tipples and lectures on dynamite at Washington U. now."

"Adam Kornfeld has two Pulitzers," said his son, proudly. "The first for his file on Trotsky's assassination, the second for a series on MacArthur and Hirohito."

"And he never comes home?"

"We have no home. I told you."

"Where is your mother?"

"You want to know?"

"I told you about my family."

"The Manhattan Psychiatric Hospital."

"Why?"

"She's been trying to kill herself since Barcelona fell to the Falange in 1939."

"She's a communist?"

"A Trotskyite," he said. "Adam is a Stalinist. Was." Kornfeld visited his mother on Wards Island. She was tied to her bed so she couldn't burn herself up, but they let him sleep over if things were quiet.

"So where do you live?"

"Nowhere. Schools, newsrooms, people's sofas. Summers I work for the *Baltimore Sun*. I stay with the editor. He's got a kid my age." He folded his paper and got up. "When are you going to come out for the *Oldfielder*? I'm serious. Stay up all night, smoke in the office, go to Harwell, city of sin, put the sheet to bed, get drunk. It's the only thing that keeps me sane. It'll save your life. Assignment meetings, every Wednesday." He was gone again, leaving the invitation to journalism hanging in the air, like a fragrance. Kornfeld wanted something from him, but he didn't know what.

After the frost drove his English class indoors, Paul Forbes stood by an open window and blew his smoke outside. It was a basement room, with doors to an inside hall and to the parking lot behind the building. He had sudden fits of impatience, with students, with faculty, but most of all with the curriculum which he despised. Manheimer and Thompson were reading the conspirators from *Julius Caesar* when Mr. Forbes abruptly threw his *Yale Shakespeare* out the window with his cigarette. "Iambic sawdust!" he shouted after the book, loud enough to be heard through the whole building and in the gym across the street. "Da-*da*, da-*da*, da-*da*, da-*da*, da-*da*. By the yard, like Telemann, like Tennyson. You can write that stuff in your sleep! Everything Shakespeare wrote before 1601 was junk." In fact, Mr. Forbes thought that almost everything written since Aeschylus was junk, with exceptions for Shakespeare, Keats, and John Crowe Ransom. He started for the door with the slight limp that some said was from the war and others from a sports accident, though the rumor persisted that his wife had shot him. Manheimer got out the door first, crawled under the rocket-grilled Studebaker of the chairman of the English department, and retrieved *Julius Caesar*. Forbes threw it on his desk.

"You know who was in Rome with Caesar the day they killed him? His mistress. CleoPAYtra." He gave her an exotic long *a*. "He had brought her from Egypt to see him crowned emperor. Imagine you're the Queen of the Nile in a strange, foreign city and your lover and protector gets himself murdered. What would you do? Pack up and scat? Hang around to see who's going to take over? Has she met Mark Antony? Has she already seduced him? Plutarch doesn't say, and Shakespeare's mum. There's a play nobody's written. I might do it myself. You guys ought to be getting your tongues around that Egyptian dish. We should be reading *Antony and Cleopatra*," he declared. "*Julius Caesar* is kid stuff. Listen to Enobarbus. It's 1606, Shakespeare's learned to ignore everything.

O sovereign mistress of true melancholy.

"That's Antony's lieutenant telling the moon he must betray his general, and it will break his heart. Literally,

> Throw my heart
> Against the flint and hardness of my fault,
> Which, being dried with grief, will break to powder,
> And finish all foul thoughts.

"End of line enjambment, syntactic runover. What's a fault? Weakness, defect, what else? Cosmic weakness, fracture in the earth's crust, a seismic event, an earthquake cleaving rock, granite ground to powder, opening the earth to receive the sinner, like Don Giovanni, into the jaws of hell."

Thompson's hand was up. Did the word "fault" have a geologic meaning in 1606? "The OED is on the shelf. Be my guest." The *Oxford English Dictionary* had bad news. "Fault" (geology), first use 1796, *Philosophical Transactions.*

"You guys are too smart. I can't teach you anything. Let's call it a day." Mr. Forbes had an unlit Chesterfield already in his mouth, and the students were pulling on their coats. "But you've got to bring me something tomorrow." They groaned. "A page about anything that suggests life's meaning—a person, place, event. Make it personal, like a bull's death for Hemingway, the full moon for Keats. Got it?"

They read their essays aloud next day in class. Most wrote about the death of pets or the divorce of parents. Henry told the tale of a sparrow who brushes against Jupiter with her wing, bearing a speck of the planet's dust a million light-years across the universe to a distant asteroid where she shakes the particle free. The sparrow repeats her journey, back and forth, until she has relocated the entire planet, a speck at a time, from one end of the universe to the other. And when the sparrow's work was done, he finished, "Eternity had not yet begun." Mr. Forbes roared with laughter. "All that just for starters!" The class didn't get it. "Tell them what it means," the teacher commanded. The sparrow's task, Henry explained, was a trope for eternity from a meditation on hell in the *Spiritual Exercises* of Ignatius. "Forever is long anywhere," Forbes interrupted, "in hell, in heaven, or with your wife. Isn't that really the definition of hell? Something that lasts forever. Joy is brief, misery has no end." He was reminded of another sparrow, in *Bede's Ecclesiastical History of England*. Bede compares man's life to a sparrow's swift flight through a door, out of snowy darkness into the warmth and light of a roaring fire in the king's mead hall, and out again into the night. "From darkness to darkness," Forbes repeated, savoring the bliss of unknowingness. "Bede's bird knows only life's brief candle, a match struck in the long night of eschatology. A bird of ignorance and, therefore, faith. But Stillman's sparrow knows all—whence, wither, and why—an Aristotelian bird of clarity and purpose. The ant that moves mountains. A Thomist like Ignatius. Am I right, Mr. Stillman?"

"You studied with the Jesuits," Mr. Forbes said as they waited for the light at Salem Street. "Whatever made you come to Oldfield?"

"My father," he answered.

"Did he go here?" his teacher asked.

"St. Paul's, and he hates church schools." He explained how his Catholic mother had sent him to the Jesuits, and his agnostic father had removed him. Schools were surrogates in their battle for his mind and soul. His father chose Oldfield because the director of admissions said there was less religion here than on a dollar bill. Mr. Forbes laughed. "Look at a dollar bill! It's all religion, Rosicrucian claptrap, a ticket to the Kabbalah. I won't have one in my pocket, I throw them away."

It hurt to learn that Joe Stillman had been outsmarted by a double-talking Yankee, and there was worse to come. Forbes laid out the whole terrible truth. "They don't tell you about Josiah Prescott and his charter or that there was a Calvinist seminary here fifty years ago. Anyone with brains became Unitarian and went to Cambridge. The dinosaurs stayed here, the Barney Nugents. Oldfield had more witches than Salem, only they didn't hang them. They're still around."

The director of admissions had taken Joe Stillman to the cleaners. And Henry too. Paul Forbes read the shame and anger in his face.

"Your unbelieving father, what does he do?"

"Teaches. The physics of solids."

"Where?"

"Washington U in St. Louis. With Compton."

"Arthur. Karl runs MIT." Henry nodded. Paul Forbes whistled. "Big stuff." Henry felt better—not so small, not so dumb.

The light was green, but Mr. Forbes ignored it. "I liked your sparrow. Ever notice how much tyrants enjoy useless labor? Move planets, roll stones, teach English. Man is God's slave. 'The chains of faith,' they say." When the light changed again, he crossed against it. He looked back. "How's football?"

Henry shouted, "Awful!"

"Keep your head down."

It was easier to stay on the bench than keep his head down. The coach was a math teacher who never forgave him for not being the killer from the Catholic ghetto that Mike Squillace had promised. During the first scrimmage, he railed like Lear. Kill! Kill! Kill! Kill! Kill! Henry stood there, head up to the sun, as aggressive as spring's first jonquil. Jimmy Bowes, who was the quarterback, tried to help him. "Keep your head down! Rush! Don't stand up!" It was the same advice Father Kirby had given, but Henry wanted to know where his death was coming from, to look it in the eye. He betrayed everyone's expectation of his large body; his teammates ridiculed him. In the locker room, they called him Ferdinand the Bull. Bowes avoided him entirely as his own star rose. From the bench, Henry watched the apotheosis of his oldest friend into a luminous jock, a "big wheel" whose circumference was greater than the equator. Whenever he looked at the field, Bowes was passing to a distant player. They were undefeated, and for the final game against Islington, they were issued the fleece-lined, hooded warm-up jackets belonging to the varsity whose season had just ended. Warm at last in a woolly nest, his ears buried in the marsupial hood, he didn't hear the coach order the whole bench into the game. Anyone who played against Exeter got a letter. Only Henry remained on the bench, asleep and oblivious of the call to greatness. Jimmy Bowes, the agile, wily quarterback, was carried off the field on the shoulders of his teammates. He was shortly elected a student deacon who marched with a collection basket to the front of the chapel in a matching maroon corduroy jacket. He had ascended so far into the stratosphere of jocks that Henry never expected to speak with him again. But that all changed the day David Greenglass was charged with giving Russia the secret of the plutonium bomb.

Henry was at a table in the lower left dining hall, trying to cut into a Salisbury steak on his tray. The first to appear was Kornfeld whom he hadn't spoken with since confessing that his family were plutocratic strikebreakers. He had twice ignored Kornfeld's invitation to heel for the school newspaper, and Henry assumed he had given up on him. He hadn't seen him at church downtown either. Kornfeld put down his coffee cup and the *New York Times*.

"You haven't been to St. Joseph's," said Henry.

"I decided to be a Jew again since we last talked. I tell them I'm going to temple in Stoneham."

"Why?"

"I can never be like you. Squirt leaves with my old slave. Break strikes. I am what I am. A Marxist Jew."

"Okay," said Henry who was indifferent to Kornfeld's doctrinal mutations.

"Of course there are no Jews on the faculty to take attendance, so we have to police ourselves like we did in the ghetto, but there aren't enough Jews worth counting anyway."

Henry didn't want to feel apologetic about his trivial and complacent midwestern family, compared with the Pulitzer Prize-winning correspondent, the Man without a Family, the suffering father with a mad wife and orphaned son. The Kornfeld Klan was epic, tragic, and grand. Joe Stillman was a button-down noodle who lived in the shadow of a Mississippi queen.

Henry's Salisbury steak slipped onto the floor; it was bonded so tightly with hay or wire it wouldn't come apart. He left it there and idly turned the *Times* so he could read it. Adam Kornfeld wrote from Hawaii that after his brilliant surprise landing at Inchon, MacArthur's rush toward Seoul and the thirty-eighth parallel was giving the Commander in Chief Pacific a great fear that the general would not stop until he got to China. Commander in Chief Pacific pleaded with Truman to rein him in or bring him home. In New York, David Greenglass, a Manhattan Project machinist who had milled the implosive lens for the plutonium bomb from sheets of explosive material, was charged with giving a drawing of the lens to Julius Rosenberg, a Soviet spy. Henry read on ravenously.

"Greenglass?"

"Yes."

"I knew the Russians couldn't have done it alone."

"Why not?"

"They got rid of their Jews. You can't build a bomb without Jews."

"They weren't all Jews," said Henry. Kornfeld thought about that.

"Seaborg, Lawrence, who else?" Kornfeld wanted names.

"James Bryant Conant, Vannevar Bush, the Comptons, Karl and Arthur, Hans Bethe, Enrico Fermi, for openers."

"Administrators. I'm talking about the real people, at Los Alamos. Oppie's people. Hungarian Jews mostly driven for revenge on Hitler, out to destroy Germany."

"But not Japan."

"Nobody wanted to bomb Japan. Not Oppenheimer, Szilard, Bohr, even Teller."

"There were no Hungarian Jews at Pearl Harbor."

"Don't be a smart-ass. Adam Kornfeld was in Hiroshima when it was still too hot to go downtown. He wrote we are all damned, the human race, for Barcelona, Dresden, Auschwitz, Tokyo, and Hiroshima. Damned to hell."

Henry was tired of lectures. "Don't be a pompous ass. Barcelona and Hiroshima, there's no comparison. The bomb ended the war."

"It should never have been used."

"My father wants to nuke China preemptively. Today."

"I think David Greenglass should get the Nobel Peace Prize for giving Russia the bomb just to stop warmongers like your old man."

"Give the prize to Oppenheimer. He's the one who let Russia get the bomb."

"Says who?"

"He and Bohr told Truman that atomic energy should be shared. There should be no secrets. He said Prometheus stole fire for everyone, for mankind, not just so the Greeks could burn Troy."

"Where did he say that? I never heard that."

"He said it to Joe Stillman."

"The coal miner in the Brooks Brothers suit? Come on, he doesn't know Oppenheimer."

"Have it your way," said Henry. He was sorry he had ever mentioned the tweed suit to a person who couldn't appreciate the style of the man or his time. It was probably the same suit he wore to Building B when he invented lightning with Steinmetz in 1910. Everyone wore ties, vests, and hats then. The vest kept your tie from getting in machinery and strangling you like Isadora Duncan, a modern death for a modern dancer. The hat kept you from knocking yourself out on projecting iron or masonry. Kornfeld challenged him. "How does your old man know Oppenheimer?"

"Arthur Holly Compton."

"Gamma rays, the Compton effect, 1923."

"Chancellor of Washington University, lives in St. Louis. They play golf."

"The Christian scientists play golf," Kornfeld scoffed.

"Gentiles. My father is agnostic."

And at that moment, Jimmy Bowes, trailed by Thorndike and Sedgewick, came into the lower dining hall looking for Henry. They had descended from the training table in the jock's dining hall on the second floor where they were having steak, buttered baked potatoes, and unlimited pitchers of milk. Bowes spotted Henry.

"Stillman!" he shouted, coming toward his table. Kornfeld turned to see who was approaching. "What do they want?" he asked. "He's a friend from St. Louis," said Henry. "I know who he is. James Madison Bowes. Thirty-one hundred yards gained passing, three hundred rushing. Completed passes, sixty percent. What does he want?" Jimmy Bowes was at their table, his roommates behind him.

"You remember the Wabigoon trip?" he began, ignoring Kornfeld who was looking straight at him. "When the Mounties seaplane sank right after they told us the war was over?"

"Yes," said Henry, trying to imagine why Bowes and his crowd were looking for him.

"Introduce us," Kornfeld demanded, still examining Bowes like excrement on a slide. Green corduroy jacket, chino pants without cuffs, scuffed and dirty white bucks, a woven leather belt made by a child in a camp craft shop, the plastered down cowlick struggling to rise like a flaccid erection from the bed of sticky hair oil, runny eczema above his lip, at the corners of his mouth, and his eyes. Leaking hormones corroded Bowes at all his orifices like an old battery.

"Jimmy Bowes," Henry said.

"Adam Kornfeld., the Inquiring Reporter. You swim?" Bowes shook his head. "Track, wrestle, hockey?"

"Baseball," said Bowes.

"First?"

"Yes."

"I voted you MVP New England secondary JV football. You can't lose."

"Gosh, thanks," said Bowes. "Cornfeld," he repeated his admirer's name, pronouncing the syllables slowly as if he were trying to remember their conjugation. Cornfeld, cornfield, cornflakes, corncob, cornhole. Kornfeld could hear how Bowes was spelling it in his head.

"With a *K*, like Kafka," he corrected him. "I like your belt. Where'd you get it?"

Bowes turned back to Henry, flustered by the reporter's interview. "When we got back from Wabigoon, you had a letter from your old man. The guys thought it was from Big Boobs Hasenclever, that's why they opened it. But I saw it. There was a page you could see through, a drawing of a ball inside a stack of boards labeled Implosive Lens, and you freaked out, you remember?"

Henry looked at Bowes like he was an addled stranger and not an eyewitness to the fact that around August 15, 1945, Joe Stillman sent Henry a sketch on onionskin paper of the implosive lens of the plutonium bomb, a sketch probably almost identical to the one David Greenglass gave Harry Gold to give to Julius Rosenberg and for which they all could go to the electric chair.

"You told everyone it was the atomic bomb."

"I don't remember."

"And then you ate it."

"Ate what?"

"The drawing."

"That's crazy," said Henry.

Bowes was confounded. "The guys were climbing on the bunk, and you ate it! Don't you remember?"

"No."

Bowes lost his temper. "It was the implosive lens! The thing this guy gave the Russians! Come on, Stillman! Your old man knows how the atomic bomb works. He helped build it, and we all knew it. I bet these guys ten dollars he did, and you're backing out? I saw you eat it, I saw you eat the goddam drawing!"

"Why would I eat it?" Henry asked him.

"So the Russians wouldn't get it. So no one would know he told you. You said so afterward." Bowes paused. It was all suddenly clear to him why Henry was refusing to confirm that he had eaten his father's drawing of the implosive lens.

"You're still protecting him! Is that it? It's still a secret?"

Henry just smiled and hunched his shoulders.

"Pay up, Bowes," said Thorndike.

"You really know his old man?" the Inquiring Reporter asked him.

"The Mad Scientist? We used to electrocute people in his basement."

"Like who?"

"Big Boobs Hasenclever. She was his girl."

"You know Arthur Holly Compton?"

"My dad does. He belongs to the country club."

"They play golf?"

Bowes realized he was being toyed with. "Fuck you, guys! What's going on? Let's go." The student deacons left.

"He'll be varsity captain, I'll bet on it." Although Kornfeld's interest in sports irritated Henry, he wanted to know what an MVP was and why Kornfeld voted for it. The Inquiring Reporter folded his *New York Times* and pushed back his chair. "Come out for the *Oldfielder* and you'll find out."

"I want to know now. Don't screw around with me."

"Most Valuable Player. MVP." He explained that MVPs were voted on by sportswriters, stringers, and coaches and that he was the New England intramural sports stringer for the *Times*, the *Inquirer*, and the *Sun*, which meant phoning in the scores on Saturday night. "It's a job. It buys me booze and cigarettes. Satisfied?" He got up to go. "I've told you about MVPs. Now you tell me. Is it true what that asshole just said, your old man sent you a diagram of the atomic bomb, and you ate it?"

"Yes."

"Why did you deny it?"

"He shouldn't be blabbing it around. My dad could wind up in the chair with David Greenglass. Me too."

"I didn't believe a word you said about Oppenheimer and Compton until Bowes walked in."

"It's better if you don't. I wasn't going to tell you."

"Tell me what?" Kornfeld held Henry's elbow tightly. He scanned the hall. "Stillman, what are you implying? How did your old man know about the implosive lens?" Henry leaned closer to him over the table to relieve the pressure. "Give me your word. This is just between us, forever." Honor and promises offended Kornfeld. "Screw honor. If you know something I should know, you are obliged to tell me. It's an insult to ask for my word. Now what's all this about?"

"He designed it. Part of it."

"What?"

"The implosive lens."

"Bullshit."

"He was on the Mesa."

"The Manhattan Project?"

"He won't even admit he was there. He says he was fishing in the Black Hills."

Kornfeld recovered his skepticism. "Why do you think he wasn't? What did he do at Los Alamos?"

Henry could only guess. Joe taught the hydrostatics of compressed fluids at Washington U, the behavior of matter under extraordinary pressure. In other words, implosion theory, shaped charges, sequenced ignition.

"What makes you think he was there if he says he wasn't?"

"A lot of things. Compton to begin with. Joe Stillman helped him get bugs out of the cyclotron at Washington U. It was separating U-238 around the clock for Fermi's pile in Chicago. He could have recruited him then."

"Played golf with Compton, helped debug the cyclotron. What else?"

"He was gone, off and on, for two years."

"Fishing in the Black Hills. What else?"

"A photograph in *Life* of Oppenheimer at Trinity. He's standing between Seth Neddermeyer and Hans Bethe. Everyone's wearing khakis and bush jackets except a man behind them who's dressed for the office in a three-piece herringbone tweed suit with an ivory slide rule sticking out of the inside breast pocket. He's wearing a felt fedora. You can't see his face. They're all holding welder's glass over their eyes, but I'd know the suit and the slide rule anywhere. Keuffel and Esser. Brooks Brothers. The same suit he wore to the mines."

"Bullshit," said Kornfeld, "complete bullshit."

"You may be right," said Henry, with a touch of rue.

"Last chance to heel for the *Oldfielder*. Wednesday, seven o'clock. We need you. I mean it."

THE OLDFIELDER

The *Oldfielder* office was a windowless basement room of the library crammed with desks, an industrial-size Addressograph machine, and steel shelves filled with metal trays of Addressograph plates for fifteen thousand graduates to whom the alumni office sent special editions of the paper. Kornfeld leaned impassively against a wall, smoking. The meeting was run by Nat Wardlow, the editor in chief, because the assignment editor was on probation for using the newspaper's telephone to talk long distance with his girl at Miss Madeira's School in Virginia.

The editor was a weary and soft-spoken senior who held his forehead in his hand and spoke into the breast pocket of his pink striped shirt. He explained that candidates for the editorial and business boards were called "heelers," which meant poor menials who do dirty work, as in the term "ward heelers." Editorial heelers must bring in ideas for stories and features; they would not receive assignments until they had proven themselves. Did they have any ideas? There were six other heelers who had been returning week after week to hear their suggestions scorned and skewered.

Henry's idea, a feature on the campus bells, put the editor to sleep when heard the word "bells." He yawned. "Done unto death. My eyes glaze over." He slumped in his chair. Henry turned to Kornfeld who looked at the ceiling in embarrassment.

Henry protested, "I have an angle."

The editor was snoring. "Wake me," he said.

"Can I just tell you my angle?" Henry persisted.

"Who is this boring, callow young man?" the editor asked.

"He is from St. Louis," said Kornfeld.

The mere mention of the twenty-sixth city caused the editor to groan. "Where do you find these people?"

"St. Joseph's Roman Catholic Church," Kornfeld told him, branding his friend a Catholic before the entire room. Henry scowled. The editor opened his eyes and examined the reporter's benign and deceiving face.

"What were *you* doing in a Catholic church, Kornfeld?" The Jew gave his reasons gladly. "Getting away from etiolated sybarites like you and your ass-licking deacons, not to mention the C-minor Passacaglia and Fugue on the Frederick C. Schwimmer Memorial Organ for the hundredth bowel-wrenching time." The editor closed his eyes and smiled, hearing himself and his favorite fugue described so aptly. His cynicism melted.

"Young man from St. Louis, you of the bells. Tell us your angle."

"Quasimodo," said Henry.

"Again?" said the drowsing editor.

"*Quasi modo geniti infantes*," Henry said.

"Stillman's a Jesuit," Kornfeld explained.

"Translate," the editor commanded.

"Like an infant. Childlike."

"Who?"

"The hunchback of Laughlin Chapel."

The editor opened his weak grey eyes and put on delicate horn-rimmed glasses. "More, more, more."

"Quintus Elmo by name."

"Who is he?"

"The janitor."

Kornfeld came to life. "Wall-eyed geezer. A hundred keys on his belt. You'd know him. Dwarf maybe," Kornfeld added. Newspapermen spoke like telegrams.

"You're making it up. It's too good."

"He's Nugent's demon," said Henry. "His Control. His Other."

"A witch?"

"An imp who does his bidding. Lights the fire, strangles babies. Elmo rings bells."

The editor was hooked. "Swings from a rope, like Charles Laughton?"

"Then he comes down to the little balcony at the back."

"And what?"

"Drinks deep at the preacher's well whose waters lighten his load and light his life. They're twins, joined at the hip. Mutt and Jeff, good cop, bad cop, savior and sinner. God and Moses, weekdays at ten, Sundays at eleven." Henry had discovered news speak.

The editor in chief was laughing and shaking his head. "No, no, no, no."

"Let me interview him," said Henry. He was guessing at all this, but why not?

"Let him try," urged Kornfeld. "What's to lose?"

"Our heads," said the editor. "Great idea, crazy idea. But no, absolutely no. Nugent's unstable, no humor, lifts weights."

"You're protecting him," said Kornfeld.

"I'm protecting my ass. I want to graduate."

"I can leave out the minister," Henry offered. "Just Quasimodo."

"Last time. No."

"Recuse yourself! Conflict of interest!" Kornfeld was shouting at his editor. "You're a student deacon, you're a Barney Nugent ass-licker! Recuse! Resign!"

"A journalist is not obliged to be foulmouthed, your Forty-third Street credentials notwithstanding," the senior editor replied.

"I like your shirt," said Kornfeld. "It's so tasteful I want to puke."

The editor in chief smiled. It pleased him more to be envied than to be loved. He turned to Henry. "You don't want to get anywhere near Nugent. He's so paranoid he makes us show him galley proofs of the chapel ear every week. Kornfeld, watch him. He's your guy." The chapel ear, Henry was to learn, was a box in the upper left corner of the front page that announced the Sunday preacher and the title of his sermon. The movie ear in the right corner listed title and stars of the Saturday night film in Josiah Prescott Hall.

"Do your Quasimodo piece when you guys are running the paper. For now, check out a rumor that's going around. A faculty wife has published or is about to publish a novel so scandalous it can be sold only in a plain wrapper from under the counter. Maia Forbes. Husband teaches English." "I'm in his class," said Henry. "Then you know. A bit weird. The war and all. Word has it she's a little queer herself. Interview her. Get her book."

Kornfeld protested again, "Don't give him that story! It's a dry well. She won't talk. A heeler wasted two weeks and never got near her. A, she's a hysteric. B, there is no book. I looked for it myself. It's a bum lead." The weary editor told Kornfeld to shut up; the lead was genuine. Perhaps she uses a pseudonym. Wardlow was confident the Jesuit would bring home the bacon. He slipped into a tweed jacket from the back of his chair, a soft garment of subtle greens and browns, double vented in the back, and addressed the room. "Who's putting the alumni issue to bed?" Kornfeld volunteered to take Stillman with him and show him the ropes and the enticements of Harwell. They would take a bus to Harwell after dinner and work all night. Wardlow twisted Kornfeld's right earlobe in a gesture of ambivalent affection. He was obviously both fond and mistrustful of the Inquiring Reporter who would probably be elected the next editor in chief in the spring.

Walking back to their dorms west of Main Street, Kornfeld again chose the defiant diagonal over forbidden grass, but this time Henry followed since it was too dark to be seen. His companion railed into the frosty silence against Nat Wardlow and the board and Prescott Academy. "Those J. Press jerk-offs are too lazy to wipe themselves. You know who runs the *Oldfielder*? The alumni office. We're their lackeys. They tell us what to print. Just wait 'til you and I get hold of this newspaper."

"I'm not an editor."

"You and I are going to run this paper, believe me."

"I know nothing about newspapers."

"All you have to do is look bored."

"I'm a hillbilly from Missouri."

"You've got some rough edges, and a really dumb name, which only makes you more believable. You're real; everyone else is an imposter. And you don't care, that's the clincher: you have complete indifference, like a god. Let 'em eat cake. You mend your loafers with friction tape. You slouch like an anteater. You piss where you please. Let's piss on the universe." In the dark, they had stumbled on the Astrolabe, a seldom-visited metal sculpture of celestial rings set on a stone pedestal in the grass where no paths led. At its center, on the polar axis of five bronze rings ten feet in diameter, was a naked family—man, woman, and child, dwarfed by the heavens around them. Kornfeld tried to piss on their heads; but Henry, from some fossil fear of sacrilege, refused to piss with him and was glad that in the dark Kornfeld probably missed.

"You want me around because my great-grandmother had a slave. That's sick."

"Not to mention your old man helped incinerate a quarter-million Japs. I gotta take my hat off."

"Nat Wardlow loves you, you're going to be the next editor in chief, and everybody knows it. You don't need me."

"Don't be so sure. Adam Kornfeld has shoveled shit for the Sulzbergers for thirteen years. You see him sailing a yacht and running the *Times*?"

"Is that what he wants?"

"Actually no. Editors are stones around the necks of writers. It's work for Georgia crackers, no self-respecting Jew will touch it."

"Aren't the Sulzbergers Jews?"

"Barely. And Jews don't like other Jews hanging around. I told you, first time we met, it's safer to mix with Catholics. Or Protestants, if you can stand them. Personally I can't. Their bowels are all tied in knots, like Martin Luther. Catholics screw and eat too much. Let me be surrounded by capon priests, them I trust."

"You're just looking for a Christian hick to front for your Marxist conspiracy."

"Young Stillman, you're more of an outcast around here than I'll ever be. You've got nothing to lose. Be my torch, we'll burn it down and take over."

He split off into the night. In a few moments, Henry saw a match blaze. But he was only smoking.

Before he called Mrs. Forbes, he checked the library and the bookstore downtown. Her name wasn't in the catalog, Books in Print, the Reader's Guide, anywhere. The bookstore had never heard of her. He phoned her from the *Oldfielder* office, and she answered in a voice that made him feel homesick for Missouri—flat as the corn, no ups and downs, climbs or slides. The accent, he later learned, was Minnesota missionary—lemon tart with no icing.

"My name is Henry Stillman. I'm a reporter for the *Oldfielder*.

"Someone from your paper already called," she said.

"We hear you have published a novel."

"Who said?"

"My editor heard it."

"Tell him I'm a housewife and a mother. They don't write books.

"Why not?"

"They don't have time. Is your name really Henry?"

"That's too bad—"

"You can change it."

"That you didn't write anything. It was exciting to think a faculty wife had written a book."

"Would that be newsworthy?"

"Teachers usually write books."

"They don't have time either."

"In the summer they could."

"Believe me. My husband is a teacher—"

"I know. I have him for English."

"So do I." Her laughter popped in his ear, like effervescence from a shaken soda. He wished he could see her laugh.

"Could we talk somewhere, like maybe Doc's?" Doc ran a lunch counter on Main Street which featured English muffins soaked in margarine and mashed flat in an electric sandwich press.

"About what?"

"Your book."

"There is no book. You've confused me with someone else, so please don't call anymore, Henry. That can't really be your name. I have to go."

"I've been thinking of changing it."

"So have I."

She hung up.

Did she mean changing her name or his? He wanted to meet her whether she'd written a book or not. Just to see her laugh.

Paul Forbes stopped him after English class. He leaned back in his chair with his fingers laced behind his head.

"My wife says someone named Henry called her and claims he's my student."

"It was me, sir—an assignment from the *Oldfielder*, to talk to her." He was blushing; he felt like a discovered lover beneath her bed. "They think Mrs. Forbes has written a book."

"Who told you that?"

"My editor."

"Who told him?"

"I don't know. He just said find the book."

"Why does he care?"

"It would be news, I suppose, that a faculty wife had written a book."

"It would be news that a faculty member had written a book, or even an article. On his goddam sabbatical." He closed his eyes and pushed his head forward with his clasped hands. Henry waited, unsure if the interview was over or if there was something wrong with his neck.

"Is there anything else, sir?"

"She wants you to call her back."

"I will, sir. Thank you."

"Don't thank me. You're opening a can of worms."

She answered on the first ring. "We're going to get you a new name."

"What's the matter with my old one?"

"No one should be named Henry."

"You don't even know what I look like."

"What difference would that make?"

"'Ichabod Crane's cognomen was not inapplicable to his mien.' People often look like their names."

"So what's your mien look like?"

"Tall, hunched over, horn-rim glasses, dark-matted hair, six-foot scarf, no overcoat."

"A William maybe, not a Henry. Why does Paul say you're interesting?"

"He laughed at a story I told. Why did he say I'm opening a can of worms?"

"The bastard!"

They agreed to meet the next day around three. She promised him nothing. There was no book. She was simply curious to see what someone named Henry looked like. He told Kornfeld about her when they met at the bus stop for Harwell, expecting praise for having engineered a meeting. Kornfeld was sour. "You won't get anything. She's a dry well, I told you that."

"You said she's a hysteric. Why?"

"She backed her VW into the lacrosse goal, got the bumper tangled in the net, took the keys, and left. They had to shoot around it for three days."

"Where was Mr. Forbes?"

"He goes off long weekends, she runs the dorm. They all talk about her nipples, but I've never seen them."

The bus took them through town, over the Pequonit Creek and up Route 24 through the rolling pastures of North Oldfield. The Marxist pointed to the whitewashed rail fences and jumps of a horse farm. "Stables of J. J. Perkins, owns world's largest cotton mills, sent them south to cheap labor, but he and his horses cling to the New England rocks. Chairman of the Board of Trustees, Prescott Academy."

The mills of Harwell stretched to the west, a perspective of long four-story stone buildings with tall mullioned windows and clock towers as far as one could see, all empty or used for warehouses. No thread of wool or cotton had been spun in Harwell for fifty years. The *Ledger-Tribune* occupied the first two floors of one such mill. The big rotary newsprint presses were on the first floor, the offset and flatbed presses for job printing were one flight up. The smell of ink, solvents, and hot lead hit them even at the bottom of the stairs. The odors triggered from Kornfeld a spontaneous rhapsody on the craft and nomenclature of printing. He took a deep breath of heady solvent and sang of the beauties of moveable type from Gutenberg to Ottmar Mergenthaler, inventor and manufacturer of the Linotype machine which was the first thing they saw at the top of the stairs, just beyond a counter that guarded an acre of columned space under wooden beams two feet square. Only one of the six Linotypes was running. Kornfeld introduced Henry to Carl, the night compositor, who typed his name on the rattling keyboard, then waited for the character matrices to accumulate in a slot in front of him. He inserted spaces by hand, then pulled a lever which sent Henry's name to a mold that filled with hot lead from a crucible above it. The mold opened, and a metal bar dropped into a tray to the left. Carl cooled it with a water spray, making the metal sizzle. Then he handed him a shiny slug of Linotype, his byline which read backward: namllitS yrneH yB.

"I hate my name," said Henry.

"Change it," said Kornfeld. They passed the Ludlow casters for making headlines with fonts larger than 18 point, the composing and makeup tables, paper cutters, and five-hundred-pound skids of paper stacked to the beams by an idle forklift. The eight pages of the fall sports issue lay side by side on a makeup table ready to be locked in chases after the final proofs had been made. There were a dozen expensive cuts paid for by the alumni office, screened photos etched on copper plates and bonded on wood. Page 8 was a three-quarter page ad for Camels. Kornfeld showed him how the ad came as a paper mat from which a plate was cast. The paper would be printed four up, or four pages at a time, on coated stock four feet square, then folded, cut, and collated. Charlie, who did makeup and pulled proof, gave them a list of problem spots and took their orders for the Merrimack Diner. They ordered hamburgers, french fries, Cokes, two six-packs of Narragansett Ale and went to work. They rewrote heads and subheads that didn't fit, cut articles that were too long, checked breaks and runovers, and proofed corrected galleys. The front-page lead under a three-column headline with a two-column photo of the quarterback making a pass had the byline of Jason Abrams, the sports editor. His story, for alumni consumption, was a roundup of Prescott's fall sweep over Islington in football, track, and swimming. It had a six-inch run over on page 6 with a montage of photos including Jimmy Bowes. Kornfeld was busy; he glanced at the front page and saw the movie ear was much shorter than its mate, which read, "Laughlin Chapel, Sunday, 10:00 a.m. Rev. B. Barnard Nugent will continue his examination of the major world religions. This week he will discuss the thought of Zoroaster. The choirs of Abbot and PA will give a joint concert." He told Henry to "dry out the chapel ear and give it to Carl." Henry chopped and squeezed until he had reduced the prolix message to a punchy twenty words. When the food came, Kornfeld paid for it, and they ate on steel stools at a makeup table, three printers and the two editors, or so Henry had begun to imagine himself. Kornfeld drank one ale in almost a single gulp and belched. The men laughed. Henry sipped his. He had tested bourbon and gin at home with no great effect but had gotten woozy with Jimmy Bowes on one beer in the dining car on the train to Oldfield.

Kornfeld opened a second ale. Ale seemed to straighten his asymmetrical face, and his mouth lost the misleading smile. He walked toward the dark end of the mill, the bottle swinging from his loosely dangling arm. The flatbed press lay dormant in the shadows with its delicate articulated arms, ending with digits of suction cups, folded to protect its dark mystery, the flatbed and rollers, at its heart. Even at rest, the press oozed fluids, oil, ink, and solvents, and suspired with compressed air in rubber arteries that swelled, contracted, gurgled, clicked, and wheezed in the dark cave of the old mill. Kornfeld stood before the ancient machinery in respectful silence, listening to its sporadic flatulence. After a long while, Henry asked, "What?" "It's seventy years old," he said. "Think of the dozens of fingers, hands, whole arms that have been mashed in this press. Stay awake," he warned, sounding like Joe Stillman on the danger of neckties around machinery. Henry thought of the chef's fingers, lost in a vat of mashed potatoes or bubbling gravy, while Kornfeld composed a threnody to letterpress printing, the brief embrace of stock and type on a nuptial flatbed. This chaste encounter of the virgin paper with the tumescent typeface left an inky visage like Christ's bloody face on Veronica's shroud. His companion became more Mandarin and obscure as he mourned the surrender of moveable type and hot lead to the cold hegemony of photo composition. "Letterpress is being killed by offset lithography and rotary presses, you'll see." He was like a western sheriff keening the obsolescence of his six-shooter. He was getting drunk.

He held the lapels of Henry's jacket and pulled his face close to his, speaking quietly, with no trace of his usual ironic games. "You've got to stay with me, Stillman, 'til the last elm falls, 'til the great lawn is gone to weed. We're gonna burn down Prescott, you and I." It was the second time he had heard that they were going to burn down the school. "You're way ahead of me," Henry answered. "Are you with me?" Kornfeld asked, pulling him even closer. Henry felt cornered. He'd been at Oldfield such a short time burning it down seemed impetuous, like his father's haste to bomb China. It was possible, Henry realized, that Kornfeld and Joe Stillman might like each other. He dodged Kornfeld's question with his own.

"Why did you come to Oldfield if you want to burn it down?"

"Not my choice."

"Your father's?"

"What are you getting at?"

"He never writes or asks how you're doing."

"Why should he? I only remind him what a crappy dad he's been."

"Maybe he ought to be reminded."

"You think he doesn't know? Jesus, Stillman. My mother makes him feel rotten enough for both of us."

"You're very proud of him. Does he know that?"

"I hope not. It would kill him."

"Why?"

"He doesn't want to know how people depend on him. That's why he ran away. Do you tell your old man you're proud he helped kill two hundred thousand Japs?"

"If he did, I'd be ashamed."

"Bullshit you would. He's a god. You worship him. Bowes licks your ass because of him. You're proud, don't fool yourself."

"I'm a complete sham, that's what I am—"

"Give me one way you're a sham."

"He wasn't at Los Alamos. Or Trinity."

"Compton, the cyclotron, the year he was away, the photo in *Life*?

"It's all just guessing."

"What Bowes saw—the drawing of the bomb you ate?"

"A sketch, a doodle."

"So why did you eat it?"

"To make them think it was top secret."

"Why, if it wasn't?"

"So they'd stop razzing me about Donna Hasenclever's tits. They thought the letter was from her, that's why they opened it."

"Your fat friend you used to electrocute."

"Yes."

"But your father wrote 'implosive lens' on it. Bowes saw it."

"He could have got it from a newspaper."

"No, he couldn't."

"How do you know?"

"Because I've looked in all the papers. There's no mention of the implosive lens in 1945. It was a secret until they caught Greenglass. The only people that knew worked for the Manhattan Project, like Greenglass and your father, or were told about it, like you and Bowes and Julius Rosenberg. Your old man helped kill a quarter-million Japs. Don't weasel out of it."

"I feel like a criminal." Kornfeld gave him a rabbit punch on his arm.

"You should drink more, Stillman. It's good for you."

Maybe it was, but it made him want to pee. The men's room was also the printers' locker room. In the middle was a ceramic basin about ten feet in diameter with a cluster of nozzles in the center which sprayed water when a foot treadle on the circumference of the basin was depressed. Henry imagined a fraternity of craftsmen, drunk on the fumes of trichloroethylene, peeing in a circle, like Indians round a campfire. He was about to perform this rite, just waiting for the urine to flow, when someone tapped his shoulder. It was Carl, who pointed to the real urinal, a long copper trough on the back wall. Henry was about to piss in the wash-up basin. Now he noticed cans of gritty powder every few feet around the tub. Carl showed him how to work the sandy soap into the ink on his hands, then rub them together under the spray by pressing the foot treadle.

Kornfeld came in with a fresh ale in his hand, headed for the toilet stalls. "Carl, babes, you're a brick," he said as he passed them. "Go slow, Junior," Carl warned, "we still got to pull proof."

"I'm super. I'm a hundred and ten percent," Kornfeld replied, shutting himself in a stall.

Charlie dropped the last slugs of Carl's corrections into the page forms and looked around for Kornfeld to give the word to pull final page proofs. He was still not back from the john. Henry shouted at him, then rattled the locked door to the stall. Kornfeld burst out like a roman candle, shouting orders and imprecations. He had obviously been asleep. It was after one o'clock when they finished the final proof. Most of the changes were last-minute scores and awards on the sports page. Jimmy Bowes was junior varsity MVP as Kornfeld had predicted. The front page was as symmetrical as the *New York Times*, the ears perfectly matched. A shift of pressmen came up from downstairs; and they wheeled the page forms, locked in chases, to the flatbed in the rear where the lights were now bright, motors whirred, and a forklift with three skids of paper threaded its way between columns toward the press. Their job was done. They called for a taxi and went home in style.

"Isn't Harwell the greatest?" Kornfeld asked. Henry agreed. Kornfeld went fast asleep, and Henry had to pull him up the three stories to his room in Tucker House and lay him outside his door.

By 11:00 a.m. eighteen thousand copies were printed and delivered to the *Oldfielder* office, two thousand for local distribution, folded in half, and sixteen thousand folded in thirds again and sealed with a round sticker for mailing to every living graduate. Heelers left stacks of the paper in the Commons and Josiah Prescott Hall and distributed it to the faculty mailboxes and departments. They would spend all afternoon and night running the folded copies through the Addressograph machine, and a truck would take the cartons to the post office early the next morning. Henry saw his first copy when he stopped at the office at lunchtime. He gazed proudly at the top half of the folded front page, the glossy stock glistening with fresh-ink smell of letterpress. The movie ear read, "Saturday Night Movie. JP Hall, 8 pm. *Sorry, Wrong Number*. Burt Lancaster,

Barbara Stanwyck, Agnes Moorehead. The fateful phone call." The chapel ear said, "Laughlin Chapel, Sunday, 11:00 a.m. Rev. B. Barnard Nugent's next piercing analysis of a world religion: **THE GREAT ZOROASTER!** With Norton and Prescott choirs." It sounded like a magic act with music. He took a copy to show Maia Forbes when they met.

It was almost three as Henry passed the lacrosse field in front of Hopkins Hall. Two teams were waving sticks that flared into latticed fans. He could not see what, if anything, they were throwing or catching with their sticks. It looked to his myopic eyes like an energetic game of semaphore, said to be Indian in origin, like smoke signals. A peculiar sport.

The dorms were divided into two entries, with abutting apartments for housemaster's families on the ground floor and thirty students in each entry on the two floors above. Married faculty had to raise families in the dorms while they waited to be assigned a big Victorian home where they could live normally with a few "house students" squirreled away on the upper floors. Hopkins Hall was red brick like everything else, with worn fire escapes at each end. The two entries, side by side, faced a quadrangle of identical dormitories with the playing field between them. Inside the entry was the door to the master's apartment, mailboxes, and stairs to the floors above. He rang several times. He knocked. Nothing. Two students coming down the stairs told him the bell was broken. "Just go in, it's always open, they don't care." Henry was reluctant to do that.

He walked around the building, looking for another door and buzzer. He passed the living room with a grand piano covered with books, an alcove with a four-leaf table sagging under more books and newspapers. The shades were drawn in the corner rooms, but in the back of the building the kitchen doors and backyards of the first-floor apartments were separated by a stake fence. The Forbes side had a scruffy lawn littered with toys, a bicycle, and a beat-up Volkswagen in the drive. He climbed three steps to the kitchen door and tried the bell which seemed broken too. He knocked. He was ready to give up when he saw a movement in the next window from the kitchen. From his height on the steps, he could glimpse, through almost closed blinds, a study or office with books and a bulletin board. A man's tousled hair appeared briefly above the sill and disappeared, then appeared again. It was his English teacher's head bobbing up and then out of sight in a slow rhythm. He needed to see just a bit more to be sure he was seeing what he thought he was seeing. Leaning on the railing, he hoisted himself on tiptoe until he saw Paul Forbes lying naked, face down, with a towel over his buttocks, between a pair of thin knees belonging to a woman invisible beneath him. Their postures shed a tiny light on a question that had vexed Henry since Kooch-i-ching: how do they do it? Some spatial and anatomical relationships were evident. He was on top, facing down; she was below, on her back, her legs drawn up. Everything else was inferential: whose thin legs they were, how they were coupled, what pelvic motion caused his head to bob, the reason for the towel.

Henry left the backyard and returned to the equally perplexing mysteries of lacrosse on the field in front of Hopkins Hall. There must be a ball or puck or stone, even if he couldn't see it. A field full of adversaries batting an imaginary ball was too bizarre. After a few minutes, the Forbes Beetle passed him, his English teacher at the wheel with his wife beside him, all gorgeous golden ponytail. She had completely forgotten their appointment in the distraction of her lust. He decided to leave the *Oldfielder* at their door to show he had kept his part of the bargain. The front door was now ajar. He knocked loudly, called hello, then dropped the newspaper on their floor and started to leave.

"Come in!" A woman who sounded like Maia shouted from the back of the house. "Sorry I'm late. Get some coffee or something. You know where the kitchen is?" Steam from a recent shower carried an intense odor of some flower, even more aromatic than the scent of gardenias that preceded Alfredo's mother into a room. It struck him, while he waited for her to return, that the women he most adored were all mothers, though never his own. Almost anyone else's. And it surprised him that Jill Bowes was high on the list and had been since kindergarten.

The living room was a bin of books, ashtrays, and unwashed coffee cups, the detritus of student smokers. One wall was stacked three feet high with what appeared to be shingles for kindling but were in fact the unopened cardboard mailers for slim volumes of verse sent to Paul Forbes for review. A scarred Mason & Hamlin grand piano was covered with music, books, and dirty cups and on the music rack the open sonatas of Scriabin. He saw quickly he could never play them.

"Do you play?" She was standing beside him; he could feel the nimbus of her moist freshness and taste the fragrance of flowers on her. He focused rigidly on the pages of Scriabin, nearly black with a dense thicket of notes. "No," he answered her. "Neither do I," she said. They stood together for a mute moment, bonded by their mutual exclusion from playing the piano. "Paul does," she said. "He must be good," said Henry. "He's good at everything," she replied in a tone neither bitter nor flattering, but resigned. He felt their kinship blossom with the addition of Paul Forbes to the world from which these two outsiders were excluded.

"I didn't think you were home. I saw Mr. Forbes leave with someone."

"That must have been Merope, my sister."

She had left his side and was patting down the papers on the piano and then every surface in the room, gliding her fingertips over tables and chairs, repeating to herself, "Glasses, glasses, glasses." They were probably under the sofa in the room behind the kitchen where her husband had surprised her, but he didn't suggest it. He had been unable to look at her while they stood at the piano; he was so frozen by her proximity and her blossom scent. Now he could enjoy her from a distance, note how the ankle-length folds of her loose striped jersey covered the thin legs he had so recently seen in the back window, and imagine how they glistened with blossom-smelling oil. Her black bangs, still glossy wet from the shower, were pulled across her forehead and behind her ear; her dark eyes searched in a constant and merry movement. She picked up some dirty cups and a paper plate with half a Hydrox cookie, its vanilla filling scraped or licked off, then put them down again and sat on the piano bench. "Sorry about the mess," she apologized. "We've kind of thrown in the towel."

A shiny red novel called *Home Front* was on the piano. He looked in the back flap to see who wrote it. The photo of the author, D. M. Evers, was definitely Maia Forbes—her eyes full of mischief and her hair over her left cheek like Veronica Lake. "D. M. Evers was raised with three sisters on the Choctaw Reservation near Ely, Minnesota, by their widowed father who ran the Indian Training School." He let the book close itself. "Where do you write?" he asked.

"I told you I don't write."

"You wrote that book."

"D. M. Evers wrote it. Back there." She nodded toward the kitchen. "There's an office sort of."

"You write under a pseudonym."

"I write under my own name. I live under a pseudonym."

"Maia Forbes is your pseudonym?"

"I'm working to change it. For a nom de guerre."

She knit her brows and squinted to focus; she knew she was missing a lot without her glasses. "Paul said you were big, but I didn't guess." Her husband was taller than he was.

"It smells good in here," he said.

"Lilac bath oil!" she said. "My sister makes it." She stopped and squinched her face horribly. "Do you really want to be called Henry?"

"No."

"Isn't there something else?"

"Not yet." She shrugged.

"If there is, let me know." She picked up *Home Front,* looked at it, and let it drop. "Is that the silliest cover you ever saw? Who are those stupid soldiers? They're not even in the book." The cover was a drawing of a nearly naked chorus line on a distant stage, a tiny patch of light and color, seen over the heads of two soldiers in the foreground who are sitting almost alone in the top balcony of a dark and ratty theater.

"What do you think of the title?"

"I can't tell without reading it."

"It doesn't make you think of radishes and carrots?"

"Carrots?"

"Victory Gardens, scrap metal, a tinfoil ball, pasting war stamps—you know, the home front."

"My father was an air raid warden. During blackouts, we stood on the high dive of the club pool to see which houses had their lights on."

"The Indians didn't have blackouts. I have to pick my son Eben up soon. You can take it if you bring it back."

"Why isn't it in the bookstore?"

"It isn't published yet. That's a review copy."

He turned to the first page.

It was my first time. A stagehand was nudging down the handles of four light boards stacked two deep in the wings. The heat given off by sixty red-hot dimmers was the only warmth backstage. The shivering chorus huddled around the boards between their scenes. "Break a leg," said the electrician. He knew it was my first time. I tossed my smock on a nail in a flat just offstage and wedged into the line between Kim and Dodo, shivering in my bare flesh. It's queer how ladylike and modest we are in front of the crew, wearing bathrobes and all. Or maybe it's just the cold. The G-string's beaded bangles bumped and tickled the inside of my thighs. My boobs bounced as I made my entrance to a three count and kick, just behind Dodo. The heat from the Fresnel lamps on the light pipe above us beat down on my nose and nipples which were erect and stippled with goose bumps. They need to put electric heaters backstage, something besides just the dimmer boards.

She was looking at him, waiting to hear what he thought. "You know a lot about G-strings and light boards."

"I've been backstage. It's no big deal."

"They have autotransformers now to dim lights. They burn less power and make almost no heat."

"This was before autotransformers."

"You write in the first person."

"I identify strongly with Martine. That's her name."

"So how does a woman from Ely, Minnesota, get to know so much about G-strings?"

"The library is one way. *Costumes of the Harem* by Gwyneth Farraday. Ottoman, fifteenth century."

Henry nodded sagely, as if the history of costume was all he wanted to hear. She laughed. "You think I've kicked in a chorus line, don't you?"

"I'm wondering." She laughed.

"Do I look like a stripper?" She didn't. The striped jersey was draped over her perfect breasts whose erect nipples he imagined stippled with goose bumps by the gamma radiation from his own hard-on which he crossed his legs to conceal. She was waiting for his answer. Her breasts were small grapefruits, not melons, not gross stripper's boobs, not big cow tits. Greek, harmonious, Venus de Milo-type tits, which were the only kind of tits he knew—the tits on statues with no pubic hair.

"I don't think you do," he said.

"'Stripping' is the wrong word. Stripping is disrobing slowly, provocatively. The queen strips, the chorus backs her up. They shed down to pasties and gadgets before the queen does."

"Gadgets?"

"That's the *G* in G-string. Same thing."

"Can I find that in Gwyneth Farraday?"

"You can find it at the Old Howard. Have you ever been there?"

"No."

"I know someone who works there. I can take you backstage if you want."

It was a curious offer, from someone he was meeting for the first time.

"It's not about Victory Gardens, your book. Not that home front."

"In a way it is. Martine and Dodo are sisters. Their guy is missing in action. *Home Front* is about war, the other war—"

"Between men and women."

"And children and pets. Everyone—spectators, journalists, the Red Cross. No one is neutral. There are no noncombatants."

"Each against all, like Darwin?"

"The home front, you're sitting in it—the killing field."

She didn't seem to notice she was crying. He must have interrupted something between husband and wife, maybe their lovemaking, and he wondered if he ought to leave. He didn't really understand much of what she was saying—about killing fields and the Red Cross. He needed to get her to give him the book and get out.

"Perhaps we should do this some other time."

"Do what?" she asked.

"Have this interview."

"This is not an interview! We're just talking. Off the record."

"Right. Just talking."

"So what do you want to know?"

"About your book, your life, why you brush your hair over your eye like Veronica Lake."

"What about my life?"

"What it's like, to be a wife and a novelist and—"

"It's hell, Henry, it's worse than being a wife and a burlesque dancer."

He didn't see the connection.

"Writers and strippers both take off their clothes, don't they? They expose themselves. That makes men jealous. They want you to be naked only for them. That's the can of worms, Henry. We've got to get you a real name."

"So men are jealous because you share your body or your mind with others."

"They call it prostitution. At least Paul does."

"How does Mr. Forbes feel about your literary striptease?"

"He hasn't told you?"

"Is he anything like the guy in your book who's missing in action?"

"He's a bit nicer, but he's still a man."

"You think a woman can be closer to another woman."

"I don't just think. But it ain't the same."

"What?"

"The sex, Henry."

"Plain sex is better you're saying—"

"Let me explain something. I didn't want to talk to you because Paul—" She stopped again. "We really got to get you another name. Hank? Hal? Harry? Where were we?"

"Sex and Mr. Forbes."

"He hates my book. He won't be associated with it, which is fine by me. I don't want to compete with him. Oldfield is his place. That's why I use my own name, why I don't want people around here even to know I'm with him because I'm labeled everywhere I go. Poet's wife, war widow, lesbian partner, pet lover—names, if you notice, that define me by who I'm with, not by who I am."

"Can't you be both? D. M. Evers *and* Maia Forbes?"

"They hate each other."

"But you're saying they're really the same. It sounds like you've divided yourself arbitrarily into two people, you and your sister—"

"Read the book and tell me."

"I don't know you."

"You will."

She chewed at her lower lip so ferociously he thought she might draw blood.

"How did you meet Mr. Forbes?"

"He was my thesis adviser. At Chicago."

"Before the war?"

"Just." She stopped again. "We've really got to get you another name."

"You were talking about Mr. Forbes—"

"I've got it!" She stood and looked at him with a face transfigured by contact with a higher power. "H." He had no idea what she meant. "It's perfect!" she said. "H., H., H.! You're H." She was talking about his name.

"Just H.?" he asked.

"Plain H.," she said. "Like K. You dig K., don't you? I know you do. Everybody does."

"I'll have to think about it."

"No, you don't." She was almost angry with him. "You didn't think about being Henry. It just happened to you, like an ugly birthmark. Now H. has happened to you. Accept it."

"You were saying about Mr. Forbes, why he doesn't like *Home Front*—"

"No. That's not true, I shouldn't say that."

She looked at her watch. "I'm sorry I was so late, but I have to pick up Eben." He was being thrown out. She would never talk to him again. It was his last chance.

"I understand Mr. Forbes was in the war—"

"He had his war, I had mine."

"Is it true he was missing—"

"Ask him. He's your teacher—"

"I guess what I want to know—"

"He crashed, H., let's just say he crashed."

"And might have been dead."

"He was definitely missing. I have to go."

She got up and began hunting for her glasses in earnest. Henry figured it was all right to keep asking things until he was out the door.

"How did he crash?"

"He ran out of gas."

"Where?"

"That's the point. He didn't know where, and he was supposed to be the navigator."

"Of what?"

"A goddam Flying Fortress." She laughed; and when she laughed, her head arched, her neck stretched long, and her arms hung loose with delicious surrender, like a dog on its back. Henry's heart danced in his throat. She was ravishing. "The fact is he didn't know east from west or left from right and never has. It's called *links-rechts* disease. Freud and Bleuler treated it with hypnosis." Her husband's spatial impairment was even funnier to her than his airplane. She laughed with complete abandon.

Mr. Forbes came in with two shopping bags and set them down. "What's the joke?" Maia Forbes tried to explain.

"He was asking what you did in the war."

"Ran out of fuel. Big laugh. So what did you guys decide?"

"We've been working on a new name for him. His is just too silly."

"Thoreau, Longfellow, Adams, James, it didn't hurt them." He turned to the current bearer of the stigmatic praenomen. "She gonna let you read her book?"

"I hope so, sir."

"Nelson Algren claims he liked it. Maybe you will."

"Paul thinks I had an affair with Nelson while he was missing in a Burmese leper colony, and that's why he likes it."

"You were in a leper colony, sir?"

"How long's it take to get leprosy, anybody know?" Mrs. Forbes asked.

"Eight or ten years," Forbes answered.

"Forty-three plus eight is fifty-one. Next year." She seemed excited by the prospect of having a leper in the family.

Henry had to ask who Nelson Algren was. His teacher set him straight. "High priest of booze and drugs. Thinks he's the Balzac of Chicago."

"My first teacher," his wife said evenly, "you'll know his name soon. His new book is terrifying."

"*I* was her first teacher," said Mr. Forbes. "She tends to forget that. So what's the story? Is Maia going to be the *Oldfielder's* new pinup girl?" he asked Henry.

"I've only read a page, but I think the editors will be very excited."

Paul Forbes took a gallon jug of gin from one of the shopping bags and put it on the piano. "'Excited' is the right word," he said. "They'll cream in their jeans. Maia's a pornographer. Only ones who don't know it are Nelson Algren and her publishers."

"You are so crude, so gauche. You're jealous the Prescott kids may like my book."

"They'll want to see you can bare ass too."

"Screw you. I have to pick up Eben." She left the room abruptly. Forbes opened the jug and poured himself some gin in a dirty glass without ice.

"Did she tell you there's a striptease artist in the family?"

"I was asking how she knew so much—"

"I can read books, that's how." Mrs. Forbes was back, holding fuzzy boots which she sat on the piano bench to pull on.

"I was going to tell young Stillman about your sister."

"I have three sisters, and I need the keys." Mr. Forbes threw them to her. She put on her parka and found her glasses, which made her look very expensive.

"What are you doing for Christmas?" she asked Henry.

"We're going to Maine," Forbes said.

"Can't he come?"

"Maybe he doesn't want to, maybe he doesn't like us, maybe he has to go home to St. Louis."

"Is that where you're from?" She was surprised and, he thought, disappointed. "H.! Tell me you're not from St. Louis."

"Who is H.?" Paul Forbes wanted to know.

"He is. Tell him," she commanded. Henry was caught between the two. He had a premonition of everything to follow, and his moment to choose passed quickly because neither Forbes waited. They answered their own questions.

"He's H.," she said. "He hated his old name, didn't you? Where are you going? I'll drop you off." She started to pull him out the kitchen door. He ran back to get her book. "Don't let Maia rewrite your life," Paul Forbes shouted as they left. "She wants to be the author of everything."

Maia watched with amusement as Henry tried to fold his ungainly frame into the front seat of the Volkswagen.

"How does Mr. Forbes fit in here?"

"He's into yoga."

"So while Mr. Forbes was hiding in a leper colony, what were you doing, if you weren't in a chorus line or sleeping with Nelson Algren?"

"Who says I wasn't?"

"Which?"

"All of the above."

Backing out of the drive, they almost scraped Adam Kornfeld who was standing a few yards up the hill from her driveway, waiting for him to come out. He was stunned to see Henry in the author's vehicle and ran after them. "We're being followed," she said.

"It's my editor."

"What does he want?"

"To find out if you wrote a book."

"You can't show it to anyone."

"Why?"

"You heard Paul. He hates it, among a million other things."

"He's too close to judge."

"He likes you. You better watch out." She looked in the mirror. "Your friend is catching up."

"Speed up," said Henry. But the light changed at Main Street, and they had to stop. Kornfeld shouted and battered with his open hands on the metal roof. "Get out! I have to talk to you." Henry waved him away. Kornfeld planted himself in front of the Beetle, leaning with his hands on the hood. The light changed green.

Mrs. Forbes was laughing. "Oh my god, what I have gotten into? You guys are crazy."

"I ought to get out," said Henry. "What shall I tell them?"

"Call me this weekend. Paul is going to Forbes Neck. I'll be stuck with Eben."

"Forbes Neck?"

"His place in Maine. His place."

THE GREAT ZOROASTER

When Kornfeld saw Henry's door open, he let the car pass. "Why did you do that?" Henry asked angrily.

Kornfeld was tied in knots, like a Protestant.

"Because, you jerk! You asshole! You hangnail! I thought we were friends." He was blowing like a hurricane, first right, then left. Maybe he was still drunk from the ales in Harwell. From the torrent of expletives, H. learned that his rage had something to do with the chapel ear. "What's wrong with it?" Kornfeld stood panting.

"You fucked it up!"

"I dried it out like you asked."

"Dry out. Make shorter, not make funny, make snide, make sophomoric. You're a putz, a schlemiel."

"I made it shorter."

Kornfeld took the new issue from his pocket and tried to mash it in his face. "Piercing analysis! **THE GREAT ZOROASTER** in caps, boldface, and exclamation point! What's that shit?"

Henry grabbed the paper and smoothed out the front page to see his handiwork. "Shorter. Twenty-four words. Count them. And you saw it last night."

"I was smashed out of my mind."

"On two beers?"

"Four. And the whole board is waiting for us at the library. You better make it good."

"Who said it was snide?"

"Wardlow, Pickering, Nugent, you name it."

"It's all in their heads."

"Nugent wants the whole issue reprinted. Eleven hundred bucks, on your term bill."

"The only thing derogatory is maybe the exclamation point. That's a typo. We can blame Carl."

"Tell them that." Kornfeld ran ahead on the path, taking the five-foot soprano poles like high jumps. The small, undernourished ascetic was a secret jock. He stopped abruptly and waited for Henry to catch up. "Okay, I'm going to handle this. Don't say a word."

"I did what you asked."

"Just shut up. Let me do the talking, and don't contradict me."

The senior editors, waiting on the steps of the Eliphalet Pearson Library in the sinking sun, were a contrast in winter fashion: Nat Wardlow in a Chesterfield with felt lapels; Pruitt, the managing editor, a Burberry; Abrams, the sports editor, a duffel coat with rope and peg fasteners, like Nugent's; and the assignment editor in an unzipped warm-up jacket. They resembled the last photo of a British climbing party, haphazardly costumed for an ascent in what they anticipated to be mild weather. A taciturn Wardlow led them downstairs to the *Oldfielder* office. Abrams asked on the way, "Were you guys drunk?" No one answered. The office was deserted, the heelers gone, the Addressograph machine silent, stacks of addressed copies destined for the alumni piled everywhere according to city and state. Wardlow swept copies of the new issue off his desk for a space to sit. He spoke to Kornfeld.

"Who screwed up the chapel ear?"

"What do you mean?"

"Someone rewrote it since the powder proof."

"I did," said Kornfeld. "It was too long."

"They printed eighteen thousand copies of the alumni issue with a front-page box that portrays our beloved chaplain as a world-class asshole."

Kornfeld picked up a copy and looked closely at the left-hand box, changing the angle of the glossy stock to accommodate the room's fluorescent light. "Show me where it suggests B. Barnard Nugent is an asshole. All I see is compliments." Kornfeld's disingenuousness stunned even the jaded Wardlow.

"Don't get smart with me," said the editor in chief. "*Piercing analysis* is a sarcastic put-down."

"To someone who believes that B. Barnard Nugent is incapable of piercing analysis, perhaps it is. Not to me."

The managing editor agreed. "Kornfeld's right. A piercing analysis is an astute dissection. That which goes to the heart of the matter. A spiritual x-ray."

"Tell that to Nugent and Pickering, they're on their way over," said Wardlow. "To me it's dripping irony. And **THE GREAT ZOROASTER** in caps, exclamation point. Makes his sermon sound like a magic act." Henry wanted to defend his handiwork, tell them that's what Zoroaster was: a magus, a magician! But he kept himself hidden behind the Addressograph machine.

"The exclamation is a typo. I must have missed it. It was one o'clock, eight pages, two galleys of overset, we were all bushed." Wardlow wasn't fooled. "Bullshit, Kornfeld! You'd shed your blood to proof a tide table. You would never, ever, do anything this unprofessional. Where's your friend, the Jesuit? I warned him about Nugent—" He stopped abruptly when he saw that Charles Coleman Pickering, the dean of students, known to all as CC, had slipped in and was standing by the sports editor. The only sound was the muffled grinding of walnuts which CC massaged in the deep pockets of the voluminous trousers of his three-piece grey striped suit. The dean acknowledged the editors with a glance over half-moon reading glasses balanced on the tip of his abbreviated nose. "Continue your deliberations. Barney Nugent is on his way. I hope you have something to say to him." Then CC whispered to the sports editor. "Who's the Jesuit?" "Some heeler." "Why do they call him the Jesuit?" "Because he speaks Latin."

Barney Nugent arrived in a varsity tracksuit and announced he had just rowed ten miles on the Merrimack and done forty laps on the track around the Cage. He exuded health and satisfaction. He was Gormely garmented and, if possible, more body-proud. Henry thought he might exhibit his preternaturally tight scrotum whose outline was visible under the soft folds of his tracksuit. Wardlow apologized for the misunderstanding about the chapel announcement. No irony or sarcasm was intended about the Reverend Nugent's forthcoming discussion of Zoroaster. CC stopped him angrily. "Slow down, young man. You can't turn a vicious smear into a mere semantic quibble. I want to know which of you libeled Barney Nugent and how you intend to wash his name clean." The walnuts in his pockets clicked ominously while he awaited their answer. Kornfeld spoke, "You need blood, sir, to wash his name clean. A bleating sacrificial lamb. Take me, if the Reverend Nugent is willing to accept the blood of a Jew."

Wardlow at last raised his voice. "Kornfeld! Shut up! I'm responsible, and I have apologized—" But CC cut him off. "You've apologized for nothing! No one leaves this room until I hear—" Nugent put a restraining hand on CC's raised arm. "Let's leave these young people alone, Charlie," his tone brimming with sweet charity. "I don't want apologies or blood from anyone—lamb, Jew, or journalist. What are a few sophomoric barbs to Barney Nugent? Nothing. I've got better things to worry about. I'm for saying the whole thing never happened. Let's forget it." And he walked out, leaving them speechless in the wake of his majestic hypocrisy. This pious forgiveness, from the man whose injured pride was demanding that sixteen thousand newspapers be shredded, took everyone's breath away, except for Pickering who was not in the forgiving mood. He held up a thrice-folded copy of the issue, with the offending chapel box just above the stamped address, and let it fall to the floor. "Correct the chapel announcement and reprint the alumni issues." Nugent had got what he wanted without appearing to ask for it. Wardlow was indignant. "But why, sir? He just said to forget it. You heard him." "Reprint them," the dean repeated and started to leave, but found he was blocked by the much-smaller Kornfeld whose necktie just grazed the dean's Phi Beta Kappa key bobbing on a gold chain threaded through the bottom buttonhole of his vest. "This isn't fair, sir." "Life's unfair," said the dean, pushing him aside. When the door was closed, Wardlow turned on Kornfeld. "Let me run this paper, will you?"

"You're too slow," said Kornfeld. "You give people time to think."

"You're gonna get yourself killed before you even grow up," Wardlow warned him. "They don't dare," said the Inquiring Reporter, brandishing an inscrutable invincibility.

"Stillman!" Wardlow shouted. Henry straightened up from his crouch behind the Addressograph machine. "You're finished. Get out!"

"Come off it!" said Kornfeld. "Show him the book." Henry gave Wardlow *Home Front*. He turned the book front and back.

"Who's D. M. Evers?"

"Maia Forbes."

"I knew it was a pseudonym. How did you get it?" But he had begun flipping through the pages and making salacious howls.

"And this Dodo. Are they dykes?" He whistled and groaned. "Unbelievable! She wrote it? Maia Forbes wrote this?" "She says so."

"She's a stripper, she's got to be."

He read to them the beginning about the "stippled and erectile nipples." The rest of the board were grabbing for the book, shoving each other.

"Write a review, do a profile, are there any pix?"

"Wait till you get to the Oldfield part."

"Jesus! Holy cow! The school will go ape-shit."

"Paul Forbes, what does he think?"

"He calls it a can of worms," said Henry.

"He's the guy who comes back from the dead and fucks it all up." Wardlow was reading a banner quotation on the rear cover.

"A woman's new life is snatched from her by a man returned from the dead. *Home Front* introduces D. M. Evers, an angry young writer and woman to watch."

"Nelson Algren. How does she know Nelson Algren?"

"He was her teacher I think," said Henry.

"Who is he?" someone asked. "The Balzac of Chicago."

"How soon can you write a review?"

"For next week."

Kornfeld pulled him from the room. On the stairs, he turned on him fiercely. "Stillman, don't ever betray me again. Never. We're all gonna be taken out and shot, so let's don't shoot ourselves, okay? You nearly got us creamed with the fucking chapel ear."

"Why did you take the blame?"

"You're too young to die," he answered.

"And you aren't?"

"I'm a vampire. The living dead. They can't touch me."

He had lived in institutions since he was six. It was mystifying how Kornfeld could derive a whole morality from sheer pessimism. Loyalty to his fugitive father and mad mother was typical of his largesse, of which the feckless Henry was even less deserving than Kornfeld's wretched parents. He tried to thank him.

"I can't talk to people when they're emotional," he said and split off across the grass where he knew Henry was afraid to follow him. He watched Kornfeld's diminishing shape with a new appreciation—a man dressed like a boy. His entire future was etched on his skewed face and wiry frame—an alcoholic, perfectionist, Pulitzer Prize winning, Marxist correspondent, loyal only to his journalist brotherhood and in flight from all personal attachment. He was his father's miniature.

Henry began reading *Home Front* at eight thirty. Lights had to be out at ten thirty, so on page 180, he moved to his bed by a window directly under a streetlamp on Main Street. With the thermostat of his electric blanket buried in new snow outside the window, and the occasional grating of a plow on Main Street muffled by the accumulating snow, he read on in the oscillating glow of the sodium vapor lamp which made the print a sickly green scum that seemed to float an inch above the pulsing yellow page. The first part was so sexy he had to masturbate twice to keep his attention on the text.

He began his review with her description of burlesque.

> *My boobs bounced as I made my entrance to a three count and kick behind Dodo . . . the heat from the Fresnel lamps on the light pipe above us beat down on my nose and nipples which were erect and stippled with goose bumps.* Martine and Dodo are sisters who are putting themselves through grad school by stripping in the chorus of a Chicago burlesque house. They believe Frank, a poet who was Martine's fiancee and tutor, has died in a PT boat in 1943. Their wartime idyll bursts when Frank returns from a POW camp in Sumatra with a prize-winning epic poem. Sexual chaos and rivalry is triggered between the sisters. He moves his seething ménage to a New England boarding school where he teaches, and the women have the run of hungry adolescents in the dormitories. It is Oldfield down to Doc's margarine-soaked muffins. Martine realizes how much she misses Dodo's warm breast and belly against hers and their life in dance. She wishes that Frank had been a draft resister and written his poetry in jail or that he had never returned. Martine is an astonishingly sad and affecting creature—a beached mermaid deprived of her element. Everyone wants to help her, nurse her, take her home, not realizing that human love will make her die.

He parsed the skimpy biography of D. M. Evers, mapping her journey from Ely, Minnesota, to the University of Chicago, to workshops and writer's colonies in Iowa, Vermont, and Massachusetts until she is gradually absorbed into greeting-card New England where she "resides" with an anonymous husband and unsexed child. It described a plastic life, not the wild ride between sex in the mudroom, lesbian sisters, crashed bombers, and warm gin that he had witnessed in Forbes House. He studied her photo. Her hair covered one eye, and she was chewing her lip. He wanted to camp on her doorstep, tell her that he loved her book, loved her life, loved her, to shout her glories to the world, to make Kornfeld, Wardlow, and all of Oldfield know that he had discovered the next Virginia Woolf, the next Hemingway.

He phoned her from the *Oldfielder* office next morning. She seemed happy he called. "Tall Henry, hello!"

"Your book is beautiful. I cried. I loved it."

"You're lying."

"It's better than *Tender Is the Night*."

"I hate that book. She's such a bitch! Say something nice."

"It's better than *The Waves*. Martine is the most fascinating woman I have ever imagined. I'm going to tell the world about her and you."

"You're putting me on."

"They will want to do a whole page on you. We'll need to take pix. I've written the review."

"H.? H.? Are you there?"

"What?"

"Please don't hate me. I've done a terrible thing. I've betrayed Paul. You can't print anything. I shouldn't have given it to you."

"I can't stop it now."

She hung up. Kornfeld was waiting for him on the wall. He glanced at the review. "This is a bombshell, Stillman. You know that, don't you? Prescott Academy will never recover, it's another *Ulysses*, a *Lady Chatterly*, a *Tropic of Cancer*! To begin with, it's completely autobiographical."

"You know that?" Henry asked.

"First novels always are. Look at it. Horny uppers goose the master's wife while he tickles his tutees—the whole sick boarding school thing."

The issue with his review and profile came out on Wednesday morning. Her photo was beautiful. The heelers all congratulated him when he came into the office to watch them fold and address the subscription copies. At their breakfast meeting, the editors cheered and elected him a member of the editorial board on the spot. Wardlow embraced him. He took the bookstore's fifty copies downtown himself and watched the owner's wife put them on the counter next to the *Oldfield Weekly Leader*. "Town and gown," she said proudly, but also let him know the *Oldfielder* was displayed purely as courtesy, and almost no one bought it. He showed her the review—*Home Front* by D. M. Evers, Mary Powell

Press, Chicago, $4.95. "You should stock a dozen copies and put them in the window with a blowup of the review." The owner's wife was skeptical; she'd never heard of the Mary Powell Press or D. M. Evers. "You say she lives here?" He pointed to the feature article. "It says right here. She's really Maia Forbes, wife of the pole vault champion. He's famous." She read the first paragraph. What did a burlesque house have to do with a prep school? She would be glad to order it if anyone asked.

Henry faced the reality that the bookstore would never stock *Home Front* and that no one would ever read it or his review. He was wrong. There was one steadfast reader of everything Henry Stillman wrote since his career in journalism had begun. He was perhaps the only person who had actually read the chapel ear, the first to react to his celebration of *Home Front* and its author, and the first to order a copy of *Home Front* from the bookstore. Barney Nugent was Henry's reader. Henry was really writing only for him.

He was late for daily chapel, which he made just under the wire. The bells had stopped, the organ prelude was about to climax, and his pew mates had spread themselves out to conceal his absence from the student checkers in the organ loft. Nugent stood somber as Ahab behind his pulpit, his hands grasping the edges of the giant Bible like the helm of the Pequod. His lesson from Psalms was a warning.

> More in number than the hairs of my head
> are those who hate me without cause;
> mighty are those who would destroy me,
> those who attack me with lies.

He closed the book and studied his captives. How many had seen this week's *Oldfielder* or noticed the Sunday chapel announcement on the left corner of the front page? He produced a copy from deep within his robes, unfolded it, and actually read Henry's stupid chapel ear out loud, **THE GREAT ZOROASTER,** exclamation point and all. The amnesty of the perfidious holy man was a fraud. Henry felt a black rage growing in him. "I'm not an intellectual," Nugent said proudly. "I went to a small college in Albany. I could never make a piercing analysis like you men will at Yale or Harvard. And I won't bore you with Zoroaster and most certainly not the coward who is sitting among you, who mocked my sermon even before it was preached and now celebrates in these same pages unnatural acts of gross depravity alleged to occur between teachers and students. I challenge this midnight scribbler to stand up before God, as I do, and admit he is a sour grape wrinkled by hate—"

His litany was interrupted by a long, fertile raspberry fart from among the upper middlers. A sibilant, flatulent, bubbling fart hot enough to lift a balloon with a gondola of passengers over their heads. The sullen congregation broke into laughter as proctors rushed toward the sound, but no farter was found. Henry took the moment to look back at the rear balcony. Quintus Elmo was in his usual place, watching his master rend his garments and cover himself with ashes. His servant seemed grieved and saddened. Henry wasn't making it up; there was something between them, and he intended to find out what it was.

The minister was unfazed. "I wonder how many of you read the enthusiastic review of a novel this critic claims was written by the wife of a faculty member. The heroine he so much admires is a modern Clytemnestra who debauches herself while her husband is at war, becomes a lesbian in the nude chorus of a burlesque house, and when he returns to teach in a boy's boarding school, the adulterous mother has affairs with the young men in his dormitory, as does he. She does everything but murder her returned war hero in his bath. What this woman has written, according to Mr. Stillman, is a lewd attack on all we hold sacred—marriage, education, patriotism, the moral contract that holds society together. The portrait of women is obscene and of students disgusting and unfair. I think the writer should be driven from the fold of this community along with the faculty and wives who are party to this cabal. They have made war on our values and must be destroyed. *Carthago delenda est.*"

He prayed.

"The bastard is obscene," H. growled through teeth gritted against a biting sleet when he caught up with Kornfeld near the library.

"I want to kill the hypocrite," Henry vowed, every detail of the aborted plan to chloroform and burn Gormely still luminous in his memory.

"That fart sure shut him up. Relax."

"When he's dead, I will."

Kornfeld was tired of his obsession with the preacher. "You're the one who made him a martyr, and we have to listen to him crow. Thanks a heap."

"Then help me kill him."

"You're kidding."

"I'm not."

"You have some deep aversion requiring his death the rest of us can't understand?"

"I guess I do," said Henry. He wished Kornfeld shared his rage, but he couldn't explain it.

Kornfeld nodded. He respected private animosities, however looney, if the boundaries were made clear. "So I'm with you, if you're with me." Henry nodded too. They had a contract: Kornfeld would help kill Barney Nugent if Henry helped him burn down Oldfield.

"How do we do it?" Henry asked.

"The way Mencken and Darrow killed Bryant."

"Who are they?"

Kornfeld shook his head in disbelief. Parochial ignorance had a limit. "H. L. Mencken, Clarence Darrow, the Scopes Trial? You've never heard of them?" He shook his head. "You are shapeless, callow, and jejune."

"Just tell me who they are."

"Darrow: public defender, greatest lawyer ever. Mencken: journalist, editor, and my godfather. Thomas Scopes: accused of teaching evolution, a crime in Dayton Tennessee in 1923." Kornfeld wandered away across the grass, lost in dismay at his obtuse friend.

HOME FRONT

Henry called Maia Forbes from the office. It rang a long time, and she answered it belligerently.

"What is it?"

"I want to bring you a copy of the paper."

"I have one."

"What do you think?"

"I want to punch you in the nose. I want to throw up."

"I loved your book."

"Why didn't you say so?"

"I thought I did."

"You said Martine was like a sick fish."

"A mermaid."

"A fish out of water. A dying fish. That's not Martine. She's a tiger in a cage. Full of life. She wants out."

"Mermaid is all wrong then."

"You missed the whole point."

"What is the point?" he asked her.

"It's so negative I thought Paul wrote it."

"Did he see it?"

"He's gone to Maine. Call me later."

Attendance at St. Joseph's the following Sunday was taken by Mr. Kiley, his Spanish teacher, whose bicycle, leaning against the wall in the freezing vestibule, glistened with condensation from tepid steam escaping from a radiator. Inside, the incense-laden air was warm with the body heat of worshipers who stood while the priest read the gospel about St. John in prison. It was the second Sunday of Advent; Christmas was coming. He couldn't see even one of the sixty students who had checked in. Henry stayed inside less than a minute, but Mr. Kiley and his bicycle were already gone. He took Main Street up the hill and stopped at Doc's grill, which was filled with students—half were Catholics from downtown and half late risers grabbing a bite before the bells for Sunday chapel. The booth by the window looking on Main Street was empty. Henry ordered an English muffin and sat at the table to save it for Maia Forbes who had reluctantly agreed to meet him with Eben.

Soon her VW parked in front; and two bundles of wool, one a third the size of the other, got out and bobbed up the steps to the shop. "I could barely hear you on the phone," she said, unwrapping the layers from Eben who turned out to be a somber boy with his father's Homeric head—a chiseled brow, imperial nose, stern jaw, and lots of brown hair.

"I hear the minister says I should be banished. I can't wait."

"He is your most avid reader."

"Paul says he's an asshole. I'm only quoting."

"That's supposed to be a secret."

"He took up the whole faculty meeting." This surprised him. She ordered a vanilla frappe for Eben.

"What was he saying?"

"That you and me and Paul should be burned. He talked so long Paul missed his train to Maine. He wanted to strangle him."

"So do I."

"You two are so alike. You get obsessed with dumb trifles."

"So what's important?"

"Who you are, who you want to be, isn't it?"

"You know that? Who you want to be?"

"Of course. Simone de Beauvoir." Another name for his list, after Scopes and Darrow. She was big in Maia's book; she and a sister had an existential ménage. Doc set Eben's frappe on the edge of the U-shaped counter, a full glass and a metal container with the remainder and a straw balanced across the top. Henry brought them to the booth.

"She is Sartre's mistress," Maia said. She blew the straw's paper wrapper in Eben's eye. He laughed. She put the straw in the frappe and sucked, very noisily. Eben screamed, "It's mine!" and would not stop crying, even when it was pointed out that there was nearly another full glass in the container. His tantrum got louder and worse until Maia Forbes had to drag him from the booth and pull him kicking toward the door. Henry collected their mittens, scarves, and coats. Mother and son were down the steps and in the street. The bell for chapel was tolling, and the students piled out of Doc's behind them. People were running up Main Street, and Eben was still screaming. She stuffed him in the car and slammed the door.

"I really need to talk to you. I'm going crazy," she said. They agreed to try again during Eben's nap, at Hopkins Hall in an hour.

Henry mingled with the last stragglers pushing into the Laughlin Chapel and stood at the back to hear about Zoroaster. The presence of faculty, wives, and children, perhaps townspeople, made the Sunday service appear more sedate than the weekday tug-of-war between Nugent and five hundred belligerent students. The minister was joined on the dais by a bald-domed bishop and an orotund Negro preacher with round gold-framed glasses. The three divines in their billowing black robes sat on oak thrones flanked by the crowded stalls of openmouthed choristers, Oldfield men on the right, Norton girls on the left, led by a calisthenic English choirmaster whose curses could be heard over Handel. "*One* and *two* and, damn your eyes, *look*!" When he slipped out, Nugent was droning on about Zoroaster's vultures which eat the dead.

Henry found Kornfeld sitting on the freezing granite steps. He sat beside him.

"How was Zoroaster?"

"Britannica stuff. Ho hum." He told him about the vultures.

"Air burial. The only way. I've specified it in my will."

"You need a platform. And birds."

"You still want Nugent dead?"

"He was talking about us in the faculty meeting Friday."

"Who said?"

"Forbes told his wife. He hates Nugent."

"You've seen her."

"Briefly, at Doc's. What are you doing for Christmas?"

"The usual. Hang around the *Times,* see my old lady."

"You want to come to St. Louis?"

"Thanks anyway."

"It's not like you think. They're all crazy. My father makes earthquakes in the basement, Mother prays for his soul in her bedroom, the cook drinks—"

"And the slave squirts leaves in the snow. I'm not a Santa Clausy kind of guy."

"It's not all just Christmas stuff—"

"I'd be like finding a dybbuk in the manger. How long does it take?"

"Twenty-three hours on the train. Five and a half on TWA." Forever. He knew Kornfeld wouldn't come, but he had asked.

Maia Forbes intercepted Henry outside the house and walked him around to the kitchen door. Eben was napping under the piano in the living room; she didn't want to wake him. "What happened to him at Doc's?"

"Couldn't you tell?"

"No."

"He's jealous."

"Of who?"

"Who do you think? You!"

"*You* stole his frappe."

"Just an excuse. He didn't want me talking to you."

"It was about his frappe."

"It was an oedipal thing. He wants to kill you."

"I'm no threat to him."

"You're almost as tall as Paul. Why do you hunch all the time?" She opened the kitchen door, and they went in.

"To look small. People my size are expected to play football and—"

She came toward him.

"Believe me, I know it ain't easy to ditch your body. Especially big people," she said, putting her hands on his shoulders and gently pushing them down.

"Let your shoulders fall, don't listen to people, and cut your hair, just a little." With her right hand, she took a hank of his hair between her forefingers, like a barber, and lifted it slowly until it slipped from her fingers. "A quarter of an inch. You'll never miss it."

He shivered and pulled away from her. "Did I do something? You don't want to be touched?"

He loved being touched, but he didn't know how to tell her he hated being told to stand up straight and to get a haircut.

"I won't touch you again, I promise," she said, and she left the kitchen. He felt more stupid and twisted than he had with Marla Starker in her garage. He had a way of turning off people, of refusing to take what he most wanted, of making them sorry they had been kind to him. He followed her into the living room where she was pouring herself a glass of warm gin from the gallon on the piano.

"Do you want something?"

"Like what?"

"Espresso. There's some left from breakfast."

"What is it?" She led him back to the kitchen and poured him a cup of very strong cold coffee—his first Italian roast—with a twist of lemon peel. He shuddered when he tasted it.

"Drink it, and don't scowl. It's a change. Welcome all change with joy," she said, laughing.

"What will that do?"

"Keep you young."

"I am young," he said.

"Oh no, you're not, O Last of Five. Your parents were old, you're old, you were never a child. Eben and I are the same age, we're having a ball, we were made for each other. He ought to be jealous. I may grow up and leave him."

"He'll leave you first."

"What a cruel thing to say!" She seemed serious. He tried to put the best face on it.

"You'll still have Mr. Forbes."

"Will I? I guess I will. He has to fit in somewhere." She bit her lip doubtfully. "Or maybe he doesn't. Maybe he's a piece from a different puzzle."

This idea appeared to account for all the contradictions in her life and gave her confidence. She was ready for questions. She said. "Where do you want to interview me?"

It was the first he heard that she consented to be interviewed. She led him to her study behind the kitchen in a room with laundry tubs full of tennis racquets and galoshes, a typewriter, cork bulletin board, and the brown leather sofa he had seen before, now covered with papers which she swept on the floor. But she closed a book carefully, marking her page with a nail file. *Le deuxieme sexe I: Les faits et les mythes*, de Simone de Beauvoir.

"Ask me anything. Do you have a pencil?"

"Tell me about Simone de Beauvoir again."

"Novelist, writer, mistress of Jean-Paul Sartre. *The Second Sex*. It will change the world. My world anyway."

"Why do you want to be like her?"

"Because she makes herself what she chooses—mistress, companion, writer, *existentialiste*, a woman in command of her life, like George Sand and Daniel Stern. Only de Beauvoir doesn't have to wear pants to be unafraid." She paused to see if he was following her. "You want me to spell anything? Stern, mother of Liszt's children, Marie d'Agoult, D-apostrophe-A-G—"

"I don't need to spell it," said Henry. "Does de Beauvoir have children?"

"Aren't you smart. You don't ask if Sartre is a father because what's important about a man is who he is—writer, radical, *philosophe*. But a woman must first prove she can jump through her vagina before you will see her as a real person. Oh, H., H., H.!" she keened for his male obtuseness. "Sartre and de Beauvoir have adopted a daughter. Does that count?"

Henry hadn't meant to irritate her, but he did wonder where the interview was going. Should he pretend he knew how anyone jumped through their vagina? He barely knew where it was. He was over his head, and she knew it. Why were they sitting on the very sofa where he had seen her underneath his English teacher? But she couldn't know that. He was beginning to perspire, perhaps from the coffee. She sensed his confusion.

"Ask me why I write," she suggested.

"Why *do* you write?"

"For company, for people to talk to. Writing is a call for help. My SOS. You answered it."

"I love your work."

"You're different, Mr. Stillman, you look, you listen. Most people are too busy winning or dying. Life is a Darwinian death camp, schools even more so. Kill or be killed. Pale virgins with black shoes read all night, whacking off on *Tess of the D'Urbervilles* and *Anna Karenina*." Or Martine, he thought guiltily. She had the power to look into souls. "Forget books. Look up, look out, touch, feel, enjoy. That's what *Home Front* is about—shedding our clothes, feeling the world with our skin, directly, passionately, like Lear—"

"I got that. I said so in my review."

"Paul didn't, and he never will—"

"He's very contained, you let go."

"Paul Forbes has demons would turn your hair white, but you'd never know it, he's so Olympian, such a redwood, a tectonic plate. He can't see himself in the book, or me. To him, Martine is just my pornographic fantasy and Frank's a marble monument she has to dynamite. Nothing to do with us. Up yours, Dr. Freud."

"Did Mr. Forbes win the gold medal for pole vault?"

"Mr. Fourteen Feet One and Three-Quarters Inches? You bet. I wanted to show him he is only six foot three, but I turned him into a stick and her into that sick mermaid you want to nurse. I ought to drink hemlock." *Home Front*, she was saying, was autobiography gone askew; and she hated Paul Forbes for saying so.

"If Martine's a tiger and not a fish, why does she cave in so easily?"

"Cave in?"

"She's this life force, full of love and promise, for herself, for dance, for Dodo. Frank comes back and BANG! She turns into a Hostess Cupcake—"

"Stop it! I don't want to hear about her."

"Why does she give up?"

"You really don't know?"

"What should I know?"

Maia Forbes was silent. Her eyes were moist.

"She loves him. She can't help herself. That's the horror of it. She's hooked, like you said."

"I didn't get that at all."

"She must choose—between a man's love and her freedom."

Tears came down her cheeks. She licked them from the corners of her mouth. She was like Eben over his frappe; she couldn't stop crying, which she did easily, like Julia Stillman. Tears are a woman's weapon and her shield. She found some Kleenex and blew her nose. Her distress appeared to summon an enormous unclipped standard poodle who came to the doorway and looked at them with doleful, compassionate eyes, like the mascot of a children's hospital. He lumbered in and put a heavy paw on Henry's knee. The claws went through his flannel trousers and, he discovered when he went to bed, drew blood. Henry flinched. "Julian! Down!" she shouted, which was the dog's cue to jump on the sofa and nestle between them. She put her hand on the dog's head, scratched between his eyes, and spoke to him, "You didn't wake Eben, did you?" Henry imagined the jealous son running him down with his tricycle just as the interview was bearing fruit.

"What are you thinking?" she asked.

"A woman's victory is snatched from her hands by a man returned from the dead."

"That's Nelson. He read the first draft."

"It wasn't snatched; she let it go, surrendered—"

"Shhh. You'll make me cry again. Nelly is de Beauvoir's lover. I met her once."

"Does Sartre know?"

"They tell each other everything."

"I wouldn't want to know everything."

"You should, and you ought to be taking notes," she said.

"I'd rather look at you."

"What do you see?"

"You always brush your hair over your forehead."

"Do you want to know why?" He did. "I grew up in my father's school in Ely, Minnesota. With three sisters. You know Minnesota?"

"I went to camp near International Falls."

"That's in summer. Mostly it's cold and dark. I was the family Bronte. I wrote three novels before I was thirteen, but I really wanted to be the mistress of Chopin and Liszt and the bride of Christ and a muse of fire for everyone I loved. So I ran away."

"How old were you?"

"Fourteen. Blood, lipstick, cigarettes, that age. We stole a car, an Indian with a harelip and me, and crashed it near Minneapolis. Neither of us knew how to drive." She touched the strands of hair that covered her forehead and went behind her ear. "I did a job on my face. My forehead."

"Can I see?"

"You really want to?" He nodded. She lifted the hair off her forehead. It wasn't the scar he expected but a deep dent, almost a pit, that caught the last golden light like a crater, all shadow on one side.

"Paul calls it Mare Maia Minor. It looks a bit like the moon, doesn't it?"

"Where is Mare Maia Major?"

She laughed. "That's none of your business."

"In the Southern Hemisphere."

"On the dark side." They both laughed.

"You are a very extraordinary woman, Mare Maia Minor included." He hoped she would infer what he really wanted to say, which she did.

"You and I could have a problem."

"What?"

"I like you too."

She took his right hand and turned the palm up and rested it on Julian's head, between his ears. He didn't believe in palmistry, horoscopes, haruspicy, or any form of divination. Maia Forbes could probably have told him the day and manner of his death, but perhaps because she felt his resistance, she turned his hand over. "Let it be a surprise," she said, but she kept his hand, almost buried in the long curls of the dog's hair.

"What does it say?"

She turned his palm over again, glanced at it, and shrieked. "Oh my god! You must get out this place. They're going to put you in a box. They're going to kill you. You'll never live to be an Oldfield man."

"I'm beginning to believe that."

"Go to Chicago. Apply tomorrow. They don't care how old you are if you can think. I know people in admissions. And don't listen to Paul. Don't even tell him. He'll try to send you to Harvard. His family runs the place."

"I have another year here."

"You won't live another year, don't you hear me? The clock is ticking. You're doomed. I want to go to Chicago too and finish my thesis. We can go together." She gave him back his hand. "Promise me you'll go."

"If you do." Leaning over Julian, her hands on his back for support, she kissed H. on his forehead.

"It's a deal," she said. "Don't tell a soul. If Paul finds out, he'll kill me."

"He doesn't know?"

"He wants to maroon me on his island in Maine. When I was pregnant, he took my sister Merope there and tried to seduce her. We all went mad. You had to take a ferry to buy a quart of milk. Paul's terrified I'll become independent like I was when he was dead. They were the best years of my life, and I still hate him for coming back. I could do anything I wanted. Won't you help me get them back?"

"Where is Paul now?"

"Writing in his cabin. It's the only place he can work."

"The cold?"

"The ghosts. His people, his demons. He probably has Merope. But now I have you."

His heart sang. She was inviting him into her life, offering to become his guide, a trellis for his growing. She was the beacon he was searching for. She curled herself on the mudroom couch between the sink and the bookcase, under the bulletin board, wedging herself closer to him around the unyielding mass of Julian who licked her knee.

"You mustn't tell anyone that we have found a way to escape before we're both safe in Chicago."

"Why won't Mr. Forbes come?"

"He hates Chicago and all my friends there. But, dear H., don't you leave us. Don't go back to St. Louis. Come to Maine!" It was the kind of extravagant act he imagined of himself, like killing Gormely or Nugent, but he had lost her attention. She and Julian had heard something; the dog was ready to spring. Eben strolled in looking benign and not a whit jealous of Henry sitting with Julian and his mother on her couch of many purposes. The dog jumped off, knocking the boy over, then stopped at the door and returned to sniff his crotch. Eben had peed in his pants.

"I'll miss dinner," Henry said while she was changing the boy on the floor. He went to the door.

"Come to Maine for Christmas. It's only a couple of hours on the B&M. I'll pick you up in Augusta." She was oracular, possessed, inspired, frightening, maybe crazy. The cold air outside didn't sober him. His mind and body were in a ferment, his being abubble with rare gases, percolating, rising, carrying him up, lighter than air, floating above the fields and trees. In love.

A figure was sitting on the low stone wall across Main Street. He saw the brief, intense glow of the ash of a cigarette. Kornfeld. Caught again, but he didn't mind.

"I know where you've been," said his friend.

"None of your business."

"You're in love."

"My brains are falling out."

"I've been thinking about Christmas. Why don't you come to New York for a couple of days?"

"I'm going to Maine."

"You're kidding."

"She kissed me."

"You are an astigmatic lump. What does she see in you?"

"What does Natasha see in Bezuhov?"

"An ungainly bear."

"A soul."

"So what did you find out?"

"She hopes the Prescott trustees throw us all out."

"She's a good sport."

"You know what she calls Paul Forbes?"

"Tell me."

"Mr. Fourteen Feet One and Three-Quarters. She says she wrote *Home Front* to cut him down to size. Six foot three."

"She said that? Can we print that?"

"She hasn't said anything we can print."

"I smell a divorce. Where did she kiss you?"

"Above the belt."

Paul Forbes must have come directly from Maine to his final examination, or almost. He stopped to pick up an armload of books in their mailing wrappers from the stacks in his living room. He walked into the building twenty minutes late, craggy and windswept in a wool lumberman's jacket. His students waited in desk chairs with blue books on the wide arms while he handed out randomly the unopened review copies of verse. He told them he was making them his first readers. Read the book, describe the work, paying attention to form and metrics, then say if you recommend it and why. "The writers probably won't be familiar to you. This is your chance to discover the next Eliot or Stevens. And don't be fooled by the blurbs. They're all written by friends and teachers who will lie without being asked."

He gave Henry an unopened package battered with travel. It had been sent to the *Mangrove Review* in Key West and returned, "addressee unknown," to *New Directions Press* in New York, then remailed to Box 16, North Haven, Maine. Inside was a slim book, *The Succubus of Adam's Neck,* by Paul Forbes, dedicated on page 3 for M. The puff on the jacket was by Delmore Schwartz. "Forbes stands the Browning monologue on its head . . . icy precision and searing self-honesty . . . makes the millstone of his patrimony seem lighter than a matchbook."

The poem was the meditation of a bareheaded man on the deck of a ferry bringing him back to his island after six month's detoxification on the mainland. The ferry stops in the dense fog, its horn echoing off unseen obstacles while the radar dish turns slowly. The mists slowly burn away and he imagines himself as a lobsterman. A voluptuous girl is sunning herself on his cabin roof while he pulls a line of traps into the stern. In one he finds a mayonnaise jar that contains a message accusing him of incest with his daughter, the golden-haired child of nature who swims nude in the quarries and maddens the natives with her freedom. He struggles with his rising lust for the unclothed girl but refuses to join the town in dampening her wild spirit by making her wear clothes. He glosses the treasures of her body, should he never see them again. The light brown hairs on her *mons venus*, each curl electric and excited by the hot noon sun. He shrinks when the succubus reaches to touch him. *Noli me tangere*, he says, not knowing whether she is a devil sent to tempt him or heaven's bride come to lift his loneliness. The fog rolls back in.

Henry suspected the succubus had to be related to Mary Magdalene, and he filled five blue books proving it. He tucked them into *The Succubus of Adam's Neck* and left them with Mr. Forbes who was smoking on the steps of the English building, a stack of verse and blue books rising beside him.

"You're such a fan of burlesque, I thought you might enjoy a girl who can't stay in her jeans either."

"I did. She's neat."

"Sit down a minute." Henry joined him on the steps, the pile of exams between them. "Keep it," said his teacher, removing the blue books and offering him the verse. "If you liked it."

He pulled the cellophane top from a fresh pack of Chesterfields, tore open a corner, tapped one out, and offered it to Henry who had to refuse. "I can't. Not here." "Sorry." He smoked alone. "Your piece about Maia's goddam book was good enough to get the preacher in a fit, which ain't all that hard. I liked the part where you called her a mermaid."

"She hated it."

"It was your best line. Caught Maia to the nines. Miserable wherever she is, gasping for something she can't name, can't remember. No one can help. She's a beached mermaid with amnesia." He spoke of Martine and Mrs. Forbes as one person.

"Mrs. Forbes prefers to think of her heroine as a tiger."

"Or a crocodile, to keep it amphibious. You know why your mermaid comment got under her skin? Mermaids die if they leave the water to make love—the feminist's fear that she will lose her independence if she surrenders to a man and loses her sexual identity if she doesn't. Tough choice. You always kill the thing you love. That's the can of worms."

"I suspect I liked her book better than you did."

"Because you're not in it," he said, "though maybe you wish you were."

"Martine is very attractive," Henry admitted. "I wouldn't mind knowing her."

"Her sister is attractive too," he said.

"Dodo."

"Merope. She's around. You may meet her. They lived together when I was gone. The early parts of her book are quite fine, when they're alone and discover their bodies, and their nakedness. That they are more than just inky-fingered grad students—a real awakening. First-class stuff. You can't wait to get them in bed."

"When did she start writing it?"

"Chicago, during the war. She stopped when I came back."

"The last half is very different."

"We tried to live in Maine first. Merope loved it. Maia hated it all—Maine, motherhood, me. She started writing again, for revenge."

His vehemence was surprising. "Revenge?"

"On me. For coming back. She was happier when she thought I was dead."

Manheimer came out and dropped his blue books and verse on the growing pile. "Who did you get?" Forbes asked him.

"William Machett," he answered glumly.

"He lives in Longfellow House in Cambridge," Forbes told him.

"It's rubbed off," said Manheimer sourly and walked away.

"Maia thinks she's Isis, and that makes me Osiris, god of the underworld. I have to be dead so she can reassemble my body parts into a bull she can adore. That's why she likes Chicago, the stockyards and all. She wants to be near bulls."

Their relationship intrigued and excited Henry the more muddy, twisted, and kinky it became. He studied the teacher's mud-caked farm boots next to his own brown loafers with friction tape holding the sole to the toe and imagined Forbes standing in a steaming bull pen, pawing the mud under the water trough.

"Are the stockyards near the university?"

"Close enough. Maia will try to make you go there."

"Mrs. Forbes thinks I will not last another year here."

"You showed her your hand."

"I tried not to."

"You have a fate line deeper than your metacarpal. You got to keep your hands in your pockets around Maia. Once she sees your palm, she'll prophesy you to death."

Paul Forbes could read his entire conversation with Maia in his face. That he wanted to transfer to Chicago of which he knew nothing because he was in thrall to a woman who read his palm and told him he would die. She was a witch, a siren. Forbes shifted his position on the cold stone step. He was trying to see Henry better in the dying December light. It would be dark by four.

"Let me guess something. Calvinist Oldfield is too flinty for you. You miss Rome—the miracles and madness, highways lined with crucifixions down to the sea, headless virgins singing in their baths."

"It's true. No beauty, no terror. I miss the purple and the cool Gregorian mode."

"Don't apologize. I was a convert myself. I know a little about the seductions of Rome."

Henry was baffled by the very idea of conversion. *The Succubus of Adam's Neck*, that was his church. "It's hard to imagine anyone wanting to be a Catholic if they don't have to be."

"You can't imagine Barney Nugent driving a sensitive man into the arms of Rome? I'll bet you can." He was right. After a dose of Deuteronomy, Henry had welcomed the sweet incense and tinkling bells of St. Joseph's. But Paul Forbes seemed too spare, too Yankee, to sit still for a mangled rosary like the one Archbishop Cushing said on the radio at breakneck speed and with no feeling. "Do you go to church?" Henry asked him.

"I did just to get my old man's goat, but he took my conversion as such a betrayal they say it killed him. Barney Nugent thinks so, which is why he wants me banished from Oldfield."

"No one takes my apostasy so seriously. I don't."

"You can't believe that you don't believe?"

"I guess not."

"You're a branded doubter, Stillman, or Barney Nugent wouldn't hate you so."

"Does he?"

"He told the faculty meeting last week you had to die. The minutes had to be emended. He was so out of control."

"I'll get him first."

"If you need a no-noise gun, I have one. Come to Maine, if you can."

He had been invited by both of them. He didn't mind sharing Maia or being the invisible ball they tossed between them, like in lacrosse. It was a game in which he got to be on both sides.

Going back to St. Louis for Christmas on the New York Central, he sat up talking all night with Jimmy Bowes as if they had been at different schools. Oldfield magnified everything about Bowes—the playboy athlete and the social climber in a corduroy coat and white bucks who paraded up the aisle of the chapel to kiss the ass of B. Barnard Nugent. Whereas Henry, in his oldest friend's disgusted opinion, had sunk from sight in a swamp of weirdos.

"Like who?"

"The guy with the smirk you always eat with. Kornfeld."

"Sometimes eat with. He voted you most valuable player."

"He thinks I'm a jerk."

"He thinks student deacons are jerks. It's not personal."

"Better than a lot of queers."

"You're saying he's homosexual? He's not."

"Weird. Creepy. Some kind of type."

"Jewish. Is that what you're trying to say?"

"I'm saying if you hang around with those types, people will start to avoid you. Your only friends will be—"

"Creeps and Jews."

"Don't tell me you and Kornfeld weren't putting me down, about you eating your old man's letter at Kooch-i-ching, because you did. I saw you eat it."

"I know I did, for god's sake! I didn't want his role advertised to the whole world, that's all. Suppose he didn't have anything to do with the bomb? Maybe he wasn't even there. And if he was, he shouldn't have been writing me about it."

"He was there. He was gone for years and look when he came back. Just after the test." Bowes was Old Faithful; you could depend on him.

"I hear you hang around Paul Forbes and his wife."

"Who said?"

"Chick Hunter. He lives in Forbes House."

"I have him for English."

"He says you're always down there."

"Exactly three times. Are the Forbes creeps too?"

"Jesus. You know who he is, don't you?"

"Poet. Pole-vaulter."

"He practically owns Maine. The Forbes gave Prescott the land for the school."

"A farm with no water, and Forbes Neck is not Maine."

"Thornhill says their island is bigger than Greenland."

"It's just an isthmus. I'm going up there after New Year's." That flattened Jimmy Bowes for fifty miles, and he sat stunned.

"Chick Hunter says she never wears a brassiere. You can see her nipples under whatever she's wearing." Henry nodded. Her nipples were hard to miss.

The Bowes and the Stillmans were waiting for their sons at the Union Station. Jimmy Bowes was a returning hero, his football exploits known far and wide. Henry was more in his shade than ever which Jill Bowes tried to compensate with her enthusiastic greeting. "Oh, Henry! Henry! Henry!" But she could not make her theme song sing as before. It grated; it rasped; it was an open sore. Maia Forbes had ruined it forever, with her new name, H., but he lacked the courage to rechristen himself. The name Henry hung on him like the dead guinea their dog, Toby, had tied around his neck as penance for killing it. He confessed to Mrs. Bowes he was thinking of changing his name. She reacted with delight. "H.! It's such a wonderful letter. You can climb it, like goalposts. But I love Henry too. It is so distant and forlorn. Henrys live alone on hilltops." Her gold hair swooped up in back in what was called a duck's ass. She grew more beautiful every time he saw her.

Joe Stillman seemed ten years older, or perhaps Henry was just beginning to notice things of long standing like Julia Chateau's grey hair the day he was expelled from kindergarten. The indentations left in the flesh of Joe's nose by the pads on the bridge of his glasses didn't disappear when he took them off. They were permanent dents because the blood wasn't circulating properly to his head or his feet.

Joe was building a television receiver in his lab with a cathode ray tube five inches in diameter, which made a screen the size of a matchbox. It received only a test pattern broadcast by KSD-TV which had yet to begin programming. The fiery optimism of the young engineer from Yale's Sheffield School of Engineering, who stood with Steinmetz and Einstein on the brink of the most exciting era in human thought since Newton and Voltaire, had begun to dim. "Was it all for this?" he asked. Henry was framing a reply that would not further dampen the old man's spirits when Joe threw him a real curve. "What happens after entropy?"

"Heat death. Minus 273 Kelvin," Henry answered without blinking. Joe had taught him.

"Funny guy, Kelvin."

"Why so?"

"He never stopped going to church."

"Darwin was a believer too. God didn't bother them then the way he does us."

"Why is that, you think?"

"They didn't confuse science and faith. Apples and oranges. No contradiction."

"I think you're wrong. Kelvin says he found the model for his thermodynamic universe in Genesis, a kind of creation explosion, then entropy took over for a hundred million years."

"I'll buy that."

"So after thermodynamic equilibrium, what?"

"Nothing. Nobody knows. The god problem."

"You kids were lucky. You had the pope to tell you what to think."

"I don't believe any of that now. I'm as confused as you are."

"But you had a structure, a place to begin—"

Henry assumed that Joe was trying to pick his usual quarrel with the Baltimore catechism, and he kept quiet. But Joe wouldn't let it go.

"I wouldn't mind talking with someone about it."

"About entropy?" He didn't believe what he was hearing.

"What happens after heat death and everything."

He had never heard Joe ask a serious question about first things or last things in his life. "Have you been talking to Mother about this?"

"She thinks you might know someone at St. Louis University, with your connections."

They had been talking. He was being set up. Julia had been trying to get him to help convert Joe since he was five, and he had refused. He liked him the way he was. Everyone but Julia Chateau thought Joe would make a ridiculous Catholic. "I'll ask around if you want." It was time to get back to Oldfield, and fast.

The telephone upstairs rang. There were two phones in the house, both black—one in Julia Stillman's study on the second floor, the other on a table in a corridor between the front hall, the kitchen, and the guest bathroom. Any telephone call was an event. The cook had to leave what she was doing to answer it, then search for the recipient. A long-distance call was like an air raid alert; life stopped. "Goddam telephone puts you at the mercy of any son of a bitch with a nickel," said Joe. The cook shouted down the stairs that it was long distance for someone named H. Henry ran up. It was Maia Forbes. She wanted to know who had answered the phone.

"Marta."

"Your mother?"

"The cook."

"You actually do live in St. Louis," she said.

"Where are you?"

"Boston. Paul is sick. We're not going to Maine."

"What's the matter with him?"

"I'll tell you when I see you. Please come soon. I need you."

He stared at the telephone handset and wondered what she would suggest next. Burn the tree, murder your family, marry me? Maia Forbes made a sort of wild sense in Oldfield, an embattled woman stranded in tight-laced New England. But hearing her voice in St. Louis, next to the kitchen, looking at Marta's rear end in front of the stove, made him realize she had no idea what his life was like or who he was besides the tall guy from the student newspaper whom she had decided to rename H. She asked for H., as if everyone in his house should know who H. was. She talked to him as if he were the master of his life. Come to Boston. He didn't know where to begin explaining that H. was her dream and that the boy who was going to Yale like every Stillman for a hundred years was the real Henry. He was ashamed of his timidity and angry at her impossible expectations.

Julia Chateau asked who phoned. The wife of his English teacher. Had he read the article about the earthquake in Peru? It quoted the head of seismography at St. Louis University, a priest named Father O'Connor. "Wasn't that the teacher your father liked, the one who limped?"

Henry phoned O'Connor and picked him up the next day on Grand Avenue. He was wearing his old army khakis and a field jacket and carried the amplifier chassis of a seismograph under his arm. Joe took him the basement, and soon the house was rattling with earthquakes and avalanches, and *Also Sprach Zarathustra* played at the threshold of pain. Julia Chateau sat at her desk on the second floor with a stoic face. It was what she had prayed for. When Henry went to the basement to say goodbye, he could barely see the men through the haze from burning cigarettes. Joe's coat sleeve brushed a wire near the magnets of the cathode tube, causing a hissing arc and the heady smell of ozone to mix with the tobacco smoke. The old sorcerer's waning powers were renewed by the charge in the air. His grey hair stood straight from his head, the hairs in his nostrils curled like a snail's antennae, and yellow sparks of static electricity jumped from his fingers to objects around him. Henry had not seen him like this since he gave the Tesla coil to Father O'Connor in exchange for Henry. Joe was in his element.

MENCKEN REDUX

Everything was topsy-turvy at Oldfield. His English class was being taught by a Harvard professor, Francis McDonough, who told them that Paul Forbes was recovering from "an attack of holiday blues" and might not be back for several weeks. McDonough's bald spot, baleful eyes, and brown suit made him look like St. Francis of Assisi. He handed back their exam blue books with an apology. "I'm giving everybody an A. You men are too intelligent to be graded." On the cover of Henry's first blue book, McDonough had written in very small block letters, like the legend on a blueprint, "Welcome to *The Succubus of Adam's Neck* fan club. I hope you are lucky enough to meet her."

He stopped Henry after class. “Paul told me about you. Maia and Eben are staying in Boston with her sister to be near him.” It was the first he knew that Mrs. Forbes wasn’t back either. “I was to visit them in Maine.”

“Paul’s had attacks since Harvard, you shouldn’t worry. Call Maia. She got a little banged up. She wants to hear from you.”

On Saturday, he took the B&M to North Station, walked past the Union Oyster House where Joe made him eat boiled lobster and the Old Howard Burlesque where Martine had done her bumps and grinds, left Scollay Square, and climbed the backside of Beacon Hill with the gold dome of the statehouse guiding him to Bowker Street. There was a note on her sister’s door: Knock Hard, Bell Is Broke. A barefoot young woman in a blood-and-gravy-stained apron opened it. “H.,” she said.

“Only you and Mrs. Forbes call me that.”

“Maia said you might come. I’m her sister. They call me Merope. She’ll be back soon.” He followed her ponytail, a shock of long blonde hair bobbing over her checked wool shirt and jeans. She was taller and younger than Maia, more his age than hers, early twenties and more athletic—the muscles and sinews showing below her rolled-up sleeves belonged to someone who chopped wood or did chin-ups. They wedged themselves past four big cans of flowers in the narrow hall to the kitchen—industrial quantities of peonies, irises, and daisies in green cylinders. Her cheeks glowed with a blush of crimson. Maia was a pale night person—a moon goddess. Merope was flush and sun ripened.

“You wrote that review of Maia’s book in the *Oldfielder.*”

“I liked it very much.”

“It’s a vicious book. I wish she had never written it.”

“Mr. Forbes says it’s her revenge for his coming back from the war.”

“Their love was a cold potato. She should never have married him.”

He had interrupted the evisceration of two rabbits on a chopping board. She put the stomach and bowels in a large pot on the stove.

“Nobody’s told me what’s wrong with him,” Henry said.

“Maia drove him mad. He tried to kill her.”

“Mad? Like insane?”

“He takes lithium.”

“What are you making?”

“Essence of lilac. Perfume.”

They heard Maia and Eben banging the front door and bumping against the flower cans in the narrow hall. "Is H. here? Where are the people?"

"Hello!"

Maia and Eben came into the kitchen, both in winter coats and stomping a light snow off their shoes. Merope helped remove the coat from Maia's shoulders, which made her sister scream in pain. Her left arm was in a cast and a sling. She dropped Maia's coat on a chair and took off Eben's wool jacket, kissing him on the forehead as she did so.

"You met my sister," Maia said.

"She hates your book."

"That's because she's in love with Paul."

"You don't want him. You should let him go." Merope left the room.

Paul had fractured Maia's humerus, and a tantalum rod had been put in the arm to hold it together. Driving was difficult, and eating. She needed lots of help, which Henry couldn't provide. He had to go to school. They drove to McLean, Paul's sanitarium, but they weren't allowed to see him. Maia left H. in Oldfield.

Kornfeld was late returning from vacation. "Merry Christmas!" He handed Henry a shiny new book. On the cover was a photo of a florid man in suspenders, his slicked-down hair parted in the middle, a cigar in his teeth, typing on a portable Smith Corona. *H. L. Mencken: Disturber of the Peace* by William Manchester.

"Your putative godfather."

"More than putative maybe. I was just in Baltimore. I met him. He's had a stroke."

H. opened the book. It was dedicated on the flyleaf, "For Kornfeld and Stillman. Good luck. William Manchester."

"How do you know Manchester?"

"He was taking care of Mencken. And picking his brain."

"You just walked in?"

"Adam Kornfeld was working for Mencken on the *Sun* when I was born. That's how he got to be my godfather. At least he doesn't say he wasn't."

"You talked to him?"

"He can't talk. He grunts. Read chapter 6, the Scopes Trial."

"How he and Darrow killed what's-his-name."

"William Jennings Bryan. You want Nugent dead, read chapter 6."

They went to the *Oldfielder* office and found Wardlow and Pruitt planning the spring issues. Kornfeld was still wearing his city clothes—an English herringbone jacket with square shoulders and side vents, full pleated trousers, a maroon striped shirt with a stiff white collar, french cuffs, gold cuff links, and a silk tie, a more elegant getup than Wardlow at his nattiest.

"Is that what you wear to your Marxist cell meetings?" Wardlow asked him.

"I was in Baltimore. Illness in the family."

"You have no family in Baltimore," said his editor.

"You're wrong. My godfather."

"Who's that?"

"H. L. Mencken, we're going to revive him." He showed Wardlow the Manchester biography. "Stillman's going to play Mencken, I'll be Darrow." It wasn't hard to see the Kornfeld strategy. They were to be the new crusaders against superstition: Kornfeld, the precise, cynical, brilliant lawyer; Stillman, the passionate, angry, bellicose journalist. The two would turn the harsh light of doubt and ridicule on Barney Nugent's bogus partnership with God, as Mencken and Darrow had exposed the anachronistic claptrap of William Jennings Bryan. This was how Kornfeld planned to kill Barney Nugent.

"We want to do a special issue on religion at Oldfield. We have dirt on Josiah Prescott that will get the state to revoke the charter if it gets out."

"When you're running the paper, you can do what you damn please. I'll be in Oxford. And what is all this about our Nobel laureate? They say he's gone crazy."

"He gets manic and breaks things," said Henry.

"Schizophrenia. Did you hear that?"

"Who said?"

"Grapevine."

Wardlow had spies, and Henry needed to be careful not to mention everything he knew.

"Who told you exactly?" he pressed Wardlow.

"Some people have nothing to do but snoop and snipe. A reporter needs to cultivate them."

"Like who?"

"My housemaster, for instance."

Wardlow's housemaster was Dr. Alden Carter, chairman of the French department, translator of Racine and Corneille, and single-handed enforcer of the ban against walking on the Great Lawn which his bachelor suite in Drayton Hall overlooked from the chapel to the Memorial Bell Tower. Kornfeld had accumulated six demerits from Dr. Carter for illicit diagonals. Wardlow apologized for Dr. Carter's style. "He considers himself a poet and rival of Paul Forbes, whom he envies for his beauty, grace, and talent. He hears Forbes beat her up. You know anything about that?"

"Where? When?"

"She went to the Newton hospital on Christmas Eve. Forbes was in jail."

"How does he know?"

"A web of Francophones in every French department around the world. Where is she now?"

"Ask Dr. Carter."

"Don't get huffy."

In his room, Henry stared at the sweat-soaked, unattractive man at his typewriter on the cover of Manchester's book. The photo was from the 1932 Democratic Convention in Chicago that nominated Roosevelt. He skimmed chapter 6 just enough to see they didn't actually kill Bryan; he died in bed. Henry resented Kornfeld pushing a fake murder and probably a fake godfather on him. He gritted his teeth and read about Dayton, Tennessee, in 1925, when it was a crime to teach anything that contradicted the Bible. Thomas Scopes, a high school teacher, was accused of teaching evolution, a crime because it asserted that man was descended from the apes, whereas Genesis stated that he was made from dust by God who blew life into his nostrils. Mencken, a journalist, critic, and muckraker, called it the Monkey Trial and suggested that apes were the injured party and ought to be the plaintiffs. He persuaded the famous lawyer, Clarence Darrow, to defend the infidel Scopes who was prosecuted by William Jennings Bryan, twice a candidate for president and a popular orator in what Mencken named the Bible Belt. Further, he described the fundamentalist circus in Dayton where Holy Rollers writhed in a tangle of muddy limbs while screaming in tongues for release from the devil. Darrow lured Bryan to testify for the prosecution as a "Creation expert" and made him concede that he was a hairy mammal who walked erect on two legs and had opposed thumbs on each hand. Mencken and Darrow blasted the world of ignorance and superstition and reduced Bryan to a lump of lard. They lost the trial, but the ridiculed and humiliated Bryan died three days later of what Mencken called "a busted gut" for which he took gleeful credit. "We killed the son of a bitch," he said later.

The sun-soaked quadrangles, white towers, and cupolas of Oldfield beckoned the groundhog from his midnight burrow. The new *Disturber of the Peace* emerged, a man like Mencken who had lost his hated Henry to the alphabet. H. was born. His partner was waiting for him on the wall along Main Street.

"Did you read it?"

He had. "They're pure killers."

"Then I'll buy you breakfast."

He treated H. to the extravagance of breakfast in the dining room of the Oldfield Inn because he'd just been paid his stipend by the newspapers he supplied with sports scores. They sat at a round table with a thick white tablecloth where Kornfeld listened to H's speculations with his eyes closed, rocking gently, his coffee and cinnamon toast untouched. H. ended with the repetition of Bowes's warning, "Nugent's gonna get you."

"He will," said Kornfeld. "We have to make a preemptive strike."

"Like Joe Stillman wants to do to China."

Kornfeld opened his eyes. "Your father is a great man. I have never fully appreciated it. I want to meet him."

"You'd like each other. Except he hates Jews."

"He got along with Oppenheimer."

"He thought he was a Gnostic."

There was a large hole in the plot to kill Nugent. Mencken had a magazine, *The American Mercury*, and a paper, the *Baltimore Sun*, and he was syndicated in a hundred more papers. The whole nation read every word he wrote. Kornfeld and Stillman couldn't even depend on the *Oldfielder* until the board changed in May. Wardlow would never let them use the paper to attack the minister; the chapel ear cost him eleven hundred bucks. They had to leave Nugent dead or leave him alone—nothing halfway. They had to hold off until they controlled the paper.

"How about the Inquiring Reporter," H. ventured. "They don't censor what you say there."

"Not if I'm sneaky." He looked around. The only others in the room at that hour were some parents and their tubby son at the next table. A white-haired Irish biddy was serving both tables while busboys set up counters for the buffet, the inn's most popular meal. All you could eat for $2.95. The waitress refilled H.'s cup. Kornfeld still hadn't touched his; he was rocking with his eyes closed again.

"Is your friend all right?" she asked.

Kornfeld stood up and went to the next table. "Excuse me. I'm Adam Kornfeld, Inquiring Reporter for the *Oldfielder*, the school newspaper. Do you mind if I ask your son a few questions?" The family was grateful for any interruption to the depressing lunch with their unhappy son. "Do you think religious observance should be compulsory at Prescott Academy?" he asked the boy.

The mother answered. "I think it's very important to keep up your good habits when there's so much opportunity to slack off. I mean, no one can watch Charlie every—"

The father intervened. "He's asking Charlie, not you."

The boy was too frightened or too obtuse to speak.

"You don't have to answer," Kornfeld told him with his crooked grin. "Or you can just tell me." He leaned over for Charlie to whisper.

"Do I think what ought to be what you said?" the boy asked.

"Do you think you should have to go to chapel or just go if you want to, like to the movies?"

"That's a terrible question to ask a child," said the mother.

"Shut up and let the kid talk," said the father.

"You shouldn't have to," said the boy.

"Can you say why you think so?"

"It's boring."

"Thank you, Charlie. What class are you in?"

Kornfeld came back to the table. He thought complaints about chapel could make an amusing column, but he was pessimistic they could ever shake the foundations of Nugent's ministry. People were stoic about daily chapel. It came with the school like the trees and the bricks and was here to stay. Laughable but inevitable. Kornfeld curled his tongue pensively and blew through it. "We'll have to come up with something potent if we want it to kill Barney Nugent," he said.

"Forbes says we should look at the last page of the school charter."

They found the original school charter in the library and took it to the archive room where other bowdlerized copies of the charter were on display. They turned to page 13 of the Charter and Articles of Incorporation of Prescott Academy, Oldfield, Massachusetts, April 19, 1779, written in the flowing hand of Josiah

Prescott himself. What they read caused Kornfeld to dance a cackling jig around the table like Rumpelstiltskin around his fire in the forest. Josiah Prescott had been an anxious man after the war, a good Puritan on a Calvinist island threatened by a sea of heresy. His charter was a dike to protect the purity of his new school from contamination.

> Only white male Protestants of good character may attend the academy, and in order to preserve it from the baneful influences of the incorrigibly vicious, the trustees shall determine for what reason a scholar may be expelled and the manner in which the sentence shall be administered. Protestants only shall ever be concerned in the trust or instruction of this academy.

"It says that? Out loud?"

"Paragraph 29. No Indians, no Negroes."

"No Jews, no Catholics."

"Better than the St. Louis Country Club."

"More better. No women!" said Kornfeld. "And there's still not a single Jew on the faculty. Not one."

"There are two Catholics," said H. "One hundred and seventy-one years later."

Kornfeld was beside himself. "This is a bombshell. The trustees are going to have shit fits." He composed the lead. "Oldfielder demands charter revision. That has real weight, not just you and me. We're feathers, but the second oldest student newspaper in America demands it. We must speak for the institution or we are nothing, just a couple of schlemiels."

H. went downtown to buy a pair of black suspenders and a cheap cigar. He stopped in his room to put on the suspenders, slick down his unruly hair, and part it in the middle. Horn-rimmed glasses spoiled the effect; his Mencken would have to be astigmatic. He was hoping for a kinetic transformation—the crippled newsboy into Captain Marvel. He put the cigar in his mouth and swaggered into the *Oldfielder* office where heelers were addressographing the last issue to subscribers and libraries. They all fell into a silent respect, maybe because he was Mencken but more likely because he was now famous for writing about Martine's stippled nipple. Kornfeld was unimpressed with his impersonation. "You need a hat."

"You wouldn't see the part in my hair."

"You look like you own a delicatessen. Reporters wear hats." H. sat at Wardlow's desk, put his feet up, his thumbs under his suspenders, and chewed the cigar, imagining himself first to be H. L. Mencken, then Big Jim Bowes behind the president's desk of his steel company and then Turner Catledge, the editor of the *New York Times* whom Adam Kornfeld detested. He lit the cigar; it tasted awful and smelled like the urinal of a crowded men's room, but he it gave him a profound exhilaration and power. Wardlow came in and stared at H. "Put out that awful thing. Who the hell are you supposed to be?"

"H. L. Mencken. And he's Darrow." He pointed to Kornfeld who was typing his Inquiring Reporter.

"Mencken is a loud-mouth anti-Semite," said Wardlow.

Kornfeld looked up. "I'm the Inquiring Reporter," he said to Wardlow, changing the subject from Mencken's anti-Semitism. "Do you believe religious observance should be compulsory at Prescott Academy?"

"Fuck off," said his editor.

He tried H. "How about you? Should religion be compulsory?"

"Religion should be as voluntary as the Saturday-night movie or Sunday breakfast," H. answered.

"Are you comparing religion to popcorn or pancakes?"

"Religion is the food of the soul. All tastes are different."

"But aren't some tastes superior to others?"

"*De gustibus non disputandum est.*"

"Translate for our readers, please."

"Concerning taste it cannot be reasoned. That's as true of the Trinity as of chocolate cake. Some like one, some the other."

"It's pure Mencken! I love it, I love it!" Kornfeld bubbled with delight as he wrote it down. H. could feel the *Disturber of the Peace* rising in him, the buoyant lift of authority, the lordly isolation of the man at the top. He liked it. It's where he wanted to be. Wardlow was deeply suspicious. "I don't know what you guys are planning, but don't do it on my watch. I'm waiting for a fellowship from Oxford, and there's no rocking the boat 'til I'm gone. Then burn the place down. I don't care."

"We're planning to," said Kornfeld.

Wardlow had a problem. He couldn't flee to Oxford without leaving someone in charge of the *Oldfielder*, and there was only one person qualified, Kornfeld, who refused to be anything but the sports editor.

Francis McDonough told his English class that Paul Forbes's recovery was so slow he felt it necessary to resign from the Prescott faculty. He told H. that Paul was dickering with Harvard about being the poet in residence there even while he was in the bin. If H. could sneak away, Maia needed help looking for a place to live in Cambridge. Her arm still made driving difficult though she was writing a second book with one hand.

"What did you think of Mrs. Forbes's book?"

"I've only seen bits and pieces as she worked on it."

"Did you like it?"

McDonough rolled his eyes toward heaven, which he did when he had to look at things that pained him, as he had just done earlier when he told the class how T. S. Eliot, faced with the discovery of his wife's madness, sat down by a lake and wept. "I think these have been difficult years for Maia. I can understand why she may sometimes appear to lack charity. Keep talking to her. She has nothing to do now but wait for Paul to get better. It must be very wearing on her." Paul was about to become an outpatient from McLean Hospital.

They had bought a bigger car, a Dodge four-door, but Maia could just squeeze her broken arm into it. There was a big bandage on her left cheek, and her right hand was useless; she couldn't raise the window or open a pack of cigarettes. She rummaged in her pockets and found a new pack of Chesterfields. H. helped tear the cellophane and open the pack for her. He looked at her tired face and wondered what new chasm Paul Forbes had dug below the bandage on her cheek, too far down to be concealed under hair and too high to be hidden by a collar or scarf. At Merope's, he hadn't been aware of the extent of her injuries. "You're looking at me. Am I ugly? Tell me the truth."

"What did he do to your cheek?"

"Nothing. A scratch."

Her eyes filled with tears that were definitely not tactical. Maia was the one he loved. The agitation, the reversals, the loops, the lies, the restless quest, all written on her face like a geodesic map with peaks and valleys, dried-up streambeds, overflowing spillways, and craters old and new. She put her cigarette in the tray and felt her latest wound with her fingers while looking in his eyes through a blur of tears.

"Go, go." She squeezed her eyes shut.

"No."

"Please don't hate me. I'm doing the best I can."

"I love you," he said.

"Please, H. We can't do this. You have to go."

"I love your scars," he said. He took her hand away and kissed the bandage. He lifted the concealing hair and kissed Mare Maia Minor.

"I love you too," she whispered. "H., H., H., H.," she mourned. "What are we going to do?"

"About what?" But he knew.

It was Maia who did all the covering up, who invented a lover with a harelip and a car crash to conceal Paul's mad destruction. He was the asteroid who had dug the crater of Mare Maia Minor above her eye. "Paul did it, didn't he?"

"He was lobstering with Merope, and he flipped."

"Was she nude on the cabin roof, like the succubus of Adam's neck?"

"You know about her?"

"He gave me the poem for an exam. I wrote five blue books on it."

"Then you know a succubus is more than some bare-assed siren. She's an allegorical figure—"

"But she's Merope too, naked on the cabin roof of a lobster boat."

"She couldn't keep her clothes on for five minutes. She was so hot for Paul—"

"She said she's going to marry him."

"She's welcome to him. Tell me about Oldfield. What do they think of Francis?"

"They think he is a saint."

"He was a Capuchin monk at Harvard."

"A monk?"

"Everyone was. Paul's tutor, his roommates, his professors were joining monasteries left and right. Paul's a convert, you know. Or was."

"He told me. I was surprised."

"Why?"

"Like you said, he's such a tectonic plate, stone, steel—"

"Well, you see he isn't. I think conversion lets something out of a person, triggers a hidden—"

"His madness?"

"Religion is the lid people use to hold in their insanity. A polite face."

She took long brain-cleansing drags of her cigarette and blew the smoke out through her flaring nostrils. "I guess I'm going to have to make up my mind."

"About what?" But he knew.

"Who I am, who I love, what I do, where I live."

She decided if Paul was going to teach at Harvard, they should live in Cambridge. H. promised to help her look when he had finished his business of disestablishing the congregational church in Oldfield.

Spring was coming, and it was finally time to change the guard at the *Oldfielder.* Kornfeld still refused to be roped in. "I won't be the goddam editor in chief."

"There's no one else. You know it," Wardlow argued.

"Adam Kornfeld says that editors are stones around the neck of writers to drag them down. If I ran the *Oldfielder*, my father would never talk to me again."

"He doesn't talk to you now. What are you afraid of?"

"People around here don't want a Jew telling them what to think."

"That's bullshit!" Wardlow shouted.

"You need a midwestern hayseed, like Stillman. He's your man. I'll be sports editor. That's final."

"I'm not qualified," H. protested.

"Nobody is," said Kornfeld. "You just have to look like an editor, and you look like H. L. Mencken. That's what counts. I'm going to take a leak." He started for the door.

"Forget Mencken!" Wardlow shouted after him. "He's a Nazi redneck, he sat out two wars with Germany without taking sides, reading Nietzsche and thinking he's the Superman. What he says about the Jews in *Treatise on the Gods* would curl your teeth."

Wardlow was baffled. "What's he talking about? He thinks a bunch of Congregationalists are anti-Semitic? That's crazy."

"The Mathers didn't like Jews either," said H.

Wardlow brooded. "What do you think?"

"Who knows? There's never been a Jewish editor in chief. A hundred and sixteen years."

"How about a Catholic?" H. asked.

"Three, all since Prohibition."

When Kornfeld came back, he said he would have quit the paper long ago, but he had to be on the masthead to qualify for his outside jobs. Wardlow made an offer: they could use the paper for their nefarious schemes to unseat the school minister, which he didn't want to know about, if they were willing to take it over. Kornfeld reluctantly agreed to be managing editor and run the paper if they made H. a ceremonial editor in chief. Then Adam Kornfeld would curse him, but not kill him. He and H. decided to room together their final year.

That summer, Maia found a house she liked on Sparks Street in Cambridge. The house was just off Brattle Street, the center of colonial America with magnificent eighteenth-century mansions set back from a tree-covered avenue. Longfellow House, a yellow manse with four white pilasters, had been Washington's headquarters during the siege of Boston before it became the poet's home. Maia's house was built in 1747 by Erasmus Darling a few blocks from Longfellow House and was in need of work. It had three floors and an unheated fourth floor where H. could put his electric chair from St. Louis and sell tickets for electrocution to tourists looking for Longfellow House. He had told Maia how much he missed Joe's basement lab—an underworld of lathes, table saws, band saws, a drill press, his electric chair, and a Lionel train with block signals and a bascule bridge that raised and lowered. Soon painters and contractors were fixing up Sparks Street. When the house was painted, Paul reluctantly left McLean where he would have preferred to remain for life. But the unnatural calm of despised lithium allowed him to leave, and he had been named the Boylston Professor of English Rhetoric at Harvard with the hereditary right to tether his cow in the Common. He was puzzled that H. had become the editor in chief of the *Oldfielder*. "I thought that was your friend's thing, the guy with the twisted smile." H. knew that Paul thought he was betraying his talent by flirting with journalism and reminded him of their common desire to destroy the ministry of B. Barnard Nugent.

H. timed his opening blast to come not long before the fall meeting of the trustees. His first editorial began, "Prescott Academy at midcentury is at a crossroads. Will it create leaders for a new world where science challenges faith, East and West compete for world domination, and all races demand their share of the planet's resources? Or will it look backward to Josiah Prescott's scheme to educate an army of white Calvinists to protect the Trinity from its Unitarian enemies?

> An institution hamstrung by its ties to the sectarian wars of the Bay Colony and colonial Massachusetts cannot address the future. Why is the school in this modern age still a god-ridden insult to every minority? Why are there only two Catholics and no Jews, Negroes, or women on the faculty? Because it was designed to be so by Josiah Prescott and kept so by two centuries of like-minded trustees. 'Only white male Protestants of good character may attend the academy . . . and Protestants only shall ever be concerned in the trust or instruction of this academy.' The Charter of 1779."

The editorial demanded the trustees amend the charter, make religious observance optional, and remove racial and religious restrictions on faculty and students. It was signed "H."

He had not learned enough about Simone de Beauvoir to give more than lip service to the role of women.

The day after the editorial appeared, Nugent was joined on the dais at daily chapel by Robert Wrigley,the headmaster, a man seldom seen and almost never in the Laughlin Chapel. The toccata from Widor's Fifth Symphony for Organ wound down, and Nugent approached the pulpit for the invocation. But instead of opening the giant Bible, he leaned over it on his elbows and scanned the congregation.

"Nice guys finish last. Leo Durocher, 1946 World Series," he said. That was his lesson. The headmaster smiled, perhaps supposing it was an ironic allusion to the Sermon on the Mount—nice guys finish last but will be first in heaven. But Durocher meant what he said, and so did Nugent. Nice guys are losers—jerks who deserve to lose.

"I'm not a nice guy, and I don't intend to finish last. God is not dead, this country is still one nation under His Benign Guidance, and Prescott Academy will always do what Josiah Prescott promised in his magnificent charter, 'to diligently inculcate upon its students the great and important scripture doctrines of the existence of One true GOD, the Father, of the Fall of Man, the depravity of human nature, the necessity of an atonement and of our being renewed in the spirit of our minds.' I'm aware of the contempt that some of you have for spiritual values. They're not in fashion. Your student voice, the *Oldfielder*, has just called for an end to faith at Prescott. I've asked the headmaster to join me here to reaffirm our commitment to Prescott's charter in the face of these attacks."

Wrigley hadn't been at Oldfield much longer than H. He wasn't Ivy League or anything close; he went to the University of Wisconsin and the Georgetown Foreign Service School, then disappeared until he emerged in 1948 as an assistant director of the recently created CIA. A campus guessing game was where and what he'd been doing for ten years and why he'd been chosen headmaster. He was a handsome dark-haired man, with steel grey eyes and a Barrymore profile. But he was also shy, seldom seen; and today he looked uncomfortable in his robes, oppressed by the thundering organ and as unhappy to be in the Laughlin Chapel as H. Wrigley was a soporific public speaker; he spoke always from notes and read them as if every word was in a carefully rehearsed foreign language that was opaque and meaningless to him. People quickly became uneasy when he spoke. H. thought his diffidence might conceal a secret atheist.

Wrigley was patiently spelling out the contingency of the spiritual, physical, and intellectual spheres on the health of the whole body when someone in the center section, among the upper middlers, snored loudly, about as loud as the fart the year before. Barney Nugent was prepared. He stood up. "Get him!" he commanded. A dozen student deacons jumped from their seats, not in their usual front pews, but peppered through the chapel. One was waving his arm and pointing. "In here, in here!" Just as the proctors collared a thin kid in a green plaid jacket, a second honking snore came from a different quarter. Religious decorum had shot its wad—rebellion held sway. But the headmaster, deep in his notes, was still affirming that the Reverend B. Barnard Nugent had the complete confidence and total support of the trustees, the faculty, and himself. He sat down and crossed his legs under the robes, giving no sign that he was aware of what had just happened. Robert Wrigley marched to a different drum.

H.'s cards were all on the table, and it was time for Mencken to appear or be forgotten. He was reading *Treatise on the Gods* between chapters of *Crime and Punishment.* Fearful men made the gods to protect themselves from an irrational universe, but as science tamed and explained the unknown, the need for the gods disappeared. Mencken fueled his growing atheism, Dostoevsky fed the anarchy that possessed his spirit and justified the murder he planned. He had brought back a straw hat which Joe Stillman wore in a 1919 photograph of him courting Julia Chateau at a polo match at the St. Louis Country Club. Worn at a rakish angle, glasses on the tip of his nose, unlit cigar in the side of his mouth, and his thumbs under loud suspenders, this outlandish garb made H. a figure people understood—a new voice on the hill who spoke for the oppressed, the masses, the little people. The student deacons left the dining hall when Henry and Kornfeld came in. The faculty, who liked to stand on the steps of J. P. Hall before assembly to watch, exhort, and scold the students as they rushed into the auditorium, stared in icy silence as Henry and his party of editors passed. The campus jocks, in their dirty white bucks and round collars looked on him as a rabble-rouser; but many more enjoyed the show. H. was the voice of reason and common sense, a populist straight talker from Missouri pushing back the darkness of Puritan gloom. He published more editorials ridiculing the charter's obsession with predestination and whether good works could merit grace and a place in heaven.

The trustees arrived for their winter meeting. Their agenda began with a dinner at the John Perkins farm in North Oldfield and ended with a final celebration on Friday at which the construction of the new gymnasium would be announced. Nelson Ransoms, the trustee who had given the necessary three million to build it, would be awarded the Prescott Medal. The Prescott and Norton glee clubs would sing. Roger Wilkins, faculty advisor for the Oldfielder, came to assignment meeting on Thursday night to warn everyone to get passes if they went to Harwell because the deans were getting uptight about the city of sin. He had been asked to look into the feasibility of using cold composition and printing the paper offset in Medford, a bedroom town near Oldfield. Kornfeld laid his head down and pounded the table with his fists. "No hot lead! The death of letterpress," he mourned. He would never write a word for photo offset. He would quit first. Wilkins took H. and Kornfeld into the hall. The charter editorials, which he loved, were causing big trouble. The faculty demanded censorship, and the trustees wanted to meet the editors. The rumor was that Nelson Ransoms was having second thoughts about funding the gym. "They want to see you guys at ten o'clock tomorrow."

They waited on a bench outside the trustees room on the second floor of J. P. Hall, Kornfeld in his spiffy herringbone suit and H. sporting elements of Mencken—the funny hair, bow tie, suspenders showing under his jacket, not a prep school type. They studied portraits of the ten headmasters on the walls until the double doors opened and the eleventh appeared. "Mr. Kornfeld? And Mr. Stillman. I'm Bob Wrigley. Come in." He introduced the three trustees who remained seated at a long table: John Perkins, Donald Overstreet, and Nelson Ransoms. The *Oldfielder* was on the table, open to the editorial page. Wrigley leaned against a window frame with his ankles crossed. The editors stood while Perkins talked. He looked more like a polo player than an industrialist, a wiry-thin man with wisps of still-blond hair and blue eyes that squinted in sun or shade. “This question about the charter comes up every eight or ten years since I’ve been chairman. It’s an albatross, no two ways about it.”

He looked at the paper before him.

“You guys certainly know your history. What Josiah Prescott wanted was a school to train young Calvinists to rally round the pilgrim faith. Unitarians were taking over Harvard, and he was out to keep New England Puritan, not to free the Negro, compensate the Indians, or emancipate women. He didn’t give a tinker’s damn for any of them. Heretics were what worried him. You’re asking us to amend his charter and get rid of all that talk. I’d like to flush it down the toilet myself. It’s pious nonsense that says nothing about the mission of Prescott today. But I have to say to you what I’ve said before. The charter of 1779, creaky and intolerant as it is, is the only guarantee of Prescott’s freedom and historic independence from state regulation and control. Open up this document for revision in the state legislature, let politicians start picking at it, they’ll grab half our property, tax the rest, and tell us how, who, and what to teach—”

Kornfeld interrupted, “So you’re admitting the charter protects the school from conforming to current state and local statutes regarding discrimination, tolerance, property ordinances—”

“Mr. Kornfeld, the trustees have ignored these restrictions for fifty years, and nobody is using the charter to get around the law—”

“So why does the racial and religious composition of the school still reflect the charter’s religious intolerance of 1779?”

“It doesn’t. We have Negroes, not as many as I’d like, but—”

“Twenty-one out of five hundred and thirty.”

“I thought there were more. We’ve got Jews—”

“A few, and there are no Jews on the faculty,” said Kornfeld.

“We’ve been slow there. No two ways about it.”

“If your woolen mills in Harwell had been chartered in 1779 like the academy,” said the managing editor, “you would have avoided the statutes regarding child labor, health, and safety that made you move them to North Carolina.”

“Three reasons why I went south, sir. Unions, unions, and unions.” Johnnie Perkins was not easy to perturb. “Listen, you guys, we’re asking you to back off this charter talk. It's fodder for the pols on Beacon Hill, it draws attention to something we don't like but can't fix and undermines our image—"

"Let's talk," said Kornfeld in his most ingratiating mode. "You say it is expedient to keep the charter, but you don't feel bound by it. So what are you willing to do?"

H. was surprised. They had agreed the charter must be revised. They never talked about making a deal, and here, Kornfeld was fishing for one.

"We can definitely shake up the faculty mix. Right, Bob?"

The headmaster nodded. "It's already in the works."

"Six Jews on the Islington faculty," said Kornfeld. "Islington 6, Prescott 0."

"We'll see about it. What else?" Perkins asked.

"Religious worship must be optional," said H. "The charter must be revised, in the legislature if that's what it takes." The trustees looked at each other. The headmaster crossed and uncrossed his feet.

"Slow down here, Mr. Stillman. You're in a minority on that."

"We don't think so."

He was trying to drive a wedge between them. Giving Kornfeld a few Jews on the faculty cost him nothing; everyone agreed it was an outrage, and the fix was in the works. Putting the brakes on Barney Nugent brought out the hardball. Perkins's tone had a sharper edge. "Look around you, Mr. Stillman. Even the School of Ethical Culture, which believes in nothing, they require some kind of meditation or prayer."

"Meditation or silent prayer is fine by us. We're talking about Congregational orthodoxy disguised as 'nondenominational' services." H. had kept his temper.

"Parents demand more than silent prayer. They want communal worship. I'm told your own mother does. There's a flag on your file that says Mrs. Julia Stillman is to be warned if you miss Mass downtown. That's why attendance is taken. You think the academy cares if you go to Mass?"

"Are the trustees letting my mother run this school? I thought you were in charge, not Julia Stillman. You're catering to the worst in parents. What other dirt have you got on me?"

"You forget, Mr. Stillman, that some people come to Prescott for its religious tradition."

"Let them. Oldfield should keep its Calvinism. It belongs here as much as the trees. But others don't come for that, so why not make religious observance optional? Separate church from—"

"It's optional now, you brainless Luddite!" Nelson Ransoms had been holding in his anger for too long. "You can go somewhere else if you don't like it. That's your option, and I advise you to take it."

J. J. Perkins pushed his chair back and crossed his legs. He'd done his best, and he left them to the bad cop. Ransoms was on his feet. A bear of a man in rumpled blue suit, he had briefly owned the Empire State Building, or a hundred floors of it. "The chairman's got a lot more patience than I have with you people. You don't wash the school's dirty linen in public, and you don't bad-mouth the place that nourishes you. If Oldfield is repugnant to you, Mr. Stillman, then get out. I've told Johnnie here and I'm telling you now, I'm reconsidering my gift to the school until I hear you're gone."

H. knew he was red with anger. He tried to slow down and not become shrill. "You're talking about the first amendment rights of a student newspaper, sir, as if you owned them. With all due respect, sir, you don't."

"Get out!" Ransoms shouted.

"I'm not leaving, and I'm not backing down. Religion must be optional!"

Ransoms commanded the headmaster. "Get that boy out of here. Now!"

The headmaster opened the door to the hall, and he and Kornfeld pulled the resisting H. out of the room. "Dean Pickering wants to see Mr. Stillman in his office," he said.

"Nelson Ransoms is a bag of wind," said Kornfeld on the stairway down. "He'll build the gym whatever happens because he wants his name on it."

H. was angry. "You're the bag of wind, Kornfeld. Your father would be disgusted with you. I don't want to know you."

CC's secretary sent him straight in. The dean looked up over his shoes which were on his desk with Henry Stillman's records propped on his knees.

"How is it, being editor in chief?"

"Difficult, sir."

"You write that editorial about the charter?"

"Yes, sir."

"Cost us the new gym I hear."

"The charter did. I didn't write that."

"If you're so smart, what's this D in Spanish doing here?" He held up a grade card.

"That's not possible. I had a B the last test." There was no way Spanish could have slipped so quickly. Something was fishy. "Mr. Kiley never said I was failing. I want to talk to him."

"We're not in loco parentis, Mr. Stillman. You're on your own. Sink or swim. The Prescott way. I've written your father, an uncommonly enlightened man, deeply concerned about your progress, that I'm placing you on academic probation. For your own good."

"I want to hear this from Mr. Kiley. I don't believe it."

"The only effect of probation is to curtail your extracurricular activities."

"You're throwing me off the *Oldfielder*. That's what all this is about."

"It's about focusing your resources, young man, and some day you'll thank me."

He took his feet off his desk and stood. The interview was over.

"I want to transfer to the University of Chicago," H. told him. The dean walked to the door and opened it.

"I wouldn't ask Chicago or any college to be interested in an unsatisfactory student." He put out his hand. "Nice chatting."

"I'm going to Chicago."

"All I have for you, Stillman, is cold turkey."

Kornfeld was waiting for him on the steps.

"I'm off the paper. You're editor in chief."

"Why?"

"Probation. Spanish, he said. Old Kiley's so afraid they'll retire him, he'll do anything they tell him."

"What's with you and religion? You really get a head of steam up. You go crazy."

"What's with you? You sold out, you caved in, for a couple of Jews."

"Can't I protect my own? Civil war between Christians isn't exactly a Jew's business."

"Our deal was to help each other—"

"I'll help you kill Nugent. Just don't ask me to take sides between heresies."

"Forget it. I've had all the help from you I'll need."

"Suit yourself."

"You always wanted to be the editor in chief. I hope you're happy now."

"I'm going to quit, if you want to know."

"I'll bet you don't. You're a sleazy opportunist, without an honest—"

"You don't know when to shut up, Stillman."

The bells for chapel began to ring. They both took the diagonal over the grass so as not to be late. The vestibule was jammed. Kornfeld, smaller and more wiry, was ahead of him. H. pushed his way out of the human stream and ran up the stairs to the tower. He went through the large room with the piano and the open door to the bell chamber. The throbbing overtones of the bell increased as he climbed toward the latticed beams of the belfry above. When his head came even with the floor of the small brick chamber, he saw a man's shoes and legs dangling a foot in the air before him. It was the custodian, with his cardigan, cap and scarf, and a yellowed cigarette clamped in his lips, hanging from a rope by his gloved hands. The rope went through a grid of beams which supported the bearings of an axle with the big bell at its center and an even larger wheel next to it on whose circumference the rope coiled and uncoiled, carrying the janitor up and down with it. When the bell came to rest, he got on a stool and jumped for the rope as high as he could grab it. He rode the bell rope until it came to rest, then dropped to the floor and quickly scrambled back on the stool to jump again. The cycle took about fifteen seconds. For the quick strokes which soon began, he used a second rope that appeared to be connected directly to a hammer which struck the rim of the motionless bell. He jumped at this rope from the floor, let go as soon as the clapper struck, and jumped again, a marionette jerked about on strings. Henry went down before he was seen.

The last students were just squeezing through the doors, and H. got safely inside. The bells stopped; and soon Quintus was in his usual place, in the balcony behind, waiting for his master and control. The inflammatory organ prelude by Karg-Elert ended in fireworks, and the minister appeared. His mark.

That afternoon, Nelson Ransoms gave Prescott three million for the gym and wore a freshly pressed suit to the ceremony to announce his gift. Kornfeld interviewed him afterward, then wrote a two-page spread on the ceremony and gift which was to be sent to the fourteen thousand alumni. H. ate early and battened himself in his bedroom with *Crime and Punishment*. He didn't come out Saturday morning until he heard Kornfeld leave. He went to the *Oldfielder* office to read his gym piece. It praised the donor, the gym and its architecture, and the noble role of sport in the life of Prescott Academy. It made him want to puke. Kornfeld came in briefly, and H. told him what he thought of his gym story. "If you were in Auschwitz, God forbid," H. crossed himself, "you would be a capo who collaborates with his killers, perhaps by publishing a death camp newspaper." Kornfeld was as wounded as H. intended him to be and left the room. There was only one other unresolved matter, besides his life. What was going on between Quintus Elmo and Barney Nugent? It was time to find out.

A JESUIT IN PETTO

H. found Elmo late Saturday afternoon in the chapel putting the Sunday programs on each seat; the religion of the week, Manichaeism, was on the cover.

H. told Elmo he was a reporter from the *Oldfielder*, which was now not true, but the custodian didn't hear him. "The school newspaper!" he shouted, but Elmo merely smiled and kept him guessing where his wall eye would wander next. Henry was so involved following the little man's gaze that he missed the approach of the Reverend B. Barnard Nugent from behind the choir stalls. "What do you want here?" he asked. H. said he was doing a feature on the campus bells.

"If you want information about the Laughlin Chapel, you come through my office. You want to speak with anyone on my staff, you come through my office. You don't just barge in. This is a holy place. Get out."

"We thought Mr. Elmo would make a good subject for a feature," said H., ignoring the minister's order. Nugent motioned to Quintus Elmo to leave them, and the custodian walked toward the back of the chapel. "You can't interview him, so please don't ask."

"Is there some reason I can't talk to him except you don't want me to?"

"Quintus is deaf, and he can't talk. Now get out of here."

"He seems to understand exactly what you're saying when you preach."

"You always turn your head. I see you."

"I turn to see who you're talking to."

"Please leave, Mr. Stillman. I don't want to talk about Quintus."

The minister positioned himself wide legged across the aisle to symbolically prevent H. from approaching the lectern of God. Nugent had no right to deny him access to a place of worship. He squared off facing his adversary. They stared at each other.

"Tell me something, Stillman. That was your doing, wasn't it? The wise crack about my talk on Zoroaster?"

"The editors said at the time that no disrespect was intended. We still do."

"But you did it. You were the Jesuit."

"I was called the Jesuit by some, yes, sir."

"And you and maybe Kornberg changed the wording."

"Yes, sir."

The minister looked at him with an unexpectedly tender, grieved face. "I thought so." He took a long pause. "Did you ever stop to think what it's like to be pastor to five hundred young men who come from dozens of religious backgrounds or even none? You ever think of that?"

"Yes, sir, I have."

"What did you think?"

"I think it is impossible and should not be attempted. That's why compulsory chapel should be abandoned."

Nugent nodded his head. He was beginning to breathe more quickly. "You're a Catholic, aren't you?"

"I was, sir."

"You go to St. Joseph's."

"Yes, sir."

"I've talked to Father Donovan down there. He doesn't know you. You don't participate in church life—the Newman Club, that sort of thing."

"No, I don't."

"You were at a Jesuit school before you came to Oldfield."

"Yes, sir."

"What made you choose to come to a school where the religious practice was abhorrent to you?"

"I was told there was very little religion here."

"You know how it feels—with a person like you sitting in the pews listening and looking at me? It's like preaching to a basket with a snake in it. I've thought about it. I said to my wife, 'The Jesuits have sent him to destroy my ministry.' Is that it? Am I right?"

He was moving closer to H. who held his ground. In a way, it was true that he had been sent by Father Kirby. Or he enjoyed pretending he'd been planted in

Oldfield, like an OSS agent in Berlin or a Jesuit in petto in the court of Ferdinand II. Maybe that was why he didn't like being called the Jesuit; it blew his cover. But he had never taken seriously Father Kirby's fantasy about his prefect of the sodality burrowing himself in the rocks of Protestant New England. How could he when even the trustees knew he had to go to Mass or his mother would make him come home?

"You really think I'm a secret Jesuit?"

Nugent did. "You've been sent to humiliate me, to make me a laughing stock."

He was very close to H., one hand fingered his lapel, the other his necktie.

"The Forbes are in on it too, aren't they?"

"The Forbes?"

"He hates me, has he told you why? His father brought me here, we built this chapel together, and I had to watch his son's conversion kill his father, I had to bury the man, and I called a spade a spade. And the wife, she wrote that depraved book you like so much, you're all out to destroy religion at Oldfield, to destroy me."

He had begun twisting H.'s necktie around his powerful palm, perhaps for emphasis. "I'm warning you, Stillman, you're going to hurt this church over my dead body." The minister was as strong as he looked; he rowed a scull ten miles on the Merrimack River three times a week before breakfast. H. tried to pull his necktie away, but there was not enough fabric left to grip, and he was making it worse by resisting. "You hear me? Over my dead body!"

"LET GO!" H. tried to say, but he could make almost no sound.

"Just tell me you've been sent."

"You're strangling me." It was a whisper. Nugent took one more turn of his necktie around his hand, and H. felt his chest caving in and his knees buckling. He grabbed blindly at the face and arms of the minister.

From the back of the chapel, he heard shrill, bleating, incoherent squeals, like a tortured puppy. Suddenly Nugent let go; he was shouting at someone. "Get off me! Get off me!" H. had fallen to his knees, but he saw Nugent trying to shake Quintus Elmo from his back and screaming at the deaf man. Nugent threw the dwarf down and stood over H. who was on his hands and knees panting, shaking, and spitting. "Get off the floor. You're not hurt."

H. looked up at his assailant and at the homunculus beside him who had saved his life, and he understood the dreadful secret that Nugent protected so violently. Quintus Elmo was Nugent's familiar. In the Bay Colony, they would both have been hanged for witchcraft. The minister was the control of an imp who served, encouraged, and inspired him and who also spied and warned him of his enemies. H. had suspected this from day one. That's why Nugent had tried to kill him. He could have commanded Elmo to do it for him, but the dwarf was the conscience of the two, the good cop. "Get off the floor, get out of this church!" Nugent was shouting at him. When he grabbed H. by the collar to lift him to his feet, Quintus must have thought he meant to hurt him again and tried to stop him. Nugent pushed the dwarf violently into a pew where he fell between the seat and the kneeler. Then he went after H. who was reluctant to fight the man. Nugent was stronger and easily got H. by the neck and one arm and was dragging him toward the exit when Kornfeld appeared. He must have been standing at the back of the chapel, just like in Hymn 519, his witness.

> Yet that scaffold sways the future.
> And behind the dim unknown,
> Standeth God within the shadow
> Keeping watch above his own.

He stepped from the shadows and said, "Let him go, sir."

"Get out of my way," said Nugent.

"Go away, Kornfeld. I don't need you." H. was furious that Kornfeld had followed him. This was his moment; it belonged all to him.

"Let him go," said Kornfeld, trying to pull Nugent's arm off H.'s neck.

"He's a sissy. I only pulled his necktie," Nugent protested.

"You were strangling him, sir. Only the dwarf stopped you. I was here." Quintus had picked himself up from the pew and was trying again to pull his master to safety back of the choirs. He nudged him toward the vestry, both his arms around him. H. couldn't loosen his mangled necktie; he would have to cut it off.

"I would never have let him kill you," Kornfeld said.

"I didn't need you. Don't go grabbing credit. Quintus Elmo saved me."

They watched Nugent and Quintus leave the chapel through a rear door.

"Your remark about Auschwitz was indefensible and obscene."

"You betrayed me with the trustees more deeply than I ever betrayed you. More deeply than anyone, including Jimmy Bowes. Then you had the gall to suck up to Ransoms."

Kornfeld smiled apologetically. "All true. How did you get Nugent to strangle you?"

"I told him I wrote the Zoroaster ear."

"What are you going to do now?"

"I haven't decided."

"I could write something like 'Nugent chokes ex-editor.'"

"You're the editor. Write what you want."

"I'm trying to do what you'd like," he said.

Kornfeld's effort to be obliging only made H. angrier.

"I don't give a fuck," said H. and walked away.

On Sunday morning, Mr. Kiley took attendance at St. Joseph's, his bicycle by his side. "May I ask you about my grade in your class?" H. asked. The teacher was surprised that Henry Stillman was his student and unable to remember him or his position on the grade sheet, which was really just a class ranking. The actual letter grade was determined by the chairman who combined the lists of several classes into some sort of curve. Whether the low man on Kiley's sheet got C or D depended on the other curves. Only the department knew. "You could have failed me and not know it?" "*Que lastima*," said his teacher. He signed in and left, getting a small pleasure from the idea that Julia Chateau thought if he signed in, he had to stay and attend Mass. It still rankled that J. J. Perkins knew his mother monitored his faith from St. Louis. "It's who we are. We don't have a choice," she had said in the Union Station. He believed strongly that he did.

On Monday, he was called into the headmaster's office. Wrigley offered him a chair.

"Can I call you Henry?"

"H. will do, sir."

"H.?"

"As in K."

"You made an impression on Johnnie Perkins."

"I thought Mr. Ransoms was more forthright."

"Perkins thought you showed character."

"It's not the school's business if I say my prayers."

"Dean Pickering says you're headed for Chicago."

"As soon as I can, sir."

"I'll be sorry to see you leave."

"I'm on probation."

"That's not why I asked you to come in."

"Why, sir?"

"Barney Nugent talked to me yesterday. He regrets his behavior with you."

"What does he regret about his behavior?"

"He says he pulled your necktie."

"He tried to strangle me."

"He admits he pulled it harder than he intended."

"Did he say there was a witness, besides the custodian?"

"No, he didn't."

"There was."

He watched Wrigley think about that; he got the message.

"Can you say who?"

"Adam Kornfeld."

"Your friend on the *Oldfielder.*"

"I didn't know he was there, until afterward."

"Do you know what angered Mr. Nugent?"

"I tried to interview Quintus Elmo, who rings the bells. He didn't want me to."

"Did he give a reason?"

"That I was trying to destroy his ministry."

"He says you're a secret Jesuit. What does he mean?"

"He believes I oppose compulsory religion at Oldfield on instructions from the pope or his lieutenants, the Jesuits."

"Do you?"

"I hope not, sir. I'm already the lapsed Catholic my mother fears I will become."

"One more question. Did you provoke Mr. Nugent to violence?"

"That's two questions, sir."

"Did you provoke him?"

"My person provokes him."

"Was he violent?"

"I said he tried to strangle me."

"Do you want to make charges?"

"I want to get off probation."

"I can't help you there."

"I want my newspaper back."

"Not while you're on probation."

"I want to go the University of Chicago."

"I won't second-guess the deans."

"Then I think I'm finished here."

The headmaster got up. "We all know Barney Nugent's job gets more and more impossible, which he courageously refuses to admit. He's old school. Not a lot of them left. We'll be poorer when he's gone. Good luck, whatever you decide."

Wrigley wasn't going to call off the deans. H. was a useful gadfly but not worth bucking the system to save. His guess was that Nugent would be taken out and shot. The headmaster was already speaking of him in the past tense. H. had expected a slower, more lingering death though, like William Jennings Bryan, his end could be quick. He did not feel Mencken's rush of triumph, but he felt no remorse either. His was not the only straw that broke the camel's back, only the last, and he had more pressing things to feel guilty about. Mail from St. Louis was piling up. He had not written or spoken with them since the summer, and he was afraid to open their letters. His life at Oldfield was over. Why stay if Pickering would not help him get into college? Why go to college if he never wanted to take another course again? Because he needed a 2-S deferment from somewhere or he was dead man. MacArthur had pushed his army so far into North Korea it was about to be cut off by the Chinese. Syngman Rhee was egging him on. He could ask Maia to phone Shapiro again to see if there was any hope for Chicago without Pickering's recommendation. She was his rock, his shelter, his love. He missed her. He was no longer a student or an editor or the buddy of Kornfeld who had betrayed him; he was barely a person. He sat in Doc's staring into a cup of muddy coffee.

THE LAST SUPPER

The first he knew that Joe was in Oldfield was a note in his box telling him to meet his father at the Oldfield Inn for supper. Joe Stillman was waiting in the dining room with a bourbon toddy. Henry sat down and took out a package of Old Golds, Joe's brand.

"When did you start smoking?"

"This fall." Joe didn't say anything; Henry could tell he was trying to remember when he had started smoking. He had smoked a pipe at Yale and General Electric and probably when he ran the coal mines, but that wasn't what Joe was thinking at all.

"It's a rotten habit," he said. "I've had to stop playing golf."

"Why?"

"Circulation, in my feet." He looked old and tired. H. wished he could blame it on cigarettes, but he knew he was the cause. Joe seemed sad, confused, and out of his depth. So was Henry. The cocky H. had all but drained out of him, and Horrible Henry was in the ascent.

"How's Father O'Connor?" he asked him.

"He's got an oscillator giving him a hard time. The rectifier tubes are German and impossible to replace."

"I mean about entropy. You wanted to talk to someone about last things."

"What's entropy got to with an oscillator?"

"Never mind," said Henry. The priest and his father had both forgotten about God, given a chance to play with their radios. It was just as well. He felt guilty about bringing them together in the first place.

It turned out Joe had been making trouble at Prescott all day. First he'd seen his new friend, Pickering. He imagined the old men comparing notes on the degeneracy of youth.

"Pickering and I have been writing."

"He said."

"He could be your staunch ally, given a chance."

"Sure. Who else you see?"

"The headmaster."

"Jesus."

"A weak sister, if you ask me."

"Why did you see him?"

"You've made enemies everywhere, tangled with trustees, deans, minister, athletic director, coaches, teachers—"

"Did Wrigley say he was my enemy?"

"He seemed to take your side, damned if I can see why."

"Because I was right."

"The man has no idea how destructive you are."

"You were hoping he'd kick me out."

"At least show you your limits, who's boss."

"I'm on probation. Aren't you happy?"

"How does anyone fail Spanish? A stupid language, a dog can speak it."

"Where's the menu?"

"And physics. Haven't I taught you anything?"

His cry of hurt and rejection was genuine. Henry was ashamed and had no answer.

"Can we eat?"

"You never even told us you were an editor of the newspaper."

"I was for a month, and it's all over. You can go home."

"When I've heard your side, I'll go."

"Okay. Remember the admissions guy who said there was less religion here than on a dollar bill? He lied. It's coming out our ears—compulsory chapel four times a week, church on Sunday plus Bible class. I wrote an editorial saying it should be optional, the trustees blew a gasket, and the school minister tried to strangle me. End of story. Now you can go."

"What's there to fight with a Unitarian about? They don't believe in anything."

"He's a Congregationalist."

"Same difference."

"If you say so."

"It's you Catholics set the tone. You see a Virgin Mary in every backyard, we poor Protestants have to come up with something—"

"Can we order?"

"You're going to have to learn to live with a lot of types. That's what an education's about. You've been too protected. It's our fault."

"He tried to strangle me."

"Pulled your necktie, the way I heard it."

"Religion brings out the worst in men."

"I want to meet him."

Henry put his head on the table, covered it with his hands, and pretended to weep. The white-haired lady brought them the relish tray and menus in order to stop him. Food distracted them from the awful reality of his marks, his attitude, and his destiny. Joe was soon drawing diagrams on the tablecloth of his latest base reflex folded exponential horn. He moved plates and glasses as formulae, graphs, curves, and drawings spread in all directions to the edges of the table.

Henry didn't understand a word, but he was grateful for Joe's obsession. It passed the time and kept attention off him.

The next day he met his father for lunch at Doc's after his classes. Joe had just come from B. Barnard Nugent's office in the back of the chapel, and his self-satisfaction with the interview was supreme. Henry had the man all wrong, just as he had guessed. Doc, who almost never left his U-shaped counter, came to their booth with a pad and pencil stub to take their order, his attempt to gussy up his greasy spoon for a visiting parent. Joe asked Doc about his scrambled eggs. H.'s shoulders began to tighten and cut off circulation to his carotid artery. He knew what was coming. Skaneateles. Joe was going to tell the old Greek about the best scrambled eggs he had ever put in his mouth in a diner in Skaneateles, a town on the Finger Lakes between the Adirondacks and Schenectady. "Doc doesn't want to hear about Skaneateles, Dad." "Who says he doesn't?" The world turned on the axis of Joe's memories. He ordered the eggs. He had reminded himself of the tricities: Albany, Schenectady, and Troy. "Barney Nugent grew up in Troy, went to Union College, Steinmetz taught engineering there, I know the place like the back of my hand. Takes a know-it-all like you to find a way to cross a decent guy from Troy."

"I'm glad you got along with him."

"Because I don't prejudge people. You make him out to be some hellfire preacher. Fact is, he's a down-to-earth guy, a Red Sox fan.

"Did he mention he tried to kill me? And only his janitor stopped him?"

"He pulled your tie and wishes he hadn't. Said you two had a run-in last year never got sorted out."

"My tie. That's what he's telling everybody. He tried to strangle me."

"I wouldn't get on my high horse, if I were you."

"What's that supposed to mean?"

"Have you noticed how you're on the outs with almost every living soul around here? You got a chip on your shoulder the size of a two by four."

"Sure. It's my fault, all of this."

"They say you're running with a bad crowd—"

"Nugent and who else says?"

"Dean Pickering says the same thing. They can't all be wrong—"

"They all hate Kornfeld."

"Your Jewish friend, with no home, no parents—"

"His mother is insane, and his father won two Pulitzers. You said a crowd. Who else?"

"Some teacher. An old family, father was a trustee, good friend of Nugent's. The son's a rotten apple, wife's a vampire."

"The Forbes. They're gone. He had a breakdown."

"Maybe you can settle down now, get on your feet."

"I'm not staying here. We're wasting our time talking about it."

"Where's Jimmy Bowes? He must know some nice people you could meet."

"Finish your eggs. You want to see my physics teacher?"

"I hear Jim Bowes is going to be on Block Island this summer."

"Where's that?"

"Just east of Gardiners Bay."

"Off Long Island?"

"Your mother and I have been talking about going back to Amagansett this summer. Stay with Phoebe."

"Swell."

"You've never been to Amagansett."

"I was there when I was five."

"What do you remember?"

"A splinter in my foot."

"You've never had a decent clam."

"Maybe not."

"Clams are all sick or dead by the time they get to market. You want to eat them straight from the sand."

"Right."

"My greatest regret was I never able to give you the sea."

"I've gotten by."

"You don't know how to sail," he said.

"I can drive."

"Almost eighteen and you can't sail."

"I sailed at Kooch-i-ching."

"In goddam Ontario. I mean sailing. Saltwater sailing."

"The wheel's kick, the salt spray spume," said Henry. He knew all about it.

"It's time we went back."

Joe hadn't been to Long Island since Button died. Henry had no memory of the place whatever, except a long dock where he got the splinter. He would join them if he wasn't in the army or somewhere trying to stay alive. His uncle Button's long painting of Gardiners Bay might be as close as he would ever get.

"We were the best goddam sailors on the South Fork. The crowd at the club claimed we had a motor."

"If you want to see Mr. Schultz, we should go."

His physics teacher, a prim German of monstrous precision, lived in a seventeenth-century farmhouse filled with Mrs. Schultz's lace. The house was not far off campus, but they should have taken a taxi. Joe's feet were worse than he said. Mrs. Schultz was waiting for them with a plate of cookies, pfeffernüsse and lebkuchen, which were Joe's favorites. He raved about them, asked how old they were, and when he learned they were baked at Christmas, he went on and on about how they improved with age. H. watched with deep disdain how Joe ingratiated himself. They adored him. It made H. queasy, as did their speaking about him in his presence. They sat in a circle taking tea with lace doilies under everything—teacups, ashtrays, cookies. Henry's difficulty with physics, according to his teacher, was haste and sloppiness. Joe agreed that bad habits were his son's undoing; he had never picked up his room or sharpened a pencil. Sloppiness reminded Joe of the parable of the slovenly shop steward. H. cringed at what was coming, worse by orders of magnitude than the scrambled eggs in Skaneateles. The steward's task was to urinate in a barge full of water anchored in the Mohawk Canal behind Steinmetz's lab at General Electric. The barge was a resistive load used in the testing of electric generators. Mr. Schultz was already laughing. "The urine varied the saline conductivity!" he chortled with glee. The slovenly steward seldom followed instructions. He peed a hundred cubic centimeters when he was asked for three hundred, and one day he just peed when he wanted to without informing the shop. Mr. Schultz was shaking with anticipation. He had a strong sensory imagination; when he had described in class the result of looking at the sun through a concave lens and allowing its rays to focus on the retina, his eyes inflamed, and he began to weep buckets and had to go home. Now he imagined the slovenly steward about to urinate in the water load with a potential difference of twenty thousand volts. Mrs. Schultz had to hold him on his chair. Joe remained dry and droll; all that was left of the steward was his buttons and garter snaps. Joe had found his audience, except for Henry who sat glum and unamused, burning with resentment at Joe's usurpation of his life.

A hour later, Joe had filled ten sheets with diagrams and formulas of exponents, contours, and crossover networks. Mr. Schultz understood everything and was excited by the quirk in every curve. Or he pretended to be. Mrs. Schultz had excused herself, and H. despaired that Joe would ever stop. He finally had to interrupt. He said he had been the test subject of Joe's Fletcher-Munson curves for five years and could vouch that his father was often carried away by his enthusiasm and assumed everyone had the same interest in Fletcher-Munson curves as he. Mr. Schultz claimed to be absolutely fascinated and begged Joe to continue. But H. had let the wind out of his sails.

Limping all the way back to the Oldfield Inn, Joe excoriated his son without mercy. "Treating me like an imbecile! Apologizing for your own father. I've never received such treatment in my life." He had seen all he needed; the dean and his teachers were right. Henry was the most arrogant, disrespectful, contemptuous, conceited ingrate on two legs. And he had no friends; that was the tip-off. Bullies have no friends. Just sycophants and toadies.

H. told him how it felt to have his own parent take the world's side against him. Joe believed the lies of his enemies and humiliated him at every chance.

"Nothing's changed with you since the rug box," Joe told him. "It's always been you against them. A lot of cheap theatrics."

They were at the inn. "Why don't you ask Jimmy Bowes if he'd like some supper? I hear he's captain of the football team."

"You keep asking. I never see him, all right?"

"If you were smart, you'd take a page from his book—"

"I did. The rug box was his idea, if you remember."

"He at least had the good sense to get out. You don't know when you're licked."

"I do too." He hadn't planned to tell Joe he was leaving Oldfield, but the old man's taunting was too much. "I'm going to the University of Chicago," said Henry.

"Pickering doesn't think you're being very realistic about that."

"He told you?"

"He gave me a letter he just sent them. Interesting guys, Hutchens and Adler," Joe mused. "What about this roommate you run the newspaper with?"

"He runs the paper. I was fired."

"Kornfeld"

"What about him?"

"Maybe he'd like a good supper."

"You wouldn't like him."

"I don't know why not."

"He's Jewish, remember?"

"I should meet some of your friends, if you have any."

"If I see him."

Joe gave him an envelope with Pickering's letter to Chicago. He read it when he got to his room. It was addressed to Maia's friend, Ted Shapiro, the director of admissions.

> Dear Ted,
>
> Henry Stillman, who affects the nom de plume H., is a journalist manqué who styles himself after H. L. Mencken. He savages the fabric of the community yet is surprised that he is resented and despised. He demonstrates the arrogance, immaturity, and self-pity of an adolescent.
>
> Though Stillman is on academic probation, he does nothing to improve his lot, save dream of greener pastures at other institutions. In this case, yours. I think you would be wise to avoid him.
>
> Best regards, C. C. Pickering

Maia was right. Oldfield would kill him. It might as well be the army, war or not, if he was going to die anyway.

He took Kornfeld to the inn with his father, partly to show the old man he had a friend but mostly as a buffer. It was risky; Kornfeld was abrasive, and he was still a Jew. He chose to interview Joe Stillman and never touched his food.

"You come from an old New England family, sir?"

"The first Stillman came to Ipswich in 1628, hated the Bay Colony and everyone in it. He followed Williams to Providence in 1637. Stillmans made furniture and clocks in Rhode Island until my grandfather's time."

"Roger Williams allowed the first Jews in the colonies," said Kornfeld approvingly.

"Quakers too, though he didn't like them either."

"What do you think of the campus?"

"Nice but no water. Schools and madhouses were built on hills that nobody wanted. The smart money moves to the water. Worst problem up here is grade crossings." Intersections were Joe Stillman's bête noire. "Have you ever seen a dog cross at an intersection? He crosses in the middle of the block because he only has to look two ways—left and right. You can get killed four ways in an intersection—left turn, right turn. Only a damn fool crosses there."

"What was Charles Proteus Steinmetz like?"

"Clearest head I've ever met. Made Edison look like a charlatan."

"Did he talk much about socialism?"

"Didn't just talk, he was on the town council and ran the school board for a dozen years. The mayor was socialist too. They both argued for a four-hour day."

"Was he an atheist?"

"He said no honest scientist could say there was a shred of evidence for the existence of God."

"Do you think Klaus Fuchs gave Russia the plutonium bomb?"

H. kicked Kornfeld under the table. They had agreed he wasn't to ask about Los Alamos.

"Even if he did, they didn't need him."

"You think they had the technology to do it on their own?"

"The only industrial secret I know is how to make Shredded Wheat."

Kornfeld pushed his chair away from the table and toward Joe's side where H. couldn't kick him. "At Camp Kooch-i-ching in August 1945, did you send Henry a drawing of the implosive lens on onionskin paper?"

"I might have. I tried to explain the bomb to all the kids."

"Was this the kind of sketch David Greenglass might have given the Rosenbergs?"

"I don't know what Greenglass knew, but the general outline of the lens was common knowledge."

Kornfeld outright contradicted him. "The implosive lens was never mentioned outside the Manhattan Project until late 1946." Joe just shrugged; it was all one to him. "Have it your way."

But H. was on his feet dragging Kornfeld out of the room. "You son of bitch, I asked you not—"

Kornfeld brushed him off. "You treat the old man like he'll break. He's tough and a lot smarter than you are. Wise up." He went back to the table and sat next to Joe. The old man loved him. He was a success. Joe invited him to St. Louis to hear his tangent tone arm and see his economic machine, a hydraulic model of the economy Joe built to demonstrate with pumps and tanks of colored waters why Roosevelt was a son of a bitch.

He asked him to come to Long Island in the summer. "You know how to sail?" Kornfeld lied. He claimed he loved to sail and accepted Joe's invitation with enthusiasm. H. refused to sit down with them. They were strangers making elaborate plans to meet at Aunt Phoebe's on Lily Pond Lane, how to take the Long Island Rail Road, what to bring—a penknife, sneakers, a jacket for dinner at the club. Kornfeld was about to usurp the remnants of H.'s sad life.

"Bright young man. Knows how to listen," Joe said at the elevator. H. and Joe could fight and blow off steam, but they couldn't talk about why they made each other so unhappy any more than they could talk about sex. Joe had gotten the wrong son; he would have been much happier with Kornfeld who wasn't afraid of him and liked him for the very reasons H. mistrusted him. And Henry wished he had a father like Adam Kornfeld who was never around and made no demands. He wanted to be left alone. By everyone. He watched the elevator lights tell him his father was on the second floor. Kornfeld was waiting for him to walk back to their dorm. "I'm not coming," he said. He went into a phone booth and called Maia in Cambridge for $1.25 in quarters.

"You still haven't heard anything from Shapiro?"

"I think he must be dead or in England."

"It's all fallen apart out here. My father had to come from St. Louis. The minister tried to strangle me, and my father took his side. Kornfeld betrayed me and is running the newspaper. I think I've had it."

They had discussed this moment a lot. "The door's open," she said. "When do you want to come?"

"Now." It was ten thirty. He had just missed a train; and the next bus was in forty-five minutes, the same bus that went to Harwell, only going south it ended in Lechmere Square where he could get a subway. He waited for the bus on Main Street in the chilly night. He had $2.85 in his pockets. He swung through the open door with the lightness and joy of pure liberation. The bus crept through the sleeping bedroom towns of Wakefield, Stonechat, Melrose, Malden, Medford, and finally Somerville and Lechmere. In an hour, he was leaving Harvard Square and dancing down Brattle Street, looking for the light in Maia's kitchen. She was waiting for him, eager to hear the Sturm und Drang of the past weeks that had catapulted him from Oldfield in the middle of the night. They stayed up all night talking and drank a gallon of coffee.

THE FAMILY BOSOM

In the morning, Paul came into the kitchen in a blue jean shirt and khakis, perhaps a bit groggy from the magic bullet of lithium that kept him calm. His hand kept contact with walls and surfaces as he moved, just in case. He didn't register the unusual presence of H. on a weekday at his breakfast table. H. was always around. But the first coffee sharpened him. "What day is it?"

"Tuesday."

"Why aren't you at Oldfield?"

Maia had been waiting to see how Paul would react. "H. is taking a breather from education. I've asked him to stay with us if he isn't in your way."

"Who knows about this but you two?" Forbes asked; and when it became clear that H. had walked away from Prescott Academy in the middle of the night, perhaps for good, he became extremely practical. H. was a missing person, and Dean Pickering would call the police who would eventually find him on Sparks Street. He made a terse phone call to the dean's office. "Henry Stillman is staying with Paul and Maia Forbes in Cambridge. He is safe and sound. Further the deponent sayeth not." He told H. he would try to get him a library card to Widener, and he instructed Maia to be certain their lodger had a toothbrush. H. and Maia drove out to Oldfield a week later and picked up his stuff. Kornfeld wasn't around. She put on Joe Stillman's straw hat, and they went to Doc's for English muffins.

He had a maid's room on the fourth floor at Sparks Street; mostly he ate in the Square or with them, Paul finagled him a library card from Harvard, and Julia secretly sent him money. He drove Eben to and from kindergarten, shopped for groceries at Sage's Market, and went to movies in the Square with Maia and Paul. He had been adopted. He had the family he had always wanted—a mother he could love and a father so august he could tether his cow in the Common. He had never been happier than where he was, but it was all coming to an end.

He had to join his real family on Long Island, and Paul and Maia were going to Maine. Paul had asked him to come; he could help Paul take care of Eben and paint the house, but he had to say no.

Kornfeld was waiting for him on Brattle Street. H. had not spoken with him since his midnight departure a month before, and he was still mistrustful of his usurping friend. Kornfeld had been accepted into Harvard and thought that H. should apply. They were looking under rocks for undergraduates because so few Depression babies were born and once-crowded institutions now had doors wide open for anyone eighteen.

He also brought news of B. Barnard Nugent who was taking a sabbatical to live in a tree on an ashram in Poona, a euphemism, Kornfeld thought, for a forced retirement. Had they killed him? They sort of had.

Julia Chateau phoned several times but refused to talk long distance for more than three minutes. He could hear her voice trail off like the sand she was watching in the egg timer and see the green leatherette notepad by her phone. Eggs, Henry's plans, broccoli, mussels, Phoebe. Joe was still intent on summering with Phoebe in East Hampton. Who was this Kornfeld he says he invited? Will he be an acceptable guest in Phoebe's house? H. told her Kornfeld's father had won two Pulitzer Prizes, sidestepping an issue everyone was avoiding. "I know the Pulitzers," she said. She did. They were a prominent St. Louis family, publishers of the *Post-Dispatch*, whose Jewishness was ignored or denied by everyone.

Summer got closer. Maia was back and forth to California, working on the screenplay of *Home Front*. H. read about the Panmunjom truce negotiations first thing every morning. "What's all this talk about the army and Korea?" Paul wanted to know. "You should go to Harvard. I have a friend in admissions. It's a lead pipe cinch."

"Who is it?"

"A guy I used to sprint with. We're joined at the hip."

He was the Harvard director of admissions. H. could call him in September if the army didn't work out.

"I never want to go to school again, but if I change my mind, thank you."

"It beats getting killed in Korea."

He met Kornfeld again in the Square, and they went to see Olivier's *Hamlet.* Kornfeld was worried whether he was really invited to stay with them on Long Island. Maybe Joe had forgotten or changed his mind. "They haven't forgot you," H. assured him with a touch of schadenfreude. "In fact, everyone is asking who you are."

"Tell them I am the Wandering Jew."

"That's what they're afraid of."

Julia phoned again. She really needed to know if he was joining the army or going to East Hampton with them. The promise of sailing with Henry had given Joe a new lease on life. H. said he never promised Joe anything. He might go and he might not.

"I won't tell Joe yet," Julia said. "You may change your mind. And what about this Cornberg?"

"Joe invited him. As far as I know, he wants to come."

"Isn't Cornberg a Jewish name?"

"You know it is!" H. shouted at the phone. "He and Dad talked about nothing else!" The egg timer had run out. She was gone.

The prospect of sailing with Joe all summer was so forbidding he couldn't face it without Kornfeld as a buffer. If they blackballed him, he definitely wouldn't go. Julia called again the next day. She had a telegram from Phoebe saying the house was too crowded for both Henry and his roommate. She had gotten Cornberg a room at the 1770 House on Main Street. Joe and Julia were about to set out for the east, she on the New York Central, he in the '38 Ford station wagon which he was driving across U.S. 40 with Charlie Adney, their yardman. Henry should meet them in a week at Aunt Phoebe's on Lily Pond Lane.

H. had a beer with Kornfeld in Harvard Square. "My aunt is getting you a room at the inn. She claims the house will be too crowded."

"No room for a Jew."

"I don't know her well enough to say."

"I'll take a pass on Lily Pond Lane. Thank your father for me. Someday I'll get to St. Louis to see his tangent tone arm." Kornfeld wasn't bitter. He was resigned.

Maia and H. went to see Marlene Dietrich in *The Blue Angel* at the Brattle Theatre. They sat together in the balcony; and when Professor Rath was dressed in a clown suit, kneeled in abasement before the nightclub singer he had fallen in love with, H. shivered and grew cold. Maia put her arm around him and her other hand on his knee. "Are you all right?" He held her hand tightly. The professor was crowing like a rooster, and Lola was singing about falling in love. Maia and H. kissed just long enough for each to understand what they wanted and to be frightened. But they continued to hold each other. On the walk home, H. said he had decided not to go to Long Island with his family. He was going with them to Forbes Neck in Maine. "You can't come with us," she said quickly. "I can't handle it."

3

GARDINERS BAY

A puff of white smoke blossomed from the barrel of the toy cannon on the committee boat and was blown over the stern in seconds, but H. thought he had seen it and perhaps even heard the faint pop, though they were so far upwind of the starting line it was hard to be sure.

"That may have been the gun," he said.

Joe Stillman was at the helm gazing out to sea, past Cartwright shoals and Gardiners Island, the glint of the white whale in his cataract-shrouded eyes. "Too soon," he said.

H. watched the dozen restlessly tacking boats of the race fleet quickly set a common course for the first mark, a long starboard reach for the fish factory across the gentle bight of sandy shore that harbored the yacht club. Joe Stillman held due north before the wind for Gardiners Island while the fleet sailed east. "You should look at what they're doing," his son advised.

His father turned his head stubbornly in the opposite direction, at the western bluffs of sloping sand with their mantle of scrub oak and pine. These were the bluffs his uncle Button had painted, in oils and water colors, fog and sun, and in a haze like now, when the colors shimmered like heat from asphalt. H. knew every detail of the western shore from the wide, horizontal canvas that had hung over the mantle in his nursery. He followed the shore from the yacht club on the left to a promontory on the right where the Indians lit fires to attract the settlers on Gardiners Island, but the focus of Button's bay was always the water towers, two oak stave tanks on iron truss scaffolds that rose high above scrub oak and pine on the bluffs behind a white mansion with wooden steps down the sand face to the beach below—the Bell Estate. He followed his father's gaze to the dark towers against the cloudless western sky; one of the tanks was missing. "Where's the other tank?" he asked.

"Must have been the Hurricane of '38," said Joe who hadn't seen the bay since he and Button buried their widowed mother, Abigail Stillman, a year before the famous storm. It blew down the chimney of her house and all the elms on Main Street. The brothers gave her home to the village library.

H. glanced toward the fish factory. The race had unquestionably begun; the boats were halfway there.

"They're all going toward the fish factory," he reported, trying not to make a big deal out of it.

Joe glanced to his right at the ripple of receding white sails heeling before the dock, vats, and sheds of the Smith Meal Company.

"Bunch of goddam sheep—follow each other to hell," he said and held his course for Gardiners Island.

He wasn't going to follow the herd. He had a plan. An engineer like Joe Stillman sailed according to scientific principles. Fluids, solids, and gases were as toys in his hands; boats and their characteristics had been mastered, like boilers and bridges, in the last century. The book was written, sailing was a science. But things were not going well so far. The trouble began during the first race when Joe tried to demonstrate for H. a principle of marine guidance, which required him to wedge himself in the forward bilge under a quarter deck over the prow of the little boat, a space used to stow sail bags and life preservers. He didn't fit; there was no air. He complained it was like being nailed in a child's coffin. As soon as he was half comfortable, his father would tell him to move—an inch here, an inch there. Finally he came out and refused to go back. He was labeled a spoilsport and blamed for everything that went wrong from then on.

Joe Stillman lit an Old Gold with his Zippo and confided his strategy. "What they don't know is the breeze is changing. We'll be to the mark before them." He held his cigarette aloft to let its drifting smoke be proof of his proposition. The smoke did indeed drift behind them, but it was backwind from the mainsail. H. looked south, across the narrow spit that separated the bay from the ocean where the high afternoon cumulus was building over the Atlantic, the clouds whose shadow cooled the lower air and made the breeze which drove back the stench of the fish factory and made Gardiners Bay habitable.

"The wind looks southerly to me, Dad," H. said.

"And the tide," said his father, pointing to a tilting buoy ahead of them. "Look at that can."

"The tide's going out—to sea," H. said.

"*Now* it is," said his father mysteriously. "But just you wait. We'll see who's sitting in the catbird seat."

"We've done this before," said the son gloomily.

"Ahh," cried his father with increasing excitement, "but we didn't do it right. You read me, Shinnecock."

He accused H. of reading him the wrong tide tables before the last race (Joe could no longer see them), mistaking a bay named after one Indian tribe, the Shinnecocks, for another, the Napeagues. Where H. came from the Indians had been named by French explorers, and few would mistake a Cadillac for a Chevrolet, but Long Island Indians were all one to him. Joe wanted him to learn the lore of salt water, the mystery of tides and habits of the wind, to be a sailor. The old man considered himself a master mariner, but for whatever reason, the hydrostatic forces that the engineer had calculated to carry them to victory in the last race had instead sucked them past Gardiners Island into the dread tide rip of Plum Gut through which surge all the waters of Long Island Sound on their way to Greenland. They were rescued near dusk by the club launch and towed home.

"Break out the spinnaker," Joe suddenly commanded. "We'll show those ninnies what sailing really is."

Spinnaker setting was a weak link in the chain of skills H. was learning from his father. In three races, they had yet to get the big balloon jib to fill and billow. The problem was to fix one corner of the sail in a fitting on the mast and the other to a pole which holds the jib away from the boat, then hoist the whole thing up the mast. A boat working against the wind is taut and steady as it cuts through the seas; but before the wind everything rattles and flaps—the stays go slack, the mast and boom shift and shudder, and the hull rises on swells and drops so deep in the troughs between that it takes water over the bow. H. hung over the water from a limp bow stay fiddling fruitlessly with obstinate hardware between submersions. The wind brought snatches of curses and commands from the stern.

"Goddam fool . . . the sheet . . . a little water won't . . . halyard, halyard . . . no goddam use . . . the pole."

After a long struggle, H. had lost both bottom corners of the sail, the pole was overboard, and the triumphant spinnaker was flying ahead of them from the top of the mast, like a trail of effluent downwind from a high smokestack. The boat was dangerously destabilized by its top-heavy load. H., being the largest moveable thing on board, was ordered aft for ballast and put to bailing the bilge.

"What a priceless performance," his father said, as if H. had planned and orchestrated every mistake for his father's entertainment.

"How do we get the spinnaker down?" H. wondered.

"You come into the wind and hope it doesn't foul the mainsail."

"Shouldn't we do that?"

The older man looked at his youngest son with undisguised contempt. "You're in a race, and you want to come into the wind? You'll stall."

H. had forgotten they were in a race. He looked for the other boats. They were on the downwind leg now, with their bright-colored spinnakers set, a dozen gay billiard balls on a table of blue. He didn't tell his father.

The first sandy spits of the south tail of Gardiners Island were on their port and tiny Cartwright Island off to starboard. H. had begun to read the charts since the visit to Plum Gut. He knew what was ahead: submerged submarine operating areas, unexploded depth charges, torpedo testing ranges, Block Island, Nantucket, and Iceland.

Long before that, they ran aground. The centerboard would have given them notice of approaching shallows, but it was raised going before the wind. The bow plowed into a sandbar, and the boat lurched to a halt, surprising even the spinnaker which fell into the shallow waters ahead like a deflated blimp.

"Old Hook Shoal!" cried his father with the delight of meeting an old friend. H. pulled in the spinnaker and pushed the boat off the bar with an oar while his father rehearsed the familiar romance of Gardiners Island—Indians, Captain Kidd, the First Lord of the island, David Lion Gardiner, an engineer, like Joe Stillman, sent by the king of England to fortify Connecticut, who got the island from the crown for his services, an engineer's reward. The island was still owned by Gardiners—the current and fourteenth proprietor being Winthrop, a playboy with two wives and no issue. Like all stories about Long Island, it ended with the cataclysm from which all recent history flowed: the Hurricane of '38. The bar had once been an isthmus connecting Cartwright with Gardiners Island until the hurricane washed it away.

The boat was free now, the mainsail luffing, but his father seemed preoccupied. He stood with the tiller between his legs, an Old Gold dangling from his mouth, scanning the dunes and grass and the narrow beach that stretched to the rising bluffs of the central island to the north. The hard glint of the white whale had been replaced by a dreamier, softer look.

"Best clamming in the bay is right around here."

He pulled in the main sheet a bit, and the boat eased along the shoal toward a white windmill up the shore. Still standing with the idle tiller gently flopping between his legs, H.'s father listened for the tug of an unseen force, like a pilot in a fog. Joe claimed he could feel the presence of clams like a dowser does water and eat a bushel at a sitting. Suddenly he kicked the tiller away from him, and the boat swerved toward shore.

"Drop anchor," he commanded his crew. H. threw over a cinder block on a rope which soon pulled taut, and the stern swung into the wind, about thirty yards from shore.

His father sat down on the stern seat and took off his sneakers and stuffed his socks in them. He removed his blue Brooks Brothers polo shirt and his undershirt. He took off his khaki trousers and folded them, making sure his keys and half-moon leather change purse were deep in the pockets. He put his Old Golds and Zippo in his broad-billed fishing hat and put it back on his head. Then he did something H. had never seen him do before. He stood, dropped his boxer shorts around his ankles, kicked them up, and caught them. H. looked away. He had never seen his father naked. H.'s family was close but reserved; they closed doors. H. was ill at ease in locker rooms and did not enjoy the camaraderie of nakedness. He believed that clothes, like fences, make good neighbors. He was utterly baffled by this new side of his father; he did not know the naked man, and he didn't want to.

He heard a splash. The old man was in the sea, up to his chest.

"What are you waiting for? Come on in."

H. was waiting for the waters of Gardiners Bay to part and swallow him.

He removed his shirt but kept on his white tennis shorts.

"Take off your goddam shorts, sissy. You'll be cold going home."

Mutiny and murder were waiting to enter H.'s heart. Had it been a proper boat—a Melville or Dana or Stevenson boat—he would have had a belaying pin or a marlinspike to hurl at the tyrant who would reel backward into the frothing sea, the white flash of a thousand teeth and the red foam on the black waves. But H.'s options on a knockabout were slender: the oar, some wood slats in the bilge, seat cushions, life vests, but no proper instrument—blunt or sharp. H. jumped overboard on the opposite side where his father could not see him. The water cooled his rebellious fever.

"They're not out there, for Chrissake! What are you afraid of?" His father was still shouting provocations from his side of the boat. H. could swim under it, grab his legs, pull him under like a turtle does the complacent swan, and drown him. It was not far-fetched, the plan—the bottom was alive with creatures that pinched if you stood still for a second. H. walked gingerly around the boat. Joe Stillman was now standing rapt: his face had the dreamy, upturned expression of a defecating dog, total concentration on something out of sight below. H. recognized the activity from the years of hearing about it; he was clamming with his toes. The old man whistled two notes and reached into the water, up to his shoulder. He retrieved a clam from his clenched toes and held it up, dripping sand and muck, for H.'s admiration, then threw it in the boat.

"Your turn," he said. "They're waiting for you."

H. hated clams; he was afraid of them. He had the born Catholic's conviction that eating fish was a punishment. He was suspicious of anyone who claimed to eat fish for pleasure. And to eat it raw—like the Japanese—that was all you needed to know about the recent enemy.

A jeep came bouncing over the dunes and headed down the beach toward them. There was a lone driver wearing a pith helmet.

"The law. We're caught, Dad. Let's go."

The jeep stopped on the sand, and the driver stood up in his vehicle. He wore khakis and a web belt with a big brown holster on it, like a safari guide. He watched the two men up to their chests in the water, the old man closer and the young one nearer the boat. Signs on metal stakes were driven in the sandy shallows up and down the beach.

His father kept at his clamming.

"On the beach, Dad, look. The gamekeeper or the clam warden. From the manor house."

The man shouted through his cupped hands, "You are trespassing. This property is posted by the owners, by the town."

"Come on, Dad. In the boat. Let's go."

His father threw another clam insolently into the stern. “Let me handle this. We were at St. Paul’s, Winthrop Gardiner and me.”

He began wading toward shore, gradually emerging, first the shriveled buttocks, then the thin legs.

H. shouted, “Dad, please. Come back.”

The older man turned to look at his cowardly son who saw for the first time his father’s uncircumcised penis, his grey and white pubic hair, and his wrinkled and sagging stomach.

“Goddam, sissy. Stay there and be quiet,” he said.

Then, like some beardless Poseidon, his father strode ashore, lured from his watery lair not by a rut for young virgins but by the lust for a clam. H. stayed near the boat. The lawman had dismounted from his jeep and stood at the water’s edge, the palm of his right hand resting on his holster, watching this primal Neptune leave the sea, his genitalia wagging, buttocks shivering, and walking more carefully as he crossed the tidal wash of smooth stones and pebbles before the sand. His father’s hand was extended to the man as he came up to him.

“Joe Stillman,” he said, explaining all.

H. was unable to watch this. He ducked under the water, and when he came up, the private policeman of Winthrop David Gardiner Jr., fourteenth proprietor of Gardiners Island, was shaking hands with the naked poacher of his lord’s shellfish.

“Glad to meet you, sir, but you’ll have to put back those clams. You passed a marker—”

“Best goddam clams on Long Island,” the old man told him. “Skip Harrington and I used to clam this beach before Little Hook broke off the point. There was a pier down a ways where the Jolly Morgan landed from Three Mile. Blew away in ’38—”

“There may have been a pier there once,” said the warden.

“Take my word there was. We came off the launch in patent leather pumps, the girls holding their skirts. They’d send a wagon down from the manor house—”

“The manor burned a year ago. There are no Gardiners here now.”

“No Gardiners?” Joe Stillman repeated.

“The island is leased to a party from Detroit.”

The lack of Gardiners was eerie, as if they too had disappeared along with the stone pier and the isthmus of their island in the Hurricane of ‘38. The certainty went out of Joe Stillman for a moment; he looked behind him for his son. H. was there; he had left the water to hear what they were saying.

"My son, Henry, he's a genuine Bonnacker."

"Don't start that, Dad," said the young man.

"I didn't get your name," Joe Stillman said to the warden.

"Solecki," the man said, a little unwillingly.

"East Hampton?"

"Greenport."

"North Fork," said Joe Stillman, identifying the inferior appendage of Long Island where a man named Solecki might live. "Henry was delivered by Doc Edwards at Green Cottage near—"

"Dad, this guy wants his clams. He doesn't care where I was born."

"Sorry to take your time," said his father.

"It's interesting to hear the local color," the man replied.

Joe Stillman had taken his Old Golds and Zippo from under his hat with one hand, the lighter held in his palm under the pack. He had a mechanic's manual dexterity. Still with one hand, he shook the pack and pressed the soft bottom with a finger until a cigarette stuck out from the hole in the torn foil. He offered it to Solecki who refused, then removed the cigarette directly with his lips. The finale to this act which consisted in getting the Zippo in front of the pack and lighting it was spoiled by Solecki who had his own Zippo waiting with a flame.

"You know Doc Richards?" Stillman asked him.

"Some of his clan, Captain Bobby and Ramsey."

"The doc used to whale with his brothers. They tried the blubber right down on the beach." He pointed to a distant landmark between the fish factory and the yacht club—a square tapered chimney rising from ruins and scrub oak.

"Hard to believe they whaled right off Napeague," said the warden, completely taken in by the story.

"They certainly did. Why, Felix Dominy and the Richards boys got their last whale only a couple of years back."

H. could stand it no longer. His father was making it up, the whole romantic fantasy.

"They didn't. They had their picture taken in a whaleboat in 1932, on land for a book. The last whale was taken in 1907. It's in the Museum of Natural History."

Both men looked at Henry.

"He doesn't want to be a Bonnacker, but he is. Just listen to him," said his father. "Delivered by an offshore whaler down in Green Cottage off Ocean Avenue, a hundred yards from the surf. His mother announced she was sick and tired of hospitals, intended to have her fifth where she damned pleased."

H. hated to be talked about. He was large enough, and being the subject of conversation doubled the space he took up. He interrupted his father, "Mr. Solecki doesn't care where I was born or who we are. He has birds to band, clams to count. Let's get out of here." And to the warden, he apologized. "I'm sorry we've bothered you. When Dad gets going, he's kind of hard to stop. We're just tourists, summer residents. We're leaving now." Joe was looking at his yellowed toenails and chewing his lip.

"Guess my boy wants to get along." He looked straight at Solecki. "We'll throw back the clams," he said.

"How many you get?" the man asked him.

"Half dozen maybe."

"Forget it," said the warden and shook Joe Stillman's hand. "Been nice talking."

While they were wading toward the boat, they heard the Rover lumber out of the sand in first gear. Joe stopped, chest deep in the tide, and turned on his son behind him. He was trembling with anger. "Don't you dare ever apologize for me again. You did it in front of that teacher at Oldfield and now with this fellow. You think you're so swell you have to be ashamed of me, is that it?"

H. had to pull his father into the boat which took away some of the old man's steam, but not much. "I've sailed this bay for forty years, and I don't need some smart aleck calling me a tourist."

"I'm not a Bonnacker."

"You were born here."

"By accident. A Bonnacker fishes for a living and has since 1603. He keeps his boat in Accabonac Harbor, not a yacht club."

"It's our bay too. We have nothing to apologize for." He was pulling on his trousers. "You talk like a Red."

When he had dressed, his father took a penknife from his pocket and pressed it against a secret place on the clam until it opened. He slipped the knife inside and cut a muscle that held the shells together and the meat to the shell. Then in a gesture of apparent reconciliation, he offered the clam to H. who recoiled. He knew exactly what his father was up to. He had been bullied with clams and oysters all his life, each one advertised as the particular clam that would put all others in the shade. Of the current bivalve, Joe Stillman proudly declared, "Here's the real McCoy. You've never had a clam straight from the sand. Tell me you have and I'll shut up."

H. could hear the syllogism being baited like a trap, but he was helpless to deny the first premise. "No, Dad. I never have."

"Then you don't know what you're missing."

"Yes, I do. That's why I want to miss it."

The logical vise was closing like the clam itself on his feeble protests.

"You'll never amount to a hill of beans if you're afraid to experiment. Edison even tried watermelon."

"For dessert?"

"For the incandescent filament, and you know goddam well what I mean."

H. may have lacked focus, but about clams and brussels sprouts, he knew his mind. He would sail, fish, try to waltz, read aloud to his parents from a terrible book called *We Took to the Woods* about a family who left civilization to live like the raccoon, but he would never eat another clam, and that was a rejection of Joe Stillman and all he believed in—salt water, the east, Thomas Edison, the scientific method, curiosity, experiment, appetite for the unknown. Worse, he was behaving like a woman, like Julia Chateau Stillman specifically. "You have your mother's thing about shellfish. No one from the Midwest even knows what a clam is. You think it's that piece of iced rubber that survives a two-week trip in a boxcar. I want you to forget every clam you ever ate." H. wished he could. "Because this is the first real, honest-to-God clam—"

"Dad, I'm not going to eat it, and I wish you wouldn't ask. I hate clams. It's nothing personal, believe me. We should start getting back." Because he was moved by H.'s plea, or more likely because he thought it would demonstrate that they were safe and good, Joe Stillman abruptly ate the divisive clam and shuddered with a palpable ecstasy. Even H. enjoyed, vicariously, the old man's pleasure. "You won't believe what that tastes like," exclaimed the older man.

He picked up a second clam.

"Dad, I believe. I really do. Leave it at that."

"You shouldn't take my word for it," Joe Stillman admonished him, inserting the blade in the clam's bowels.

"But I do. I take your word for everything. I believe it all." The Creed of Gardiners Bay rushed from his lips.

"I believe I was delivered by an offshore whaler, that the 1914 Packard ran on gin in a pinch, that you changed tires six times in white flannels between New York and East Hampton without getting them dirty, that you wore pumps with bows to Gardiners Island and danced 'til dawn in the manor house. I believe you can command the wind to blow for you when everyone else is luffing in irons, that reindeer fly in formation and rabbits lay colored eggs."

He wished he had shut up.

"I didn't mean that," said H.

Joe Stillman threw the half-opened clam overboard and closed his penknife. A distinct boom rolled over the water from the south. Joe Stillman didn't look. He threw the remaining clams in the water and kicked the weed and sand into the bilge between the wooden slats. H. looked toward the club. Twelve boats were staggered along the horizon, two just passing behind the committee boat. The race was over.

H. raised the mainsail, and they started the long, silent tack home. The only words spoken the first hour were "coming about." The club lay directly in the wind; they crossed the bay six times—Louse Point to the Napeague buoy to the water tanks to the fish factory to Barnes Landing to the Mackay radio towers. On the tack toward the chimney, the old man finally spoke, "I don't see you have so goddam much to brag about. No college will even touch you, and why should they? It was a mistake ever taking you away from your mother's Jesuits. You were better off wearing skirts. You're not man enough to meet real people."

It was Joe's old song; if you had his mother's religion, you had her mind and were ineducable, like all women. None of his sisters had been allowed to go to college. Joe couldn't believe that the theoretical basis of nuclear fission had been discovered by a woman. He thought that Lise Meitner's nephew, Otto Frisch, must have pointed her in the right direction, though he allowed that Madame Curie had isolated radium, a brute labor of endurance like housework, or Edison's search for the electric filament; he tried seven thousand materials including watermelon rind before stumbling on tungsten. Joe Stillman was a fossil of the steam age, a deadly rock that should be marked in red on every chart. H. was learning to steer around him.

"You're probably right," he said. Sailing with the old man was worse than driving with him. There was no place to escape, not even a filling station.

"Coming about," said his father, not much before pushing the tiller away from him. H. ducked. "That poor minister is in Tibet, I hear. You made his life such hell."

“About time he discovered hell. He’s on a paid vacation.”

“You’re riding for a fall, in my opinion. Someone’s going to cut you down to size.”

“I wish they would,” said H. He longed to be small and agile, like the wily Odysseus or Jimmy Bowes. Anything but this lumbering whale whose broad back was filling with harpoons and enemy hardware. Joe didn’t hear his son’s irony, but he caught the pain and backed off a bit. “I guess it’s not much fun for you here. You need people your own age.”

He didn’t need people of any age. He needed to be alone, back home in his father’s basement shop and lab, making holes in things with the drill press—the whirr of the one-horsepower motor and the finely focused power; the micrometer precision of the rack and pinion gears that moved the chuck; the rising pile of filings, like worm spore, where the bit entered; the wisp of smoke if the drill was dull. He had once watched his father use a tiny bit in the drill press to make a hole in his own thumbnail to release the pressure of a blood blister where he hit it with a hammer. The black blood spurted up and suffused over the nail. The pain was gone. He wiped off the blood with the same scorched and yellowed rag he used to clean the tip of his soldering iron after plunging it in a cup of acid flux. That was the man he loved and admired.

H. caught the mooring the first time. No praise from the helm; his father was really angry or hurt. He told H. not to furl the mainsail but to pull it off its track, pull out the battens, and stuff it in the sail bag. And the jib. And the rain gear. Everything was going ashore. “Dad,” H. began, not knowing where an apology would lead, but Joe cut him off.

“Time to cut our losses. Never too late.” Joe Stillman was quitting. He lashed down the boom and stowed the rudder as if another hurricane was coming. H. wished it would. Joe blew the Klaxon horn to signal the launch to pick them up. They had to sit there and wait.

“You better think what you’re going to do with your life before your options run out.”

“I’m going to join the army. I’m never going to school again, so please, please get off my back.”

“I felt the same way after St. Paul’s—” Joe began, but H. wasn’t listening. He had dived into the water and was swimming toward shore.

He reached the deserted beach just as the club launch was leaving the dock to pick them up. The sun was low behind the water tanks; the nannies and children had gone home. It was cocktail hour on the clubhouse deck.

GODPARENTS

Frankie Cromwell was sitting at her outdoor table under a striped umbrella. Behind her, the glass-paned doors to the dance floor were open to the afternoon breeze. Frankie was exactly where her chauffeur, Fitzwilliams, had placed her at lunchtime when he brought her to Gardiners Bay from the ocean where she had watched the children swim at the Maidstone Club all morning. Frankie could not move without Fitzwilliams and whomever else he could enlist to help him at moving time. She weighed over three hundred pounds, and her ligaments had stopped holding her together. Garmented in layers of diaphanous silk, she spread like the Nile wherever she was not impeded. They built dikes before setting her down, stuffing pillows in the interstices of chairs to contain her.

She wore a giant straw garden hat tied with a pink bow under the many rolls of her chins where freckles and moles rippled like waters stippled with pebbles and trout. Frankie was a glittering carousel festooned with baubles and trinkets on chains. Among the bric-a-brac on the fields of her bosom were pictures in oval frames, whistles, fans, sunglasses, amulets, salts, pince-nez, lorgnettes, and a pair of 800 x 20 power binoculars from Abercrombie & Fitch.

Frankie was H.'s godmother, and she was waiting for her men to return victorious from the races which she had watched from her table as she did everything else—the children and their nannies in the sand, the junior yacht club practicing seamanship in dinghies, the members eating hothouse tomatoes stuffed with chicken and avocado under the awning, the adolescents carrying Coke and ice cream from the snack bar window to the ping-pong room, and her husband, the commodore, mixing drinks for the vice commodore's wife in the cockpit of his ketch, *The No Nonsense*. Frankie was reading *Love in a Cold Climate* and eating cinnamon toast when her godson emerged dripping from the sea. She spoke with the throaty voice of the foghorn at Montauk.

"What were you two doing on Gardiners Island?"

"Clamming."

"Your father is insane. They shoot baymen who go out there."

"He talked the game warden out of six clams."

"Joe Stillman was the most dashing devil this island has ever seen."

H. had nothing to add to that. He shook the last water off and took a chair before a pile of cinnamon toast.

"What went wrong with your spinnaker?"

"We lost the pole."

"What were you doing before the wind anyway?"

"Dad had a plan." H. shifted uncomfortably. He was not an informer. She pushed the plate of cinnamon toast even closer to him.

"No, thank you."

"Indulge yourself," she commanded. "I do. I am a woman who has never been denied."

H. knew that wasn't strictly the case. She was making up for once having been denied, but she did have an enormous store of affection to lavish upon her godson. They had never met—until this summer. He knew her only as the source of the mint julep cup that arrived in a light blue box every birthday. "I intend to save you," she told him when they first met, but she had not yet told him from what.

"Are you going to Yale like your father or Princeton like Button?"

"Can you keep a secret? Because I may not, and Dad is going to have a major fit—"

"Look at me, child. Life is one terrible secret."

"If worst comes to worst, and the army is too risky, I might go to Harvard."

"Oh my god, never tell him. The first Stillman hated Harvard so much he moved to Providence."

"Ezra Stillman left the Bay Colony before Harvard was even founded."

"Harvard. It's full of Reds. Hooray! What a black sheep you've turned out to be. And what about you wrestling with the school minister in the chapel?"

"I never touched him. He tried to strangle me with my necktie."

"The last I heard you were going to be a Jesuit. Your father was ready to shoot you." H. winced to realize she knew about his brief vocation. "I ought to be taken out and shot. I never should have told him."

"You know he'd be happier living in the east. We'd take care of him. They don't understand him out there in the corn. Why doesn't your beautiful thin mother come to watch you race?" she asked him.

"It bores her, I think."

"She has never approved of us. Catholics turn up their noses at us Yankees. They think we boil everything, like Germans—beef, cabbage, fish, lobsters. She may have snared your father, but it isn't right for her to keep you all prisoners out there wherever it is—don't tell me." H. could see she wasn't really trying to remember.

"St. Louis," he said. His mother's city.

"Are you having a good time? I want you to be happy or you won't come back."

H. took a piece of cinnamon toast and told her about the clams which he had refused to eat. He felt guilty all over again.

"He wants you to love Gardiners Bay so much," she said.

"I can't sail with him anymore."

"He hasn't got his sea legs back yet," she said.

H. looked up the walk toward the bathhouses and lockers where his father was still changing. He leaned close to Frankie so the other tables couldn't hear.

"Frankie," he asked her, "does Dad really know how to sail?"

"What did you say?"

"He says he used to win every race, that nobody could beat him."

"He goddam well did." Her affirmation was like a sonorous belch you could hear in the parking lot. "Joe Stillman was so far ahead of the pack, people said he had a motor."

"We could use a motor," said H.

"Stay with him. He'd be lost without you."

"I make it worse, Frankie. I'm driving him crazy. And vice versa."

She put her hand with a dozen rings and bracelets on his. "I looked at you two going out on the tender and fiddling with the gear on the boat. He's so happy. It's just like it was when—"

She stopped herself and looked at him. "You don't know how much he misses Button. You never knew him." H. shifted uneasily. "I'm not going on about how you resemble him. I know you don't want to be told any more than I like to hear how thin I was in 1919."

She was right; he didn't like it that he was a copy of someone he had never known. "He wants me to be Button, he wants me to eat clams like Button and skinny-dip off Gardiners Island like Button. I'm not Button. I can't be, and I won't. I hate sailing. I'm sorry."

"It's taken your father all he's got to come back. You can't desert him now."

"I'm not sailing with him anymore."

"Hold your horses, young man. Button and I took a solemn vow in that wretched church where your mother dragged us to be your goddam godparents. Now Button's dead, it's just me. And I'm telling you, no one jumps ship. Not now. When someone dies like Button, it makes everyone of us feel like we're responsible. It's terrible. Think what you father is feeling, coming back here. No wonder it took him eight years."

H. heard her. Dies like Button did. She was saying Button had killed himself. It wasn't a stroke or a heart attack or whatever.

"How did Button die?"

"He hanged himself. Didn't you know?"

"We thought he killed himself somehow. But none of us were sure."

Frankie was appalled. "They never told you?"

"No. How did he do it? Where?"

"From the furnace. In the basement on Lily Pond Lane."

H. had always imagined he used a gun. They were staying in the house where he did it. At Aunt Phoebe's.

"Why?" he asked her.

She shook her head; she didn't know. Then she said, "Maybe they were just all too close—Button, Joe, your grandmother Abigail. She was a terror. The hurricane in '38, that was Abigail coming back to find her teeth. It was her dying I think. They were all split up. Joe was gone to the west. Button was all alone."

"What about Phoebe?"

Frankie looked at him. "What about her?"

H. knew what Frankie meant. "She's a child, Henry. A sweet child. That's not company."

His father was coming along the boardwalk, showered and spiffy in a tweed jacket and grey flannels. He flicked his cigarette into the sand as he came up the steps to the deck. Frankie caught him before he had even sat down.

"You boys need some help."

"How so?" he asked innocently.

"You need a crew."

"I've got Henry. Is he complaining?" He looked at the tattletale.

"He didn't say a thing. *I'm* saying."

"We're doing fine, Frankie, just fine."

"Joe Stillman," she fairly bellowed, "you can't even get your goddam spinnaker up!"

There was a brief hush among the members; even the waiters were silent. But it was water off a duck's back. "We nearly had it up. If Henry hadn't dropped the pole." He lit a cigarette.

Frankie almost stood, which was thought to be impossible. Instead she took her lorgnettes from the shelf of her bosom, and holding the mother-of-pearl handle, she moved the glasses back and forth until she had the villain pinned like a specimen in the focus of the lens.

"Ahab," she hissed at him. "Peg leg."

"We're done with the goddam boat. So don't get your wind up." He looked around for a waiter.

"That is childish, Joe. And ridiculous."

"Henry should be meeting people his own age. We're all agreed. Nothing more to say." He ordered a bourbon toddy.

A second hush fell over the deck whose tables were filling for cocktails. A couple had just come up the steps. The man was tall and elegant in a double-breasted seersucker jacket and red pants. She was familiar—a small, compact blonde woman made almost his height by what looked like glass platform shoes. The continuing silence was caused by the fact that she was wearing a cellophane dress. They took a table near Frankie's, by the railing of the deck. The man nodded to her as he sat. The woman arched her neck and looked out to sea, turning her back on the thick censure that hung in the air. Her handbag was on the table, a Plexiglas cube whose contents seemed frozen in ice—a box of English cigarettes, compact, lipstick, car keys, Kleenex. The cellophane of her dress was a clear window on the woman within—the slip, the brassiere, an inoculation scar on her upper right arm.

"That's young Gardiner, Winthrop Jr.," his father whispered to his son, then leaned over to Frankie. "What in god's name does he have with him?"

"Number Three," she shot back, "and you both know who she is."

Lana Turner? Rita Hayworth? Irene Dunne? They couldn't guess. Frankie had to tell them how the island's childless heir, Winthrop Jr., had sold it to his aunt to finance frivolities whose latest instance was Number Three—the world-champion figure skater, Sonja Henie, who now gazed forlornly at her new husband's lost patrimony, the paradise leased only four miles away.

Joe Stillman turned and stared, unabashed, at the perfidious heir, his classmate's son, Winthrop Jr.—three wives, no issue, the manor burned, the island leased to duck hunters from Detroit. "There's a rotten apple in every barrel" was his judgment.

H. felt the beam of his father's scorn leave the unworthy scion and his cellophane mate and slowly sweep the circumference of the club like the Montauk Light. It was about to fall upon him, the quintessential rotten apple, when Frankie did her most remarkable thing.

She made a piercing, oscillating shriek on a silver police whistle she picked from the junkyard around her neck—her summons to Fitzwilliams. The club members ignored the blast. The chauffeur appeared with several waiters who helped him to raise and bear Frankie to her limousine—a landau touring car with an enclosed driver's cab, covered with black crinkled leather, and an open rear seat nested in the canvas folds of the retracted roof—an assassination vehicle for a Hapsburg prince. Frankie raised an immense multicolored parasol over herself and was driven away very slowly, at a walking pace. She was never hurried.

Julia Chateau Stillman and her sister-in-law, Phoebe Carter Stillman, sat under hanging baskets of fuchsia enjoying the afternoon breeze from over Hook Pond that bent from view behind rushes and reeds until it reached the far dunes. They were on Phoebe's porch having their second bourbon toddies when the men came home from the sea. "How was the race?" "Bad wind," said Joe. "Henry lost the spinnaker pole." H. had held his temper long enough. "I wouldn't have lost it if Kornfeld was here. We need more crew. There was plenty of room in the house for him." He directed this to Phoebe, who was a delicate small woman with a face prematurely wrinkled and aged as if she had seen a ghost, which H. now understood to be the body of Button hanging in the basement. It changed everything.

"We're not racing anymore. Boat's going back to the yard. Henry doesn't want to sail."

"You don't sail! You run aground, you poach clams, you bore strangers with how I was delivered by an offshore whaler between chases, you make me lie in the bilge."

His mother was distressed. Though Julia was tall, even stately, she was a far cry from the thin vampire Frankie Cromwell imagined her. Both she and Phoebe had married into South Fork; they could take it or leave it alone. Neither had the native's primal lust for clams, surf, the wheel's kick, or snappers on the breakwater. Their passion, if any, was for box hedge.

Julia Stillman described Aunt Phoebe as a Carter from Virginia as if that accounted for everything, and Phoebe probably thought of her as a Chateau from St. Louis. Julia could have survived without her pedigree, but Phoebe's only armor was the Carters. She was an aspen leaf; if you blew on her, she danced, shimmered, scattered light like a sequin. The first day they stayed with her, she asked H. to drive her to Bohacks, the nearby market, because her car was sitting broken in the garage. She was ashamed to have it towed, but it wasn't safe to drive.

"What's wrong with it?"

"The horn won't work."

H. pried the cap off the horn button and cleaned the salt corrosion from the contacts. It honked like new.

Looking at Phoebe through the eyes of his newfound godmother, H. found her innocence not charming but dangerous. She had failed Button. And she had failed H. as well. He needed Kornfeld to survive.

Joe had just settled into a wicker chair with a toddy when the phone rang. Phoebe answered it in the pantry and returned to say Frankie Cromwell commanded everyone's presence at cocktails the next day. The commodore would be there. Phoebe had declined and sent Julia to answer for her family. Joe refused loudly to go. "They're your friends, not mine!" Julia shouted. "You chose the woman for a godmother, not me." She accepted for them all. Phoebe screamed at her. "I said I'm not going, and I won't!" The Carter from Virginia wanted no truck with Frankie or her commodore. All they did at the yacht club was swap wives except for Frankie who was referee and scorekeeper for obvious reasons. Joe Stillman smiled. "There's a new girl on the block. You ought to go out and have a look."

"Sonja Henie, I heard," said Phoebe. "Winthrop Gardiner should be ashamed of himself." Julia's ears pricked up at the mention of her favorite actress after Deanna Durbin, the Catholic Woman of the Year.

"Sonja Henie? Where?" H. burrowed into his wicker chair while they dissected the hapless Gardiners, their island, their bay, and their women.

The next day, Phoebe went to a meeting of the Ladies Village Improvement Society to discuss the snapping turtles in the pond that were grabbing the feet of the swans and pulling them into a watery grave, as H. had thought of doing to Joe at Gardiners Island. She sent her regards to Frankie and the commodore who met them on Lily Pond Lane as H. was parking in the lee of a hedge ten feet tall around Frankie's house. Jack Cromwell was a beautiful man, tall with snow-white hair curling from under his yachting cap and wreathing his ruddy and weathered face. Not just the double-breasted blue blazer and white trousers with subliminal ivory stripes but the cravat embroidered with his ensign, a swallow-tailed flag with red stripes, all proclaimed the commodore. In real life, he was a surgeon who never left his hospital, just as in summer he never left his boat. His appearance on dry land meant something was in the wind.

"Frankie put you up to this. What does she want?" was his father's accusation as he got out of the station wagon. The commodore ignored the provocation and opened the gate in a fantastical topiary hedge of hounds nipping the skirts of dancing gingerbread girls. Within these antic battlements was concealed an ivy-covered cottage with thatched roof. Frankie awaited them, laid out on a chaise in the patio. Behind her, the French doors to the living room had been permanently removed to allow entrance to the ivy which covered the ceilings and walls and festooned the bannisters; the chamber was like a rabbit hole, alive and growing with roots and vines.

After a slight hesitation, as if she were looking for an undiseased patch among acres of flesh, Julia Stillman kissed Frankie near her ear. His mother had always been wary of her; she had known her when the latter weighed ninety-four pounds and was her chief rival for the hand of Joe Stillman, the young electrical wizard who drove his Packard back and forth from Lake Placid to East Hampton to court the women and dance until dawn. They had both been beauties in their flapper days, and Julia still preserved a hint of her past. It was Frankie, she believed, who had sent Joe Stillman the autumn leaf in a pale envelope which had cast a shadow on the first September of her marriage to the engineer. They had chosen Frankie and Button for his godparents, two Protestant hedonists still reeling from the bootleg twenties, and made them responsible for H.'s Catholic upbringing if Julia died. It was a nightmare arrangement she regretted every day since. "I must have been under the influence of all that gas they gave me for the baby to agree to such a thing," she once told H., in an attempt to explain away his dreadful godmother.

But a stranger from St. Louis had no choice, she didn't know a Catholic in all of New York state except the laundress; all she knew was Joe and Button's gang—Episcopalian friends from school and college and the women they squired. Julia had first met Frankie at the Lake Placid Club in the Adirondacks before the first war, when they were both chasing the dashing Joe Stillman who brought along his St. Paul's roommate to squire the "other woman," whichever she turned out to be, and eventually that was Frankie. She danced away her beautiful, thin youth with Jack Cromwell and married him when she despaired of catching Joe. It was Jack Cromwell who lied about the midnight skating at St. Paul's when only Joe was expelled and Joe never really trusted Jack after that. Asking Frankie to be H.'s godmother was Joe's attempt to put things right. But Frankie remained bitter, more so after Button died, and it was Julia Stillman's suspicion that Frankie's present ruin was her living rebuke to Joe Stillman for marrying a Catholic from St. Louis and moving west, and her grand revenge would be to seduce his son with sugar and immoral ideas and bring him east. H. knew his godmother's saga by heart, hence his reluctance to accept her cinnamon toast. He was a pawn in a war between women, which made him understand why men kept themselves far apart, in offices, clubs, forts, and boats. Even now, Joe Stillman and Jack Cromwell were talking on the lawn, fifty feet from the women on the patio. H. joined them.

"You and Henry could use some help out there," the commodore was saying.

"The hell we can," his father replied.

"Joe, these little knockabouts, they aren't like the old Star boats—"

"I sailed a knockabout on Buzzards Bay before you ever saw one."

"Listen to me, Joe. Those old Stars had a half-ton keel. The truth is they sailed themselves—"

"Don't tell me how to sail, goddam it. Is that what all this is about?" Joe Stillman's voice was rising. The women were looking.

"Come on, Joe. You didn't even cross the starting line yesterday. Or Saturday either. You went off on some tangent downwind—"

"That's a perfect lie," said his father. "Take it back."

"There are five judges to say you didn't. Christ Almighty, Joe, we can't sit on the line all day waiting for you to make up your mind whether you intend to race or go to Nantucket—"

"I don't mean to inconvenience your goddam race committee. Not that you've got anything better to do but sit on your rear ends all afternoon and fire a toy cannon."

"We fire it three times, Joe. Warning, start, and finish," the commodore reminded him, still in good humor.

"A real day's work," his father replied, unsmiling. He turned and walked toward a small bear, about three feet high, alone in the center of the lawn. It was Winnie the Pooh sitting on a chair reading a copy of A. A. Milne, the whole thing a topiary sculpture from box hedge. The commodore went into the house. Julia Stillman put on her blue-tinted glasses. Frankie watched Joe talking to Pooh Bear.

"Don't you dare corrupt that bear!" she shouted at Joe who didn't even turn. "Pooh was made for you, Henry, your first birthday present," she said.

"Nineteen thirty-three, what a dreadful year. First Hitler and then Roosevelt. We were desperate for relief. And you arrived, just like the Redeemer, while your beautiful mother was on sojourn, not quite in a manger but in that dreary cottage on the beach, delivered by the town doctor between whale chases. It called for celebration, something really special. I told the gardeners, 'Make me something gay, make me laugh.' Mr. Edward Bear, a.k.a. Pooh."

H.'s mother smiled at the description of her fifth and final accouchement.

"You didn't expect me to stay in St. Louis in the summer, I hope, just to have Henry. The British consul gets hardship pay for roughing it in our little backwater and the jungle kit—malaria pills and mosquito netting—"

"If it's so terrible out there," Frankie asked, "why have you stayed away from us for ten years?"

"The war, or was it the hurricane—," began his mother, very vaguely, with an anxious glance toward her husband who was still talking to the hedge. It was her rule never to be caught alone with Frankie who was looking at her through her lorgnettes, just as she had her husband. "It was Button," Frankie said. "Why don't you say so?"

Julia ignored her. "I remember. We tried to come, in '42, and look what happened. The Germans landed right on the beach at Amagansett where the children play. They left dynamite, and Lord knows what else buried there in the sand where Henry or Joe Jr.—"

"Julia," said Frankie, "the saboteurs didn't land in Amagansett just to kidnap Henry."

"They had a submarine waiting just off the bar, didn't they?" Julia countered. "They could have taken the children back to Berlin and held them for ransom."

"Roosevelt would never have paid it, not for Republicans," said Frankie.

"It just seemed safer to stay in Missouri, and where was Joe? Off fishing somewhere, in Wyoming," his mother said, becoming unexpectedly sad and serious. "They bomb Dresden, they bomb Coventry and Monte Cassino, but who wants to bomb St. Louis? We'd have to pay to have it bombed, and we're the ones who really need it. St. Louis never had a really good fire." She was genuinely rueful.

Julia Chateau's ancestors had settled in St. Louis. Her family had owned blocks and blocks of riverfront. To a young girl in 1904, the city of St. Louis and the Louisiana Exposition were the center of the universe. But she had watched the city grow shabby in the decades following the fair while Chicago and San Francisco rose from the ashes of fire and earthquake with new vitality. She still owned property downtown, but she was serious about bombing it. She mourned St. Louis, this city she loved, because it had never burned, just as she mourned Dresden because it had. Behind her blue-tinted glasses, there were tears. Her firm belief that there was a life to come did not give her the comfort it gave others. The same God who allowed the current state of affairs was also in charge of the hereafter. Why expect any improvement?

The commodore returned, wearing half-moon spectacles on his nose and carrying an open book, *The Rules and Bylaws of the United States Yacht Racing Union*. He went straight to Joe Stillman who was sitting on the grass facing Pooh. Standing over the two men, the commodore read them the rules of the starting line. "A boat shall rank as a starter, which, after the starting signal, crosses the starting line within such a period as will permit the committee boat to proceed to the next mark prior to the lead racing boat." The commodore thought that the issue was very well stated. Joe Stillman said he liked Pooh's book better. He pulled himself to his feet and stooped for his empty toddy glass.

"What do you want, Jack?" he asked him.

"Just this. Henry here is pretty new to the water. I want to find one of the juniors, someone his age, to show him the ropes."

"We're done sailing, so you can stop all this goddam plotting, all of you," he said loudly for the ladies too. "Henry's going to play ping-pong, tennis, meet people his age, like he ought to. Now leave me alone." He walked through a hole in the hedge and was gone.

These old friends had started the little yacht club as a place for their children to learn to swim and sail. Joe had endowed the Stillman Bowl for Most Improved Seamanship in the junior yacht club. With Jack Cromwell, they had scuttled the Star boats in storms to keep them from being blown to Connecticut and lured a first-class maitre d' from Manhattan to run the restaurant. No one thought an interpretation of silly rules could come between them. But everyone was relieved that Joe Stillman had sworn off racing.

Frankie called H. to her side while the commodore was walking Julia to the car. "Go to the snack bar before the race tomorrow. Ask for Albert." "Who's he?" said H. "Someone who wants to meet you," said his fairy godmother.

H. and his mother combed the surrounding lanes looking for Joe Stillman without success. He had walked back to Phoebe's and gone off in her Dodge.

They were making dinner when he returned. He got out of the car with a big shopping bag, but he never came inside. In a while, they heard hammering in the basement which was reached from a stairwell outside the house. H. was sent down to call him for supper. He thought they ought to leave Joe alone, but he obeyed; he wanted to see the basement and what Joe was doing. From the bottom of the stairwell, he couldn't see his father at first; there was a stack of fertilizer bags and garden lawn seed just inside. Near the door was a bench with a board clamped in a vise and a clothesline leading from it into the dark recess of the basement. Joe was back there holding the other end of the rope. H. could just make out the ganglia of the furnace behind him. It was ridiculous to imagine he had interrupted Joe Stillman preparing to hang himself. But he did.

"You want some swordfish?" H. asked.

"You want to see something cute?"

"What?"

"I'll show you tomorrow."

"Where?"

"The starting line."

"I'm not sailing, Dad. I mean it."

Joe emerged from the darkness holding a galvanized steel bucket in which he coiled the clothesline, without any hint that he had been about to attach the line to a furnace duct like the branch of a dead oak in the shadows. Button must have used one of the ducts; they were the only things high enough to loop a rope around. The hot air ducts looked flimsy; rusty hanger straps were nailed to the old beams, any sudden weight would pull it down. H. definitely would have chosen to shoot himself. Joe nested the bucket he was holding with another on the bench.

"What is all that?" H. asked him.

"Come to the race tomorrow, you'll find out."

"Dinner's ready."

"Jack will take you on the committee boat. You ought to see a proper start. It'll give you a kick." Joe began to drill a hole in the board in the vise, and H. left.

H., his mother, and Phoebe poked at their swordfish. A half hour later, Joe still hadn't come up. It was quiet below. "What's keeping him? What's he doing?" His mother's voice had an edge. Phoebe cut around the brown part of the fish with her knife. She was sitting directly over the furnace where Button had hanged himself. H. would have moved to another house. Suicide is hereditary. It runs in families.

Then they heard him slam the basement door. H. was ashamed of what he had been thinking. Joe Stillman wasn't going to kill himself; he was just trying to get away. His father had to have a basement, a place where he could be alone. A laboratory where women didn't follow him. And H. saw he was no different; he had the same feeling of suffocation, the same need to escape. He had seized the rug box to escape the adoration of Donna Hasenclever and Ms. Finch and her clay. H. didn't want to be like his father, or Button. The thought scared him, that he was like Button; everyone said he was. He would rather have been like Jimmy Bowes, the life of the party, but he would never be like Jimmy Bowes in a million years. When Joe Stillman came to the table, H. excused himself and went to the only telephone in the house, in the pantry, to call Jimmy Bowes. It took ten minutes for the operator in Riverhead to reach Block Island about twenty miles and four ferries away. Jimmy Bowes answered, but the connection was bad, as if the signal was leaking into the water around the wires. H. wanted to come to Block Island for the weekend, but Bowes was going to Nantucket on somebody's boat.

"I have to get out of here. I'm going crazy. I'm going to kill someone," said H.

"Your old man?"

"Myself," said H.

"Don't you know anybody?"

"No." Bowes knew everybody in every city of America. It was his vocation. He was never alone.

"Where is this place? Amagansett?"

"Southwest of you about twenty miles."

"I mean what's it near, Southampton?"

"East Hampton. It's east of East Hampton."

"I've never heard of it. Who goes there?"

"I don't know. I don't know anyone. I told you."

"Try this. I forgot where she lives exactly. Alberta Bang. Try her old man. Constantine Bang, he owns ships. They may not be listed."

"Bang?"

"B-A-N-G. She's the hottest piece I've ever met. I mean she's got knockers like basketballs."

"B-A-N-G," H. repeated dubiously.

"It's Norwegian. And don't screw this one up, babes, you hear me? Don't pull another Marla Starker." Bowes knew him. If anyone could, he would screw it up.

"Where did you meet her?"

"Bermuda. She's sensational."

He was looking for Bang in the Suffolk directory.

"I don't see it."

"Oh shit. He's not her father, he's her stepfather. I don't know what Constantine's name is."

There was no Bang in the Suffolk County directory, from Amityville to Montauk.

THE EAST WIND

The ensigns of three commodores were flying from the yard arms on the yacht club mast. Knockabouts from clubs on Shelter Island and Orient Point had crossed Gardiners Bay for the regatta, the great race of the summer, followed by the regatta dinner dance. The parking lot was full, and the dock was crowded with visitors. Julia drove H. to the club because Joe had taken the station wagon before anyone was up. She let him out by the tennis courts. He had agreed to take lessons and to let the pro arrange a match for him with someone his age. He might actually make a friend before the summer was over. When he opened the car door, it was apparent the wind had shifted. The overpowering stench of the fish factory hung over the bay like phosgene at Ypres. It was a sweet and rotting smell that went directly to the stomach and pulled its contents back up the esophagus. Seasoned members ignored the stink like they did Frankie's police whistle.

The pro introduced him to his opponent, a taciturn sun-bleached girl whose name he did not catch and which she would not repeat. H. played tennis with his mouth tightly closed to keep down the taste of vomit around his Adam's apple. The girl had a vicious serve. H. lost the first set 6-0. In the second set, his father, wearing his sailing clothes, appeared on the sand-covered walk between the courts. He had a curious load; the paper bag H. knew contained the buckets, a hank of clothesline, some boards, the sail bag, and a new spinnaker pole. H. double-faulted four times. "You want something, Dad? I'm trying to play tennis."

"I bought a new spinnaker pole. It's aluminum, it floats."

"I see."

"If you want to come—"

A whistling serve shot past him.

"You're not breathing," said the old man.

"I can't breathe. The stink," said H.

"Good for your lungs," said his father, taking a deep breath. He loved fish in any form.

His opponent won the second set and left the court without speaking to him.

Walking around the clubhouse on the sand, he saw her sitting at a table outside the snack bar with two equally thin and brittle girls. Their heads were together to suck straws from a single Coke bottle. H. did not go up on the deck but leaned against a piling where he could hear them talking above. No matter how sensational their gossip, they pretended to be bored. He expected the victress to be ridiculing his tennis, but the whispered subject was the Whore of Napeague. They wouldn't be her for a million dollars. Name one real thing about her. Her tits were full of Kleenex, and all that hair—it was peroxide, or even a wig. No one respected her; it was really disgusting the way she sucked up to the commodore. Did you ever see such a dirty old man? A real fanny pincher. Everyone knew why she got the Whosie Whatsis Cup last year—for Most Improved Ass Wiggling. Wouldn't you try to hide it if you had all that fat? She was pathetic.

H. left his concealment to find something at the snack bar to take the fish taste out of his mouth. The three girls watched silently as he came up the steps. The snack bar was a long window into the kitchen with a hinged shutter that hooked on a beam above, exposing a rough counter. A young man leaned with his elbows on the counter behind him. He was talking to the rear end of a girl next to him who was stretched so far into the kitchen over the bar that her crossed legs were in the air. Her white shorts were rolled up as far as they would go, an inch above the crease of her buttocks. She slid down from the counter and on to her feet, a big girl—ripe and overflowing—licking a double-dipped vanilla and chocolate ice cream cone encrusted with red-and-green sprinkles.

She was a double-dipped cone herself—two chins and apple cheeks around lips that were pink as a white rabbit's nose and frosted with chocolate cream.

A white man's shirt with its tails tied in a knot above her navel was losing the battle to contain her. The dimple of her belly button rolled from below, and the buttons above strained to retain her breasts, which pressed every seam for an exit. Golden hair was caught up in two pigtails but elsewhere tumbled over her freckled face from under a striped engineer's cap. H. had to look away; he leaned over the counter to find the Filipino who ran the bar.

The young man on her left was leaving, angrily. "He should have told you sooner," he complained.

"I'm really sorry, but you know Constantine. He won't sail in an east wind."

"See you around, Albert," he said, taking the three steps to the sand in one stride.

H. looked around. There was only the girl licking her cone. "I'm Albert," she said.

"I'm H.," he said.

"I can call you just H.?" He nodded. He had seen her once before, just her head, above the topsides of a boat while they were jockeying for position before the first race. They had never been that near another boat again.

"Where you guys going today?" she asked him.

"Where?" said H. in surprise.

"You're number 9, aren't you?" Maybe they were; he couldn't read the number on their sail from the deck.

"You got caught in Plum Gut."

"That's us," he said, pleased to be famous.

"They almost called the coast guard."

"The coast guard?" He hadn't known.

"Will you tell me the truth? Are you really racing?"

"My father is a physicist. He tests theories."

"A physicist?" She looked dubious.

"An inventor really."

"What's he invented?"

"I can't tell you."

"It's secret?"

"I shouldn't be talking about it at all."

Albert whistled; she understood secrets. "I knew something was queer. You didn't even cross the starting line last time. You went to Gardiners Island."

"We did, yes. We were poaching."

"Poaching, Jeeeee-sus." She was impressed.

"Clams. And skinny-dipping."

"Skinny-dipping." Her eyes, which were immense, dilated to twice their size. "My brother and I skinny-dip at Napeague," she admitted, then blushed. Violet, cherry, orange.

"Napeague," he repeated as if the part about her skinny-dipping didn't interest him.

"We live there," she explained, "on top of an old coast guard battery."

He was talking to the Whore of Napeague. It wasn't Kleenex in her tits, and it wasn't a wig. She was a Fragonard, a Renoir, a vision from the age of flesh, a sunburst of vitamin C. And she seemed to find his exploits wonderful, all the boring hours of tyranny with Joe Stillman on Gardiners Bay. He hoped she would never finish her ice cream cone, but he could see the club launch filling with boat crews to be ferried to the moorings. It was race time.

"I guess you better get to your boat," he said.

She shook her head midlick. "Constantine won't sail in an east wind."

"The smell?"

"He won't even leave the house. And it's worse on the water." She ate the whole cone.

"You better go, you'll be late."

"I'm not sailing either," he said.

"You aren't?"

"I can't sail with my father anymore."

"Why?"

"I want to kill him."

"Your own father?" The idea interested her.

"So do I," she said. "I make hangman's nooses all over the boat when he isn't looking."

H. shook his head. "You should drown him, make it look accidental."

"But you have fun with your father, you do crazy things—"

"Science is not that fun, believe me."

"I have to pull Constantine off the sand and mud all day long. And off me," she added.

"A dog?"

"My stepfather. He's Greek."

Albert was transfigured by a thought; she forgot to close her mouth, and her eyes dimmed. "Would your father let me crew for him?" she asked.

"I don't think so."

"Why not?"

"He says women shouldn't be allowed on boats."

"He wouldn't go skinny-dipping if I was there. Is that what you mean?"

"Boats are for getting away from people—women in particular."

"I'm different. He'll see."

"It's no fun, believe me."

"Anything's better than hanging around here. Can I ask him?"

"You can try." She was already running down the steps past the three thin girls with their Coca-Cola who stared as H. ran to catch up with her on the long dock. He overtook her by the sailing dinghies that hung off the dock on davits, the fleet of the junior yacht club. The launch was about to leave, already top heavy and listing from the load. Albert shouted, "Wait for us!"

The tide was out, and the launch, a wide whaling dory, was a big jump down from the dock. As they appeared at the dock's edge, the occupants looked up and shouted back, "Don't let her on!"

"No room. We'll sink!"

"Overload. Napeague Albert's coming!"

"Her jelly rolls will keep us afloat!"

"Look who's talking, lard ass!" Albert cried merrily as she jumped into their midst, landing on a pile of sail bags and life vests.

The benches along the hull were filled, and they squeezed into a space atop the engine housing as the wide whaleboat began its circuit of the moorings. Albert was popular; she talked and joked with everyone, even the few fathers aboard. She had grown up over the summers in this place; they knew each other.

H. had been the largest of his peers; even in kindergarten, he was a mountain among mice. At eighteen he was tall, but not the sore thumb he had once been. He could tell that Albert had always been large and precocious for her age. The jokes had begun in summers past, but the jokers now failed to see what H. saw—she had become a voluptuous woman. He had the luck to see it first, but he would not be alone for long.

The commodore waved to them as they passed his ketch. He was standing at the helm, one hand on the binnacle, talking to Sonja Henie. Winthrop Jr.'s tall figure emerged through the hatch from below with a bucket of ice. When H. told

Albert who they were, she exclaimed how beautiful the Norwegian athlete was. He remembered the silence on the clubhouse deck for the world's champion figure skater and was glad the commodore had invited her aboard the *No Nonsense.* The committee boat was pulling alongside the ketch to take the commodore and his guests aboard. It was all teak and striped canvas with a knifelike prow and a mast with yards and halyards from which dozens of flying pennants told the racecourse for those who could interpret them.

Beyond the ketch, they caught their first sight of Joe Stillman's boat. It looked deserted—no sails, no activity, no Joe Stillman. "I saw him going out. He had a ton of junk with him," H. said uncertainly. Only when they came alongside did they see the old man, flat on his back on the floorboards with his head and shoulders under the stern seat. He was surrounded by a cat's cradle of tangled rigging, clothesline, pulleys, pieces of wood, and, on the seat above him, the two galvanized buckets upended with ropes coming out of holes he had punched in the bottoms. H. shouted at him, "Someone wants to crew for you!"

"Just in time," the old man said, his head still under the seat.

"Not me. Someone else."

Albert jumped into the boat, pulling H. with her. "You can't leave," she said. The pilot gunned the dory and left them. They were stuck.

"Do you see a pair of long nose pliers around?" His father's right hand was already raised in expectation. He handed his father the pliers.

"Someone here wants to crew for you," H. repeated.

"Can you put a little tension on that line by your feet?" his father asked. H. picked up the rope and pulled it taut.

"What is all this?" he asked.

"The Stillman Bucket Drag," said its inventor. "Now slack off on that line."

Joe Stillman wriggled from under the seat and felt with both hands for his glasses. H. nudged them into his reach with his foot. The old man sat up.

"It's time to stop playing around. I'm going to show this crowd a thing or two."

With one hand, he hooked a flexible wire stem of his glasses over his left ear, laid the pearl nose pads on the bridge of his nose, then pulled the other stem over the right ear. He got to his feet. Now he saw Albert.

"Who you got with you?"

"This is Albert."

"Alberta Bang," said the girl. H. turned.

"Bang?" he asked.

"You're dead," she answered, unsmiling.

It was the girl Jimmy Bowes had told him about, with boobs as big as basketballs. He had found her, by accident. Joe took the rope H. was holding and jerked it. It came free.

"Goddamit," he swore. "This is no time for visiting. The warning cannon is about—"

"She wants to crew for you."

Joe dismissed the offer. "I don't need crew. I may not even race. I haven't decided." He got back on his knees to crawl under the transom seat.

"I can sail," said Albert. "Let me show you."

"Thanks just the same." Joe's head and shoulders had disappeared again.

H. looked apologetically at Albert. Her presence made him almost forget the stench of the fish factory. "I'll stay if she does. Okay?"

Joe pushed himself from under the seat and looked up at Albert. "You look like a smart girl," he said. Albert may have been smart, but she didn't look smart. His father was saving face, looking for a way to justify an exception to his law. No women.

"A race is won at the starting line. Did you ever hear that?" he asked her.

"I've heard it, yes, sir," she answered politely.

"Well, I was the best goddam starter this bay has ever seen, and I'll tell you the secret. Keep your wind. Never let it go."

"Keep your wind, right," said H.

"The trick is to be on course at the cannon, come hell or high water. You want to charge that line like sixty, like an Indy 500 skidding into the curve. What do you need to do that? Brakes, you're going to say. But a boat's got no brakes. It's got to lose wind to slow down. That's when you need the Stillman Bucket Drag."

Alberta Bang was mesmerized by the old man. H. was suffocating from the increasing odor of the fish factory on the stiffening wind but mostly from Joe Stillman's patented bombast—smothering and didactic, like being under the tailgate of a dump truck full of cotton. And he knew who his audience was. He went straight for Albert.

"I'm going to show you how to cross a line, and you're going to see that tin-pot admiral eat his goddam words."

"What admiral?" Albert asked.

"The commodore," H. said, hoping to head off his father on the subject.

"The son of a sea cook claims we didn't cross the starting line on Wednesday," Joe told her. Albert listened with a poker face. She knew they hadn't crossed it.

"Jack Cromwell is a tinsel sham," said his oldest friend and St. Paul's roommate. "He hasn't weighed anchor on that boat of his since '38. All he does out there is make ice."

Joe Stillman laughed at his own joke, and Albert laughed too because the whole junior yacht club knew that the commodore made more than ice on the *No Nonsense*. Even H. knew that. But Albert had passed Joe's test, and he made her a proposition. "How would you like to be my test engineer?" he asked.

H. was primed to explode. He was Joe's test engineer, ever since he'd been expelled from kindergarten. He had worked his way up—first locating burning cigarettes that Joe left on the edges of desks, shelves, and machinery; then as the subject of the bass-treble loudness perception curves, six months of numbing noise at the threshold of pain when even the dog ran away; and finally a full-fledged test engineer responsible for calibrating the square wave generator, for marking graph coordinates on x and y axis with the sharpest pencil. They had invented the electric chair and discovered gunpowder; he had guarded the laboratory and waited for him during the secret war years. It was malice and spite to make a girl he didn't even know his test engineer. He was just looking for someone he could boss around, someone to listen to his bullshit.

"She can't. We have to be somewhere. We have to go."

"Hold your horses," said Joe. He picked through things under the deck, looking for the Klaxon to call the launch. "I just thought you could spare me a minute to help rig the drag. Christ, you think I want a bunch of kids aboard all afternoon?" He found the Klaxon and blew it ferociously.

His father dug in his pockets and brought up a silver stopwatch on a black shoelace. He checked the ancient Bulova on his wrist and handed the stopwatch to Albert. "Just do me this until the launch comes. Start the clock at the first cannon. I may not have a hand free."

The old man meant business—stopwatches, milliseconds, the mysterious bucket drag. All he wanted, Joe Stillman said, was to show those sons of bitches on the committee boat what a real start looked like. The race boats were beginning to chase and play around them. The committee boat had taken its position on the starting line riding gently behind its anchor chain. The afternoon was brisk and bright, the August sun warm on the face and arms, a day worthy of Monet or Marie Cassatt, if you couldn't smell it. But the putrid oils of the slimy menhaden poisoned the air and made the beautiful bay the vestibule to an abattoir.

At the warning cannon, Albert, with the stopwatch around her neck, had shinnied up the mast to rig the spinnaker halyard which had come off its block at Old Hook Shoal. She stood on H.'s shoulders, her knees clutching the mast and her bare feet on his shoulders. H. could look up at her glorious bottom or down at her feet, the toenails painted the same rabbit's nose pink as her lips. Perhaps it was the interior of the pedigreed rabbit's ear—a soft and velvety pink, flecked with mica that flashed in the sun.

"What is your real name?" he asked her.

"Albertine Bang."

"What is that?"

"Norwegian. My great-great-grandfather was Christian Bang. Have you heard of him?"

"No."

"He was bishop of Oslo. And a theologian."

"What kind?"

"Protestant, I guess." She reached for something above her, and her toes dug into his shoulder blades. It was struggle not to kiss her feet in a Muslim gesture of adoration, but he was saved by the cannon. They had ten minutes.

The bucket drag, it turned out, was just a bucket on a rope thrown overboard to slow down the boat. The Stillman variation had a tandem yoke and bridle for two buckets and a trip line that allowed an operator to vary the drag effect by tilting the buckets or dumping them entirely to resume speed. Albert was appointed operator of the trip line while H. was to throw the whole apparatus overboard without fouling the rudder. It was never suggested that the whole business was illegal. The fleet was now on the line, squeezing each other for a coveted space on the windward end near the committee boat. There was barely time to run tests and train the operators.

To know the limits of a system, the engineer must exceed them. Joe Stillman asked two questions of a thing: how will it break and when? Only the destruction test could tell. By contradictory orders and impossible commands, Joe whipped his assistants into a frenzy of mistakes and errors. H. snagged the towline on the tiller, the apparatus jammed the rudder which brought the boom around suddenly and knocked off Albert's engineer's cap, releasing a cascade of shimmering blonde filaments that seemed to swamp the boat. H.

was so transfixed by the sheer quantity of her tumbling hair that he didn't even hear his father's curses. Albert's trip line was a treacherous mechanism that flipped the buckets entirely at the least pressure, causing them to surface and bob behind the boat like beach balls. The inventor pushed her without mercy. "Not up. Down. Now up. Dammit. Up. Keep awake, watch what you're doing." She bit her upper lip and held back tears as she tried to find the precise tension that would keep the buckets underwater.

Joe Stillman glanced at his stopwatch and abruptly declared the test a success; they knew the weak spots. He had lavish praise for Albert and gave her his favorite golf hat to hold in her hair. A celluloid window in the floppy brim shed a green path across her nose and cheeks. They were ready to assault the starting line.

In his final briefing to his crew, the skipper declared that being first over the line was secondary to being closest to the wind which meant closest to the committee boat on the windward end of the line. Nothing must come between them and the teakwood relic that carried the despised committee or they would forfeit "the freshest air," a euphemism that made H. smile. The bucket drag was to be deployed in only two circumstances—if they arrived on the line prematurely or to avoid collision with a boat that had right-of-way.

The race committee had chosen a two-legged course whose windward reach lay directly toward the fish factory with the east wind in the yachtsmen's noses. H. groaned. With stopwatch in hand, the old man set straight for the first mark, a buoy near the factory, that would take him under the lee of the committee boat. He never intended to ram it or to foul number 21, a race boat belonging to Asa Goodrich. But he intended to come very close.

Joe was bearing down, calling off the seconds, H. was poised over the stern with the buckets balanced on their yoke, Albert was in charge of both sheets and the trip line. Number 21 came suddenly out of the wind from the wrong side of the line, like a Jap zero diving from the sun, intending to run broadside to the line toward the committee boat and come close to wind at the gun. Joe was aiming for the rapidly narrowing space between the committee boat and Goodrich who was coming from starboard with right-of-way. Joe Stillman's failure to give way began to alarm everyone. The committee's crew blew their loud diesel trumpet. Asa Goodrich and his son were shouting. But the old man was pure granite; he could have been a skeleton lashed to the helm. No one on the Goodrich boat knew that Joe Stillman had a secret weapon; they thought he was mad and would ram them or come about and ram the committee boast. "Twelve seconds, eleven seconds, ten seconds, BUCKET DRAG." H. hurled the drag aft, and their boat suddenly slowed without changing course or losing wind.

It was too late for Asa Goodrich who had lost his nerve. Afraid of being rammed or forced to foul the committee boat himself, he chose to jibe and pass Joe Stillman downwind. But he had to jibe too quickly, the boom lifted parallel to the mast, then swung forward, taking the stays and the mast with it into the water. The crippled craft lurched wildly into the boats behind which scattered to evade him before he took so much water over his leeward gunwale that he capsized. Joe Stillman slid quietly into the lee of the committee boat, alone.

"Five seconds, four—," he called, and to Albert, "Good girl. Good girl. Keep her down. Full drag." The committee in their blue blazers stared stonily at the triumphant Joe Stillman passing beneath them, happy as a clam. A question was answered. What makes a clam so happy? Its secret. The submerged bucket drag.

"Two seconds, one," said Joe Stillman. The cannon fired on cue. They could smell the powder, feel the heat and the ring in their ears. A perfect start. A handshake away was the commodore, beet red with anger under his white cap and hoary hair, his arm supporting Sonja Henie who was sickly green from the unfamiliar stench. Winthrop Jr. was on her right with a frosty glass in his hand. As the stern passed, the commodore's eyes followed the rope disappearing into the wake.

"What the hell are you trailing, Joe?" he shouted.

"Can't hear you!" the old man shouted back.

"What's that line behind you?"

Joe cupped his hands behind his ears to signify he didn't hear. The commodore thundered something unintelligible, and then they were out of earshot. They were a boat length ahead of a blue knockabout way downwind that had not been involved in the fracas up the line. They were first. "Hooray for our side!" Joe Stillman shouted to his crew. "Cut loose the drag!"

H. uncleated the line to the bridle, Albert let go the trip line, and the ropes slithered over the stern.

"I think the commodore was asking something about the buckets."

"None of his goddam business," said his father to the wind.

"The boat that turned over, he was trying to get out of our way."

"Didn't touch him. Didn't even come close."

"He thought we were going to hit him," said H., trying to elicit a trace of remorse.

"We bluffed him good," said the helmsman, savoring the fatal encounter. He lit an Old Gold and studied their situation. The fleet had recovered from the demasting of number 21. A dozen boats were over the line, and the blue boat appeared to be gaining. But they were, incredibly, first. Albert was leaning far back over the water, her feet braced against the opposite bench, straining at the main sheet. She was racing.

"What's-her-name is a real find, a good trouper," Joe Stillman confided to his son.

"She says her name is Alberta Bang."

"Where have you been keeping her?" the old man asked.

"We just met."

The two men talked about Albert as if she wasn't there. It was a miracle that she was; women didn't sail in Joe Stillman's days. They grew fat eating petit fours on the yacht club deck, waiting for their men to come home from the sea. A boat was no place for a woman.

Albert ignored them. She watched the mainsail and checked the boats behind. "Number 11 is gaining," she said. They let out the jib, they pulled it in, they tinkered with the mainsail. The old man ordered H. forward; the stern was too deep. H. bummed a cigarette and a light from his father and had to endure being told he smoked too much. He'd had one cigarette since breakfast and judged the old man to be on his second pack. He sat next to Albert and shared the smoke. Each drag briefly blotted out the fish factory. They were getting close enough to see men unloading a long metal ship, a bunker boat, with a wooden wheelhouse on its bow and a cabin and stack at the stern. Boom hoists raised nets full of bunker, or menhaden, from the hatches and dumped them behind the ship.

"Where is the stink from?" H. wondered.

"From the shed, the big one behind. I've been there," said Albert.

"You have?" It was almost unthinkable to be so close.

"They press out the oil in there and boil it down. Then they grind the flesh and bones and dry it in vats. That's what stinks, that and the oil." The progress of the menhaden into fertilizer fell like music from her lips.

The blue boat passed them before the first mark. The old man blamed their centerboard; the slab of zinc steel was too heavy. Other boats had lighter alloys. Joe Stillman predicted they would be back in business before the wind; he still had a few tricks up his sleeve. The committee boat was making a wide berth around the race fleet on its way to the first mark where it waited a hundred yards off the buoy.

They were second round the mark on the downwind leg toward home. Before they left the mooring, Albert had rolled and raised the big spinnaker and lashed it to the mast. Now she pulled the tie strings, and the big jib was instantly filled and billowing. The boat jumped forward, and the men cheered the new mate and her vast pregnant spinnaker.

The sun beat down from behind them, the wind at their backs was warm and gentle, and the boat rocked like a cradle in the swells. Albert sat on the narrow edge of the quarter deck, leaned against the mast behind her, and untied the knot in the tails of the white shirt over her navel. She began unbuttoning the front. H. couldn't believe his eyes. Was she planning to undress? She leaned forward and took off her shirt. She was wearing the top of a turquoise bathing suit. H. was both disappointed and relieved. He had thought for a moment that the Whore of Napeague was going to strip in front of him and his father. Then he saw how crazy that was. He had been having strange spells all summer, but they were getting worse. He had nearly kissed her feet.

His father stared at the blue boat ahead and at another gaining on the port; he studied the trim of the mainsail and the magnificent spinnaker ahead and shook his head. "Son of a bitch," he said softly. He was now looking at Albert with her half-green face under his old golf hat, her deep tan, and her turquoise bathing top. H. knew what the old man was thinking. "You're a big girl," the old man said.

Albert smiled.

"I weigh a hundred and thirty-eight," she said. Her tone neither confirmed nor denied his statement.

"That's just perfect," said the old man. Albert smiled again. She was used to compliments.

"How would you like to try an experiment?"

"Don't," H. said quickly. "Don't listen to him, I know what he's trying to do, and the answer is NO."

Albert was baffled at his outburst. "What's the matter?"

"He's trying to stuff you under the deck, get you to lie in the bilge—"

"What for?" she asked with fatal curiosity.

"Let me explain it to you," said the engineer as if his voodoo scheme was the fruit of pure reason. And he told Albert how, when he was a boy on the St. Lawrence River, he sailed a skiff without a rudder that was steered by shifting one's weight in the hull. Movement of ballast forward pushed the bow down and tilted the mast, which caused a change of course. If they could do the same thing with a knockabout, the need for a rudder would be reduced; and the less tiller, the more speed. But the distribution of weight had to be constantly fine-tuned for the desired effect. Dead ballast wouldn't work; he needed a willing body of the right size and shape. Albert.

Albert listened with wide-eyed credulity. The old man was sweet-talking this glorious sunbeam into the dark hole of the bilge where cold water sloshed forward every time the boat nosed into a trough.

"I won't let you do it, Dad. Take us to the dock like you agreed. You showed us your start. It was wonderful. Now let us go."

It was H.'s turn to be treated as if he didn't exist. "Henry used to be a good test engineer, but he's got timid. He's afraid to get wet, won't even try a fresh clam."

"I don't mind getting wet," said Albert. She had to hold her breath to unbutton the fly of her shorts. H. held his breath too as she wiggled out of the very small pants. The turquoise bottom of the bathing suit appeared, something larger than a G-string but not by much. She got down on her knees and prepared to go under the deck.

"Screw it. *I'll go*," said H.

"I don't mind," said Albert.

"*Now* you want to go," crowed his father. "It takes a girl to show the way. What a specimen you turned out to be."

The dormant parricide within him was awake and battering to get at the old man's throat. Albert had crawled into the dark hole; only her feet were sticking out. H. went in after her.

"Good," said Joe Stillman, "the more weight the better, but keep it to starboard. And further up. As far as you can go."

The space abreast the centerboard well and the mast step was the most cramped. Ahead of that was a four-foot width that rapidly diminished as the ribs grew smaller toward the stem. Albert had wedged life vests in the bow to cushion her head. It was dank and fetid, but you could barely smell the fish factory.

"I'm sorry, Albert, I really am," he began.

"I'm okay. Did you see the white flag on the committee boat?" He hadn't. "There's been a protest."

"The guy we sank?"

"Asa Goodrich. Number 21."

"Did we do something illegal?"

"I think so, but it was fun."

"More to starboard" came orders from the helm. H. who was in the center pressed against Albert whose back was to the strakes of the hull. By balancing on the narrow ribs, they could keep out of the water in between.

"Beautiful. Stay there. Don't move," said Joe Stillman.

"If it was dark, I'd kill him, I swear," H. whispered.

"Maybe it will work." Albert had faith.

"He's crazy," H. said firmly. "He kept me down here for an hour last week."

"But he really invents things."

Albert believed in the powers of the old engineer as H. once had until his eyes were opened. He wanted Albert to like him. Maybe her liking his father would help.

"Dad was Steinmetz's test engineer at General Electric."

"Whose?"

"Charles Proteus Steinmetz, the wizard of Building B. A hunchback socialist dwarf with a pointy beard."

"What did they invent?" she asked.

"Lightning."

"Holy cow."

"Man-made lightning. The first million-volt discharge, 1911. Dad was almost killed." He exaggerated. The artificial arc turned all the oxygen to ozone. The young assistant, fresh from Yale, was pulled unconscious from the lab.

Albert bit on her sucked-in cheeks. "You are the strangest people I have ever met," she said.

H. scowled. His object was not to be strange but to be loved. He didn't want to be some weird curiosity. He wanted to be Albert's friend, her ally against the world. They had things in common; they were large and therefore misunderstood. That's why they were condemned to be human ballast in the bilge, why the envious beanpoles on the deck said cruel things about her, and the men in the launch made bawdy jokes. He wanted her to know that he believed they were wrong.

"You let people put you down."

"For instance?"

"My father, the guys coming out in the launch—"

"We were just horsing around."

"You're not so big or whatever, that's all."

"I weigh a hundred and thirty-eight."

"Is that a lot?" Numbers meant nothing to him.

"I'm five foot eight," she said.

"I think you're beautiful," he said, taking a bold shortcut through her statistics.

"How much do *you* weigh?" she asked him.

"A hundred and eighty-one." She whistled. "You're *big*."

"Don't I know it," he confessed.

She punched him hard on his bicep with the second knuckles of her middle fingers. "Hey, I mean it. It's all right. I like it, you know?"

H. heard her. The Whore of Napeague liked him, and he liked her. He tried to explain to her that Alberta Bang was real and everything else was fake and undernourished. "Those girls by the snack bar, the thin ones—," he began.

"*Brearley*," she said.

"A school?" He had heard of it.

"In New York. They teach them to talk that way and not to eat."

"They're jealous," H. said.

"What did they say?" she asked. He didn't want to tell her.

"Tell me. Come on. What did they say?"

H. should never have mentioned them. She hit him again with her knuckles, on the same spot.

"Ouch."

"Tell me."

H. was in a torment. He bit his lip.

"They think I put out, don't they?" she said.

"I told you they're jealous."

"Well, I don't. So don't get any ideas."

Alberta Bang turned over in the bilge, depriving H. of the nearness of her bosom and replacing it with her cold, wet shoulder. Her motion also knocked the Stillman compensatory bow wave into a cocked hat. The boat veered into the wind, and the old man cursed.

"Jesus Christ. Stop moving, goddamit. What are you doing in there? Starboard. Starboard. Like you were."

The two of them lay there, like fugitives, not daring to speak or move. "We were doing just great and you go and ruin it," his father lamented.

"He's making it all up," H. whispered. "Now if it doesn't work, it's all our fault. I've been here before." The old man fumed and fussed. A torrent of orders, one canceling the other, issued from the helm. Finally H. challenged him.

"Is this doing any good?" he shouted to the stern.

"You bet. Don't move."

"Where are the other boats?"

"All over."

"How many are ahead?"

"One or two."

"I don't believe you. There were four."

"You're talking too much."

"I want to see."

"Stay put. You've done enough damage."

"He's lying," H. told Albert.

"I believe him," she said.

The boy and girl lay in the dark, their bodies pressed together against the bilge strakes and their spirits separated by the gulf between skepticism and faith. They listened to the seas rushing past the seesawing hull, fast and full of bubbling air. They were moving.

"One of you should come about three or four inches to the stern," his father said.

Albert offered, and as she moved, H. felt her tail slip off the supporting ribs and sink in the water between. "Damn," she said quietly. "Good," said the helmsman. "Stay right there," and after a while, "Boy oh boy. We got the blue one." H. was too beaten down to care.

Joe Stillman called down to them, "I think you all ought to come up for this." Albert started first. She was working her way backward past the mast step, and H. had turned gingerly on his knees when an explosion detonated on the portside, like a depth charge near a submarine. H. thought of the unexploded munitions left in Gardiners Bay when Montauk was an off-limits torpedo testing range during the war. He scrambled topsides, bruised and lacerated in his haste, to see Sonja Henie waving at them and clapping her hands from the stern of the receding committee boat. The cannon was still smoking; they were the only boat across the line. The blue boat was behind them. They had won.

Klaxons on boats in the harbor and autohorns in the parking lot honked their accolade as they approached the mooring. From the club deck came the shrill scream of Frankie's police whistle. How had Joe Stillman done it? For the rest of his life, he would tell one and all only what he had not done on the windward leg of that famous race. "I never touched the tiller." And now he stood preening himself with the unused tiller gently rocking back and forth between his wide-planted legs. Albert was lowering the spinnaker and stuffing it in a bag when the committee boat, now flying only the white protest flag below the club ensign, returned to its nearby anchor. "White flag," Albert observed. "There's been a protest." Joe would not look in its direction.

"Can they take it away from us?" H. wondered.

"Over my dead body," said the victorious skipper. "Let 'em try."

"What can they do?" H. asked.

"Not a goddam thing. We won fair and square."

"You're sure the bucket drag's not illegal?"

Joe was adamant. "I used a drag since I was half your age. They're perfectly legal."

"When you were half my age, but what about now?"

"All right, know-it-all, be a wet blanket if that's what you want." Joe hurled the tiller into the bilge under the quarter deck.

"Congratulations!" shouted the young man who brought the club launch alongside. When they were aboard, he said he had been instructed to take the skipper of number 9 to the committee boat where the protest of boat number 21 was being heard.

"Who's that?" said Joe.

"Mr. Asa Goodrich, sir."

"He's just a sore loser." The deckhand waited for instructions.

"Goddam the committee," said Joe Stillman. "Take us to the dock." Albert pulled H. into the bow. "They're going to disqualify him, I know it. I feel awful for him. He's so sweet." It wasn't the word H. would have chosen to describe Joe. "How do you know they'll disqualify him?"

"We had to learn the rule book in the junior yacht club."

H. was divided. He savored their victory, but he was also looking forward to a reckoning that would take Joe Stillman down a peg or two. He had it coming for a long time.

SORE LOSER

Frankie was waiting for them. She had watched it all through her binoculars—the commodore pinching Sonja Henie while Winthrop Gardiner was getting ice below, the mysterious doings on the stern of Joe Stillman's boat prior to the cannon, his suicidal plunge toward the committee boat, and the mayhem on the starting line when poor Asa Goodrich lost his mast and his boat. She had ordered masses of cinnamon toast, tea, and bourbon for her glorious men and for Constantine Nikolaides's stepchild with the ridiculous name who must have set that spectacular spinnaker; the men couldn't have done it alone in a month of Sundays. And where in the world were the children on the windward leg? They just disappeared. But most of all, Frankie would go to her grave remembering the commodore's face when his oldest friend had the nerve to use a bucket drag under his very nose.

"What the hell are you talking about? What's wrong with a bucket drag?" Joe asked. Frankie put down the piece of cinnamon toast almost to her mouth and looked at Joe.

"Are you serious? Are you asking what's wrong with a bucket drag?"

"Oh Jesus," escaped from H. who had suspected this all along. Albert punched him. They were standing behind the adults waiting to be dismissed.

"What do you think that white flag is all about? You can't have anything aft, nothing below the waterline. But I loved it. I haven't seen such a thrilling start since you and Button in the old Star boats."

Joe stared out at Gardiners Island and shook his head. Frankie reached up and squeezed Albert's hand. "I like a big girl, don't you, Joe?" In fact, she spoke to the entire club in case anyone present entertained a mistaken bias for thinness. "So don't let anybody sell you short." The metaphor from brokerage finance could be understood at every table. "I saw your fanny up the mast when you set that magnificent spinnaker. So don't deny it."

Albert blushed, a chromatic fantasy from red to yellow. But Joe hardly noticed. "I think you brought my boys a lot of luck," said Frankie. "Do they know you won the Stillman Bowl last summer?"

Albert shook her head. The donor of the Stillman Bowl for Most Improved Seamanship finally broke his gloom and looked up at the award's Designee for 1950. "I'll be goddamned," he said.

Frankie lifted her binoculars to her eyes.

"The commodore cometh." They all looked to sea. The club launch was speeding toward the dock bearing the commodore who stood in the bow like Washington crossing the Delaware. Soon they could hear him on the boardwalk below, even before he bounded up the steps to the deck with the energy of a ten-year-old and came straight for Frankie's sweets-laden table.

"Joe," he was shouting, "what the hell were you trailing off your transom?"

Joe kept his seat next to Frankie. "What are you talking about?"

"Asa Goodrich has lodged a protest—"

"I didn't touch his goddam boat."

"He claims you used a bucket drag—"

"He's got only himself to blame. He lost his nerve."

"We all saw the line off your stern. What were you trailing?"

"Asa Goodrich is a crybaby and a spoilsport."

"He's got some names for you too. Come on, Joe, was that a drag?"

"What if it was?"

"It's illegal."

"Button and I used a drag on the Star boat. So did you."

"Twenty years ago. Not since we joined the race union."

"Go ahead, Jack, change the rules. You're the goddam commodore."

"You're disqualified, Joe. I'm sorry."

"You've been a goddam cheat since St. Paul's, and I—"

"Joe, shut up." Frankie had enough. "You won, you made fools of all these stuffed shirts, now don't spoil it. Don't be like them."

His father raised himself from the canvas deck chair and stood his full five feet eight or nine inches, a small man in the shadow of his old St. Paul's roommate. "Sorry to get you off your boat, Jack. I didn't mean to spoil your afternoon." Then Joe looked at H. "I guess all this makes you happy," he said and went into the clubhouse.

Jack Cromwell stood with his hands deep in the pockets of an Abercrombie windbreaker with his ensign stitched on the breast. "What was he raving about, do you know?"

Frankie did. "The time you let him take the blame alone for something at St. Paul's. Ice-skating in the middle of the night." Jack Cromwell lived insulated from guilt and could not understand why others allowed themselves to be tormented. "He used a drag, Frankie, we all saw it."

"So what," she murmured and blew her police whistle practically in his face. Her husband turned and walked briskly to the dock where the afternoon race results were shortly posted. Number 11, skippered by Anthony Hyatt of Shelter Island, was in first place. Number 9 by Joseph Stillman was disqualified.

Fitzwilliams and the waiters had borne Frankie off to her vehicle, and Joe Stillman had not returned. H. and Albert searched for him on the beach, the lockers, and the clubhouse, but he was gone. Albert laughed when she saw the Stillman's station wagon in the parking lot. H. had to ask what was funny. "It's so old. It's an antique."

"It's the best vehicle Ford ever made." The claim didn't upset Albert. As they were leaving, H. saw Phoebe's Dodge parked at the sand's edge facing the bay and Julia Stillman sitting behind the wheel wearing her blue-tinted glasses. Had she seen them win the race? She could take Joe home. H. borrowed the station wagon.

Albert's house, perched alone on a dune looking seaward, was reached from the highway by a winding lane in the sand that passed two other houses. They stopped behind a foreign sports car parked in the driveway below the house. It had room only for the driver. The first thing he saw when they went in the front door was a painting two stories tall, between narrow windows that looked over the dunes and the sea, a swirl of color and angular slashes of black. "It's by a guy from around here," said Albert. "He changes it every summer." On the wall opposite was a painter H. recognized; the gallery at Oldfield had one with red and black and silver dribbles. This one was black and white. Pollock. He also lived nearby, on the Old Stone Road. H. wondered if Julia and Joe Stillman knew there were artists in the woods painting canvases as big as houses. Even Frankie's omnipotent binoculars might have missed what was happening deep in the scrub oak under the water towers behind the Bell Estate.

A counter divided the living room from the kitchen where Constantine Nikolaides, a small man with a bushy black mustache and an enormous appetite, was splitting lobsters and stuffing them with liver pate, crabs, and anchovies. He owned ships and lived everywhere. Victoria Nikolaides had returned to the city until the wind changed. Constantine insisted on making them a rum drink to celebrate their victory. He worked at a counter covered with bottles of liquor H. had never heard of, and he squeezed juices from fruits H. had never seen. He shaved ice in a machine and built the drink in careful layers of many colors—red, green, yellow, orange, pink. It took him half an hour to fill two tall cylindrical glasses. The completed drink looked like a core sample from sedimentary deposits at the bottom of the ocean. H. was drunk before he finished a quarter of his glass. Albert drank hers like milk.

They took their drinks to the gun chamber to watch the surf. The foundation of the house was an abandoned artillery emplacement built on the dunes to repel an Axis invasion during the war. The concrete walls were three feet thick, with a narrowing slit through which the cannon and sights had faced Napeague beach. Nesting terns and swallows flew out as they rolled back the steel door. In 1942, the saboteurs had come ashore in rubber rafts just down the beach toward the coast guard station.

Albert and H. sat in the gun aperture and listened to the sea.

"Constantine seems okay. I mean he—"

"He's been very good to me."

"But he gives you a hard time."

"I shouldn't have said that. He's a man. He doesn't look who he's pawing."

"He ought to. What do you do?"

"I smack his hand, I tell him to stop it. He does mostly. I shouldn't have said anything."

"What happened to your father?"

She shook her head. "I don't know."

"Where is your brother?"

"In Finland. Working for Constantine. Are you going to the dance tonight?"

"I don't dance very well."

"I can teach you," she said.

"La Raspa. I can do La Raspa."

"The Mexican Hat Dance. I love it."

They were silent for a while. H. found an Old Gold he had filched from his father and lit it with matches he took from Frankie's table at the yacht club. They smoked it together.

One thing had troubled him all day. "Did Frankie ask you to sail with us?"

"No."

"She said look for Albert at the snack bar."

"She told Constantine you guys had fun, that's all."

"Did you have fun?"

"Sure. I'm sorry about the buckets. It was a great idea."

"I think he knew they were illegal all along."

"Your father's secret invention, was it for the war?"

"Yes."

"Will you ever tell me?"

H.'s head was dancing over the surf with the gulls. Had Alberta Bang asked him to take her to the regatta dance? No, but she offered to teach him to dance—where else but the club dance? Everything in the world seemed to be within his reach. His most secret wishes could perhaps come true.

"You wouldn't understand. Or even believe me."

"I will. I promise."

H. looked at her for a long time. At last he spoke very carefully, giving everyone their proper due. "Neddermeyer, Kistiakowsky, and Stillman designed the implosive lens." She didn't understand. "For the atom bomb," he said.

"You know how the atom bomb works?" she asked.

He exhaled smoke slowly through his nostrils.

"You must never repeat this."

"I won't," she vowed.

"The implosive lens was the trigger."

"For the atom bomb?"

Joe Stillman's test engineer nodded. "It was designed by Seth Neddermeyer, George Kistiakowsky, and Joseph Stillman."

"You give me the shivers," she said.

He intended to, shivers like he had got when he first unfolded the drawing of the plutonium device—a drawing like the one David Greenglass gave Ethel Rosenberg to give to the Russians.

"I have goose bumps," she said. She showed him an expanse of stippled flesh like a fresh plucked chicken. "Feel them." He ran his fingers over the deeply tanned skin. She was only the second person he had ever told.

"Did he talk to you about it?"

H. shook his head. "He can't tell anybody. It's still a secret, or they hope it is."

"The Russians might kidnap him?"

H. nodded. "We didn't even know he was on the Mesa, not even my mother. We thought he was fishing in Montana."

"How did you find out, about your father?"

He was on dangerous ground. "I'm talking too much. I should shut up."

"I understand, I really do. You shouldn't have told me—"

"I pieced it together, from little things."

She jumped from the gun aperture where they were sitting to a stool that rolled on a track around a long metal chart table fixed in the concrete. Albert and the stool shot off for the end of the table, cornered recklessly, and returned on the far side where they crashed into a second stool that H. caught as it passed him. Albert reversed direction, and they hit each other at the corner.

"My brother and I used to do this all night."

Before they went skinny-dipping, H. supposed. "Will you come to the regatta dance with me?"

"I thought you already asked me. We're going to do La Raspa."

As H. turned west on the Montauk Highway from Albert's driveway, he felt light headed with the prospect of returning in a few hours to pick her up for the dance. The fog was rolling over the dunes and across the pine barrens and bayberry bushes, covering the narrow highway, the railroad track beside it, and blocking out the Mackay radio towers—now ghost antennae sending coded messages to subs at sea. Somewhere on the right was Gardiners Bay. The fog condensed in rivulets on the windshield. He turned on the wipers. It was wet inside as well. While he tried to wipe the glass with his hand, he drove off the road and into a mailbox which remained standing. He got out to look at the scraped right fender. He felt a curious indifference, like a spectator. The rear wheels were still on the road; he was able to back out and keep going, but he still couldn't see. The fog was in his head. His brain was full of rum and Albert. He drove with his head stuck out the window, letting the moist salt wind blow in his face. The wind had turned southerly; the reign of bunker stench was over. Lights of oncoming cars came out of the fog only in the instant they passed. It seemed appropriate that having just found happiness he should die. Everyone had gone to the Sea Spray Inn for dinner. He didn't have to answer Julia Stillman's questions.

H. knew only the box step. His box had four corners, and it required four beats to get back where he started. The sound of castanets or beans in hollow gourds spelled disaster—some asymmetrical, syncopated, three-beat rhythm he could not handle. H. was trying to pull Albert off the dance floor in the face of a rhumba, but she wouldn't come.

"Hold me," she said. "Close your eyes. Don't think of anything. Forget your feet."

He moved without effort, without knowing what he was doing. Rhumba, samba, tango, he didn't know the names. He opened his eyes and glanced at other couples. *Are we doing what they are doing?* he wondered. He was afraid to look down; he might fall. Albert wore white; when she let go and spun around him, her hair and her skirt lifted. He could see her white underpants, and her golden hair brushed his face. She had kicked off her shoes early on. And then came La Raspa. He knew what he was doing; and he abandoned himself to the energies he had been controlling all day long, while holding her on his shoulders by the mast, lying in the bilge, sitting in the gun mount. He held her waist tightly from behind, his head nestled in the cushion of soft hair at the nape of her neck as they kicked left and right in the conga line that snaked around the room, then he pulled her around to face him; he hugged and lifted her screaming off her feet and spun her around. Then they locked arms in the frenetic swing left and right which reversed itself over and over until they were staggering, dizzy, sweating, and laughing; and finally in a manic crescendo, gasping for breath, they fell on the floor, dripping with sweat, Albert's white dress sodden and dirty. They lay there panting and laughing. It was enough to provoke the commodore to leave his table and start toward them. Albert crawled under the tables on her hands and knees looking for her shoes.

"Get off the floor and act your age," the commodore commanded. "Go to your lockers and tidy up." On their way off the dance floor, they decided to leave. Who needed a commodore to tell them how to have fun? Passing the trophy case near the office, Albert ran her fingers along the top of the glass-paned doors and glanced at the second shelf to enjoy her name on the Stillman Bowl. She stopped and stared. "It's gone." On the second shelf crowded with cups and plaques was a big empty space in the middle, about eighteen inches wide. It was there yesterday; she had seen it. Maybe they were putting the next winner's name on it, though that was always done during the winter. Someone had stolen the Stillman Bowl. It was creepy. They decided to tell the commodore in case someone at the dance had it. He was about to stop the orchestra to make a speech when they left.

They haunted Route 27 in the ancient wooden station wagon. They went to Bowdoin Square, a jazz spot in Southampton, but got thrown out, half because they were underage and half because of Albert's feet; she had never found her shoes. The Shinnecock Inn was surrounded by police because Indians had fired shotguns at the bar. In Watermill, the Seven Ponds Inn let them stay, and they closed the roadhouse at three o'clock, dancing to the music of Lester Lanin without rebuke and consuming bourbon and gin until they ran out of money. They ran out of gas in Bridgehampton and rang a bell to wake the attendant who lived over the garage and came down to lend them a gallon can. He was the only Negro east of the Shinnecock Canal. They gave him their last dollar.

It had been a crazy day; they barely knew each other. They began to talk a little, exploring warily the ground between them. Albert had no consciousness at all that she was preposterously beautiful. H. wondered if perhaps he was mistaken, that he had made her up. It was impossible. They watched the sunrise from the dunes below Albert's house. A walkway and steps of bleached wood led through the grass and over the dunes. H. imagined them skinny-dipping, Albert and her brother racing over the splintery slats, leaving a trail of clothing behind them like Hansel and Gretel as they dashed into the surf, their fannies and flying hair, their windmilling legs and arms disappearing in the spray, and then just their heads bobbing on the water. He asked her where she went to school. She didn't. She went to a conservatory, a music school. He wanted to know more, but she asked about him. Fact for fact, tit for tat. Her turn. Where did he go to school? Oldfield, but he had left.

"Prescott Academy? Do you know Jimmy Bowes?" she asked quickly, jumping his turn.

His first impulse was to say he didn't. He had lived in the shadow of Jimmy Bowes and his women all his life. But she could easily find out they were friends. Bowes had given H. her name. He had to tell her.

"Sure. I know him."

"He thinks he's a big wheel, don't you think?"

"We're both from St. Louis," he said evasively.

"He isn't all that great, if you ask me."

He couldn't tell what she really felt. Maybe she didn't like Jimmy Bowes, or maybe she wanted H. to think she didn't, or she wanted to find out what he thought. He didn't have to tell Albert how well he knew him. He could play it cool.

"He likes people. He's very persuasive."

"Like Constantine. He's a wheeler-dealer." She had Jimmy Bowes's number. Maybe he had a chance.

"I'm more of a loner," said H.

"So am I," she replied. There must be a side of Albert he hadn't seen. It was hard to imagine her in a corner brooding about life.

"What goes on in a music school? You play, you listen, you compose?"

"Will you show me where you got the clams?"

"By the windmill, but it's patrolled. We got caught."

"We could take a picnic in Constantine's boat."

"When?"

"Tomorrow. He's going to Rome." They were walking back toward the house. A shutter opened on the second floor. Albert ran into the house.

Julia Stillman was still at the breakfast table when he woke up. Phoebe was in the kitchen, and Joe was gone off in the station wagon. Where was he all night, she wanted to know. He named the villages that he and Albert had visited, beginning with Hampton Bays and working east.

"You took the station wagon."

"Dad let me have it."

"You abandoned him. How was he to get home?"

"You were in the parking lot. I saw you."

"I might not have been."

"I looked all over for him. Where was he?"

He didn't get an answer. She had an intensity he could not quite figure out. Frumpy blue dress, probably for church. Gold pendant locket containing a chip of the femur of Blessed Madame Sophie Barat, founder of the Order of the Sacred Heart, but she couldn't be foraging for miracles in East Hampton. She spoke to a piece of untouched toast on her plate. "You were on the boat with your father." He admitted he had been.

"And someone else."

"Alberta Bang. I met her at the snack bar."

"Not tennis."

"No."

"Then, in words of one syllable that I can understand, who won the race?"

"We won. We came in first."

"I'm glad you say so because I saw him win with my own eyes."

"We were disqualified, Mother. Afterward."

"They took it away from him. They stole from him the one thing on earth he cared about."

"He cheated. He used a bucket drag."

"Buckets of hogwash. I know why. Because they've wanted to punish Joe Stillman ever since he came to St. Louis, because he got out of their rut and did something with his life besides drinking in the cockpit and philandering in the cabin. I never want to hear of a Cromwell again as long as I live."

Aunt Phoebe applauded from the kitchen. She came into the dining room with a basket of stale bread. "You show 'em, dearie. I'm going to feed the swans." She left by the French doors that opened on the lawn and the pond below. Julia followed her onto the patio, shouting to her sister-in-law, "I may be a hayseed from the Corn Belt, but I've got their number." She came back in.

"A bucket drag is illegal, and he knew it," H. said. "He got caught, but he had fun."

"Fun for you. He's crushed. He's destroyed."

"He's not. He made fools of the whole committee."

"Do you know where I found him last night? Do you know what he was doing?"

"I'm waiting to hear."

"He was sitting in the beach locker—"

"I went out there. I called."

She circled the table in agitation, first looking through the kitchen to the driveway, then out the French doors for Phoebe, and back to the sideboard behind H.

"He was sitting in that little cubicle with wet bathing suits and towels, holding this on his lap." She opened a door of the sideboard and took out a large silver bowl, about twenty inches in diameter.

"Oh Christ," said H., feeling cold. He took the Stillman Bowl in his hands and read the inscription, "In Memory of Henry Alden Stillman by his brother, Joseph Stillman. Awarded to a Member of the Junior Yacht Club for the Most Improved Seamanship."

"In memory of Button. I didn't know."

"They loved to sail. It was all they did, all summer long."

The last name in the list of winners was "Albertine Bang . . . 1950." There she was in print. It was really her name. He savored the letters as lasciviously as he had admired her toes and breasts.

"You know what this is?" Of course she did; Julia helped him buy it at Black Starr and Gorham.

"And you let him take it? It belongs to the club."

"It belongs to Joe and Button," she said, taking back the bowl and hiding it again in the sideboard. "I don't want Phoebe to see it."

"I'm taking it back," said H. "He stole it from the people who won it."

"If they can steal from him the way they did, he can steal back his own bowl. They don't deserve it." The depth of her hatred of Joe's old friends, even his own godmother, was greater than he had guessed. Maybe she believed that Frankie and Jack Cromwell had helped to kill Button, the way that Frankie somehow held Joe and Julia Stillman responsible. It was time to find out.

"Nobody ever said Button killed himself."

"Frankie Cromwell told you."

"She thought I knew. Naturally. Who wouldn't?"

"You knew. Don't pretend you didn't," she whispered.

"Why the big secret? Why didn't Dad tell us, or you?"

"There are things it doesn't help to talk about." Julia Stillman pursed her lips and took a deep breath. "Your father's so unhappy. He should never have come back."

"Mother," he surprised himself with his anger. "Why didn't anyone tell us? What are we? You think it doesn't matter?"

"Shhhhh," said Julia, looking outside. Phoebe was coming up the hill with three enormous swans waddling behind her.

"Why did he do it?"

"This isn't the time to talk about it."

"I'll ask Frankie."

"Judas," Julia said soundlessly, her eyes blazing. This was no morning for tinted glasses but for clear-eyed rage.

"We're crazy," said H., "we're all crazy. That's important to know. Stillmans, Chateaus, Carters, we're all looney as jaybirds."

"Henry, don't ever say that again. Not even in jest."

She was holding the locket with the relic of the Blessed Sophie Barat in her clenched fist and probably beseeching the madame to intercede on behalf of her fevered son.

"Where is Dad?"

"At the club getting his things."

"Why?"

"We're going home."

"Home?"

"St. Louis."

"When?"

"As soon as he can get the oil changed. Today. I'm taking the train. You and he will drive the station wagon."

"Whose idea is that?"

"Your father wants to leave. I don't blame him."

He should have drowned him at Gardiners Island when he had the chance—the perfect holiday tragedy. "Nude Engineer Drowns while Clamming, Son Struggles to Save Him." But he had let him live only to see him dragoon the most wonderful woman he had ever met into lying in the bilge, he had taken back her sailing award, and now he was ready to go home. Never mind that H. was poised on his life's greatest adventure. Joe had had enough. H. stared into his coffee cup, at three days on U.S. 40 at forty miles an hour. Over the Alleghenies and into the corn to the obbligato of Joe Stillman's recollection of auto tours past—the Pierce Arrow at Ausable Chasm, the Stanley steamer at the Water Gap, the '38 Ford in the Black Hills. He couldn't drive with him, and he couldn't leave. He should never have said he wouldn't sail with him; it was all his fault.

"I'll sail with him. I'll eat clams. We don't have to leave."

"He never wants to sail again. He told me."

H. had ruined the old man's summer. It was simple as that.

"I know how hard it is," his mother said. "I've been doing this for twenty-nine years," she said.

Whatever misery was between them for twenty-nine years, it was a fresher grief that was on his father's mind. It was the indiscussible Button whose spit and image he was said to be; whose oil study of Gardiners Bay with the two water towers, painted on a darker day than the version in St. Louis, was looking at him from over Phoebe's sideboard containing the purloined bowl; whose widow was trying to coax the swans back into the water by hurling stale french bread over their heads.

"I'm staying," said H.

"You can't."

"I'm not going home."

"How could you be so selfish? He needs you. You have your whole life ahead of you."

"I'm not the one who's being selfish."

Nor was it certain he had any life ahead of him at all. Not at his present rate. He reached for a piece of cold toast. Julia watched him butter it.

"You can't go to communion if you eat that."

It was Sunday. H. not only didn't go to communion but also didn't go to church at all except when he was with his mother. But he was as reluctant to proclaim his apostasy as she to confess his uncle's suicide. Joe Stillman had a theory that women couldn't be taught to use a hammer. His theory was all wet. Julia Stillman had nailed him in a box.

They heard the station wagon on the gravel. "Please help him," she pleaded as if he had to be bribed to act decently. He went to the back door. Joe was not alone.

"Look what I found!" he shouted, getting out his side. His passenger was Alberta Bang.

"She was hiding under a table at the club."

"I was looking for my shoes," Albert explained. Julia and Aunt Phoebe met them in the kitchen. Joe introduced her as his new test engineer, the best bucket drag operator on Gardiners Bay. A real find. H. could hear the implied comparison—a plain girl succeeded where his defective son had failed. Julia gave Albert her frostiest welcome. Aunt Phoebe was warmer; she offered her some hot cocoa and asked her where she went to school.

"The Curtis Institute," she said. Everyone pretended they knew what that was.

"How lovely," Julia exclaimed. "Do you like it?" Albert said she liked Philadelphia.

H. and Joe went out to unload the car—the sail bags, life preservers, oars, the Klaxon horn, and toolbox. He did not look like a man in the straits of despair as Julia had advertised.

"Where'd you go yesterday? I looked for you," H. asked him.

"Your mother gave me a lift."

"She says you want to leave."

"Time to break camp. Get back on the trail." He gave his whim the force of natural law.

"You were going to show me how to catch snappers off the Three Mile breakwater. We could sail over. And clam at Accabonic."

"Clams have been around longer than we have. And snappers too. They'll have to wait."

"Come on, Dad, we can still have some fun."

"It isn't the same, not since '38."

"Since Button," added H.

"Button too," said Joe, and he went around the house toward the basement with a load of boat junk. H. grabbed an armful of life preservers and followed him. Joe had set down his load to open the cellar door.

"Frankie told me Button hanged himself."

Joe nodded. "That's what he did."

"Was there a note or anything?"

"He was seeing a doctor. They said he was getting better. Everyone was surprised by what happened."

"Where was Aunt Phoebe?"

"In New York. It was around Easter. The house was closed." He stopped speaking. H. imagined Button taking the Long Island Rail Road three and half hours to walk on the beach, think things out, paint the water towers in the spring haze. Joe opened the door.

"I thought maybe we'd circle home by the Finger Lakes, best time of year up there about now. I know a roadhouse outside Skaneateles has the goddamest scrambled eggs you'll ever put in your mouth."

H. put the life preservers on a shelf where they would stay dry. "Frankie says Button was lonely," he said.

"Frankie has her own axe to grind."

"What's her axe?"

"We were a gang. Frankie, Button, and me. And Jack too. She's always been mad I moved away. Frankie's a stubborn girl. She wants things her way, same as your mother." He seemed resigned to living in proximity to such stubbornness from which he took refuge in basements as they were doing now. The women could be heard overhead. Both men knew they were playing hooky. They couldn't sail together, but they were still in the same boat.

THE WHORE OF NAPEAGUE

"What is the Curtis Institute?" he asked Albert as they walked down to the pond.

"A conservatory. I told you."

"You play an instrument?"

"Your mother doesn't like me, does she?"

"She doesn't like anything east of the Shinnecock Canal."

"She should leave if she doesn't like it."

"We are leaving, today maybe."

"Your father said. I came to say goodbye."

"He's pissed off at the commodore for yesterday, that's what my mother says."

"It was a great race, the buckets and him not using the tiller and all. Your dad's okay."

"I can trust you," he said. "Do you know about my uncle?"

"Who killed himself?"

"Do you want to see where?"

They let themselves into the dark basement with great care, then stumbled over rakes and hoses until they stood by the old hot air furnace like a hollow oak with stumpy branches over their heads. It had been converted to oil, but there was still a bin of coal behind it. Albert reached up and lifted herself by one of the ducts. As she chinned herself, it creaked, and rust and soot fell on her face and hair. Her arms were as strong as a gymnast's because she was no feather. H. was impressed. "Jesus, what do you do?"

"He must not have been very tall," she said. She was right; the ducts weren't high enough for Albert or H. to hang themselves.

"My father is kind of short."

"Your mother's tall. She runs your house. I can tell."

"Who runs yours?"

"Constantine."

"He's shorter than my father."

"He's Greek. He has to be king or he goes crazy."

"Dad goes to the basement."

"Your uncle too," she said. He remembered Joe Stillman rigging the ropes of the bucket drag in this cellar on Friday night while the swordfish got cold upstairs and the brief moment at the doorway when he thought Joe was doing something else.

"What was Button's real name?"

"Henry. I'm named after him."

"I'd hang myself too if I was named Henry."

"You should talk."

"My real name's Albertine. Proust's lesbian lover."

"I haven't gotten to Albertine."

"Neither have I." They both laughed. They probably hadn't read a page of Proust between them.

"Why did your uncle kill himself?"

He shook his head. "I just found out. From Frankie."

"They didn't tell you? That's weird."

"There's something I don't know."

"Like what?"

"The Stillmans may be mad. Sometimes I think I am."

"Why?"

"I feel trapped. I'd blow up the whole world if I could, to get out." Like Joe Stillman.

"I would too," said Albert.

Albert didn't seem like someone who was going crazy. "You're so, so carefree."

"You don't know me." Albert's brows furrowed. "When are you leaving?"

"I'm not going."

"You can stay with us, in my brother's room. I'll ask Mother."

A ray of the morning sun suddenly came through a dusty window and struck Albert's hair. It was speckled with flakes of metal from the rusty duct. H. started to pick them from her hair, but Albert shook her head vigorously, and the flying hair grazed his face as it had at the dance the night before. It was too much. His hands burrowed through the mane of hair to find her face and lips, and he kissed her gently, savoring the spearmint taste of her lipstick. Suddenly her tongue was in his mouth. This was an epiphany for which nothing in his life had prepared him. Her kiss was improbable, unexpected, a wonder so bizarre he wanted to light a votive candle, fall on his knees in gratitude. He learned from her quick tongue what he could do with his own, find the inside of her front teeth and the moist membrane under her tongue. His mind was afire, but when he tried to put his hand on her breast, she took it off and turned her head away. "Not now," she said.

"Why?"

"Your uncle."

H. pressed against her tightly, his breast against hers, their crotches together. Had Jimmy Bowes done this with her? Was she really the Whore of Napeague? He loved her anyway.

Overhead they heard Julia Stillman calling for him from the porch. She thought they were at the pond. "Henry! It's time for church." His erection melted like chocolate in his pocket. Religion, sex, and death. There, on the spot where his uncle died, he had an intuition why it gets harder and harder to live.

Julia Stillman was summoning her son to the church where he had been baptised. In the 16 mm home movie, they are all there—Frankie, his godmother, looking stocky but not yet fat; Button in a straw hat and a double-breasted jacket with a carnation in his buttonhole; Abigail, his grandmother, leaning on Button; Aunt Phoebe; and the commodore. These black Protestants have motored out the Sag Harbor Turnpike, following handwritten instructions like clues to a tacky treasure hunt, to St. Perpetua Catholic Church in the quarter behind the summer cottages where baymen and the indigenous gentry live. Not across the railroad tracks, but along them. The ostensible object of their homage is a bronzed and fatted baby, held by a hatchet-faced nurse brought on from St. Louis for his birth, who is about to be christened Henry Stillman. But the real cause of their pilgrimage is the tall and slender woman under the disc of a vast garden hat like a halo by Giotto. Julia Stillman gazes at her admirers with the serenity of the Virgin Mother at Lourdes owing to the five tanks of anaesthetic gas she has inhaled since she went into labor. She is the Sleeping Beauty awakened to a party in her honor. Only Joe Stillman is missing; he is behind the lens.

"Do you have to go to church?" Albert asked.

"No," he answered defiantly. "Henry!" his mother called from further away. It wasn't easy to ignore her.

"You should go if you have to. Why are you so angry?" Albert asked. She didn't want to get him in trouble.

After a while, Julia stopped calling. They still held each other, but Albert's face was buried in his breast where he could not reach her lips. Finally they heard Julia drive off alone. She bit him on his breast. "Come to Napeague," Albert whispered. "No one will bother us."

"Someone has to drive back with Dad."

"Your mother."

"She gets carsick."

"Come to Napeague. Constantine's going to Rome. Mom's still in New York."

"There'll be a bloodbath if I don't go."

He was scared. He wasn't at all certain what Albert wanted, why she had stopped kissing him, or what she was promising at Napeague. He needed to talk to Jimmy Bowes. What a wretched apostate he had turned out to be, a man who trembled to miss Mass with his mother.

"Are you all Catholic?" Albert asked.

"Mother is. Dad's agnostic, and I'm a Manichean."

Constantine Nikolaides's XKE 5000 was still in the drive. Albert promised to ask her mother if H. could stay with them and ran indoors. H. bought the *Times* and the *Tribune* at the news store on the way home. The Soviets had tested an implosion bomb, and the Panmunjom peace talks had been suspended. The war was on again. H. would have to go to college unless he could get the army to send him to Germany. He gave the newspapers to Joe who wasn't surprised. "We've lost our chance for good," he said and went for a walk on the beach. Salt water had improved his circulation.

The phone rang just as Julia returned from church. It was Veronica Nikolaides in New York City who called to invite her son to be their houseguest at Napeague. She would be down Monday after she put her husband on the plane to Rome. "She sounds foreign," said Julia. "Who are they? What does he do? The girl doesn't look Greek. Who is the father?"

"Her great-grandfather was bishop of Oslo."

"It's better not to know any more," said Julia who knew a losing battle. She had done some outrageous things when she was about his age, and she knew he could not be stopped—just lasted out. All that interested Julia was getting Joe Stillman away from Gardiners Bay, the past, and his old "friends" who were out to undermine him. If she had to drive home by way of the Finger Lakes and eat the legendary scrambled eggs in Skaneateles, so be it. It was her cup; she would not let it pass. By bedtime, their bags were packed and stacked in the hallway.

As soon as they left early the next morning and Aunt Phoebe had gone to feed the swans, H. looked in the sideboard. The Stillman Bowl was still there. He put it in a shopping bag. Albert picked him up in an open Land Rover like the clam warden's vehicle on Gardiners Island. They passed the pond, the flagpole, and the village cemetery where the stone effigy of David Lion Gardiner, the first lord of the island, rested in full armor on the lid of his tiny sarcophagus under the gabled roof of a Gothic gazebo. He was about four feet long. Albert took the shortcut to Amagansett, a back road that ran past the Maidstone golf course. She floored it, and the Rover left the links behind like a driven ball. Albert liked speed. She slowed down only at the first Napeague radio tower to check whether her mother's car was in the drive to their house. It wasn't, and they resumed speed for the Montauk clam shack. While they sat in the Rover waiting for their onion rings to crisp in the bubbling oil, she noticed the shopping bag at his feet. She screamed when he showed her the bowl. "My bowl. Where did you find it? Who took it?"

H. still had not decided whether to admit his father had stolen it. He was ashamed of Joe for letting an old crock like Jack Cromwell get under his skin. But Albert had seen Joe run from the commodore, and she had helped look for him everywhere. She could guess. "Your dad took it. That's why we couldn't find him. He was hiding it somewhere."

"We've got to put it back," said H.

Albert furrowed her brow. "The race was great. I didn't think he was really so pissed off."

She drove back through the Hither Hills park toward the club even faster than she had come. H. waited with the brown bag outside the club for her to give the all clear. The trophy case was opposite the door to the club office where the secretary was adding up chits on a noisy adding machine. H. leaned on a counter in the doorway to block the woman's view while Albert replaced the Stillman Bowl in its ring of dust and walked quickly away. H. followed her, and near the snack bar, they were frozen by the bellowed command, "Children, come here." Frankie was ensconced under her umbrella with all her paraphernalia to which was added a Zenith Transoceanic portable shortwave radio on which she followed the progress of a tropical storm off Bermuda and the recapture of Seoul while she watched the commodore teach tactics to four girls from the junior yacht club in the cockpit of his boat and read *Home Front* by D. M. Evers in a new edition with a much sexier cover of the chorus line.

"How do you like it?"

"It's delicious. I can't put it down."

"I know the author. She's the wife of my English teacher."

"Well, she's a very, very naughty woman," said Frankie, which was a high compliment from someone as jaded as Frankie.

The commodore saw Frankie talking to Albert and H. and called to them through a bullhorn.

"*WHERE IS JOE STILLMAN*?"

"*THEY WENT HOME*!" H. shouted back.

"*WENT WHERE*?"

"*ST. LOUIS*!"

There was much scurrying on the deck, and soon the commodore was rowing his tender toward the dock. H. assumed he was sorry for having to disqualify Joe in Saturday's race and embarrassed by his sudden departure, but he was wrong. Jack Cromwell had forgotten about that; he was only worried what Joe would say when he learned the Stillman Bowl was missing. It had been stolen on the commodore's watch, and he was full of excuses. "Bunch of drunk punks from Greenport. We'll never invite them to Regatta Week again. I've ordered a new bowl. You tell him I apologize for these louts." He seemed relieved that Joe had left because he didn't have to face him.

He started to go, then remembered that he had meant to "pick Joe's brain about the Russkie bomb." He looked around the deck and lowered his voice to conspiratorial intimacy. "There's been talk, since the Reds got the bomb and with Korea heating up again, about the advisability of living in New York City. We have an excellent bomb shelter in Greenwich, but in the city, we're sitting ducks."

H. spoke even more softly so as not to cause a panic on the deck of the yacht club. "Dad says New York City is a primary Soviet target, and it's safer to live in the Midwest or the South." The commodore looked at his wife. "We could take the *No Nonsense* down to the Caribbean." "You take it," she said. "I'd rather see a mushroom cloud." Cromwell rowed slowly back to his tactics class.

Frankie was unhappy. "I think everybody has lost their way." She took H.'s hand in both hers. The gems and baubles on her pudgy fingers flashed in the midday sun. "I'm glad you stayed. We have to stick together. With Button gone, I'm all you've got for godparents. If you get bored with St. Louis, you can always live with me. Five eleven Park Avenue at Sixty-ninth Street, the fifteenth floor, and the door from the elevator is always open." She turned to Albert. "Please, for god's sake, will somebody have some fun? If the world is going to end, you must enjoy it while you are young. You can come live with me too. I mean it. And bring your harp."

"Do you play the harp?" he asked her as they drove along Gardiners Bay past the ruined chimney. She laughed. "She knows I don't. I hate harps."

"So what do you play?" He had nothing to lose; he had asked her three times. He imagined it was the flute.

"Frankie has a heart bigger than she is. That's what my mother says."

"My mother hates her."

"She hates everyone."

"I think Dad was engaged to Frankie, and Julia Chateau stole him."

"If Frankie had married your father, she might not have got fat."

They were on a road that wound around the Mackay radio towers and onto the main highway. Albert's drive was in sight. She slowed and squinted into the afternoon haze over the ocean. "Shit!" she shouted and gunned the motor. The sports car was in their driveway. They passed her lane and zoomed west on the highway. H. looked back to see what had disturbed Albert, but scruffy pines and bayberry had closed the view.

"What was it?"

"Constantine didn't go to Rome. He's come back," she said grimly.

"How do you know?"

"His Jag. Mother can't even start it." She made a reckless left down a steep road that ended at the coast guard station on the dunes. She paused at the edge of the asphalt to shift into front-wheel drive, manipulating the levers like the operator of a steam shovel. The Rover lumbered onto the sand, and when she was out of sight of the coast guard, she stopped.

"Shit," she said again.

"Why didn't he go to Rome like he said?" H. asked her.

She was breathing through her nose in short breaths. "I knew he wouldn't go."

"Why?"

"I don't think you should come," she said.

He had been expecting this since they kissed by the furnace. He was surprised that he felt relief. He wasn't up to it, not to the Whore of Napeague. She had too much experience, too much expectation, and she had finally seen that he was a pebble in the shade of a rock like Jimmy Bowes. She was going to leave him in the dunes with his suitcase, looking like a German saboteur from the U-boat that the coast guardsman's son met on horseback while he was patrolling for bodies washed up from Jones Beach. It took the current three days to carry a body to Amagansett. H. had twenty-five dollars and nowhere to go.

"I can stay with Jimmy Bowes on Block Island," he said. The Bowes would put him up even if Jimmy was off in Nantucket or somewhere.

"Oh, god. I'm sorry, I'm sorry. I didn't mean it."

His heart soared. He was a yo-yo on her finger.

"What's the matter? What's happened?"

She shut her eyes. Her mouth was open; he could see the line where the pink lipstick ended and the real liquid smooth pinkness of her mouth began.

"It's your father, isn't it? Why did he come back?"

"Because of you. And he's not my father."

"He doesn't want me to come, does he?"

"He doesn't want me to have any friends."

H. was intruding on some quarrel between them. She had told him she wanted to escape, just as he did. Was she really wild? The possibility frightened him. He thought of what she said about her stepfather pawing her and what the thin Brearley girls said about her at the snack bar and what Jimmy Bowes claimed to know. He didn't believe it. She wasn't the Whore of Napeague but probably a virgin. She was making Constantine a monster, but he had seemed quite nice when he made them the enormous drinks. She turned to him, her mouth open and her eyes closed under the long blonde lashes. "Where are you?" she asked.

He was struggling to get to these lips from the valley of his bucket seat over a mountain of transmission forested with gear shifts. Against all obstacles, their lips met for the first time since Phoebe's furnace. Strawberry, the flavor of her lipstick.

"You're going to hate me," she said.

"Why?"

"Who I am. Me."

"I love you."

"Don't say that."

"It's true."

"You don't know me."

"Saturday, when you were standing on my shoulders, I wanted to kiss your toes."

She screamed. "That's perverted! Why?"

"They were pink."

"You're a pervert."

"It's a Muslim gesture of respect. Jews wash the feet of an honored guest and kiss them and rub them with oils and unguents. Chinese—"

"What's a Manichean?" she asked.

"Forget I said that. It was a joke. I didn't mean it."

"What is it?"

"A heresy. Manicheans believe the flesh was created by Satan and the spirit by God. Dark versus light. The body and the soul are at war."

"Aren't they?"

It was strange that Albert of all people should be a dualist, and he told her so. "You seem so happy in your body."

"I wish," she said and looked at her left hand. Holding it perfectly flat, she separated the little finger from the remaining four, then moved one finger at a time to the left until all had joined the little finger. "Can you do that?" He could not get even the fourth finger to join the fifth without bending them.

"The mind can imagine more than the hand can perform. Is that Manichean?"

"If you believe the body limits the soul's flight," he said, "you could be a Manichean or just a Gnostic."

"I know it does. We're both Manicheans." They kissed again. Her tongue searched his gums and the back of his teeth and began moving toward his pallet. The organ was prehensile; she could type or play the piano with her tongue. He put his hand over her breast. She let him keep it there. He tried to feel her nipple through the fabric, but he couldn't find it.

"You're not a Manichean," she whispered. She took his hand and guided it into her shirt and placed it on the nipple of her breast. It was erect and hard. He made gentle circles around her erect nipple with his fingers. She put her own hand over his and pressed harder.

"Neither are you," he said.

"I believe the soul flies on the wings of the body." She breathed. "What do you call that?"

"Hedonism."

"You have so many names for things. Tell me some more."

"Origen, the first church father, castrated himself to be free of lust and perfect for God."

"Monks," she said. "That's what we are. Musicians are monks. That's what they want us to be."

"It isn't that a Manichean doesn't enjoy the body," H. explained, "but that he feels guilty because he does."

That excited her even more. "That's how they control you. They make you feel dirty and disgusting."

"Your teachers?"

"Everyone. To get what they want, to keep you in a box. I want to go to Oldfield. I want to learn something real."

"Oldfield's just a bigger box. You'd hate it."

"You know everything. You must have learned it somewhere. I haven't even been to high school."

"What do they teach you at the Curtis Institute?"

"Solfège, harmony, counterpoint, *basso ostinato*, French, German, Italian, and the history of music. Nothing about life. I can't even spell."

The thought of the conservatory sobered her. She sat up and started the Rover. "Ohhh, where is Mother? Why has he come back? I had this all planned." She didn't say what she had planned, and H. never learned. As they came down the lane to her house, they could see Constantine at his weather station on the roof. A tower with guy wires supported an anemometer and radio antennas high above him. He waved to them with a conical strainer. "He's a weather freak," said Albert. "He gets up and reads his meters and gauges and says it's going to rain or it's going to blow. It's always bad, and he goes back to bed or talks on the phone or the radio." When Albert first spotted his Jaguar XKE from the highway, he had just returned from the city. The front seat of his sports car was still filled with packages of meat and fish wrapped in a variety of butcher's paper and dripping blood on the leather upholstery. Albert gathered the food and ran inside to get a sponge.

The barefoot Constantine met them at the door wearing bell-bottom sailor's pants tied with a rope and a fishnet undershirt whose wide interstices were choked with the bramble of black curly hair on his chest. Albert walked straight past him to the kitchen.

"Why aren't you in Rome?" she shouted.

"Something very exciting came up. I'll tell you about it."

"Where's Mother?"

"She's waiting for us in New York." That stopped her. "For *us*? I'm not going to New York. She's coming here."

"I have wonderful news, but I want to discuss it calmly at dinner. I'm waiting for phone calls."

He went into his study off the living room. H. could see a transmitter rack and big Hammarlund communications receiver on a table.

Albert shouted at him, "I have a guest. Mother invited him. I can't leave." The door closed softly. She ran to a telephone and started dialing. Then she realized that Constantine was on the line. "Hang up!" she screamed into the receiver. Constantine appeared in the doorway.

"Albertine, please put down the telephone. Your mother's not home. You can talk to her later." Albert stared at him with the phone in her hand. "I will if you tell me why I have to go New York."

"When you know, you will be on your knees begging me to take you."

"I want to know now."

She was spoiling Constantine's surprise. H. felt sorry for him even if it meant he might have to leave.

"The duke d'Alessandri has offered to sell us his Goffriller, but he wants to hear you play it first. Now put down that phone. I have business." He closed the door again.

Albert was stunned. She replaced the receiver on its cradle and stood with her hand on it and her head bowed. H. put his hand on her shoulder; there was no reaction, no life in her. "What is a Goffriller?"

"He's doing all this just to get rid of you. And trap me."

He tried again. "Who is the duke d'Alessandri?"

"Some old fart from Tuscany." She tried to open Constantine's door. It was locked, and she banged on it. "I'M NOT GOING, I'M NOT GOING!" She ran upstairs, and H. followed her, but she blocked him. "That's your room, she said, indicating a room over the kitchen which was reached by a few steps off a landing on the front stairs. Albert was in a rage. "I want to kill him!" she screamed and ran up the stairs.

H. went back to the car to get his suitcase. His room had pennants from Hotchkiss and Yale and a bookcase with *Ulysses, Lady Chatterley's Lover,* and back copies of *Popular Science* and *Mechanics*. He sifted through D. H. Lawrence looking for juicy parts while Albert thumped, ran water, and threw herself on the bed over his head. It was quiet for a few minutes, and then he heard something that changed his life. It began as a low rumble like a sixty-cycle hum in an amplifier with an unshielded audio output. At first H. thought it was a phonograph; but the rumble acquired overtones, double octaves, and a strange lower harmonic that fluttered like the buzzing edge of a Jew's harp or toilet paper over a comb. Then it took off, a gravel-like sweep of sound that set the whole house in sympathetic vibration, like being inside a drum. Everything loose was rattling and skittering. The house was alive. It was Albert.

He went to the landing and up the stairs to her door, which was half open. Albert was sitting on the edge of her bed playing the cello between her legs. Her hair had fallen over her face and the upper half of the instrument between her legs. She held her bow arm far from her body, crooked at a right angle; but her left hand that fingered the strings behind her ear was invisible, covered with hair, until suddenly she threw her head back to let her fingers slide all the way to the bottom of the fingerboard. Her hair tumbled after her, and he could see her face. Her eyes were closed, her mouth half open, and she sang with herself in the same daa-dee-daa language that Brother Alfredo had used when he accompanied himself. Her sun-tanned knees were almost as dark as the stained wood that rested against them. Why hadn't she told him? How could anyone able to make such beauty not want the world to know?

From below came a plume of smoky odors, garlic-coated molecules of blackened butter and the fumes of brandy bonded with crystals of fresh chopped rosemary and sugar. Constantine was cooking. H. went quietly back to his room, a dry Manichean anchorite sandwiched between two sensualists. "And softly with that marvelous swoonlike caress of his hands . . . he stroked the silky slope of her loins, down, down between her soft warm buttocks . . . She felt his penis risen against her with silent amazing force . . . she yielded with a quiver that was like death, she went all open to him." He closed the book. It was hopeless. He would never get there.

Albert came to dinner in a white dress with a high collar. He barely recognized her. Her hair was wet and pulled back in a ponytail. She was severe and chaste—no pink, no orange, no red except the mottled dun of her freckles. She hadn't dressed for him; he liked her in shorts and the tight blue-and-white striped shirt. It had to be for Constantine or for his supper. He had opened a bottle of white wine, lit candles, and set a steaming covered tureen on the table. He stood by his chair in a red vest and his chef's apron rubbing his hands in expectation. Albert told him to wipe his mustache which was fringed with flour or whipped cream. He squeezed lemon on his hands, washed his face at the table, dried it with his apron, and threw it in the kitchen. Albert poured the wine, and Constantine toasted their guest. He uncovered the tureen to reveal a cornucopia from the sea floating in tomato stew.

Constantine served H. before he could prevent it. He watched squid, clams, scallops, a lobster claw, shrimp, and hunks of white flesh ribbed with delicate bones being ladled into his bowl. He could not pretend to eat it; he could barely sit in front of it. Constantine passed him a dish of creamy pink sauce which he used to conceal the fish and tentacles. "It's hot," the cook warned him. They were both looking at him. Albert didn't know about H.'s thing with fish.

"I have an allergy," he apologized.

"To shellfish?" asked Constantine.

"Almost any kind."

"What happens?" Albert was skeptical.

"My heart goes into fibrillation. I grow a dorsal fin."

They gave him a plate with bread and a pile of cheese as repulsive as the stew; it was white, crumbly, rancid, and sat in a puddle of its own milky fluid. He wished he were in St. Louis or even in the beanery at Oldfield eating boiled sausage on mashed potatoes. He tried to follow the conversation and hold down the cheese. The wine helped. Constantine opened a second bottle and toasted Matteo Goffriller.

"I don't want a Goffriller," she said. "I am happy with my Oberdorfer."

"What is a Goffriller?" H. asked.

"Matteo Goffriller, 1659 to—," Constantine began.

"A cello," said Albert. "It isn't right. It doesn't suit me."

"What do you mean? It suits Casals."

"They're too big. I would look silly."

"Casals is half your size. Does he look silly?"

The cello in question, Il Gigante, had belonged to the Alessandri since Goffriller made it for them in 1728. Cherubini and Boccherini had performed on Il Gigante while serving in the duke's orchestra. The present duke was deep in debt. He had leased Constantine a thousand acres of his estates near Mestre for a dry dock and shipyard, and now he was selling off the contents of his Palladian villa. His dignity required that it should be owned by an artiste. Albert would have to audition for him. The duke was waiting in Rome with the instrument. Albert didn't believe any of it. "Why suddenly now? Why not last month or next year? Because I have a guest is why. Because you don't want me to have a life."

"Not so, my sweet radish. Forgive us our little quarrels, Mr. Stillman. Because the Prix Elisabeth is in November, and the Russians will have Amatis and Strads owned by the state, and you play on a toy."

"I'm not going to Brussels, and Jan would lend me his Goffriller if I did."

"And because the duke must sell quickly. Jews from Beirut are camped on his doorstep. They smell carrion."

"How much does he want?"

"The Soviets will give him twice what I offer. It is tomorrow or never. He expects us." Constantine took H.'s plate to the kitchen. Albert was tight-lipped as she cleared the remainder. She returned and whispered from behind his chair. "He's known about the Goffriller for months. Jan told me."

"Who's Jan?"

"My teacher. I'm going to call Mother." She went to Constantine's study.

Dessert was a raspberry mousse with the whipped heavy cream that had been in the cook's mustache. In Albert's absence, he argued his case to H. Matteo Goffriller, 1659-1742, a Venetian violoncello maker originally from the Austrian Tyrol, apprenticed in the studios of Bregonzi to whom his own instruments were misattributed until the early twentieth century. Goffriller's violoncellos were now considered equal or superior to the Cremona instruments of Amati and Stradivari. They were distinguished by a lustrous red stain, enormous size (102 cm), immense sound, and a warm tone. Casals had played a Goffriller since 1910. Albert's teacher had one. Many Goffrillers had been shortened and their sound boxes made smaller to accommodate the style of the late eighteenth century. Only fourteen unmodified instruments were known to exist; the opportunity to own a true Goffriller did not occur once in a century. A great instrument was a challenge to an artist's dedication. Albert's indifference showed how unworthy she was of the greatness within her. She was more interested in how she looked than how she played. "You are intelligent. What is her duty, in your opinion?" Constantine had brought him a fresh glass of after-dinner wine. He was drunk.

H. was a student of disobedience to a whole hierarchy of duties—to parent, teacher, state, church, and God. But he had never thought of duty to one's art. Albert's rebellion became instantly comprehensible and absolutely necessary. She was the slave of her talent, and *non serviam* was her only defense. She was a fallen angel struggling to free herself from God's awful mandate. That's what he loved in her. "Her first duty is to herself," H. said. "Of course," cried Constantine. "To her gift. Please tell her so." That was not what H. had said or meant.

Albert had been talking to her mother for more than an hour when the men went to their rooms. She came into H.'s room after one o'clock and lay on his bed. She was wearing a terry cloth bathrobe, and he couldn't tell what else because she stopped him. "Let's just lie here."

"You've been talking to your mother."

"She thinks I should go."

"For the Goffriller."

"She says Constantine won't be around forever."

"He seems very involved in your career."

She laughed. "That's why he married her."

"Why did she marry him?"

"Mother worked in the gift department of Bonwits. BC. Before Constantine."

"What did your father do?"

"He was a violist for CBS. Gangbusters, quiz shows, the CBS symphony. He worked harder than Haydn, he never slept, he never smiled.

"When did you start to play?"

"When I was four."

They were quiet while that sank in. Twelve years. Enough time to become a Jesuit priest or do postgraduate physics at Göttingen.

"Jesus," H. spoke with reverence.

"I know," said Albert gloomily. She had been rigid on the bed, staring at the ceiling with wide eyes. Now she turned and snuggled close to him. "But I've made up my mind. I won't take it anymore."

"Music hasn't made you happy."

"I love music. It's all I know. It's the only place I feel real."

"You know spinnakers and how to dance."

"That's my normal act. You've seen it—boats, cars, and samba. I want to be a real person, read books, have ideas."

"You've had too much school. You need to live, and so do I."

Her eyes were on fire and her body full of sudden energy. "Yes, yes, you know. Thank god. Someone who knows." She was on her knees, pounding on his chest. "I'm not going, I'm not going to Rome if he chloroforms me. No Roma, no way."

"What are you going to do?"

"Leave."

"When?"

"Tonight. Tomorrow. Will you come with me?"

"Where?"

"We'll figure that out. The important thing is to live, isn't it? I know that now. I'm not going to play for anyone but myself, for two years, maybe three. I'm going to get a high school diploma. You'll tutor me. And read all I want. You'll show me what. And maybe have a baby. Wouldn't that be wonderful? I'll make music for both of you. Am I crazy?" She fell on top of him and squeezed him with a secret strength. Her arms were steel.

She was definitely crazy. Their situations weren't the same at all. She was trained since four to be a particular thing, and she deserved time out before her life was cut in stone. But he was nothing, and he had no inkling of what he ought to become. He was a seed without genes, a blank page for anyone to scribble on. Albert saw him closing his covers. "Don't be afraid. You've got to risk everything to live. I mean, how can you understand the soul of Bach or Mozart if you haven't loved and been hurt? Or Beethoven and Schumann. They knew so much suffering and loss. Don't we owe it to them to live with courage and beauty and freedom?"

"What do you want to do?" he asked.

"Is there some place where we can hide, just 'til he goes to Rome?"

"You can't say no to him?"

"It's very hard."

"I don't think you can hide and be truly free," he said. She let go of him and rolled toward the wall. "Ouch," she said. She fished out *Lady Chatterley's Lover* from under her ribs. "Jesus, you even sleep with books."

"Sorry."

"You don't need this. It's a stupid book. I can show you everything you'll ever learn from D. H. Lawrence. What do you want to know?"

"How to do it."

"Have you ever been inside a woman?"

"No."

"Not with your finger?"

"I can't find the way in."

"Close the door. Turn off the light. Give me your hand."

She lay back on the bed and raised her legs. Her pubic hair wasn't golden blond; it was dark like his. He saw where her bush ended and the slit of her vagina began, much further down than he expected. H. thought he had figured out the position of the vagina from the instructions in a box of his sister's Tampax he had found in her bathroom, but he had missed by a mile. Albert took his forefinger in her hand and drew it slowly up her vulva between the labial folds until it stopped just inside the top of her slit. "That's my clit. Has anyone ever told you about the clitoris?" He had read about it. "Rubbing it turns me on. With your finger, touch it, gently." He stroked the moist flap of flesh inside her. She shook and howled. "Oh! Oh! Oh! H.! H.! H.! Stop! You're killing me!" She pulled down his pants and kissed the prepuce of his penis until he begged her to stop. She taught him the secrets of her body like parts of a Goffriller—the neck, the tailpiece, the sounding board, the pegbox. She grasped the tangle of his hair and pulled his face to hers, her open mouth to his. Her lips and the tip of her tongue made a ticklish track over his cheek and his ear filled with her warm breath as she whispered, “Come inside me. Let me guide you.” He went down, down, down into a cave with no end; and then they made love, slowly, deeply. He expected and feared a premature ejaculation, but it didn’t happen. They both came, not together but not far apart, like two depth charges, like the blast in their ears of the cannon on the committee boat. They had won. The peace that followed passed all understanding. They lay exhausted, he sucking her nipples, then her clitoris and her earlobes, surprised by how oral he was; he wanted everything in his mouth. He bit at her breasts when she let them hang over his head and was alarmed when she lay back and they disappeared. He didn’t understand the properties of fat in a woman. She leaned forward on one elbow to blow on his eyes and nose, then lick the corners of his lips. Naked beside her, their toes tickling, knees rubbing, revealed a new heaven to him.

“This wasn’t really your first time,” she said.

“It was.”

“I don’t believe it.”

“Why?”

“You were so understanding, so gentle.”

“I’ve thought about it a lot. And read some.”

“Some people get so excited, they can hurt you.”

“Have you had many partners?”

She seemed surprised by the question or perhaps by the answer. “Very few actually.”

“I can’t live without you.”

“People say that the first time.”

“You can’t go to Rome.”

“I’m not. No Roma, no way.”

“I have friends in Cambridge. With a house. And Harvard if I go there. We can hide out a while.”

“We’ll hitchhike. I don’t want Constantine saying I stole his Rover.”

“We can leave early, before it’s light.”

It was settled. They kissed. She went to sleep, and he watched her breathe until he nodded off too. She was gone when he woke up.

There was no one in the house, and the sun was high. The Jaguar and the Rover were in back, and the door was open to the deck and boardwalk over the dunes.

H. took a mug of coffee and went to the beach. The south wind was warm, and the steel blue sky had a band of yellowish haze near the water. From the top of the dunes, he could see three trawlers offshore dragging for flounder. Constantine and Albert were lying on beach towels on the wide white sand, and as he came closer, he saw they were nude. He stopped, but he could not avoid looking. Constantine was black with hair; he was simian. His foreskin was pointing to the sky, and H. at first thought he had an erection, but he later saw his penis was small and the foreskin held it up. Constantine saw him and waved.

H. was alarmed that Albert's breasts had disappeared as they had the night before. But then she sat up, and they reconfigured; the aureole and nipples exploding on his retina and coursing through his body like a discharge of static electricity. The extraordinary wedge of dark pubic hair was another shot of electrolyte in his blood. Albert nude. He had to leave or go mad. And he was angry, cheated of his innocence. They were Adam and Eve, driven into shame.

He should speak for himself. Albert showed no shame whatever. She rose languorously and leaned down to put her sunglasses in her hat, showing the men the incredible curve of her ass with its succulent bifurcation. She was still in paradise. "Come in the water," she called to H.

Constantine got to his feet; he was compact and muscular, a shortened version of Bob Gormely. He looked capable of exotic and daring physical things, like an acrobat or an aerialist. He belonged in a circus where Picasso might paint him. "We must leave at noon," he said. Then he ran across the beach and dove into the surf.

Albert waited for H. "Come in the water with me," she said. He tried to be stern and angry with someone he really wanted to lick and devour.

"You're going to Rome," he said.

"I have to. Come on." He had never intended to swim; he had on frayed white ducks and a tee shirt. What was he to do, unzip his fly, kick off his pants, and run naked with her into the sea? "Let's go," she said. He took a sip from his coffee mug and put it down carefully in the sand. He looked at the mug between his feet.

"I'm sorry. I can't."

"We do this all the time at Cap Ferrat. It doesn't mean anything."

"I know," he said, and he really did. He knew everyone did this on the Côte d'Azur. It didn't mean a thing. "But I can't." He picked up the mug and walked back toward the house. From the top of the dunes, he saw she was already in the water.

He had eighteen dollars and a ticket to St. Louis, but he never intended to go there again. Joe and Julia were still on their way to Skaneateles. Kornfeld was working in Baltimore. Jimmy Bowes was on Block Island. He got a ride with a truck full of cantaloupe and called Bowes from a gas station in Greenport. Mrs. Bowes answered; Jimmy was at a tennis tournament on Martha's Vineyard. She commanded him to come to Block Island; he should phone when he got there. A woman going to Boston took him to Orient Point and the New London Ferry. The Block Island ferry left New London from the adjoining slip and passed the same red lighthouse in the harbor before turning to port.

Five minutes after he called her from the ferry slip, Mrs. Bowes drove up. She wore a lemon yellow dress and big straw hat, but there was clay in her fingernails. She had been working. Block Island was a place where you dressed up to go to the ferry. Big Jim was playing golf on Long Island with people who wanted to buy Bowes Aircraft. The men who had been striking for four years would be replaced by nonunion workers. It made Jill Bowes sick. He put his suitcase in the backseat. Jimmy had gone to a dance on Martha's Vineyard and stayed over for the tournament. She just hoped he brought back his tuxedo and didn't leave it on the beach. And there had been two phone calls from a girl named Albert in the past hour.

"Albert? Called here? For me?"

"She seemed very upset."

"Where was she?" he asked.

"At Idlewild waiting for a plane. She was sorry you left."

"Bullshit," he said softly. They were on a street of large Victorian houses under immense and shady trees. The Hurricane of '38 had spared Block Island. Mrs. Bowes stopped the car; they were home. She turned in the seat and looked at H.

"Tell me about her."

"Who?"

"Albert."

"I barely know her."

"Please, H., I want to know."

"It's nothing, I swear."

"I have a hunch, and I want to know if it's right."

"What is it? I'll tell you."

"That you're going to fall terribly in love with someone you can't have, who's going to hurt you very much—"

"I'm not in love."

"And that you'll let this hopeless love rule your life for years and years—"

"You're all wet."

"Because it makes you feel special and doesn't ask anything of you. Because you enjoy it."

"You're crazy."

"But am I right?"

"I don't know."

"Tell me about her. What is she like?"

"She seems like an all-American cheerleader—ice cream, boobs, belly button busting out all over. But it's a cover, a complete disguise."

"What is she really?"

"A prodigy. She's played the cello since she was four, and now she's going out of her mind."

"Her body has taken over her life. That's what happens to girls. It's awful. At any age. I can tell you." She shuddered dramatically as if she'd been doused in a shower of ice, opened her car door, and got out. "So what happened? Why did you leave?"

"She has this stepfather—"

"Who is in love with her too."

"Who's taking her to Rome—"

"Away from you. Don't let him. Get her back, H."

"You've been talking to her."

Mrs. Bowes swore she had told him everything Albert said. There were things women understood about each other. They didn't need to talk.

"*I hate women*!" he shouted into the trees.

"Oh, H., H., *H.* I always said that when you fell in love, it was going to be like a house falling down." In the cool interior, there were high ceiling fans turning lazily, big chairs, sofas, and tables all of white wicker and oval braided rugs. He was very happy to be there, even if Mrs. Bowes wouldn't stop asking about Albert. He didn't really mind. He loved to listen to her; she was so intense, so determined that she couldn't let anything go. She made him feel like the most important, most interesting, most necessary person in the world. You'd think the earth would stop turning if he didn't get back together with Albert.

"Are you hungry?" He was. They went through a long pantry toward the kitchen, Mrs. Bowes in the lead. She stopped and turned; he almost ran into her. Her eyes were blazing. "Alberta Bang better be good to you, she better know she's got the best guy, the most caring, most understanding, most intelligent—" She blew air through her pursed lips, trying to control her feelings. She took a deep breath to hold down her rising pulse and held on tighter and tighter to his loose tennis shirt with both hands. "Oh. Oh. I am just so mad—"

"It's going to be all right," he tried to soothe her.

"No, it isn't." H. was missing something. Mrs. Bowes couldn't be this steamed up over someone she didn't even know. But her anger made her more beautiful than ever. She was a smoking gun, a shiny pistol. The pistol was in his pants. They were very close, touching. He could almost see her nipples, just covered by the loose fold of her thin yellow dress and maybe a brassiere. He pulled her against him and kissed her, his tongue deep into her mouth. Her hand had already unzipped the fly of his khakis and was cold on his flaming penis. His hand under her dress had encountered an obstacle, a very tight elastic girdle. "We shouldn't, we shouldn't," she was saying as she gave short, gentle pulls on his prick. Between her stomach and the rubber girdle, his hand found a bushel of stiff hairs. He searched with his fingers, separating this bush root from root, looking for her opening. "Further down, further down," she murmured. "I know, I know," he replied impatiently, but the girdle acted as a modern-day chastity belt, a barrier between his searching fingers and her moist opening. She screamed anyway, just as he ejaculated in her hand, too soon like with Alfredo's mother. It must have been a weird sight, them standing that way in the kitchen pantry.

When Jimmy called from the ferry, Jill Bowes was up to her arms in clay, so H. picked him up. He was wearing tennis whites and carried two racquets—he had won the Martha's Vineyard tournament—and his tuxedo. H. didn't even bother trying to tell him about the skinny girl who aced him twelve games in a row at the yacht club. Bowes wouldn't find it funny; he'd say it just showed how pathetic he was and why didn't he do something about it. Besides, what Bowes really wanted to hear about was Alberta Bang; did he meet her? They had met.

"So tell me, did she put out?"

There had been a lot of people around. Bowes groaned. "Another Marla Starker."

"Where did you meet her?" H. asked him.

"On a beach in Bermuda. How about those knockers? Have you ever seen tits like that?" H. confessed that he had never seen such knockers in his life. He wished he hadn't.

HARVARD

H. had to borrow twenty dollars from Jill Bowes for trains and ferries to Cambridge, but Sparks Street was deserted until Maia returned from California, looking more desirable than ever. Something was different. She was aware that he was staring at her. "I'm pregnant," she said. "It's Paul's," she added as if he might think it was another. He admired her new belly curving toward her womb. His destiny denied. Betrayed by her fidelity to the mad and profligate Paul who was still in Maine, probably with Merope. He felt her tummy, and she put her hand over his, he thought inching it a bit south. "You came back earlier than I thought. It's weeks until Labor Day."

"Everything went wrong. Kornfeld couldn't go because he was too Jewish, my father was caught cheating in a sailboat race, lost his temper at his oldest friend, the commodore, stole back a sailing trophy he donated to the club thirty years ago, and drove my mother to St. Louis in their ancient Ford station wagon."

"But you stayed."

"I am in love. With Alberta Bang."

"A Norwegian."

"Her great-great-grandfather was the bishop of Kristiania, now Oslo, but she was called the Whore of Napeague by the kids at the club. I made love to her, and we were going to escape together—she from the tyranny of her profession, she's a cellist, me from the mess I've made of myself."

"You didn't escape."

"In the morning, I found her and her stepfather nude together on the beach."

"Did they ask you to join them?"

"Yes, but I left. He was flying her to Italy in an hour to buy her a famous cello. It was all over."

"If you say so. Was her stepfather jealous?"

"He wants her to have no life but music and him."

"So you didn't go swimming."

"I was afraid to take off my pants. I should have, shouldn't I?"

"Things might be different. So what are you going to do?"

"Join the army, drive a truck, maybe go to school if I can find one, I don't know."

"Houghton Mifflin has optioned my next book. It's about a lobsterman's wife who suspects he has women on the water because he won't let her work on his boat. She becomes a mermaid who spies on him as he pulls up his pots. The bay is teeming with hungry mermaids who wait in the traps to seduce the men when they are pulled into the boat. I need to know lots about mermaids and lobstering. About shedders, culls, their age, and all the lore about the traps, whether they really use kerosene-soaked bricks for bait. I need a researcher I can trust. It's a real job. I can pay. What do you say?"

She mistook his speechlessness for reluctance. "It's magic realism," she apologized. "What's in now. Casteneda and Vargas. I know it sounds silly."

"What I want most in the world is to stay here and work with you," he said.

Paul came back from Maine the next week to put Eben in the Buckingham School. When the Boylston Professor heard the plot of Maia's next novel, he shook his head in wonder. He knew she wrote pornography, but its commercial success surprised him. He advised her research assistant to check out what happened when St. Patrick drove Ireland's snakes into the sea. Some say that mermaids killed and ate them. Paul also informed him from the cloud of Chesterfield smoke engulfing him that Maia's research assistant had one choice of profession if he wanted to stay with them in Cambridge. Go to Harvard. If he wanted to flirt with the army or any other waste of time, he should do it elsewhere and out of his sight. Franklin Perry, the director of admissions, was ready to talk with him anytime. Paul suggested the next day at eleven. He was not kidding around.

When H. tried to explain why Dean Pickering refused to recommend him, Perry stopped him. "Paul Forbes says even the school minister tried to kill you. Your transcript has been lost, so we'll have to take you on faith. Congratulations."

Someone withdrew a week before classes, and H. was slipped into a suite in Wigglesworth Hall with Adam Kornfeld. He called Julia Chateau to tell her he was going to Harvard and to expect a term bill. Julia had given up trying to influence him but was willing to support his education if he stayed out of jail. She didn't think Joe Stillman, whose heart was still set on Yale, was ready to handle the news. She would break it to him slowly. "Isn't Harvard full of communists and homosexuals?" she asked. "Please be careful."

Kornfeld had been in Wigglesworth for a week and was already working nights for the *Crimson*. Their rooms in the old dormitory faced half on the Yard of trees and squirrels and half on the Square and Massachusetts Avenue. The miscarriage of his invitation to East Hampton had caused Kornfeld to scrap his theory that Jews were safer in the company of Christians. He had become a belated Zionist, and *Time* magazine was sending him to Israel as a stringer the next summer.

They went to the Freshman Union to be welcomed by Harvard president James Bryant Conant. The hall was packed with the national press and two hundred fifty freshmen. Conant had just been named the high commissioner and ambassador to Germany. He called for universal military training and two years' public service for everyone over eighteen. "None of you gentlemen should be here." And he called for a national priority to develop contraception by pill in two years. "This room should be filled with women who are masters of their own bodies." The press rushed for the phones. Conant talked for an hour and was never seen again.

Nobody warned H. about the freshman physical training requirement. He was told to report to the Indoor Athletic Building for posture photos, fire rope drill, and swimming test. The IAB was a block square tomb of pools, showers, gyms, padded rooms, and offices where he was told to strip and get in line. In the next room, a naked man at a typewriter wearing a watch and a baseball cap asked him for his name and allergies. Another man, on his knees behind him, was fixing a dozen wire tabs to his spine, from his nape to his coccyx, at ninety-degree angles to show his defective posture. He knew what was coming. He would be made to walk naked in a room of mirrors looking at the pretzel of his spine while a voice reminded him that the stomach was like a bucket. He tore off the tabs and refused to be photographed.

He was sent to speak with Folsom G. Wicker, director of freshman hygiene, who sat naked at his desk near the swimming pool eating a sandwich, making out reports and handing them to assistants who filed, phoned, and typed, all naked in paradise as if the Fall of Man had never taken place. Wicker had the stiff tummy and tight scrotum of his predecessor, Gormely, a whistle around his neck and a clipboard on his knee. H. told Wicker that in Harvard Square, for ten dollars he could buy the posture photos of the entire freshman class at Radcliffe, front and rear elevations, tiny buttocks, splayed asses, pendulous dugs or atavistic paps, anomalous as dorsal fins.

"Photos of my spinal lordosis will not be for sale." Wicker reminded him that the freshman physical training requirement was mandatory and advised him to choose a sport, swim a lap, shinny down the fire rope, and not make trouble. "What sport?" H. asked. Wicker mentioned a few: swimming, tennis, skating, indoor calisthenics. H. said he preferred something solitary. The director suggested rowing and H. saw quickly that rowing would allow him to smoke, read, and exercise simultaneously. He wore a six-foot J. Press wool scarf, smoked Viceroys, and read *The Brothers Karamazov* while he rowed. He had become convinced that in Dostoevsky, he would find the solution to his life. He was content to be despised by the jock-strapped crewmen of the eight-oared shells and their coaches.

General education at Harvard made most of the freshman curriculum mandatory. Everyone was now expected to learn the difference between good and evil and science and culture. For electives, H. took Paul's course on Wordsworth and Walter Savage Landor and a course called Gloom about Nietzsche, Kierkegaard, and Dostoevsky.

Landor was a poet of whom H. remained resolutely ignorant to the bitter end. Paul lectured to a seminar of six graduate students and H. who never understood a word he said about Landor. He should not have been allowed to take the course. Wordsworth was a different story. The poet's romance with Annette Vallon, the French revolutionary, their love child, their abandonment to the Terror, and the poet's fraught meetings with them on a channel beach was the stuff of the grand romantic agony and a far cry from the Wordsworth of "a violet neath a mossy stone." H. saw himself in the great poet—torn between love, revolution, beauty, and terror. He waxed so passionate on Wordsworth he earned the brief respect of the graduate students.

Paul Forbes knew he was flying blind and reading nothing. "You'll have to write something soon, and everyone will know." H. tried to read Landor instead of Karamazov while rowing backward on the Charles River in a heavy training craft called a wherry, with a seat that moved back and forth on a track as the knees bent and unbent with the oar's stroke. He ran into weeds and other boats and could not concentrate. Knowing a little about Landor was worse than knowing nothing. He considered taking an incomplete in the course, but Forbes refused. "I wouldn't have let you take it if I thought you wouldn't learn something." "That I'm a fool," H. lamented. "That's something."

A thick envelope from France addressed to the wrong school in the wrong state had somehow gotten to St. Louis and been forwarded by Julia. It was a letter from Alberta written two months before on many folded sheets of scented blue paper. He got lost in the pagination trying to read it. It was mostly about the duke d'Alessandri and how disgusting he was. It turned out the Goffriller cello wasn't even in Rome but at his summer villa in Porto Santo Stefano. When they got there, Constantine discovered he needed to see someone in Milan and left her alone with the duke. He began skipping around trying to learn if she got the cello, but the numbering of the folded sheets was all screwed up. It was obvious the duke was trying to get into her pants, if she was wearing any. He couldn't make out whether he had or hadn't, though she must have gotten the cello because on page 17 she is in Perpignan, in the south of France, at a master class with Pablo Casals who says her Goffriller has a warmer sound than his own. The letter seemed to be missing a folded quarto sheet with pages 5, 6, 15, and 16 on it. On page 17, she is sorry Constantine made her leave so suddenly, but she tried to call him at Jimmy Bowes's house, figuring he might have gone there. She hoped he had a good time on Block Island. She is coming back to Curtis soon for a concert in Altoona and is desperate to see him. "I love you. A." H. wrote her back, in the only letter he mailed all year, that he loved her too. It was returned from France three months later.

The next week, two concert announcements arrived together, the first from the Altoona Public Library for a chamber recital three weeks earlier in the Main Reading Room featuring Alberta Bang, violoncello, and Peter Pelagius, piano. The second card announced a violin recital by Sing Sang Woo, accompanied by the same Peter Pelagius, at Town Hall in New York City on the coming Saturday night. The cards were on top of a stack of unopened letters from people who expected to hear from him. Julia Chateau knew he wasn't opening his mail except to look for checks, so she wrote headlines on the envelopes, "Joe wrote Yale magazine. You are at Harvard. Secretly proud!"

He had two days to decide if he would go to New York. Sing Sang Woo's photo on the announcement showed a girl with a razor-sharp bangs and straight black hair trimmed like a hedge just below her ears. Written right over her mouth and cheek were three words, "Please come! A." It was the siren's call. He couldn't go. He had to write two papers and read for exams or perish. And what did he care about Peter Pelagius and Sing Sang Woo? But the important thing was she wanted to see him. He was in love with the Whore of Napeague. Denying it was useless. He hadn't seen her since she bobbed on the swelling breast of the surf at Amagansett, where his life had stopped in the moment it had begun. She was back now.

He met Maia at the Hayes Bickford in the Square for coffee and rice pudding. He told her that Alberta Bang was back, and he didn't know what to do. Why?

He was still furious and humiliated with himself that he had abandoned her floating naked in the surf with her nude stepfather. She was the only woman he ever loved who wasn't older, married, or a mother. She could have been the beginning of a new life, and he had walked away from her and from all that was good in himself. He showed Maia her mispaginated letter. She read it. "She's more embarrassed than you are over what happened. She wants to see you. You should go."

"She just wants to show me her Goffriller cello."

"She wants to know whether she loves her cello or you."

"I'm going to fail Paul's course. And Countercurrents of the Nineteenth Century too. I have to work."

He focused on the Bick's excellent view of pedestrians battling vehicles to cross the square. Maia turned his face toward hers and studied his eyes. "We should have gone to Chicago like I wanted. You are disappearing already in this terrible place. Harvard is stupid, humorless, and pretentious. It doesn't care who you are. It only wants to make you a Harvard man. Who cares? I'd rather sleep with a cello than a Harvard man. Forget this place. Go to her. You deserve a woman or you will rot."

"You deserve a man who loves you too."

"Oh, H., H., H. Do you think I don't know that? So watch out. Find your Alberta Bang."

The new scar Paul had left on her cheek was a thin curving line about an inch and a half long. He stroked it with his finger. "I'll try."

"Let me know." He watched her leave, hunching into her lumberman's wool jacket which she pulled tight around her shoulders against the increasing cold. Maia was a warm stove in a cold room.

He met Kornfeld for a beer at Cronin's, the campus hangout with two television sets over the bar. The *Crimson,* where Kornfeld worked,was just around the corner.

"I'm going to go find her," he told him.

"The dame from this summer. She's bad news."

"Nevertheless."

"So what's to stop you?"

"I'll fail Wordsworth and Landor, be thrown out, drafted, and die in a rice paddy."

"Be absolute for death. Find her."

"Either death or life will thereby be the sweeter," said H. He would have preferred to know which, preferred to know what would happen between him and Alberta Bang redux.

"My old lady tried to burn herself up again. I should see her. I'll go to New York with you."

TOWN HALL

His mother was a curse, but at least Kornfeld had no army problem; he was deaf in one ear, legally blind, had terminal jock itch, premature loss of pigmentation, and pacifist tendencies. He brought Fairbank's *History of China* with him on the train. It weighed fourteen pounds.

There had been an ice storm in the night along the Connecticut coast, trees bent and wires drooped with the weight of a crystal shell of ice. Cattails and dock pilings in the inlets glinted with a stipple of ice. The frozen world sparkled in the morning sun still low in the south over the Long Island Sound. As they crossed the Thames at New London, he saw the tip of Block Island and later, leaving the station, he glimpsed Plum Island, Orient Point, and maybe the north side of Gardiners Island—a land as mysterious to the South Fork as the far side of the moon. The islands sat on the horizon, the stunted trees and the water tower of the animal quarantine facility shimmering like hairs on his arm held up against the sun. Behind the cliffs of Gardiners Island was the yacht club, the narrow isthmus of Napeague, and then Albert's house and the beach where he had last seen her. He had to shift and cross his legs; he was getting a hard-on. It was stupid of H. not to have taken off his pants and gone swimming. That much he had figured out with Maia's help.

Kornfeld readjusted himself under the weight of Fairbank. The *Times* was also open in his lap. A judge had declared that David Greenglass could introduce his drawing of the implosive lens as evidence at his espionage trial. And with MacArthur returned from Tokyo in disgrace, Adam Kornfeld wrote much less. He sent a stringer to cover the off-and-on-again truce negotiations in Panmunjom. "Maybe Adam will come home now," H. suggested. "Not unless Mother dies," said Kornfeld.

At Grand Central Station, Kornfeld offered to walk H. to Town Hall which was on Forty-third Street just a block from the New York Times where he was hoping to scrounge a bed from an editor or stay in his mother's hospital on Ward's Island. If H. missed the last train back, he would probably call Frankie Cromwell, but it was better if he got back. It was too early for Town Hall, and he hadn't been able to reach Albert; Constantine's phone was unlisted.

They emerged into a chilly wind on Vanderbilt Avenue across from the Biltmore Hotel. Kornfeld suggested they watch the plutocrats mate under the famous clock at the Biltmore, the weekend meeting place for prep school and college students. The clock was a rococo-gilded ornament over the entrance to a cocktail court in the center of the upper lobby with elevators and shops on either side. A perimeter of plants and leather banquettes enclosed several dozen small tables and chairs. "Some Enchanted Evening" was being played on a piano at the back. Carefully combed girls in cocktail dresses sipped gimlets and sidecars and tried to seem a little drunk. Though everyone wanted to look like they were in college, it wasn't hard to tell those who really were. The real college men wore beautiful grey flannel or pinstripe suits, Chesterfield coats, and homburg hats. Some had leather gloves, and all had shining and pointy black shoes that would have been death in a prep school. The undergraduate population had their uniforms from Brooks Brothers and J. Press—tweed jacket and grey flannels, regimental ties, and round shirt collars held in place by a gold clip, loafers, and white bucks.

Fashion was a subject of Kornfeld's Marxist critique despite the dapper degeneracy he affected for himself—french cuffs, his father's Phi Beta Kappa key from City College on a gold chain, a double-vented Saville Row Harris tweed jacket that smelled of the sheep urine used to fix the dye. H. was converting his rumpled journalist into a frugal bohemian, the poet in *La Boheme* who pawned his overcoat to buy medicine for Mimi. The six-foot green wool scarf was the centerpiece, but he had added a large double-breasted suit coat that he never buttoned. His shoes were still the broken loafers whose flapping soles were held on with friction tape around the toes. They were a bizarre pair—the messy tall one and the jaded small one.

They stood by the elevators where they could watch the babbling mob through the potted palms. Jimmy Bowes was sitting at a table talking to a girl whose back was to him. All he could see was a big beret that locked up her hair. He moved all the way around the court, passing the piano and the waiters station, to the other side of the lobby where he could get a look at Bowes's date. She wore dark wrap-around Swiss ski glasses, and her lips were painted a deep purple, but he would have recognized her in a gas mask. It was Albert. What had she done to her golden hair? Why was she so thin? Where were her glorious breasts? They were talking intently over the little table. Bowes was shaking his head. It was the first time he had seen Bowes since he went to Princeton. They lived on different planets and would for the rest of their lives. Bowes, like Kornfeld, was 4-F. He had a hysterical eczema that was tamed only by a miracle drug called ACTH. Albert took a pack of Benson & Hedges from her purse, and Bowes lit her cigarette with a silver butane lighter. She seemed to have lost forty pounds; gone were the jelly rolls of delicious fat and the double chins.

A girl screamed his name—his St. Louis name. "Henry! Henry Stillman!" From the direction of the clock, Donna Hasenclever was wedging herself between the potted palms to get to him. She was too stout to fit and more so as she was covered with the fur of a thousand rodents. "Everybody's here!" she shouted. "Pook and Linda. And Jimmy Bowes. Have you seen Jimmy Bowes yet?" Donna had once invited him to a tea dance at Rogers Hall, a girl's school near Oldfield, but he never replied. "Nobody believes I went to kindergarten with you, that I knew you and Jimmy Bowes when you got expelled for taking over the rug box. It was the most exciting day of my life." She begged him to come to Wellesley sometime and show people that she really knew him. He walked with her toward the clock, promising her anything, to get her away from Jimmy Bowes and Albert. He didn't want Albert to know he had seen her. Kornfeld saw him leaving and joined them under the clock. H. looked back. Albert was gone. "Who was the girl with Bowes?" Kornfeld wanted to know. "That was Albert. Alberta Bang."

His friend was surprised. "I thought she was this blonde bombshell, Miss America, that sort of thing."

"She's done something to herself. She looks like death."

"That's what they do. Women are crazy." He spoke from the deep experience of a mother who had tried to burn herself up on every anniversary of Trotsky's birth.

They walked west on Forty-third Street. Everything in New York City was on Forty-third Street—Grand Central Station, the Biltmore, Town Hall, and the New York Times. Sing Sang Woo's picture was in the glass cases between the doors of Town Hall, and below the photo was her program—Bach, Schubert, Beethoven, and Prokofiev. Her accompanist was the ubiquitous Peter Pelagius. Kornfeld studied the selections and made the sound of vomiting. "Schubert—a bog, an unconscious swamp. Like being trapped in the dream of a drunk. And Beethoven. I once saw a Beethoven holograph of the bagatelles at the Morgan Library. It was covered with blood, excrement, semen, and vomit, then shredded by the talons of a shrike. There's no music after Palestrina." He shook his head sadly and waved goodbye. H. watched him walk away toward Seventh Avenue. The closer he got to the New York Times, the lighter his step; he skipped, he dropped his cigarette, and he broke into a trot. The ink in his blood was lusting for home.

H. was still early; the lobby was deserted. He bought the cheapest seat in the balcony for $2.50. It was empty except for an old man turning the pages of the topmost of a lapful of scores. H. read his program. Sing Sang Woo was making her Town Hall debut fresh from her triumph in Milan where she won the coveted Applefarb Competition. The past summer, she had made an extensive tour of South America. Ms. Woo, a native of Los Angeles, was a student of Carl Horner at the Curtis Institute in Philadelphia. Peter Pelagius also studied at the Curtis Institute with Mieczyslaw Horszowski and Rudolf Serkin. He had been associated with the Casals Festival Orchestra at Perpignan the past summer, was a native of Amsterdam, and played the Steinway piano. It was the longest piano H. had ever seen.

Ushers were showing people to their seats in the orchestra. Many of the center-aisle seats were empty, saved for the critics who came only at the last minute; they never want to be kept waiting; a Town Hall debut was the most important moment in the life of a soloist. The lights dimmed, and the critics were quickly seated just before the performers entered. Sing Sang Woo came from the wings, followed by Peter Pelagius. She was wafer thin and dressed in black. The pianist was a cadaver himself with sunken eyes and sandy blond hair down to his shoulders. He carried some music, which he put flat on the piano and never opened. H. imagined Albert seated with her Goffriller in the Altoona Library Reading Room and Pelagius at his enormous piano behind her. They had been together in Perpignan too. Or she could be in love with Jimmy Bowes. He had been afraid of that from the day he met her. Everyone loved Bowes, even poor Donna Hasenclever. H. was tied in jealous fits for a woman he barely knew. Was he making it all up? He had the flyer in his pocket. "Please come!" Exclamation point. The dozen people in the balcony had all moved down to the ten-dollar seats in the front row. He was alone in the $2.50 section.

Her hands covered his eyes from behind. "You came." She sat down, wiggling out of her coat. "It's a furnace up here. Why are you sitting here?" "It was cheap," he said. "Oh, Henry, I left you a ticket at the box office." The name was like a stab. "Henry's dead. Call me H. or anything." Peter Pelagius barely acknowledged the audience. He sat quickly, adjusted the leather bench a half turn, and struck a chord. Ms. Woo sharpened a string by a hair and glanced at Pelagius.

"I hear you were a terror at Oldfield," Albert whispered loudly, "that people crossed the street when they saw you coming. They were so afraid of you. Why didn't you tell me?"

"Who says?"

"Jimmy Bowes. You were the editor of the newspaper—"

"What's up between you and him?"

"What do you mean?"

"You've been talking to him, about me. And what else?"

"Why shouldn't I?"

"I saw you with him at the Biltmore."

"I tried to call you at his place on Block Island before I left."

"Mrs. Bowes said."

"She hates me. I could tell. Why did you leave?" she asked.

"*You* left."

"Are we going to accuse each other?"

"What have you done to yourself?"

"I was fat. I hate it."

"I loved your fat."

"You're really going to love me then. I'm pregnant."

"How pregnant?"

"Three months."

She didn't look pregnant at all. He wanted to hold her, to feel her tummy, her breasts. She was saying the child was his. What else was she saying? The icy shadow of fatherhood darkened the landscape of his life.

"Is it mine?"

"Ours."

"Why didn't you tell me?"

"I wasn't sure. I just got back from France."

People in front turned and glared at them. The Bach partita had begun. Albert tried to be quiet. "Isn't that beautiful, the repeat? She does that so beautifully, don't you think?" And in the next breath, she wanted to leave until the Prokofiev. "She's so good, so incredibly good. It's so easy for her. She doesn't have to work like we do, like Rudi breaking rocks in Opus 111 or Casals stretching his thumb until it almost comes off. You can hear his pain, can't you? That's what I love about him. He doesn't pretend it's easy."

Albert was saying that Sing Sang Woo was a soulless technician.

"What are you going to do?"

"What do you mean?"

"About the baby."

"That's why I didn't tell you. Because you'll just make me get rid of it. You can go to hell!"

A man in front started climbing toward them. Albert ran into the hallway with H. following. In the light, he saw again the death's head she had painted on herself—the dark hair, black makeup, the pallor. They faced each other just out of sight of a smoking usher.

"I want to have your children but not yet."

"When?"

"When we're ready."

"You don't want to be tied down. I understand. You have to go to Harvard and fight the cold war."

"I feel responsible."

"Don't pride yourself. Just give her some lipstick when she's eighteen. You have nothing to do with this kid. She's mine."

"If you have an abortion, I'll pay for it."

"Don't get in my way with a goddam abortionist!"

The usher came down the steps. "Hey, you guys, they're trying to make music down there." H. tried to pull her away from the usher. She broke free and ran into the hall. "I'm tied down now. A baby is my freedom. I want it!" Albert ran down the stairway, leaving H., the usher, and a balcony of music lovers. He lost her at each landing, and in the lobby, she was gone. He went into Forty-third Street and found her banging her head on the top of a parked car. It was cold, but she wouldn't come in. She pulled down her sunglasses which had been in her hair. Her coat was still in the balcony. H. gave her his scarf which he wound around her.

"What are you going to do?"

"I'm not having an abortion, if that's what you're asking." She put her head on the car and was still.

"Are you having this baby by yourself?"

"No. I'm getting married." She was crying.

"To who?"

"Peter Pelagius." She turned her head to him. "You're going to like him. He's very kind."

"He looks like Dracula."

"He said he'd live with me and help take care of the baby."

"I have a better idea. You say you want to go to high school, be a real person with your own ideas and opinions. I have friends in Cambridge where you can stay. He's a poet who teaches at Harvard, she's a novelist. You can take classes around Cambridge, and they'll tutor you or I will. You can play your cello or not. You'll be free. If we want to have children later, we can. Nobody has a gun to our heads." She was looking at him like a dog who has unexpectedly brought her a duck.

"I know someone at the New York Times right now who can find the best abortionist in New York. Do you want me to talk to him?"

Years of brave posturing dissolved with her running makeup in her tears. She couldn't answer him. "Give yourself a break. Let me love you." He licked her cheeks and held her tight.

"You'd stay with me?"

"Absolutely. I'll be back in five minutes."

"I'll be inside. There's a party in Chinatown afterward." They kissed.

People started to fill the lobby for intermission. She ran into Town Hall and up the stairs. He jogged across Forty-third Street, getting cold without his scarf and wondering what Jill Bowes would say about his chasing after an abortionist for the woman he loved. It was just what she predicted.

A guard in the lobby of the New York Times finally let him explain to someone on the phone that he was the roommate of Adam Kornfeld's son who was visiting in the building somewhere, maybe the foreign desk. Kornfeld met him at the elevators on the third floor and took him to a long smoke-filled room where several men stood at clacking teletypes scanning the accordion folds of punched paper that refolded on the floor. They tore off sections and passed them around. "Here's Morgenstern from First Corps. Did you find the First Cav?" They were trying to piece together where General Van Fleet's decision to cease offensive action would leave the Eighth Army and First Corps if there was really another truce. Others were debating whether Fuchs had named Rosenberg or just a man named Raymond and why they had indicted Ethel. The room vibrated with the great issues—the presidency, Caesar and imperialism, separation of powers, treason, and espionage. Did Truman have the clout to keep MacArthur off the ticket? Could Eisenhower be drafted? It was embarrassing to bring up a mundane thing like where to get an abortion.

Kornfeld introduced H. as a friend whose close relative worked on the implosive lens. They all wanted to know if this relative ever mentioned David Greenglass. Or Harry Gold or Morton Sobell. H. grimaced as if their questions caused him acute discomfort. "No one from the Mesa was surprised it only took the Russians four years to make a bomb."

Everyone began to shout.

"Greenglass?"

"Sobel?"

"Fuchs?"

"Who else?"

H. measured his words. "Several members of the project did not believe it was right for the U.S. to have a monopoly on atomic energy."

Everyone was shouting again.

"Who?"

"Haakonen?"

"Oppenheimer?"

"His wife? Jeanne?"

Kornfeld pulled him away. "Give him a break. He can't talk. He'll get his source killed."

"Did Greenglass know what the lens was for?"

H. couldn't resist. "Spherical hydrodynamic compression."

"Of what?"

"U-238?"

"Plutonium?"

"Of anything," said H. calmly. "It doesn't matter what."

"Corncobs, shit, uranium?"

"Anything. Hydrostatic compression. Period."

"But could he have guessed?"

Kornfeld intervened. "He can't answer that." H. didn't need help; he was in control. He had imagined this interview many times. He stood lost in thought, weighing whether David Greenglass could have guessed that the layers of explosives he crafted were designed to compress a core of plutonium the size of a grapefruit into a critical mass smaller than a golf ball.

"Does anybody know where I can find an abortionist?" he asked. The editors laughed, but Kornfeld was furious when he realized why H. had followed him to the New York Times. "This guy's broad is bad news," he told the smoky room. "Anyone with a name like Alberta Bang has to be bad news." He kicked himself for letting H. risk everything on a whacko nutcase. It called for an antiphon.

K.: The readiness is all.

H.: The ripeness is all.

Both: He who risks nothing is bound to lose all. *Merde de tresieme*.

The editors laughed, and someone suggested that Janet St. Janeway was the one to ask. The ferocious lady, who had won a Pulitzer for her account of rivers choked with bodies in the India-Pakistan war, was on the phone in her cubicle. They scribbled to each other. "Abortion?"

"Where?"

"NYC"

"Dr. Howard Raymond, Police Surgeon, Union City, NJ. Nutley 6-0123. $500. No fluids twelve hours. *Bon chance*."

H. sprinted back to Town Hall. The lobby was empty and dark, but a group standing on the sidewalk waiting for a cab looked like they might be going to Chinatown. They were Sing Sang Woo's sisters from Los Angeles and a violinist named Noah Glaser. They hadn't seen Alberta, but they offered to take him to the party in Chinatown where she must be. The Laughing Gingko Cantonese Family Restaurant was down some steps in a basement. There were two rows of long rough tables in the narrow room, like a refectory, and a kitchen you could see behind a wide serving window at the rear. The menu was handwritten in Chinese on a blackboard, but it didn't matter because no one ordered; it was a private banquet. Noah Glaser identified some of the guests: Sang's parents and sisters from Los Angeles, her teachers from Curtis, Carl Horner and Efram Zimbalist, Mme. Tourquet, and a dozen friends—Karen Tuttle, Fred Lawrence, Julius Katchen, Jaime Laredo, Boris Manheim, Myrna Yi, Jacob Lateiner. As they came in, the eighty-year-old Horner was just making a high-pitched tinkle with his chopsticks on his water glass. "Pardon my triangle," he began and gave a toast in several languages, which made everyone laugh. Glaser said it was about what Bach would have said to Prokofiev if they had heard Sing Sang in Town

Hall. He couldn't see Albert anywhere. Glaser guessed she was in the ladies' room, if there was one.

Peter Pelagius was even taller than he looked on the stage where he was somewhat diminished by his thirteen-foot Steinway. Now he stood in a First World War army great coat that came down to his ankles, his long blond hair covering the coat's epaulettes. He nodded and spoke with everyone, but his eyes were searching the room. Perhaps he was looking for Albert too. H. was more angry than anxious that she wasn't there; she had brought him all the way down to Chinatown and disappeared. Someone toasted Sing Sang and Peter, and he replied in a accent that veered between French and German and may have been Dutch. He had a mellifluous tenor and seemed like a gentle person. Noah Glaser passed H. and said he should sit down and eat. "I've never had Chinese food," H. admitted.

Glaser was amazed. "Where have you been?"

"St. Louis," he explained. He watched the sweating cook in the kitchen juggling deep round pots in clouds of steam and tongues of flame. An old Chinese lady stood between the tables, talking to everyone as she carried dishes from the counter. Glaser said they were Sing Sang's aunt and uncle; they owned the Laughing Gingko. The tables were becoming covered with steaming dishes.

"Where do you think she is?" he asked.

"Pelagius should know. Ask him."

Glaser pulled H. over to the musician. "This is a friend of Albertine's." Pelagius excused himself to Sing Sang's parents and stepped close to H.

"Where has she gone? Was she with you?" Pelagius asked.

"I haven't seen her since the intermission. We thought she was with you."

"She was to meet you here?"

"Yes. I went to get something for her, and she said to meet her here if you all had left."

Sing Sang Woo joined them. She had seen her companion's anxiety talking to H. She put her arm around Peter Pelagius. "You're H. Stillman. Thank you for coming. Albertine told me about you."

"Thank you, it was wonderful."

"You're not Jimmy Bowes," said Peter Pelagius, showing some relief.

"He's Albertine's friend. They sailed together last summer." Sing Sang Woo was lively and spirited; he was sorry he had missed the concert.

"You are Albertine's friend," Pelagius repeated.

"She says you have been very kind to her."

"Do you know Constantine? Her stepfather?"

"I met him."

"Albertine must have shelter from such a man."

H. considered whether he had turned his back on Albert when she needed him most. If it was true, he hadn't known it. She looked like she was having fun, an otter playing in the surf. The sea otter is said to be the happiest animal in nature; it floats all day on its back eating abalone.

"I hope she will come back soon," he said to Pelagius who embraced him and kissed him on both cheeks. H. said it was a wonderful recital. Peter kissed him again and sat down. "I am very worried. Where is she? You saw her when?"

"At the intermission. We were in the street."

Peter Pelagius stood and called for quiet. The guests tapped on their glasses. "Dear friends," he said, "has anyone one here seen Albertine Bang since the concert?" No one had seen her all night except H. She had disappeared. He had a chance at catching the last train to Boston and finishing his term papers. But Sing Sang's aunt stopped him as he tried to leave. "You no eat, young man?" He apologized for his rush. "I make you fortune cookie. You eat." She held a pinched and folded cookie with a homemade fortune on squared paper sticking out, all wrapped it in a paper napkin. "You eat soon," she said again. He put the cookie in his pocket.

NEWARK

The cold wind off the Hudson blew down Canal Street as he hunted for the subway to Grand Central. The chill made him wish for his scarf. It was his overcoat. While he waited on the empty platform, he took out the now-crumbling fortune cookie. The squared paper was folded three times and pushed inside the dough. He ate half the cookie, his first food in hours, and unfolded his fortune. It was handwritten in pencil. "Bang pen station." From Grand Central, he took the Times Square shuttle, then the IRT to Thirty-fourth Street. Penn Station's arching space of stone and intricate steel, like a cathedral made from an Erector Set, was as deserted as the subway. She was sitting on a bench in a small waiting room, reading a pocket score. She jumped into his arms and smothered his face with kisses.

"Why did you run away?"

"I changed my mind. I want my baby."

"I almost went back to Boston."

"You should go."

"Why did you tell Sing Sang's aunt where you were?"

"I was afraid without you."

"I'm here. Now what do you want?"

"You're going to say no."

"Try me."

"You and the baby."

"One at a time."

"Did you find your friend?"

He gave her the scratch sheet with Dr. Raymond's name and number. "Five hundred dollars."

"We'll find it."

"Is it too late?"

"They must work at night." He tried to get her to stand up.

"Did you meet Peter?"

"He's very worried about you."

"I've known him since I was ten. At Curtis."

"We should phone this guy." He made her stand and walk with him to a bank of telephone booths at the entrance to the waiting room. She had washed her face of the black mascara and chalky makeup and looked more like Albert, though a far cry from last summer's ice cream cone. Her dark hair and flat tummy snuffed out the Bang in her.

He dropped a dime in the phone and dialed. An operator asked for forty cents. A voice answered and said to call back. He began dialing person to person. After a half hour, someone named Louie answered and refused the charges. H. called him back for forty cents and handed the phone to Albert. Louie had never heard of Dr. Raymond. How many months was she pregnant? Three. He told her go to a particular bank of phone booths in the Newark Plaza at eleven tomorrow morning and dial a number. She'd be told what to do next. Anyone with her should wait on a bench in front of the phones while she called. She should bring a towel, extra underwear, and six hundred dollars in used twenties. She was crying with big heaves and shaking. He held her as tightly as he could while he wondered where to spend the night and where to get six hundred dollars.

They went back to their bench. It was cold, but he had back his scarf which he wound around them both. Agreeing to lose the child had made her miserable. "I can't live with a killer. I can't play for a killer. They all know at Curtis, I can't face anyone again, Peter, Sing Sang, or anyone—"

"Leave Curtis. You say you hate it. Come to Cambridge. That was the deal. A new life."

"I keep forgetting." Albert and H. hugged each other on the bench and tried to generate a protective envelope of body heat. Penn Station had turned off the furnace.

"Where is your house? Where do you live? Can we go there?"

"Some friends of Constantine are staying there."

They tried to imagine a future after the abortion and Curtis Institute and Harvard. They fell asleep trying. H. was awakened by a policeman shaking his foot. He and Albert were wrapped in each other, prone on the bench.

"You gotta keep your feet on the floor," he said. It was seven thirty by an enormous clock in the far waiting room. People were walking by, and the benches were filling up with families and suitcases. "I'm hungry," Albert said. They had orange drinks and two Nedick's hot dogs apiece, with spicy tomato relish, at a stand off the main concourse. Dust danced in the shafts of morning sun before bisecting the lacy iron girders that supported the structure above them.

"I should go back to Curtis. I haven't got fifty bucks. Six hundred is crazy."

H. had been thinking. "We'll call Frankie."

"You can't tell her."

"She's my fairy godmother."

Albert said she was going back to Philadelphia, find the money, and come back next weekend. It was only an hour and a half.

"But you won't have me."

He went to the telephone books hanging on a rack between the booths. Dr. John Cromwell, 511 Park Avenue. A servant answered and left him waiting for many minutes and nickles. He imagined a phone line being installed for his godmother or four strong men bearing her to a telephone on a litter. "H. Stillman. How wonderful," roared Frankie. "You must stay with me. Find 511 Park Avenue. Go to the fifteenth floor and follow the orange peels to your room." She was determined he wanted to spend the night and only reluctantly accepted that he wanted to see her now. "I am at my levee, but come if you must." He told her he was with Alberta Bang. "BRING HER."

Albert protested all the way to Sixty-ninth Street. Frankie would tell Constantine, the commodore would tell the police, Frankie wouldn't have that much cash around on Sunday, Albert looked awful. Only the last was true. How could they ever get Albert's hair back? And her ass and her boobs and tummy? The new Albert in bright sun was a fright. It would take years to restore her, like the *Last Supper*. She balked at the front door, then at the elevator. It opened directly into the Cromwell apartment, opposite a marble staircase. A maid met them and took them down a long hall to the solarium. They saw Frankie first; she was facing a roof garden and beyond that a view of water tanks and the trees of Central Park. Frankie's winter mode was larval. She was semipermanently installed on a chaise in a leafy bower of verdant plants growing almost perceptibly from hydroponic fuses in an endless fluorescent day. In the glassed greenhouse, the metabolic heat of vegetable consumption around her pupal couch was even steamier than in her peripatetic summer months, which seemed abstemious by comparison. Amid all that chlorophyll, Frankie looked like a forced tomato. She was reading a spy story by Graham Greene about microfilm baked in a chocolate cake.

"ALBERTA BANG. What have you done to yourself?" She turned on H. "Henry Stillman, how could you allow this? You should all be ashamed. Oh my darling Albert," she keened in her richest diapason. "I know exactly what you're up to, my pet. You think nobody takes you seriously because you're beautiful and happy and enjoy yourself. Look at me. What does Frankie know except her appetites? Has she suffered? Has she despaired? The words are not in her vocabulary. Come here. Come here, let me look at you, let me touch you." Albert approached Frankie with great care, like Julia Stillman did in East Hampton, as if her flesh hid whirlpools that might suck you in. She was still tightly wrapped in her wool overcoat which had been her night's blanket. "Take off that terrible thing, let me see you." Frankie spun a siren's song, a beckoning web of words, drawing Albert ever closer. She brushed aside orchids and anemones to make a space for Albert close to her. "I know all about Constantine living with the *princessa* in Milan and leaving you in the maw of that repulsive duke." To H., she explained that Constantine had used Albert to occupy the duke while he ran off with his duchess. They were all disgusting. The news that Constantine had abandoned her mother for the *princessa* must have been buried in the lost quarto pages of Albert's mispaginated letter.

The commodore swore, according to Frankie, that the *princessa* Francesca d'Alessandri would never set foot in the yacht club, but he had said the same thing about Sonja Henie. "Mother is better off without him," said Albert. "We would all be better off without any men, except for Joe Stillman," said his father's most loyal admirer. Frankie now had Albert firmly in her vast embrace; she was feeling the dark hair ("it will grow back"), running her finger along the scalp and behind her ears, but the left hand was exploring her ribs and breasts and pausing over her stomach. "Alberta Bang, what are you hiding?"

"What?

"Does H. know?"

"Yes."

"Is it his?"

"Yes."

"Turn to me, dear." Albert obediently turned her ravaged body toward the Great Mother. Frankie put her open hand on Albert's stomach. "It's a boy."

"We need six hundred dollars," said her godson, "in used twenties."

"All I have is crisp bills for the staff Christmas gifts."

They just had time to get to Newark. Albert attacked Frankie as soon as they were in the street and didn't stop 'til the train crossed the meadows and wetlands of reeds and cattails and a thousand gulls bobbing on mucky water, just a minute from Newark.

"I don't think Frankie Cromwell has any right to say how I should present myself as an artist. If she wants to be a clown and make fun of herself, that's her choice," Albert spoke fiercely, with unexpected pride in her image. It made him wonder what her real family was like. "Tell me about your father. Where is he?"

"Who?"

"Your real father. Bang."

"Norway."

"Is he still alive?"

"I suppose." He was chilled by her response.

"How old were you?"

"Eight."

"The great-great-granddaughter of the bishop of Oslo."

"My father was a violist at CBS. A nobody."

He gave up trying to be nice. The plaza was just outside the terminal. It was five minutes of eleven.

"Will you come back to Philly with me afterward?"

"I've got exams tomorrow."

"If I'm sick?"

"I won't leave you."

They walked to the plaza and found the bank of phone booths and the row of benches Louie had described. The skyline of Newark was like St. Louis around the Union Station. Grand public works from the Depression dwarfed by urban decay. The plastic Christmas wreaths that flapped on the concrete lampposts were ridiculous, a mockery of birth and renewal. H. felt like a grinch. He hated the world.

Albert went into a phone booth to call Louie. A bald man in a blue overcoat was talking in the next booth. When Albert came back, she reported that Louie had asked if she was alone, what she was wearing, and whether she had the money, then told her to wait, he would come. They watched as the bald man left the adjacent booth where he had been talking and approached them. "I'm Louie. I'll take you to the doctor." To H., he said, "You stay here. I'll bring her back."

"How long?" H. asked him.

"About two hours." He asked for the money. Albert had the envelope in her hand.

"Where are we going?" she asked.

"A motel, not far. I have a car."

"What kind of anaesthetic?" she asked him.

"Demerol."

"How much?"

"One hundred fifty cc."

"That's not enough."

"It's too much. If the cops come, you have to be able to move, you have to clear out, you can't be all zonked." Albert put the money back in her purse. "I've changed my mind," she said to the man.

"You two talk about it." He walked away toward the phone booths and stood with his back to them.

"What should I do?" She was asking him. H. felt like a rat. He wanted her to have an abortion; he had from the moment she said she was pregnant. He loved her, he wanted to marry her or at least live with her, and he didn't want her to have a family yet. "If you can handle 150 cc, you should do it. That's why we came."

"Abortions should be in hospitals. There's this doctor in the Alleghenies. He runs a sanitarium, with nurses and beds, and everyone has to stay at least one night or as long as they need. Abortion is some mystic and political thing with him, but for all the love and kindness and care, it's still terrible. It's murdering something that's alive, some hope inside you that gets killed." H. had suspected it. "This isn't your first, is it?"

"I'm always pregnant. I must be Mother Earth." She sounded like the helpless spectator of her own body.

"We should go back there, to that doctor in the mountains."

"I tried to when Peter and I were playing in Altoona, but Pennsylvania had a big crackdown, and he was closed."

She took the money out of her pocket and counted it. "Louie, let's go." She kissed H. quickly, and Louie put her in a Fairlane parked just off the plaza.

He was accomplice to his child's murder in every way. Had he promised her anything for doing this? They had passed a Chock full o'Nuts in the station. Whole wheat sugared donuts were what he needed to set the world right. He was returning to the plaza with a bag of donuts for Albert when he saw the Fairlane parked where it was before. They had only been gone about twenty minutes. Albert saw him and got out. Something must have been wrong with the money. Frankie's new bills were too easy to trace or she had balked at the Demerol. "What happened?"

"He wouldn't do it."

"Why?" Albert began sobbing soundlessly. She held him tightly, leaning on him with her whole weight, her knees sagging. H. pulled her to the bench and tried to get her to sit, but she slumped to the ground between his legs. "What is it? What did he say?" But she only sobbed. Louie got out of his car and came over to them. He explained what happened. "The doc won't scrape anyone after ten weeks, eleven at the outside. It's for her own good. She's too far gone. She told me she was three months." Albert let out a howling "NOOOOOOOOOOOOO!" and then another and another. A man on a near bench looked at them with alarm, prepared to help if necessary. A woman left a phone booth to see what the trouble was. "How far gone?" H. asked Louie. "He thinks at least four months, maybe more. Her cervix is three fingers. I have to go." Albert unleashed a last shattering NO. Louie went into the same phone booth where they had first seen him. The woman who had been staring at Albert returned to her phone booth, and soon she and Louie were talking. She was Raymond's next client.

It wasn't his baby, not if what Louie said was true. It was conceived before he knew her. Albert was terrified he would accuse her of entrapping him. "You think I planned this, to make you think the baby was yours."

"I wish it was. It made me very happy—to be entrapped." He stroked her face and tried to lift her from the ground.

"I discovered how much I loved you and needed you."

"What are you going to do?" he asked her.

"I have no choice."

"You can get married."

She laughed.

"Do you know who the father is?"

"I can guess."

"Will he help?"

"If I blackmail him. Which I wouldn't."

"Do I know him?"

"You hate him."

"He was my best friend."

"He thinks you're a god."

"So what were you talking about at the Biltmore?"

"You mostly. How you electrocuted your fat friend over and over."

"Donna Hasenclever. We took all her money, then we did it for free."

He offered her a whole wheat donut which she accepted greedily, a welcome hint of the old Albert. They walked to the station where they exchanged partially masticated donut dough while they kissed on the platform, waiting for a train to Philadelphia. "I love you," she said.

"Where are you going to go?" he asked her.

"France maybe. Study with Casals, wait for the baby, Peter Pelagius will be there. He said he would help."

"You're not going to tell Bowes."

"It's nothing to him. Why bother?"

She tried to return his scarf, but he held her hand to keep her from taking it off. The train came in, but it didn't stop long. No one got on or off. She stepped into the vestibule and tried to pull her hand away from his. "Be free," she said from the already-moving train. He walked, then ran beside her, holding her hand. "Let go," she said, pulling her hand away. She loved him, and she was leaving him. He couldn't let go. Watching the train disappear, he knew he wasn't free. He should have gone with her.

It was six when he returned to Wigglesworth. He was sipping Cointreau and thumbing Landor when Kornfeld came out of his room in gym shorts and sneakers, on his way to do squat-thrusts at Sweat, Swim, & Shower, an exercise class that met at six thirty in the Indoor Athletic Building.

"Did you find the abortionist?"

"He wouldn't do it."

"For five hundred bucks?"

"Six. She was too pregnant. Four months."

"Didn't she know?"

"She says she didn't."

"Is it yours?"

"I wish."

"No, you don't. Whose?"

"You saw him under the clock."

"Bowes?"

H. nodded.

"You don't want to have anything to do with this woman."

"I love her."

"She's a monster."

"She's a genius."

"You don't know the first thing about music."

"I know."

"You've never even heard her play."

Except in Napeague, he hadn't. But he believed. Kornfeld went to the gym. H. tried to get a couple of hours' sleep before the Wordsworth exam. Why was he even here? Why was he taking a test on Walter Savage Landor and Wordsworth when he should have got on the train with Albert and gone with her to Philadelphia? He had deserted her again. That's what Maia was going to say. He had left her in Newark just to get back to Harvard to show off his Walter Savage Landor for

Paul. A note on the door of the seminar room said the exam was rescheduled for Wednesday. And there was H., chock-full of the hateful poesy of Walter Savage Landor and no place to dump it.

Maia had just put down Eben and was finishing a glass of red wine at the kitchen table when he opened the door. She jumped up in excitement; she had been waiting all weekend to know what had happened. Does she love you? Does she want you? He had rehearsed the moment, but it did no good. He couldn't tell her. "What? What happened?" she demanded.

"She was pregnant."

"Alberta Bang? Pregnant?"

"You're all pregnant," he said forlornly.

"Was it yours?"

"She thought it was."

"And it wasn't?"

"She lost track of her periods."

"How did you all find out?"

"The abortionist wouldn't touch her. She was too far gone."

Maia was miserable for him. "Oh, baby, you must feel awful. You went down there to get your girl and wound up taking her to an abortionist. Do you still love her?"

"More than ever." He knew it was ridiculous.

"Why?"

He looked at her, chewing her lip as she struggled to make sense of his tormented life. How had he been lucky enough to find her for a friend? Maia was about four months pregnant herself. Could he tell her he wanted to put his head on her stomach and listen to her child? Or open her blouse and suck on her nipples? His appetites embarrassed him. Was it possible that there was something fundamentally wrong with him? Why had all of Oldfield turned against him, everyone but Maia and Paul? He wondered if the same thing was about to happen at Harvard. He could feel the anarchy and hate rising in him. He appealed to Maia.

"Is there something wrong with me? Am I crazy? Be honest."

"Have some wine," she said, pouring him a glass. "You're having a tough time. You'll be okay when it's over."

"Alberta Bang you mean?"

"Alberta Bang just doesn't see what a wonderful, sexy person you are. You hide everything that is beautiful, you slump, you tell the world you hate yourself."

He drew her toward him, and they kissed. His hand expertly found her clit, and she moaned. "I can come ten times. Did Alberta Bang teach you that?"

"She or you have taught me everything I know."

They closed Eben's door at the top of the stairs as they went to her double bed. He left her sleeping and drank the last of his wine as he went through the kitchen. He felt ten feet tall. Maia would be furious that he was going to Philadelphia to look for Albert.

They met at Philadelphia's Thirtieth Street station. She looked a lot more like her old self except for her hair. She wore a bulky sweater, a bright wool skirt, and matching cap that held in only a small portion of her hair's volume. The thick wool concealed how thin she had become. "I told Peter Pelagius the baby wasn't his," she said the very first thing after they met.

"What did he say?"

"What I expected. He wants to marry me anyway."

"I hope you don't."

"He's a beautiful person."

"He is a complete innocent."

"It's true, he is. He was surprised we had had sex when I told him."

"Maybe you didn't."

"What's that supposed to mean?"

"That you thought you did. You said he's homosexual."

"Well, he isn't."

"You wanted him to be the father. You hoped he was. Let's leave it at that."

"You're saying I deliberately lied to him."

"I'm saying you didn't know how pregnant you were. It was a genuine confusion."

"I thought I'd never see you again. Why have you come back?"

"I'm still in love with you."

"Why?"

"That's what I want to find out."

"I never should have told you about Jimmy Bowes. You hate him."

"He as much as told me himself. You made love on the beach in Bermuda."

"He's a shit."

"An attractive shit, the life of the party."

"You're telling me I should have his baby alone."

"What would Bowes say if you told him?"

"He doesn't want to hear about babies."

"Even his own?"

"He wouldn't believe me, he'd say I'm a whore, which I probably am."

"You should tell him anyway. He should be helping you now, not Peter Pelagius."

"Will you still talk to me when I'm a mother?"

"Why wouldn't I?"

"You're so angry."

"Not at you. At Jimmy Bowes. I want to kill him."

The possibility of some kind of relationship was in the wind if he wanted it. Perhaps that was what he had come to find out. He could imagine living with her but never playing father to a child of Jimmy Bowes.

"Walk me to Rittenhouse Square. It's just across the river." They looked into the water from the bridge. A light snow swirled in cyclonic patterns over the Schuylkill.

"I could give the baby away for adoption."

"Have it and see." She was thinking of ways to make room for him in her life. Adoption was no more radical than abortion, maybe less. Either way, the child disappeared. They crossed the river and could see Rittenhouse Square ahead.

"I'd be bored to death living with Peter Pelagius. It was stupid to think I could."

"Tell me something," H. said to her. "How can an innocent like Pelagius, with no experience of life, understand the anguish of Beethoven so perfectly?"

"Theory classes claim you don't need experience to understand music. A musical statement is complete. It explains itself. It's mathematical. That's bullshit. Look at Mozart, look at Casals. How age changes, how we grow. I want my baby because I hope it will make me a more feeling person and a better musician."

The snow was barely noticeable in the city until they came to the square whose bare trees were limned with white on their weather side. Albert named the burghers who built the grand mansions on the square—Biddle, Cowles, Fields, Sibley, Drexel, Curtis Bok. The Curtis Institute was a Renaissance palace on the corner of Locust Street. She lived a block away in an apartment on Latimer Street she shared with

Sing Sang Woo and Karen Toskowitz. She left him to wait inside the front door while she ran upstairs. "You can come up if nobody's there." His mind danced with possibilities of being alone with her in her apartment, even four months pregnant. She was gone a long time, and when she came down, she was almost hidden behind a big cello case she carried in front of her. "They're rehearsing up there," she said. She made him take back his scarf. "It's all you have to wear."

"Where are you going?"

"To Curtis. They have practice rooms. I want to be alone with you, to play for you. I want you to hear the Goffriller." He couldn't think about music. Damn her Goffriller. He wanted to be alone with her to hold her in his arms. She was walking very quickly in the snow, with her arm around the cello like a pet bear.

"Hurry up. He shouldn't get cold." "He?"

"Il Gigante. Wait 'til you hear him growl." They were at the iron gate doors to the Curtis Institute that opened into a warm wood-paneled room with a wide fireplace and mantle and a high ceiling. It was a common room with sofas and tables where students were reading, talking, and drinking coffee. A short-haired girl that H. had seen in the Laughing Gingko called to her.

"Albert, where did you go? What happened?"

"I got sick."

"Peter was looking for you everywhere."

Albert pulled H. down a corridor and into a gilded practice room with a grand piano, chairs, and music stands. She opened the case and took out the fiery red Goffriller and bow. The deep stain had highlights of yellow and orange that shimmered in the light like tongues of flame. "The Il Gigante," she said, opening her thighs wide to receive the instrument between her knees so that her skirt rode up her legs. Il Gigante was her man. She tightened the hairs of her bow, plucked a string, then swept the bow down to her left shoe and drew it back and into the air behind her in a broad theme that began with an innocent question whose answer rattled and growled and resolved itself in a low whisper that shook his soul. Albert was smiling at him, her head and neck stretching toward him, drawing him to her, asking him to enter her world of sound.

"Beethoven," he said.

"Shhhh." She was smiling. She played on, her head bent close to her fingers on the strings, then thrown back wild, joyous, free. He didn't hear the door open or shut; but a tall man in a hooded grey tracksuit went by him, stopped by Albert's chair, and leaned his head way over to hers. It was Peter Pelagius. She raised her face to him and kissed his mouth without stopping. Peter sat down at the piano behind her, kicked off his soggy sneakers, and began playing with her, barefoot. It was the Beethoven Opus 69 that had brought them together; but she continued to play for H. as if he were the only person in the room, in her head, her heart, her world. She smiled at him, closed her eyes, and quickly opened them to make sure that he was still with her. She rejoiced that he was her audience. He tried to return her smile, to let her know what happiness she gave him; but instead of the joy and wonder he intended to express, he cried. Kornfeld was right. It was not his world. He would always be an outsider looking in on a beauty he could never enter. Before she could see his tears, he left the room. The snow was sticking in Rittenhouse Square deep enough to leave tracks. He felt the flecks of ice crystals on his cheeks melt under his warm tears.

"H.! H.! Where are you going?" She was calling to him from the iron gates. He didn't look back.

IVAN KARAMAZOV

H. was folded into the fireplace in their living room smoking a joint with his head just below the damper and *The Brothers Karamazov* and a bottle of Cointreau on the blackened brick between his legs. He had just finished The Grand Inquisitor, and in an exalted state of lingering orgasm and spiritual ecstasy, he unraveled his frame from the fireplace and stood. He had to talk. Kornfeld's door was closed; he was a sleeper on nights when he wasn't working at the *Crimson*. H. had just made the astonishing discovery that he was not, as he had always thought, the young Alyosha, a novice in a monastery who brings love and understanding to his vicious, violent brothers. Far from it! He banged on Kornfeld's door.

"What do you want?"

"I am Ivan Karamazov."

"It's two o'clock."

"There is no God."

"I know that, you asshole. Go to bed."

But he couldn't. H. was incandescent with the epiphany of doubt and hate he had found in the chimney with Ivan Karamazov. Chaos and conflict was his medium, alive and potent. He was the Superman. He was god. The shambles of his life was revealed to him as the true incarnation of his spirit. He was possessed with the unexpected, surging power of negation—a glorious, purgative NO, *non serviam*, Satan's liberating cry as he tumbled through the void into hell.

He shouted at Kornfeld's door. "Open the door! Henry Stillman, pious prig and servant of God, must die, over and over, as I have just died in the arms of love. Henry Stillman is no more. Trofim Lysenko has shown that the genetic destiny of a potato can be altered in a single generation. I can undo my genes. I can choose new parents or none at all. I am the author of myself, the orphan I have longed to be. Gone is the Chateau, rooted out the altar boy, the honor cards and medals, gone the gentleman in white gloves bearing an orchid corsage to the debutante who will someday give him twelve children.

"And death to the Stillman in me too, to the young man who is the spit and image of his uncle Button. I will not wait until I am forty-six to hang myself from a furnace duct or sixty-two to bury myself with my toys in a basement tomb like a pharaoh. All is gone, obliterated, and from the ashes arises H., outlaw and destroyer, condemned and friendless, parricide, adulterer, defiler of mothers and Madonnas, betrayer of friends."

H. opened Kornfeld's door. The bedroom reeked of tincture of benzoin with which he coated his body to suffocate the jock itch fungus that lived in his pores.

"Open a window, for god's sake. This is a gas chamber."

"Nice image, Stillman, really tasteful. Somewhere in Poland perhaps?"

"*The Grand Inquisitor* is a hundred years old. He burns heretics for breakfast."

"For heretics read Jews and Muslims."

"And Christ comes—"

"Messiah Visits Warsaw Ghetto; Advises Residents to Turn Other Cheek."

"*The Grand Inquisitor* throws him in jail."

"I've read it."

"Classic comics. What happens next, smart-ass?"

Kornfeld got out of bed, pushing hair over an incipient bald spot. He went into the living room, put on a rumpled tweed coat, and folded himself into the fireplace as H. had done earlier. Shivering, his chin rattling on his drawn and naked knees, he picked up a pipe and lit it. After two deep breaths, he took up H.'s challenge.

"The Inquisitor visits Jesus in his cell in the middle of the night and talks him to death. I hate Dostoevsky. All his men turn to religious mush and fall in love with whores. Near death fried his brains. I must forgive him."

"Wrong thought," declared H. "Raskalnikov turns to mush, and the Underground Man, and Alyosha, but not Ivan. He holds fast to nothingness. No whores, no monks, only madness. And the Grand Inquisitor, what a saint. He's your kind of hero, Kornfeld—a Lenin, a Stalin, a colossus, a giant who takes on himself the burden of good and evil, frees man from the curse of his freedom so he can be happy and productive, redeems Christ's errors, and makes human life possible. I met a Jesuit who knew God was dead but kept on going."

"Don't mention Lenin in the same breath with your god-sotted clerics." Kornfeld was racked briefly with a consumptive cough. "Lenin demanded the highest, the best man can give."

"The church and socialism are the same thing—"

"Bullshit."

"Ideologies that explain everything and leave nothing to the individual. Ivan rebels against this paternalistic slop. He will not serve—God or Mammon. He is the Superman."

"Why in hell are you reading Karamazov? You've got term papers due."

"For the answer to my life."

He went into his room. They blessed each other with their private antiphon.

H.: God is dead.

K.: The divine corpse stinks in putrefaction.

Both: *Merde de tresieme.*

Kornfeld shut his door.

4

ST. LOUIS

He was woken by the telephone. It was Julia Chateau, and for the first time, he couldn't detect the egg timer in her long-distance voice. "Your father wants to be baptised."

"Is he sick?"

"He just wants to be baptised."

"You must be very happy."

"Of course I am. I'm thrilled. But I want to ask you. This Father O'Connor, is he really a Jesuit?"

"Yes, Mother."

"I don't think he's a real priest."

"Why?"

"He always wears old clothes, like you do."

"He was a chaplain in the army, he taught me physics at St. Aloysius, he's a Jesuit."

"They just make noise down there."

"That's what they do, Mother."

"Make noise?"

"The Juggler of Notre Dame just juggled, but he made the virgin smile."

"Your father wants you to be his sponsor, his godfather."

"Dad asked me to find someone for him to talk to, and I did. That's as far as I can go."

"Your own father is asking you."

It was a trap, set by Julia or Joe, their cunning scheme to make him live the life they chose for him and behave in their image of him. They were hard to resist. Ivan Karamazov has risen in him not a minute too soon. He had broken every vow he had ever made to himself. He swore he wouldn't go to East Hampton if they made Kornfeld wear a yellow star and sleep in the barn, he swore never to go back to school, he swore never to return to St. Louis, but above all, he had vowed never to sell Joe to the church, however many pieces of silver his mother offered him. "I have an exam, I'll call you later," he lied and hung up.

The issue was muddy in his mind whether he had broken his vow by finding Joe a priest. It wasn't Julia but Joe who had approached him, but he had betrayed him nevertheless. He had to draw the line at the godfather business or live a hypocrite forever. He was an atheist, at least an agnostic, with nothing but contempt for Joe's newfound religion. He couldn't be anybody's Catholic godfather. Father O'Connor would back him up. He had never confessed to Julia Chateau that he had left the church, but it was time to lay his cards on the table. He had to go home and tell them. It was Christmas anyway.

He met Joe at the breakfast table. He hadn't spoken with him since August.

"So you decided to go to college after all."

"It was the only place I could get in."

"I could have got you into Yale."

"You didn't. And without Pickering's reference, I doubt you could."

They watched the toaster smoke in silence.

"Did your mother tell you I've decided to call myself a Catholic?"

"She was very excited."

"We thought you might be willing to be godfather."

"You and who else?"

"It was my idea."

"I can't be your godfather. I'm not a Catholic."

"Neither am I."

"The blind leading the blind."

"But you were."

"Why are you doing this?"

The old man spread Dundee marmalade on his burned toast.

"There's a devil in me. I want to get him out."

"Untrue. It's common sense."

"I don't know what damn fool thing he'll make me do next."

"Make you join the church, if you ask me."

"Father O'Connor thought you might be a help."

"Being a Catholic is serious stuff—faith versus reason, grace against sin, god in three persons—"

"We don't get into all that."

"The god business, you mean."

"Waves and their propagation. That's what O'Connor and me have in common."

"I like you as you are. The Great Wave Propagator."

"I'll still be the same. I'm not going to change."

"Did Julia Chateau put you up to this?"

"Even if she did, it's no reason not to, is it?"

"Getting religion to make her happy?"

"I don't see any harm in that."

"I do, but I have my own history with her."

H. was relieved that Joe knew what he was doing and why. He had feared the old man was going soft in the brain. "I thought O'Connor had sold you some medieval proof of the Trinity, and I got worried."

"I was hoping we could all be together on something, for a change." He was clearly very disappointed. "Maybe you can think about it."

The second piece of toast burned. H. felt like a heel.

He walked along the driveway to Jill Bowes's carriage house where she had her studio. It was three o'clock. Big Jim would still be at the steel mill, and Jimmy Bowes was at Princeton. H. hadn't seen her since summer, and he knew something was not right about what had happened or been happening between them since kindergarten. It wasn't right that he had slept with the wife of his English teacher, but it seemed even less right that he wanted to sleep with the mother of what was once his best friend. They hadn't touched each other again after the moment in the pantry on Block Island.

H. had begun to wonder if his passion for Jill Bowes was a kind of jealous revenge on the sins of her son. Jimmy Bowes had all H.'s women first. H. got the dregs he left behind. H. was ashamed he had lost Albert to Jimmy and decided not to tell his mother what had really happened. He found Mrs. Bowes in her studio working on the bust of a horse's head. She was surprised to see him.

"H., H., I thought you were dead. What did you do? Where did you go?"

"Harvard. But I'm about to quit. Join the army, do something real."

They kept a careful distance. Both knew. He held out a twenty-dollar bill across the divide between them.

"I owe you."

"Tell me about the girl with the funny name who was on her way to Italy. Did you get her back?"

"Alberta Bang. She came and went. It's all over."

"You were in love with her."

"She's pregnant."

"But not yours."

"I wish."

"How could that happen? I talked with her on the phone. I could tell she loved you."

"It was before I met her."

"Do you know who?"

"She was wilder than I thought."

"I'm sorry."

"How's Jimmy?"

"He loves Princeton. He's the female lead in the Triangle show. They tour eight cities before Christmas."

She put down a palette knife and brushed clay off her smock.

"You really want to quit Harvard?" She was saddened by what she saw as the downward spiral of his life. "You were first in your class with the Jesuits. You had everything. I don't understand."

"The first shall be last."

"That doesn't explain it."

"I am corrupt, dishonest, and cynical."

"For example?"

"My father asked me to find someone to talk with him about God."

"Julia Chateau has been trying to get him to do that since you all were in kindergarten—"

"I swore I would never help her convert him, and I did."

"That was wonderful of you, and you condemn yourself?"

"I knew a Jesuit who saw God die and return as a land mine during the Battle of the Bulge. They became friends. Dad is getting baptised next week, and he wants me to be his godfather."

"I think that's beautiful—"

"It's ludicrous. A charade."

"He wants to be close to your mother and to you. Is that a crime?"

"There are better ways, if that's what he wants. Being a Catholic means something—that you believe in a set of things, the Trinity or the transubstantiation, like he believes in Ohm's law or the conservation of energy. And I'll bet a hat he doesn't."

"The proof is what works for a person, isn't it?"

"No. It's what's true, it has to be."

He was shaking. She came close to him; they touched, and the shaking stopped.

"You become so ferocious about faith, you scare me."

"It's gotten me in a lot of trouble."

Jill went to an easel and began sketching him in charcoal. "Just hold still." She worked furiously—rubbing, blowing, scratching, breaking lots of charcoal. "Okay," she said.

The picture was of a large hunched man with a scowling face like a black cloud. He was wearing a priest's cassock.

"That's how you see me?"

"That's how you are."

"You've made me a priest."

"Oh, Henry, Henry, I want to say something I should have said to you a long time ago. Remember back when you told me you were planning to become a Jesuit? I felt you were closer to your true self more than any time since I've known you. It was thrilling. It was the real you."

Was she right? Would the Jesuits take back a lapsed prefect of the sodality? Could he ever rededicate his life to the greater glory of God after going so far astray? What was once natural and simple now seemed immense and impossible. Like being a godfather. They were side by side looking at him in her big sketchbook. He drew her to him, and they kissed. Through her skirt, he slipped his hand in her underwear and pressed it against her pubic hair. There wasn't the tight girdle she had on before, and his fingers explored her crotch easily. She put her hand over his, stopping him.

"No further, please, or I'll die. That's fine, right there, that's wonderful, just like that."

Julia Chateau was waiting for him at her desk when he tried to sneak past her to his room. She nailed him.

"Don't run away from me. Is a word of what your father told me true? You refused him? His own son? The poor man is crushed."

"If you had seen that poor man in his knockabout stuffing everyone in the bilge to test his loopy theories of sailing, you wouldn't be so sorry for him. He can take care of himself."

"Give me one reason why you can't do this simple thing for him."

"I'm not a Catholic, and I don't think he is either. He's doing it for you."

"You are a Catholic too. You're just going through a phase, like everyone does—"

"I should no more be his godfather than Frankie Cromwell should be mine. You say so yourself."

"It's not the same. You were a baby. He's an old man who deserves your love and respect. Try to forget yourself for once and think of others."

"I take what Joe believes a lot more seriously than you do. I love him for his belief in reason. I'm protecting the man I love by refusing to cater to his whims about the church. It's not the real Joe Stillman."

"He wants to come up, Henry, he's frightened. You've got to help him."

He agreed to drive them to St. Louis University to talk to Father O'Connor about baptism and godparents. O'Connor really wanted to show them his seismograph, a surprisingly small device for something that measured such cataclysmic events. A round pendulum above a roll of graph paper was attached to needles that recorded squiggles and waves on the moving paper under it.

"Earthquakes?" H. asked.

"Eight hundred a day, but you're probably looking at freight cars coupling in the Mill Creek yards three blocks south." The pendulum had been designed by Press and Ewing, but the rooms of electronic filters and amplifiers which interpreted the needle's motions were designed and built by O'Connor.

As they were leaving, he told the Jesuit about his reluctance as a lapsed Catholic to be Joe's godfather. "A godfather is completely unnecessary. Don't worry," he said, which only confirmed Julia's conviction that the priest was an imposter.

Joe was baptised in a garden directly over the seismograph anchored in the bedrock under Grand Avenue. O'Connor wore a black suit and clerical collar which assured Julia that Joe's original sin was in fact wiped away by an authentic man of God. Only she, H., and his sisters were present. Nobody had asked either sisters to be godmothers.

Joe the Believer was not a lot different from Joe the Doubter. He wore the same necktie and pursued the same obsessions in his lab. He did not come out of the basement as Julia prophesied, and he didn't go to church with her. H. wondered if she was disappointed. She said what made him happy made her happy.

Maia called from the Lambert Field Airport. She was laid over in St. Louis for two hours between planes. H. met her at the bar near TWA. She looked tired and anxious and bit her lip more than ever. "Never sleep with a woman just once. They think you hated them. You never called, you never came back. You just left me in Sparks Street thinking I had made you my enemy."

He tried to persuade her of the ecstasy she had wrought, of the new man he had become. It wasn't enough. The experience had changed her whole life. H.'s body tightened. He was afraid she was going to unwrap some grand plan like her fantasy of escaping with him to Chicago. He feared being swallowed by another of her unbridled enthusiasms. She said their lovemaking had revealed to her the shoddy emptiness of her ambition. She was going to leave Paul, move to California, have an abortion. She wanted a new life. H. had always assumed that their weird marriage was an arrangement they had worked out. Her sweeping disaffection surprised him though it made perfect sense. Paul ignored her, he had a bizarre arrangement with her voluptuous sister, and now there was the lithium-soothed mind disorder of the Boylston Professor of Rhetoric. His only connection to Maia's world was Eben and perhaps H. He watched over their education with a father's sharp and critical eye. Maia lived in the same pulp-fiction world she wrote about. Soft edges and cream filling. She hated New England; it was time to leave. The lush warmth of California was the right place for her. She was having lunch soon with Ingrid Bergman who might play Martine in the movie of *Home Front*. Maia had already found another life.

"An abortion?" he asked.

"I can't have Paul's baby. I doubt I'll have any more children. It depends." It was hard to believe that just sleeping with him had caused this sea change in the woman.

"You're not sorry we did what we did?"

"I'm sorry I didn't do it long ago," she said. "Why are you still here? Christmas is over."

"I've been mending things with my family. I'm going back soon."

"Take care of Paul. He's very fond of you."

"Do you know why?"

"It has something to do with the bird you wrote about who moved planets. He said he had never met anyone who enjoyed Ignatius until you."

"When we first met, you were coming from a shower. I had just seen you making love with Paul in your office. Through the window."

She remembered the afternoon well. "I never made love in my office. It must have been my sister."

"While you were in the shower?"

"Then he bought a gallon of gin. Please don't feel sorry for me. Visit me in Hollywood." She was going to buy a house with a room for H. just like Sparks Street. He promised he would come, but he knew he was lying. This was his farewell to Maia as it had been to Alberta Bang in Rittenhouse Square. His world was shrinking, but he was growing. He didn't mind being alone.

The day H. was to return to Cambridge, Joe got sick. Maybe he had been sick before, and they hadn't told him. Perhaps his whole conversion was all a fear of death. Maia believed that getting religion triggered the nascent illness in people. They removed twelve inches of Joe's cancerous colon.

He was in St. Mary's Hospital surrounded by nuns who put out his cigarettes before they were half burned. He was miserable, and H. could see why. The boredom in Joe's hands went straight to his head. He loved tools and objects. His fingers longed to caress reamed holes, beveled edges, and fractured surfaces. They itched to touch and feel about for which things went together and what things could be teased apart. H. bought the largest Erector Set they had in the toy department of Famous-Barr. His own set had been lost or given away. Joe's eyes lit up when he saw the large red metal box with a handle and the picture of the Coney Island parachute jump on it. They had made it together ten years before.

H. broke the plastic covering and removed girders and plates, nuts and bolts, and the small tools that came with the set—a screwdriver and a wrench. He spread the instruction book on the pillow next to Joe and arranged the parts for the base on his bed table. Joe's high spirits lasted about five minutes. He couldn't see the manual, his fingers had lost the agility to thread the little nuts on the tiny bolts, and frustration soon overwhelmed him. H. put the set away and worked on it himself when he visited. The parachute jump was soon about five feet tall, and he was just beginning to lace the strings that guided the chutes and their little jumpers. It was almost finished. He cranked the drum of the lift line, and two of six parachutes rose up until they tripped a release and floated gently to the floor with their passengers. Joe clapped his hands.

A chair that crawled along a rail had been installed along the front stairway to help Joe get to his bedroom on the second floor, but no one had thought about the basement. When he got home, Joe couldn't manage the steep steps to his lab, and he instructed his test engineer to bring the test bench to the first floor and put it in the sunroom off the living room. He watched his mother's face as she heard Joe's plan. For as long as she'd been trying to convert him, she had been trying to get Joe Stillman to come out of the basement. They were really the same thing. But she had never considered that if he came up, he would bring his laboratory with him. Joe's earthquakes and avalanches moved out of the cellar and took over the house. She watched with resignation as the oscilloscopes, the square wave generators, the Klipsch horn, and tweeters spilled from the sunroom over her blue carpets and chintz. Father O'Connor helped H. move the grandfather clock to make way for a folded exponential woofer.

Julia retreated to the second floor from the war zone of her blue living room. She barely acknowledged Father O'Connor when he came to the house bringing parts of his seismograph, which the two engineers repaired in the sunroom laboratory.

Kornfeld called to see if H. was ever coming back to Harvard. When he heard Joe was sick, he flew to St. Louis, and H. picked him up at the Constellation's gate. Kornfeld claimed deep admiration for the upward thrust of Minoru Yamasaki's vaulted airport terminal, which he believed had cast its shadow on Saarenin's gateway arch for which excavations had begun. He wanted to see the exact spot on the levee where H.'s ancestors had landed with bags of fur in 1764. Julia Chateau met them in the parking lot. She was astonished by the elegance of the person she had despised since she first heard of him. Kornfeld was wearing his three-piece Savile Row herringbone suit out of respect for his hosts and the twenty-sixth city.

"I am delighted to be in St. Louis. I am hoping to see your slave squirt leaves." He kissed Julia's hand.

"There are no leaves in January," said H., dragging his roommate into the house to meet Joe Stillman.

"How'd you get here?" Joe wanted to know.

"TWA."

"Where'd you sit?"

"At the back."

"The cheap seats. You know why?"

"View obstructed by the wings."

"Too far from impact. You buy a gun, you want to know it will kill you."

Joe was sitting on a rattan chair in his lab, a jeweler's glass on his right eye, fiddling with a pump on a giant assembly of brass, glass, pipes, motors, and colored fluids.

"What does it do?" asked Kornfeld who admired the etched calibrations on the glass, the bright enamel of the tubing and gleaming brass of the pumps.

"Proves that the New Deal won't work, and Roosevelt was a son of a bitch." Joe turned it on; a dozen pumps whirred, and colored waters flowed from tank to tank. "I discovered Ohm's law of economics. C equals P over R. Consumption function over gross production is inverse to raw material." Soon the yellow, red, and green waters had all amassed in tanks at the bottom of the machine, and it stopped.

"Ah hahhh! The economy has consumed more than it can produce. We must prime the pumps! Henry, get some water."

H. ran to the kitchen for a silver pitcher of water. The machine whirred briefly, then stopped again. "Nineteen thirty-nine. New Deal runs out of steam. Roosevelt has to go to war."

"You believe Roosevelt declared war to end the Depression?" Kornfeld was blown away by the audacity of the man, his machine, and his opinions.

"Nothing jump-starts a factory like war parts. Put them in here"—he reset levers on the machine—"and they show up here." The machine sprang to life.

Kornfeld applauded. "You seem very well, sir. Henry says you've been ill."

"Got a glitch in my power supply. Stomach's not getting the right amperage. H. listened carefully for any hints Joe might die of natural causes. Then he wouldn't have to kill him.

Kornfeld examined every machine on Joe's test bench, twisted all the knobs, and asked dozens of questions about his methods, experiments, triumphs, and failures. Joe was the lost father of all his friends. Alberta Bang hung on his every word, Jimmy Bowes believed he was a genius, Kornfeld came a thousand miles to sit at his feet. What was wrong with H.?

They went back to college together. In Cambridge, the Charles River was frozen and the boathouses closed. He could not row. He tried to do calisthenics with Kornfeld to meet his PT requirement but was again repelled by the sights, odors, and mentality of physical exercise. He quickly lost interest, and it was spring when he was informed by a postcard from the dean of freshmen that he was on probation for failing to satisfy his requirement. Jonquils were in bloom, the ice on the Charles had melted, and eight-oared shells were racing from MIT to the Larz Anderson Bridge at Harvard. H. returned to the water. He was rowing upstream in his heavy wherry, reading *Crime and Punishment,* when he was passed by two eight-oared shells racing in a heat from the MIT basin to the bridge, being followed by their coaches in a motor launch. Over his shoulder, he saw them go through the center arch of the bridge and stop in the middle of the river, their oars floating loosely in the water. The coaches harangued the fatigued crewmen through an electric bullhorn while the men fought to get their breath. H. rowed his wherry through the right-hand arch, which he had seen to be unobstructed. He struck the *Gift* of the class of 1931 broadside, and it sank in less than a minute. Everyone who was in the water had to have plague shots at the Mt. Auburn Hospital. The Charles was famously polluted. It was generally believed around the Weld boathouse, among crews, coaches, and staff, who all despised H. for his costume, smoking, and reading on the water, that he had rammed the shell deliberately. The staff of the boathouse would not issue him rowing shoes or a boat. He had no sport, and probation was hanging over his head. The Harvard corporation charged $18,000 for the sunken shell on his term bill.

H. told Paul about his athletic problems over coffee in Sparks Street. Maia was in California, but there was no hint that she had abandoned ship. Merope had not replaced her as H. presumed she would. If she was around, she was invisible. Eben and Julian were much in evidence. Paul listened to H.'s woes and suggested they talk with a professor of constitutional law who lived next door. The professor said that the university's business practices had always been suspect. They charged Henry Thoreau a dollar for his diploma, which he refused to pay. He sued, lost, and never graduated. The lawyer counseled H. to ignore all Harvard's demands unless served on him by a sheriff. That's what he did, and he was still on probation for lack of a physical training credit when he received an empty red envelope instead of a diploma at his commencement. Like Thoreau, he never graduated.

Joe Stillman's cancer metastasized to his liver. It was mistaken for jaundice, and by the time it was diagnosed, he was almost dead. H. flew home. Joe's mind, though narcotized, was alert to his condition, which he continually analyzed. He believed his intestines were part of a short-circuited preamplifier, and he asked H. to get him another preamp from his desk in the laboratory, his number 7 with a new feedback loop. He held the aluminum chassis on his stomach under the sheets, H. put *Also Sprach Zarathustra* on the turntable, and Joe declared his stomach was working again. Sisters from the Sacred Heart Convent brought a relic of their founder, Mother Duchesne, so effective she had been beatified. Hoping an additional miracle would secure her canonization, they wanted to pin the gold locket containing her hair on Joe's pillow. Julia Stillman had her own piece of the femur of Madame Sophie Barat, Mother Duchesne's superior, and she wanted none of it—no relics, no miracles, no divine intervention, only for Joe to die quickly. She asked the sisters to leave and take Mother Duchesne's hair with them. She was in high gear.

Joe died in the night, and things began to fall apart as if he had been the rusty wire that held them all together. First Marta, the cook for twenty years, quit before the body was out of the house. She had stayed only to take care of Joe, whom she loved. She hated Julia Chateau with an unexpected ferocity and refused to take her last week's wages. She kissed Joe on the forehead and put pennies on his eyes. Julia removed them as soon as the woman left the sleeping porch where he died. H. drove Marta to the streetcar at seven the next morning with two suitcases. At the undertakers, Julia said the silk-lined metal coffins on display made her sick. She demanded a wooden coffin, which was difficult to find. The funeral director tried to shame her into buying what she called a tasteless bronze submarine, then she trumped him by saying that Joe's remains would rest in her living room at home in a plain woodbox until the funeral, and not in the undertaker's chapel. Julia knew the director thought she was being cheap, and she walked out, almost taking Joe with her. The undertaker tried to help H. and his sisters write the death notice and obituary information, but they couldn't agree on anything. Was it a long illness or a short one? Did he teach hydrodynamics at Washington University or just give a couple of lectures a long time ago? Was he the president of the Symphony Society, or did he just head the maintenance fund and quit over the salary of the conductor? H. was surprised by how little they knew or how much he had imagined about Joe and his life.

Later the *Post-Dispatch* called the Stillman home for an obituary photo and to check the funeral home's confused account of Joe Stillman's life. H. told the editor that Joe had been the Mozart of glycerine fuses. He invented the microswitch detonation sequencer for coal seam blasting in the thirties and was called to Los Alamos to help design the firing sequence of the implosive lens. Did he have any photos of Joe on the Mesa or at Alamogordo, the editor asked. No. His father had been reticent about his part in the Manhattan Project and didn't like to talk about it. As far as Joe Stillman was concerned, he was never there. The *Globe-Democrat* called soon after, and he told them essentially the same thing.

The undertakers found a polished teak coffin lined with red velvet more expensive than anything Julia had seen on the display floor. They moved the piano to the library and installed Joe's coffin at the end of the living room in a curtain of smilax not nearly as lush as the greenery around Alfredo's father in the Shoreham Hotel. They opened the coffin. Joe wore no glasses, which made him seem naked even in his three-piece Brooks Brothers tweed suit. He had a rosary entwined in his laced fingers. The man had probably never held a rosary in his life. Late that night, while Julia was dozing at her desk upstairs, H. found Joe's glasses in his highboy and took a pair of wire cutters and his tack hammer from the shop. He clipped the rosary in five or six places to remove it from Joe's frozen fingers. Then he slipped his favorite tool under his folded hands—the maple-handled tack hammer. The hammer's head just below the knot of his necktie looked like a holy icon. He was a Brooks Brothers version of St. Joseph. And lastly he hooked the steel-rimmed bifocals over Joe's ears and rested the bridge on his nose where the dents made by the pads were waiting for them. Joe Stillman was now a man who appeared to have done something important with his life. H. was pleased and slept soundly. When Julia saw H.'s improvements in the morning, she did not mention them. She knew the rosary had been ridiculous, and the tack hammer was almost pious. The bifocals were a matter of taste. Joe probably hadn't worn glasses in the last months of his illness, and Julia may have gotten used to seeing him without them.

Mourners at the wake assumed that Joe was laid out the way Julia wanted him to be. What they really wanted to talk about was the obituaries. Many had never realized Joe was at Los Alamos. Others had suspected it, and a few said they had always known he helped make the bomb. H.'s eldest sister had been Joe's favorite and known him better and longer than any of her siblings. She had fished with Joe in the Black Hills and ridden with him in the Adirondacks. She had never believed Joe was trout fishing in the Black Hills in August of 1945. It was too hot. But she didn't think he was at Los Alamos either.

"All that bomb making is just your invention," she told her youngest brother. "You've always wanted to make him into some earth-shaking god that he wasn't. And now you have everyone believing it."

"So where was he?" She had promised Joe never to tell.

Julia ignored it all, like she did the tack hammer. If someone had told her that Joe was Jack the Ripper, she would have smiled.

The undertakers brought a blanket of white carnations to cover the teak coffin for the funeral. H. told them to take it away and replaced the flowers with a wood crucifix from the bathroom. Walking down the aisle on H.'s arm, Julia Chateau looked neither left nor right. But from behind her black veil and blue sunglasses, she saw them all as she passed and noted their grid coordinates with such precision she could have called in a mortar round on any one of them—Marta weeping in the last row, Jill Bowes in a swank black sheath between Jimmy and Big Jim, fat Donna Hasenclever still pining for H., and Harriet Fordyce with her forty-year crush on Joe Stillman. And lastly she saw the bare coffin in the aisle with the bathroom crucifix on it—H.'s last contribution to Joe's departing.

Father O'Connor said Mass while Etienne McBride prayed at a kneeler at one side. O'Connor spoke less than a minute about Joe. He said it was the other way around, Joe Stillman had converted him. His experience as a chaplain in the war had persuaded him that heaven was empty and God was missing in action. Joe believed that the Creation in Genesis was in fact the big bang, which still rumbled after twelve billion years of evolution. The day of rest was yet to come when life's struggle to survive would end in the silence of entropy, every particle in the universe resting in cold slumber, equidistant from its neighbors. Thermodynamic equilibrium. Absolute Kelvin. The absent god returned in a cosmic quiet that any seismologist or inventor of dynamite fuses could respect. Joe Stillman and Father O'Connor had found their lost faith hidden in each other.

Julia leaned toward H. She whispered loud enough for his sisters on her left and several rows of Chateaus behind her to hear what she said. "He's got a missing screw loose if you ask me. Even if he says he's a priest."

Jimmy Bowes approached H. outside the church where they were waiting for the coffin to be brought out. He looked good; his eczema had dried up, and his skin was clear. They hugged a long while. Bowes had been a genuine friend and loyal admirer of Joe Stillman who was a second father to him. "I always knew he worked on the bomb, since Kooch-i-ching."

"What do you hear about Alberta Bang?"

Her name caught him off guard. "Alberta Bang. I haven't seen her since—"

He paused to think.

"The Biltmore," said H.

"The Biltmore! How did you know?"

"I was there."

"When you were in the Hamptons, I gave you her name."

"You met her on the beach in Bermuda."

"She had the greatest knockers."

"You hear anything about her?"

"She may have had a kid, but I'm not sure."

"She was pregnant."

"When?"

"When you had drinks with her at the Biltmore."

"She didn't tell me. Who was the father?"

"You."

"Bullshit."

"She didn't know it then. She figured it out later."

"Why didn't she tell me?"

"I don't know."

"You seem to know everything."

"I was in love with her."

Jimmy Bowes quickly saw the tragedy of her pregnancy for H.

"I'm sorry. I really am."

"I got over it."

"She played the violin, did you know that?"

"The cello."

They kicked dirt for a minute or so, and Bowes said, "I'm real sorry about Joe Stillman. I liked him."

"He liked you." They hugged again, and Bowes gave him a rabbit punch on his upper arm in the same place Albert had. The spot was still tender.

END

Made in the USA